THE VICTORIAN ARMY AT HOME

THE VICTORIAN ARMY AT HOME

The Recruitment and Terms and Conditions of the British Regular, 1859–1899

ALAN RAMSAY SKELLEY

CROOM HELM LONDON

McGILL–QUEEN'S UNIVERSITY PRESS
Montreal 1977

Croom Helm Ltd., 2–10 St John's Road, London SW11

British Library Cataloguing in Publication Data

Skelley, Alan R
The Victorian army at home.
1. Great Britain. Army – History
I. Title
355'.00941 UA649

ISBN 0–85664–335–1

McGill-Queen's University Press
1020 Pine Avenue West, Montreal H3A 1A2

ISBN 0–7735–0304–8

Legal deposit third quarter 1977
Bibliotèque Nationale du Québec

Printed in Great Britain by offset lithography by
Billing & Sons Ltd, Guildford, London and Worcester

CONTENTS

ACKNOWLEDGEMENTS

I should like to record a debt of gratitude to the many people whose help at various stages made the preparation of this book possible. I am indebted to them for their inspiration and direction, but any shortcomings and failings are of course mine alone. Those who made my work easier are so numerous that I cannot unfortunately mention each and everyone, although I do wish to thank them all. In particular, I am grateful to Professor Geoffrey Best who supervised my work while he was at Edinburgh University, and to Dr John Brown, also of Edinburgh University, whose tireless criticism helped to shape my writing. I have relied extensively on the work and advice of Brian Bond of King's College, London, and it is largely through his encouragement, and that of John Brown, that this book has been brought to publication.

I am very grateful for the kind permission of His Grace, the Earl of Dalhousie, to quote from the Panmure Papers. In addition I should like to thank the several librarians and other officials whose cooperation greatly facilitated my research, especially Mr D.W. King, OBE (Central and Army Library, Whitehall); Mr J.K. Bates (Scottish Records Office); Mr B. Mollo (National Army Museum); the curators and directors of the British Museum, the Public Record Office, the Kent and Suffolk Record Offices, and the staff of the National Library of Scotland. Very special thanks are due to a number of people. Mr W.F. Boag (Scottish United Services Museum) put a great many sources at my disposal, and gave me the benefit of his considerable knowledge. The Gordon Highlanders' Association was extremely helpful, and I am particularly grateful to Major George Slater for his hospitality. The late Lieutenant-Colonel C.G. Mort showed a great deal of interest in my research, was a ready source of help and information, and provided me with numerous contacts in the army. I am grateful for having known him for even a few short years. I am most indebted of course to my wife Margaret, who helped me in so many ways, and who never failed to encourage me.

ABBREVIATIONS

The following abbreviations, apart from those more commonly known, have been used:

CAB	Cabinet Papers
Colburn's	*Colburn's United Services Magazine*
DNB	*Dictionary of National Biography*
EHR	*English Historical Review*
JRUSI	*Journal of the Royal United Services Institution*
JSAHR	*Journal of the Society for Army Historical Research*
NAM	National Army Museum, Chelsea
PP	Parliamentary Papers
PRO	Public Record Office, London
RAMC	Royal Army Medical College, Millbank
RHMS	Royal Hibernian Military School, Dublin
RMA	Royal Military Asylum, Chelsea
WO	War Office

To the memory of
No. 3405 H.T. Skelley, Colour-Sergeant

INTRODUCTION: THE VICTORIAN ARMY

> Until young men entering the army can count upon a certain fixed reward for the faithful performance of certain prescribed duties, the number of improvident and comparatively useless men who enter the Army will continue to be considerably large. . . Men will rough it to a certain extent in the army, but if there be too great a contrast between the amenities and decencies of life which he is compelled to live as a soldier and those of the life to which he is accustomed as a civilian, he will not become a soldier. . .
>
> H.O. Arnold-Forster

> The English soldier on enlistment is suddenly lifted into a higher sphere entirely at variance with his former modes of life and habits of thought. He is free from his previous sordid cares of providing for his daily bread and from the anxieties entailed by sickness, injustice, and the mutability of civilian callings. Organised regularity instead of haphazard disorder; self-respect applied both to his dress and his demeanour; the development of his intellectual faculties through travel about this wonderful world; reverence for, and pride in, his officers, his regiment, his profession; the spur to distinction; and, above all, constant association with education and refinement beyond his former experience, all are grafted on him. . .
>
> Colonel Henry Knollys

The history of Britain's military affairs during the century after Waterloo has always struck me as involving an essential paradox. For a nation which seemed much of the time so little interested in such matters, the record of the British Army is a surprisingly distinguished one. The wonder is not that so many needless, costly mistakes occurred but that even under conditions of extreme adversity the army proved to be so dependable and effective. While an explanation must involve tactics, training and equipment, and of course opportunity, the pervasive influence of national character cannot be altogether ignored. National traits were reflected in the army and to an extent they preconditioned its response to particular circumstances and delineated its strength and weaknesses. In effect, the character of the army itself had an important bearing on its abilities. This professional character was in no small part influenced by the outlook and behaviour of the privates and non-commissioned officers of the forces. Recruitment and service conditions are vital issues because they, in turn, as much as anything, helped to shape the man in the ranks.

The forces in Britain cannot be separated entirely from those that were stationed in the colonies, but because of the large numbers involved and the uniformity of conditions and experiences there in contrast to the variety found overseas, particularly where active service was involved, it is worth attempting to single out the regular home army. The subject is further limited by concentrating on the rank and file, that is the privates and junior non-commissioned officers. The conditions experienced by the officer corps were markedly different and by rights form a separate subject in themselves. The time period is an important one; bounded by two major wars, it comprised a span of years in which there was a great deal of activity in the field of army reform, and in which a number of important changes was made affecting the structure of the forces.

The role the army was required to play in this period was a major one. Responsibility for the defence of Britain throughout the century was shared between the land and sea forces of the Crown, although neither in theory nor in practice was the division an equal one. For geographical and historical reasons the navy was usually considered to be the first line of defence, the army the second. The 'Blue Water School', that body of opinion which supported this division of responsibility, remained in the ascendancy throughout the century, and indeed the primacy of the Royal Navy was a common principle of public policy and a matter of pride for the nation as a whole. The army was seriously touted as the first line of defence only when, in the face of increasing naval competition from other powers, the navy seemed to have lost its edge. This was the situation at times during the 1870s and 1880s, and more especially when the century drew to a close, and the wisdom of placing too many eggs in one basket was widely queried. The 'Blue Funk School', as theorists of this persuasion were called, questioned the ability of the navy to guarantee totally the inviolability of British shores, and warned against being caught with land forces unprepared.[1] The fears which they aroused in the face of rising naval expenditures by foreign powers led during the late 1880s and 1890s to several invasion scares, and to the building of an extensive programme of fortifications to cover London.[2]

Continental war never reached the shores of Britain, and in the end it was the Victorian army, not the navy, that saw the most action. The reason of course was that the nation fought its wars overseas. This alone was to have a tremendous influence on the army, encouraging, even demanding, the development and use of tactics wholly unsuitable in a conflict with another principal European power.[3] As Brian Bond has argued, Britain's gamble that she would not be involved in a major war succeeded only because the Boer War in time underscored fatal weaknesses.[4] As an implement of foreign and colonial policy during the Victorian years the army was at the very forefront of the action. It was primarily upon the army that the security of the Empire depended, and world-wide colonial commitments ensured it full employment.

The second half of the nineteenth century witnessed the heyday of the British Empire and the rise of the United Kingdom to the zenith of its power. These years were to prove to be of vital significance for the army not only because of the actions in which it was engaged, but for the varied reforms which were introduced and which affected its every fibre. The Crimean War left a legacy of concern with the terms and conditions of service of the rank and file, which in later years along with the recruiting problem and rising civilian standards was to serve as impetus for a number of attempts at reform, not all of which were to be successful. The engagements of the Boer War at the other end of the period initiated a second major military crisis with some startling revelations about the results of the previous half century, particularly in the failure to improve training, tactics and recruitment.

The military forces of the Crown in this period comprised a number of branches of arms, each differing from the others in either the functions it performed or the terms of service of its men. Not only were there the obvious tactical differences between for instance cavalry and infantry, but the auxiliary forces, militia, yeomanry and volunteers, played a separate strategic role, and were enlisted under different terms of service.[5] The regular army, small though it was by European standards, formed the backbone of the British military effort. The Crimean War was fought almost exclusively by the men of the regular army, as were the numerous colonial campaigns of the next forty-five years. The South African War of 1899–1902 saw the employment of vast numbers of auxiliary forces and of colonial troops only because the regular army was committed to the hilt and was unable to meet on its own the demands which were made upon it. Foreign service was a major responsibility, and had a deep and lasting effect on the army. Between 1856 and 1899 a large proportion of the forces, as much as one-half at times, i.e. anywhere from 90,000 to

110,000 men, were stationed in Britain, however frequent rotation with units serving overseas broke up the continuity of home service. India especially left its mark in the development of tactics, the growth of a division within the officer corps, and the experiences particularly of the men in the ranks.

Just as the military forces of the Crown were divided into a number of constituent parts, so the regular army too comprised in its make-up different branches. The army in 1856 numbered approximately 236,000 NCOs and men.[6] This was a standing somewhat inflated by the numbers raised to fight in the Crimea and who were still on strength. In later years the establishment fell gradually by as much as 60,000 men, but by the end of the century the strength of the army had begun to climb again. In 1899 the total NCOs and men in the army numbered 216,000.[7] The greatest proportion by far were in the teeth arms. In 1861, the first year for which there are comprehensive figures available, the total force maintained at home and abroad was 221,604 officers and men. Of these 75.2 per cent were infantry, 8.9 per cent cavalry and 12.4 per cent artillery. The service corps were the Royal Engineers who made up 2.0 per cent, the military train (transport) 1.0 per cent and the Army Medical Department 0.5 per cent.[8] Other supportive tasks or logistical duties were performed by men seconded in small numbers from the fighting arms, a practice which these figures do not take account of. As it became clear that the need for these services was not temporary, more service corps were founded and army support staff grew at the expense of the teeth arms. Since many of the supportive functions were now performed by special corps, this may well have had the additional effect of increasing the proportion of effectives in the infantry, cavalry and artillery. In January 1899 the bulk of the total army establishment of 224,609 officers and men were infantry, cavalry and artillery who made up 66.2 per cent, 8.6 per cent and 17.6 per cent respectively. A slightly higher proportion than previously of men in the service corps were in the Royal Engineers (3.6 per cent); the Army Service Corps, responsible for transport and supply (1.5 per cent); the Army Ordnance Corps, with duties of weapons supply and maintenance (0.6 per cent); the Army Pay Corps (0.3 per cent); and medical services (1.6 per cent).[9]

While historians have not neglected the Victorian army, their treatment of it has been somewhat uneven. For the most part, the many reforms which so greatly altered the fabric of the army between

1856 and 1900 are well known. Yet discussions of the major questions do not as a rule deal in any depth with the rank and file but rather concentrate on such issues as the development of a general staff, the abolition of purchase, and broader questions of strategy and preparedness for war. Brian Bond has done important work on the Cardwell reforms and others have looked at certain specific points, notably aspects of the recruiting problem. In beginning this work I was nevertheless struck by the need for a comprehensive study of the conditions and terms of service. It became obvious too that the question of recruitment was a central issue and one that could not be dealt with separately. Much of the Herbert-Nightingale-Cardwell part of the story is well known, as are many of the efforts which were made to adapt the army to the needs of empire. Too often however the army is seen in terms of upper-class pressure groups, with no understanding of the scope and actual effect on the rank and file of the reforms carried out. These after all had wide repercussions and implications. The military forces comprised a sizable body of young men, and played an important role in Britain, economically as a source of employment and politically since they must have influenced the attitudes of those who served in them. In addition the army was at times a focal point of public concern, and in various ways a political issue. In the colonies soldiers were the leading edge of British civilisation, and left deep and lasting impressions upon those societies with which they came in contact.

The absence of a general treatment of conditions of service and recruitment reflects in part the historians' fascination and involvement with the many other aspects of army reform. Another factor clearly is the difficulties which must be encountered in the primary material available for such a study. Official enquiries into recruitment and conditions of service and the reports of the various army departments are useful, although statistics from different sources are sometimes conflicting, and on occasion inaccurate. It has not always been possible to isolate the home army, nor even to provide figures covering all of the years in question. In addition inconsistencies in the manner in which statistics were originally compiled make their interpretation difficult. Moreover there are many gaps which statistics are unable to fill.

Army regulations and official manuals are valuable although they too have their limitations. It is easy enough to outline what official policy was and what were the rules set down; to describe conditions in the ranks however is a different matter. The army was such a large organisation that in many respects there was a great deal of diversity from unit to unit. Regulations said one thing, but how they were applied by the officers on the spot and to what extent official policy was out of touch with particular conditions is another question. To strike a fair balance, one is forced to rely on the accounts of men who served in the ranks, and on pertinent observations made to committees of enquiry, particularly by serving officers.

The private papers of public figures are not as rich a source of material as might be imagined; in fact a great many other specific interests distracted the attention of the leading soldiers and politicians of the day from the condition of the rank and file. Moreover, an examination of newspapers, principal contemporary journals and parliamentary debates reveals how little attention in general was devoted in ordinary times to the private soldier and his problems. This difficulty of mobilising a generally uninterested public opinion was faced by all those anxious to reform conditions within the army. 'We all profess anxiety for a better state of things,' Lord Wolseley wrote in 1887, 'but until the public is taken into confidence, our complaints against the present system will have no practical result.'[10] In spite of these efforts interest and reform were too often followed by bouts of conservatism.

Notes

1. See for instance E.F. Du Cane, 'Do we Need an Army for Home Defence? ', *The Nineteenth Century,* XLIII (1898), pp. 23-9.
2. See Colonel John K. Dunlop, *The Development of the British Army, 1899-1914* (1938), p.12.
3. One of the most recent works to deal with this question is Edward M. Spiers' 'The Reform of the Front-Line Forces of the Regular Army in the United Kingdom, 1895-1914', unpublished Ph.D Thesis, University of Edinburgh (1974), pp.1-42.
4. Brian James Bond, 'The Introduction and Operation of Short Service Localisation in the British Army, 1868-1892', unpublished MA thesis, University of London (1962), pp.260 et seq.
5. See Colonel John K. Dunlop, *The Development of the British Army, 1899-1914* (1938), pp. 42-66.
6. *Report of the Royal Commission on Recruiting for the Army,* P.P., XV (c.3752), 1867, p. 271; cited hereafter as *Report of the Commission on Recruiting* (1867).
7. *General Annual Return of the British Army,* P.P., LIII (c.9426), 1898, p.8.
8. *General Annual Return of the British Army,* P.P., XLIII (c.1323), 1875, p.8.
9. *General Annual Return of the British Army,* P.P., LIII (c.9426), 1899, p.9.
10. Lord Wolseley to Edward Stanhope, 31 May 1887, Stanhope MSS., 1372.

1 THE HEALTH OF THE RANK AND FILE

> Those who enter our Army are picked men, in the prime of life, their period of service varying from 20 to 30 years of age. They are examined by a medical man, and must, before their admission into the service, be reported free from malformation and all tendency to disease. How comes it to pass then, that among that class of men the mortality is greater than among those of the same age in civil life?. . .In my opinion,. . .they are generally badly housed. . .
>
> Sidney Herbert

> Having the honour of commanding one of Her Majesty's regiments, and holding the position which I do now, [Inspector-General of Cavalry] I have had peculiar opportunities of knowing the facts connected with a large number of barracks in various part of the country, and I must say that the statements which have gone forth to the public of the discomforts experienced by the soldiers have been much exaggerated. . .
>
> The Earl of Cardigan

Although the sufferings of British troops in the Crimea were probably no greater than in many of the earlier campaigns in which the army was engaged, the publicity they engendered led for the first time to public awareness of and concern with the condition of the forces. Throughout the remainder of the nineteenth century the army never entirely escaped the stigma attached to it by the chaotic administration of the war effort. To a large extent this was unjustified, for the years 1856–99 saw a great many improvements in the condition of the forces; among the most important were those changes which bore heavily on the health of the rank and file.

The question of army health inevitably involves military-civilian comparisons, and these present a number of problems because it is difficult if not impossible to isolate civilian groups which correspond in age, social class and circumstance with the rank and file of the regular army. Moreover crude mortality rates are the only basis for comparison.[1] Nevertheless the evidence does seem to show that if the comparisons between military and civilian health were to the army's disadvantage at the start of the period, they were to its advantage at the end. This appears to have been the result of improvements in the conditions of military service.

1. The Statistics of Army Health, 1856–99

Common sense would seem to suggest that in 1856 the British regular home army would be one of the healthiest groups in the Kingdom. The bulk of army recruits were young men between the ages of seventeen and nineteen. On enlistment they were inspected by a surgeon who rejected those having any serious bodily infirmity or sign of disease. Any man might also be discharged for medical reasons within three months of enlistment or at any later date if ill and unfit for military duty. During 1854 alone, 20.8 per cent of the infantry stationed in the United Kingdom were invalided from the Service.[2] Most duty was performed in the open air, troops were supposedly well-housed and fed, and constant medical care was readily available. In the circumstances it might be expected that sickness and mortality in the army would be minimal, certainly better than that of comparable age groups in the civilian population. There is ample indication however that this was not the case and that ill-health within the forces at this time was very serious indeed.

In 1857 a Royal Commission was appointed to enquire into the health of the regular army, and one of its goals was to make valid military-civilian comparisons. By contrasting the crude death rate within the forces from accident and disease with that of certain groups of civilians, it was possible to point out the unhealthy state of the rank and file and to show that it resulted primarily from conditions that were peculiar to military service. The commission discovered that the mortality rate in the army was considerably greater than that of (a) the civilian male population of approximately the same age, and (b) the more strenuous civilian occupations, mining included. Moreover, within the same urban area of London detachments of the army had a much higher death rate than that of the surrounding civilian population.[3] Comprising as it did a select group of young men, the army should have had a significantly smaller mortality rate than each of these groups. Civilian males of army age included men in all states of health, the occupations included many much older men, and the nearby civilian population was made up of children and adults of both sexes and all ages. The unduly high rate of mortality within the regular army therefore could not be due solely to either the strenuous work soldiers were required to perform nor to the areas in which they were quartered. Clearly the causes were more directly concerned with the conditions of military service.

Within forty-five years of the Commission's enquiries an outstanding improvement had taken place in the health of the army. The mortality rate from accident and disease dropped significantly by 1860, then continued to decline progressively throughout the remainder of the century. This improvement was experienced by all the arms of the Service. With a large body of men like the army living under a variety of local conditions throughout the United Kingdom, annual fluctuations in rates of mortality were unavoidable.[4] Yet as the following Table shows, mortality rates throughout the whole of the Service declined markedly between 1857 and 1899.

Table 1–1 Mortality Rate per 1,000, All Ages

Year	Household Cavalry	Foot Guards	Cavalry	Infantry	NCOs & Men Home Army
1857	11.0	20.4	13.3	18.7	17.5
1860	3.2	9.5	6.1	10.0	9.9
1865	8.2	5.9	4.8	7.5	9.0
1870	9.9	9.2	8.5	7.9	9.5
1875	7.4	7.7	6.3	8.9	9.3
1880	7.5	7.5	5.7	5.8	7.5
1885	2.4	10.0	5.5	5.8	6.7
1890	4.1	6.4	5.9	4.8	5.5
1895	4.1	4.3	4.1	3.8	5.5
1899	1.8	5.7	2.6	4.4	4.3

Source: *Annual Reports of the Army Medical Department,* P.P.

Medical statistics which trace the decline in the number of soldiers hospitalised for medical treatment each year are another indication of this same trend. Table 1–2 shows a significant decrease in the proportion of troops admitted to hospital annually between 1860 and 1899. In fact, during the forty years in question hospital admissions dropped by more than one-third.[5] By modern standards the percentages of men hospitalised for treatment even in 1899 were very high, but this may be in part a reflection of the availability of medical care in the Service and the extent to which it was taken advantage of.[6]

An indication of the way in which health had improved by 1900 can also be had from examining the evidence of the more important diseases afflicting soldiers. The extent to which the more serious diseases had become less of a problem and required less medical care is illustrated by Table 1–3 which lists the four main classes of disease and shows the decline in their occurrence after 1860. There was a lower incidence of the more serious diseases by 1872, and by 1880 respiratory and tubercular diseases which had been so virulent in 1857 and are normally the product of an unhealthy environment caused only slightly more than three deaths per 1,000 annually. Fevers which attacked nearly a quarter of the rank and file (24.6 per cent) in 1860 hospitalised only 3.6 per cent by 1899.

Table I–2 Hospital Admissions, Home Army, 1860–99

Year	No. of Hospital Admissions per 100 Men	Year	No. of Hospital Admissions per 100 Men
1860	105.2	1884	87.0
1864	96.7	1888	74.1
1868	89.4	1892	76.1
1872	78.4	1896	64.5
1876	81.3	1899	67.1
1880	89.6		

Source: *Annual Reports of the Army Medical Department,* P.P.

There was a number of possible reasons for the vast improvement in the health of the forces after 1856. Because invalids were discharged from the Service regularly it might be suspected that a high mortality rate could be concealed by an increase in the number invalided annually. Yet although the basis for medical discharge remained for the most part unaltered after 1856, the proportion of men invalided from the Service was less in 1899 than it had been in 1860.[7] The answer is not tied up therefore merely in the interpretation of statistics; a central problem is that in general the condition of the army cannot be divorced entirely from that of the civilian population. Absorbing as it did some 20,000 to 40,000 young men each year, the forces could hardly remain unaffected by civilian conditions. Civilian mortality rates had begun to register a significant decline by at least 1880. By this time consolidations of law and local administration were having an important effect on public health, and scientific knowledge had begun to leap ahead. The period after 1880 was remarkable for the success which was achieved in the control and in some cases extinction of infectious diseases, especially those like smallpox and cholera resulting from an unhealthy environment. Not to be ignored either is the influence of dietary improvements which may have increased resistance to disease. Certainly the army seems to have benefited from these improvements, for as Table 1–4 shows, the second half of the century witnessed a parallel and progressive amelioration in the health of the army and of society as a whole.

Table 1–3 Incidence of Selected Diseases, 1860-99

	Tuberculosis %		Respiratory %		Fevers %		V.D. %	
Year	Hosp.	Death	Hosp.	Death	Hosp.	Death	Hosp.	Death
1860	1.8	0.35	10.6	0.18	24.6	0.12	36.9	0.008
1864	1.6	0.29	8.9	0.14	19.4	0.14	29.1	0.012
1868	1.4	0.32	6.8	0.13	17.5	0.09	28.2	0.01
1872	—	—	7.7	0.1	4.8	0.07	—	—
1876	—	—	9.0	0.1	4.3	0.05	—	—
1880	1.1	0.19	7.6	0.14	4.9	0.04	31.8	0.002
1884	0.8	0.18	5.6	0.09	3.1	0.03	27.0	0.001
1888	0.3	0.18	6.3	0.13	2.0	0.04	19.8	0.01
1892	0.3	0.08	6.9	0.13	3.3	0.03	18.8	0.006
1896	0.2	0.06	3.8	0.06	1.8	0.03	14.4	0.005
1899	0.2	0.06	5.4	0.09	3.6	0.03	11.2	0.006

Source: *Annual Reports of the Army Medical Department,* P.P.

Evidently however, improvement was more rapid in the army. The mortality rates of civilians and of soldiers aged twenty to twenty-four years were all but equal in 1860; by 1899 that of the soldier was significantly less. Moreover, the lower working classes suffered rates of mortality higher than the national averages[8] which would seem to make the army figures even more striking. One apparent anomaly is that the average recruit in 1899 in terms of physical size was certainly smaller than he had been forty years earlier. This was due to the forced reliance on a larger proportion of recruits from urban areas and to successive lowering of minimum physical standards. An examination of the physical stature of the British soldier between 1866, when first figures were available, and 1899, reveals a steady decrease both in height and size of physique.[9]

Table 1–4 Military and Civilian Mortality Rates, 1860–99

	Deaths per 1,000								
	Military Age Groups (Home Army)						Civilian Age Groups Male (Eng. & Wales)		
Year	Under 20	20-24	25-29	30-34	35-39	40 & Over	20-24	25-34	35-44
1860	3.2	8.5	8.3	15.0	16.8	20.5	8.2	9.0	12.4
1865	5.1	4.1	7.1	11.5	19.4	17.3	9.2	10.6	14.2
1870	2.2	6.3	6.4	13.7	21.7	23.7	8.0	10.0	13.8
1875	3.6	4.4	8.9	10.8	17.2	22.2	7.6	9.7	15.0
1880	3.0	4.8	5.8	10.2	16.0	21.9	6.1	7.9	12.5
1885	3.5	4.8	7.5	10.7	5.6	28.9	5.8	8.0	12.6
1890	2.6	5.7	5.9	8.5	11.9	14.0	5.7	8.0	13.2
1895	2.4	4.4	5.1	6.1	9.7	14.8	5.0	6.6	11.0
1899	2.2	3.7	5.9	7.2	10.1	15.9	5.0	6.7	11.6

Source: *Annual Reports of the Army Medical Department*, P.P.; B.R. Mitchell, *Abstract of British Historical Statistics* (Cambridge, 1971), pp.38-9.

Army Medical Department statistics also show that after 1860 proportionally more recruits were able to pass the initial medical examinations and suggest therefore that healthier men were coming forward. Moreover, comparison of the reasons for which recruits were rejected during medical examination in 1860 and again in 1899 reveals a reduced incidence in the latter year of virtually every serious disease and infirmity.[10] There is also evidence of efforts to make medical examinations more searching after 1870.[11]

Table 1–5 Percentage of Recruits Rejected as Unfit for Military Service, 1860–99

Year	Percentage	Year	Percentage
1860	47.9	1885	40.0
1865	42.6	1890	39.7
1870	33.7	1895	41.1
1875	25.7	1898	34.6
1880	40.8	1899	33.1

Source: *Annual Reports of the Army Medical Department*, P.P.

A lower rate of rejection by medical examination at the end of the century did not lead contemporaries to congratulate themselves on enlisting a superior type of recruit. The sheer number of men rejected each year in fact caused authorities a great deal of alarm. Because of the increase in the number of recruits taken annually 4,600 men were turned away in 1861[12] while in 1898 rejections totalled 23,370.[13] Concern during the Boer War with Britain's exposed military position heightened public concern, and the alarmist writings of Major-General Sir Frederic Maurice and others stressing the number of men rejected for military service each year aroused fears of racial degeneration.[14] On the instigation of the Director-General of the Army Medical Service and of the Presidents of the Colleges of Physicians and Surgeons an Interdepartmental Committee was appointed in 1903 to enquire into charges of physical deterioration. Although the findings of the committee discounted such fears, they did point out that shockingly poor health was fairly general among the sections of the urban working classes from which most army recruits were drawn.[15]

Clearly then, the very significant improvement that took place in the health of the regular army between the years 1856 and 1899 was due only partly to the influence of civilian conditions. Arguably the army was healthier in 1899 than was the corresponding civilian population. Moreover, because the army remained in many respects an entity separate from the rest of society, most of the conditions such as environment, food and clothing which affected the health of the soldier were different from those experienced by civilians. This independence from civilian influence underscores the need for a closer examination of the conditions of military service and of the changes they underwent in the half-century before the South African War.

2. Army Barracks and the Soldier's Environment

In 1856 it was the soldier's environment more than anything which contributed to the extraordinary amount of sickness in the forces. Tuberculosis, respiratory ailments and fevers, diseases directly connected with living conditions, were responsible together for hospitalising 37 per cent of the rank and file in 1860 alone. The connection between environment and more highly infectious diseases was not as close, but neither should it be discounted entirely.

Permanent quarters for the army were a relatively recent concept in 1856. In 1792 the whole of the accommodation in charge of the Board of Ordnance for troops in Great Britain and the Channel Islands was sufficient for only 20,487 men distributed in forty-three fortresses and garrisons.[16] With the outbreak of the French revolutionary wars extensive barrack construction was undertaken. These buildings and those that were erected during the next fifty years were far from adequate. Lack of concern with the health of the soldier, financial stringency and inadequate medical knowledge of the true causes of disease were hallmarks of the period. By the middle of the century, poor design and faulty construction coupled with overcrowding, inadequate ventilation and sewage disposal, neglected sanitation, and faulty lighting and heating contributed to a rate of illness which yearly sapped the army of much of its strength. These were features common to barracks at home as well as abroad, where the soldier often had to endure extremes of climate and questionable water supplies, was tempted by native food and drink, and was exposed to a frightening range of endemic diseases.[17] Men sent to India directly from Britain found the heat intense, and when an oppressive sickness set in were often driven to suicide. Of one such occurrence a soldier recalled:

> Great numbers began to die very suddenly from cholera. The regiment not being used to the like of this, the whole began to look melancholy, and fear was seen on every face, as much as to say, 'it will be my turn next.' Some gave themselves up to utter despair and died. I was very low in spirits myself once, and the more so because I had never been confined to a sick bed in my life. It was dreadful to see fine, stout, healthy young fellows, well and dead in a few hours. . . Not a day passed but we had some one to put in his last resting place. Oh, how often did I wish. . . that I had died when young. I accused myself of being an ungrateful wretch, who deserved no better than what he now suffered, for not obeying his old parents. I now felt completely lost, and did not care what became of me.[18]

In 1855 when proposals for the construction of permanent barracks at Aldershot were being considered, an advisory committee, later known as the Barrack Accommodation Committee, was formed to look into future accommodation for groups up to 1,000 men. After examining many of the barracks and quarters which were then in use, the Committee noted that

> . . .the accommodation hitherto provided in barracks notwithstanding an improvement in those built of late years, has been generally inadequate both for the comfort and convenience of the soldiers, and for the creation of a higher tone of social habits amongst them. . .
> . . .considerations of economy. . .have been allowed to overbear the demands of a sanitary and moral character, the importance of which is being everyday more fully recognised and acted upon in reference to the class of society from which the privates of the army are generally recruited.[19]

Although minimum limits of space for each soldier already existed in army regulations,[20] it was found that they were regularly violated and that overcrowding was common.[21] The enlisted men themselves objected strongly to these conditions. Non-commissioned officers questioned by the committee described in unequivocal terms the 'wretchedly bad; most unhealthy' state of ventilation, the overcrowding, and poor sanitation that was characteristic of many barracks.[22] It is not clear whether these views reflected the general opinion of the rank and file, but they do indicate the weakness of the argument, voiced by a number of senior officers, that because conditions outside the army were so poor the enlisted men did not object to the state of their army quarters.

In 1857 the investigations of the Royal Commission on army health produced similar findings. Even for the middle of the nineteenth century, some of the instances it discovered of the careless disregard of the most elementary principles of sanitation were startling. In fact ventilation and sewage disposal were so bad in some of the barracks that they were almost uninhabitable. Fuel for fireplaces was usually short and to keep in the heat men closed windows and stopped up ventilators. Wooden urine tubs were left in the room all night and in the morning merely rinsed out.[23] By then, the smell, as one soldier was to recall, was nearly overpowering.[24] In some cases these same tubs may have been used even to carry in the day's rations.[25] A deputy inspector-general of hospitals, when asked if non-commissioned officers and men ever complained of the foul air in barracks, replied:

> The sergeant-major of the invalid depot at Chatham has told me that when he goes to open the door of a full barrack room the first thing in the morning, he always stands on one side to let the

'whiff of foul air' pass him; and that he has frequently seen men stagger and hold on by the rail of the verandah as they come out.[26]

A sergeant describing how he found the morning air in the rooms under his supervision stated:

> . . .in a very thick and nasty state, especially if I come in out of the air. If I went in out of my own room sometimes, I would not bear it till I had ordered the windows opened to make a draught. I have often retired to the passage, and called to the orderly man to open the windows. The air was offensive both from the men's breath and from the urine tubs in the room; and, of course, some soldiers do not keep their feet very clean, especially in summertime.[27]

Testimony by senior regimental officers confirmed these impressions.[28] Contemporary reliance upon the miasma theory of infection explains the preoccupation with fresh air.

For the married soldier and his family conditions in barracks were, if possible, even worse. Separate married quarters were virtually non-existent in the forces. Instead wives were given a bed in the corner of the barracks, shielded from the view and attentions of others only by the protection of their husbands, and a blanket hung on a cord. For half rations they washed, cooked, cleaned and 'mothered' the men in their barrackrooms. Children lived with their parents, usually occupying a vacant bed or sleeping on whatever furniture was available. If a young daughter sent out as a servant lost her position she might return to stay with her parents until something else could be found. Small boys were treated by the men as a species of mascot or performing monkey and were soon taught to drink, smoke and swear like their elders.[29] Army statistics for May 1857 show that in just seven camps, including among them Aldershot, Dublin and Colchester, there were 3,087 soldiers' wives and 3,685 children.[30] Of the 251 stations of the army, separate quarters were provided for men and their families at only twenty.[31] Nor was this the whole of the problem. Unlike most civilian employers, the army restricted the number of men who were permitted to marry. Under normal circumstances, a maximum of six men per company of 100 might receive official permission. The families of soldiers married without permission or 'off the strength' had no security, since the government refused to recognise them and made no provision for them. Instead of quarters in barracks they were forced to live in semi-permanent isolation in lodgings outside the base, their only means of support the pittance their husband could spare them from his meagre pay and the small sum the wife could earn as a seamstress or a servant. When the regiment's turn for a transfer came, especially to an overseas posting, transportation was provided only for some of the wives and children who were 'on strength'.[32] No count was taken of the men who had married secretly but contemporaries estimated that at times the number may have equalled those who married with permission.[33]

The report of the Barrack Accommodation Committee in 1856 was the first to awake concern. Then with the cessation of hostilities in the Crimea, a large group of reformers including army officers, MPs and others concerned with the welfare of the forces determined that current sympathy with the plight of the rank and file should be fully utilised. Subsequent improvements to army barracks were very much an expression of the reforms in public health and sanitation which marked the latter half of the century. Reformers whether interested in the health of the army or that of the civilian population were contemporaries with similar backgrounds and similar goals. Hopes for an improvement in the health of the forces were placed on the application of established sanitary standards and medical principles to the question of army barracks and hospitals. If the environment could be cleaned up, ventilation and sanitation improved, an improvement in health, it was reasoned, would result automatically.

These views were on the whole right for the wrong reasons. At the mid-point of the century misconceptions about the cause, detection and cure of disease were common to military and civilian practitioners alike. The origins of infectious diseases especially puzzled doctors. In 1853 *The Lancet* moaned

> . . .all is darkness and confusion, vague theory and speculation. What is cholera? Is it a fungus, an insect, a miasm, an electrical disturbance, a deficiency of ozone, a morbid off-scouring from the intestinal canal? We know nothing; we are at sea in a whirlpool of conjecture.[34]

Three principal theories sought to explain the phenomena of infection: the germ theory of infection by a living organism, not widely accepted in Britain until the 1860s; the theory of spontaneous generation of disease within the blood and the atmospheric or phthogenic theory which contended that illness was caused by miasms, a noxious emanation from a diseased source which passed through the air, clung to walls and was present in stagnant water.[35] This latter theory enjoyed a large currency for many years and even after medical science had come to accept the presence of germs in causing infection, influential sanitary reformers clung to it obstinately, placing great importance on ventilation and drainage.[36] Nor did army doctors fail to notice for instance that a patient's chances of survival in a regimental hospital set up in a windblown tent were decidedly greater than in a large stuffy building. As the one certainty they could grasp, and anxious to apply the benefits of an age of science to medicine, many came inevitably to look upon large-scale drainage schemes and vigorous ventilation as an essential element in both prevention and cure. Each of these figures largely in the improvements to barracks and hospitals which were introduced after 1856. Ventilation especially was at times overdone. In 1860 for instance sanitary inspectors could complain of barrackrooms overheating to a temperature of 70 degrees and yet record indoor temperatures of 46 degrees with no comment.[37] Twenty years later the danger of excessive ventilation was just being realised.[38]

Of those who were the closest involved in improving army health, the most pre-eminent and probably the most influential were Florence Nightingale and Sidney Herbert. Florence Nightingale had become famous throughout Britain for her efforts in the Crimean hospitals and her prestige in 1856 was immense. Her meticulous research, prolific writings and constant badgering of any and all who could improve conditions in the army lent a powerful impetus to reform.[39] Sidney Herbert, as is well known, was a gifted and capable politician and administrator and one who through his own efforts and position in public life achieved a very great deal.[40] He died in 1861; Florence Nightingale lived until 1910, though her influence waned after Herbert's death. There were other influential reformers who were much less well known; among them Douglas Galton, Sir John Sutherland, Sir John Richardson, Thomas Longmore, T.G. Balfour and J.H. Lefroy. Indeed Florence Nightingale's correspondence with Sutherland, who was a noted army surgeon, shows her dependence upon him and, it might be argued, raises questions as to the originality of some of her own work.[41]

Between 1856 and approximately 1862 under the leadership of Herbert and Nightingale, efforts to bring about reform were welded into a well-directed campaign. The secret, as J.H. Lefroy realised, was publicity.[42] Because of inertia, parsimony and opposition to change,[43] the government could only be persuaded to act by a combination of private influence and a public campaign in the press, journals, and in Parliament.[44] Their goals, as we have seen, were to publicise conditions within the army by dramatic military-civilian comparisons, and by the sensation these revelations would create. These efforts bore fruit with the appointment of the Army Sanitary Commission.[45] Its report in the later part of 1857 called for not less than 600 cubic feet of space per man in barracks and guard rooms, with a minimum of three feet between beds. The existing regulations specified a minimum 450 cubic feet that was rarely obtained; in Scottish poorhouses the pauper was allowed 480 cubic feet or more. Urine tubs in barrackrooms were to be replaced by adequate facilities separate from the barracks and by the proper chamber utensils. The provision of better water supplies, more efficient lighting, heating, ventilation and sewerage of barracks and other facilities used by the troops was outlined and the Commission urged that whenever possible ablution rooms, baths and day rooms for the use of troops be provided.[46]

In a campaign for publicity, those who would receive a copy of the report were carefully selected, journalists were urged to review the Commission's findings, and in some cases even the reviewer was chosen.[47] Herbert went as far as to ask Gladstone for an article, but was unsuccessful.[48] Partly through such efforts and partly because of public interest and sympathy the report received considerable attention. *The Times* wrote:

> There can be little doubt that the chief cause of the evil is the deficient accommodation and the consequent overcrowding in barracks. . .the closeness, the dirt, the indecency spoken of remind one of a slave-ship more than of a place for English soldiers to inhabit.[49]

Three days later an editorial remarked: '. . .if a man is anxious to get rid of his life without having recourse to measures of direct suicide, the most honourable way to obtain this desirable end is to enter as a private in any one of these [Guards] regiments'.[50] *Punch* observed:

> Those who survive [life in army barracks] are the bravest of the brave, and we may add too, the toughest of the tough. Their courage and their constitutions have alike been tried, and may be pronounced perfect—that is Barrack-proof. . .so long as they continue to do duty on home service, they are trained to face death by living constantly next door to him.[51]

Privately published pamphlets,[52] and military and civilian journals devoted a great deal of space to the report as well. Sidney Herbert reviewed forcefully the Commission's findings for the *Westminster Review*[53] and the prevalent opinion was summarised by J.T. Howell, another of Florence Nightingale's nominees, in *The Edinburgh Review*. 'The truth is', Howell wrote, 'that the barrack accommodation of the United Kingdom is utterly insufficient to provide healthy quarters for any considerable body of troops. . .and the health and efficiency of the army peremptorily require that large additional barracks shall be erected in good sanitary principles.'[54]

The main opposition to change lay in the heavy weight of conservatism among senior army officers and administrative officials. 'Few beyond those immediately behind the scenes', commented a writer in 1889, 'are aware of the powerlessness of the thinking part of the army to move the administrative officials, and of the terrible dead weight of tradition and blind conservatism which opposes every movement in the direction of progress.'[55] With civilian conditions as dreadful as they were, many senior army officers and government officials failed to see why special efforts were necessary for the soldier. In 1855 there were objections to even the most common-sense recommendations of the Barrack Accommodation Committee. Colonel T. Wood of the Grenadier Guards for instance opposed the suggestion for separate day rooms in barracks on the principle that there was nothing wrong with doing everything in one room as was the habit of the cottagers of the country.[56] He furthermore denied that barracks were overcrowded and felt that the men had all the comfort it was desirable they should have. Separate married quarters were unnecessary and baths were rather luxurious for mere soldiers.[57] The Earl of Cardigan, fresh from Balaclava yet insensitive to the conditions in which the private soldier lived, could see no problem either in terms of ventilation or of noise from below in having men quartered above stables.[58] Cardigan assured the House of Lords that the discomforts of the soldier's existence were much over-exaggerated.[59] The Commander-in-Chief of the Army, the Duke of Cambridge, also argued in the Lords about the same time that contrary to what was claimed the soldier had not been neglected in the past but was merely more appreciated by the public at the present.[60] The attitudes of Cardigan and Cambridge were no doubt shared by a large number of officers throughout this period.[61]

Apathy had to be contended with as well, and as time passed public and political interest waned. After Sidney Herbert's death, Gladstone remarked that he knew nothing at the time about either his colleague's wishes or his plans.[62] The press too remained for the most part silent on the question of the health of the forces until the late 1880s when an outbreak of fever in Dublin barracks temporarily revived concern. Nor on the whole was Parliament any more vigilant or any more concerned. The universal desire to get on with the business of army reform which was so evident in the Parliamentary debates of 1856 and 1857 was by 1860 already being countered by the demand for reduced expenditures and the opposition of conservatives to change.[63] From the later 1860s, any interest in the soldiers' welfare was increasingly a result of either recruiting difficulties or of some particular unforeseen crisis. Questions in either House as to the state of particular barracks were minimal and indeed governments met with continual opposition to any increase in army expenditures. In any case, successive administrations were keen to keep down spending and complacent about the progress which had been made.[64]

What progress then was made both before and after interest waned in the early 1860s? Cecil Woodham-Smith in her biography of Florence Nightingale has suggested that by 1865 efforts to improve the environment of the soldier had been largely successful.[65] This is only partly true. Very considerable improvements had been made in some areas but in others a great deal remained undone. For example, on the approved minimum of 600 cubic feet of space in barracks per man the major stations in the United Kingdom were in 1861 anywhere from 25 to 45 per cent deficient in accommodation alone.[66]

In 1855 the Barrack Accommodation Committee had set out guidelines for the disposal of sewage, the improvement of hygiene, and for better ventilation and lighting; and had called for a reduction of overcrowding in barrackrooms.[67] Its report was accepted by the government which agreed to consider their recommendations with regard to some of the new barracks under construction. This left untouched the state of those that were already in use. More than two years later the Army Sanitary Commission found that while some of the new barracks constructed in the meantime incorporated the earlier recommendations, it was clear that no change whatsoever had been made in the accommodation furnished for the vast majority of troops.[68]

The Royal Commission itself seemed initially to promise rapid results. The government was urged by reformers to appoint a number of sub-commissions to carry out its recommendations.[69] The War Office agreed, and in 1858 four sub-commissions were appointed.[70] The most important of these was called the Barrack and Hospital Improvement Commission and later became known as the Army Sanitary Committee. It was charged with the supervision of sanitary works, and in 1861 was granted permanent status as a standing committee to advise on barrack and hospital construction.[71] The three other sub-commissions created by the government looked into (1) the establishment of an army medical school, (2) the organisation of the Army Medical Department, i.e. the army's staff of doctors, and (3) the reorganisation of army medical statistics.[72]

Between 1858 and 1861 the Army Sanitary Committee visited every barrack and hospital in the United Kingdom and reported in detail on all structural improvements and improvements to ventilation, sewage disposal, water supplies and washing facilities which were considered necessary. The first interim reports again showed how little had been done. Overcrowding, inadequate ventilation, heating and lighting, poor sanitation, and insufficient facilities for cooking and washing, all of which had been underlined by the Army Sanitary Commission, were general. Separate married accommodation was still a rarity and several cases were found where soldiers' daughters up to the ages of fourteen or fifteen mixed in with the troops.[73]

In March of 1858 Sidney Herbert became Secretary of State for War and under his direction and with the help of the army medical services considerable progress was made in the ventilation and warming of barracks, the introduction of drainage and gas lighting and extension of water supplies, and in the remodelling of kitchen facilities.[74] Separate married quarters especially were proceeded with, so that by 1890 some privates had two or three rooms for themselves and their families. Where finances allowed, structural improvements and even reconstruction were undertaken. Parliamentary returns show that in 1854 £118,276 had been spent on the construction and enlargement of barracks in the United Kingdom while £115,600 was spent on ordinary repairs.[75] By 1859 expenditures under these headings had risen to £602,804 and £154,037 respectively.[76]

The annual reports on the health of the forces by the army medical services seem to indicate that progress along the same lines continued during the next forty years. The medical officers' reports from the major stations draw attention to any sanitary defects in barracks and other accommodation, outline necessary improvements, and often detail changes that had been or were being made. Well into the 1880s conditions that cannot be regarded as anything but serious were reported, but by the middle of that decade it appears that sanitary deficiencies at the military stations in Britain were being dealt with and that those remaining were of a much less serious nature.

But how accurate an impression is this? Medical officers, as Lord Stanley was to charge, frequently understated what was still needing to be done.[77] It would be a mistake to overestimate the rate at which all of the barracks were being transformed. Opposition to reform from influential parties in the army, in the government and elsewhere; a reluctance by governments of all flavours to underwrite large expenditures for improvement; frequent lack of concern with conditions in the ranks; opposition from civilians to the construction of army barracks in their neighbourhood;[78] and equally important, the magnitude of the task at hand, when 97,863 troops were quartered in the British Isles alone in 1898; all these effectively slowed the rate of progress.[79] Moreover advances in minimum standards of public health, hygiene and sanitation reduced the importance of many of the gains that had been made.[80]

The final reports of the Army Sanitary Committee on barracks, published between 1861 and 1863, surveyed 111 major barracks and 59 hospitals. They show that by 1861 ventilation had been introduced in 2,996 barrackrooms, 346 NCOs' rooms, 86 guard rooms and 67 school rooms, libraries and workshops; roughly three-fifths of all the barracks. In one-third, baths with water piped in had been provided, and at nearly one-half latrines had replaced privies and cesspits, and sewerage had been improved. Better water supplies were available at seventeen barracks, and at thirteen stations where cavalry were situated above stables, ventilation shafts had been introduced to prevent foul air penetrating the barrackrooms.[81] The principles that had been followed were those laid down by the original sanitary commission of 1857. Arguably without Herbert's influence and that of the Army Sanitary Committee they might well have been departed from by the Royal Engineers who normally oversaw such work.[82] At this stage the committee was optimistic and looked forward to a time when 'all barracks and hospitals' would provide 'a proper extent of space for their inmates', and benefit from the 'full operation' of 'the various sanitary reforms'.[83]

The War Office allowed the Army Sanitary Committee to lapse into disuse and resisted all attempts to have it revived [84] although its final reports did show the survival of a number of very black spots.[85] With much of the urgency for immediate action gone and with the Army Medical Department seemingly on top of the situation, other interests gained priority.[86] Increasingly measures for the improvement of living conditions in the army settled into the familiarity of regular routines. The danger was that these routines themselves were not fully adequate. In some cases army barracks deteriorated from neglect, in others there was a failure to improve conditions and to keep pace with rising public standards of health and sanitation, and clearly unhealthy conditions were allowed to persist at many stations.[87] Expenditure on barrack construction and repair which had exceeded £610,000 in 1860 was allowed to run down significantly within just a few years, and although there was a slight increase in the amount spent on barracks during the late 1870s, it was not until the last decade of the century that the level of 1857–60 was again approached.[88] Then the ramifications of a controversy surrounding the state of Dublin barracks again shed light on army living quarters and provided a new stimulus for improvement.[89]

In 1859 the Army Sanitary Committee had found Dublin barracks crowded, unhealthy, 'an excellent illustration of what ought to be avoided in barrack construction'.[90] Although improvements were later carried out,[91] a serious outbreak of enteric fever occurred in 1879. An enquiry in 1880 by the Army Sanitary Committee related the fever to its incidence amongst the civilian population in Dublin.[92] In spite of additional sanitary measures, however, a considerable resurgence of fever occurred in 1886 and occasioned further investigations.[93] Reports on the epidemic were made to the government by the Principal Medical Officer, the Commanding Officer of the Royal Engineers in Ireland, and the Royal Engineer Division Doctor, all of whom laid the blame for the outbreak on poor lighting and ventilation, the overcrowding of men and horses, and faulty drainage. The demolition of buildings and the improvement of ventilation and lighting were called for.[94] Various improvements again were carried out but the number of cases of enteric fever in barracks increased and the following year another enquiry was held, again with little result. Investigation by a board of officers confirmed the insanitary state of the barracks but was unable to account for the extent of sickness. A second enquiry that same year highlighted poor drainage, bad latrines and other minor nuisances.

On its recommendations latrines and ventilation were improved and floors raised although no buildings were demolished. In 1889 a civilian engineer was commissioned to prepare what was to be the last of the reports to deal specifically and only with Dublin's Royal Barracks. In very clear terms he laid the blame for the epidemics on poor sanitation, hygiene and ventilation and on the construction of the buildings themselves.[95]

News about the state of Dublin barracks led to a revival of interest in the conditions under which troops were housed in Britain. Although much of the controversy was well-contained by the government, pressure on the War Office to take effective action increased rapidly, and the problems in Dublin raised the question of conditions elsewhere. Queen Victoria expressed frequent concern with the health of the army both in Dublin and other centres.[96] Senior army officers pointed to serious conditions at stations other than Dublin as well.[97] Yet when questions were first raised in Parliament about the Dublin barracks, the government initially asserted that everything was under control,[98] partly because of instinctive concern for economy.[99] In 1888 there were further questions in the House, and demands for action were more persistent. This time the Secretary of State for War, Edward Stanhope, was forced to admit that there had been at least thirty-nine deaths from enteric fever in 1887.[100] Concern continued to mount throughout the year, and in August, Stanhope promised to increase expenditures on barracks and to consider the general question of accommodation.[101] When by 1889 more outbreaks of disease indicated that immediate government action was necessary, further investigation revealed the desperate state of many of the nation's barracks. It was soon clear that quite a few were in a very bad state of repair; others, such as the temporary huts built at Aldershot after the Crimea and designed to last twenty years but still in use, had never been meant for permanent occupation at all.[102] Deficiency in the elementary requirements of sanitation and comfort was a common fault.[103]

The comparison with civilian conditions is striking. During the preceding thirty years the circumstances in which the working classes lived had been subject to a parallel measure of reform and neglect. On the one hand it is clear that there was very considerable progress made in public health and sanitation, yet improvement was piecemeal and imperfect leaving many evil and unhealthy places to be cleaned up in the future. Seebohm Rowntree's study of poverty in York in 1899 revealed that at least 15 per cent of the working proletariat lived in conditions of primary poverty, many in crowded insanitary housing, sharing water and privies with many other families.[104] Robert Roberts' childhood recollections of Salford at the end of the century are ones of extreme hardship and misery.[105]

The situation in Dublin resulted in increased concern in Parliament for the health of the forces. MPs demanded action without any regard to the cost involved. Lord Randolph Churchill, for example, argued that most of the present accommodation was insanitary and detrimental to the health of the troops and told the House he was convinced a large expenditure was necessary.[106] Many others expressed the same opinions.[107] As a result the Army Sanitary Committee was revived in 1889.[108] By February 1890 a comprehensive scheme of barrack construction had been prepared and presented to Parliament. Since the sums required were too large to be included in the annual army estimates, a series of large loans was resorted to. Objectives were the concentration of troops in certain strategic areas, the demolition of condemned and reconstruction of decayed barracks, and the meeting of urgent sanitary requirements. They were immediately approved by Parliament and an ambitious programme of works was put into operation. Yet the sheer size of the task at hand as before limited the rate of progress. By 1900 £3,809,590 of the original £4,100,000 had been expended, an impressive figure, but considerably less than the £9 million estimated as necessary for repairs alone by Lothian Nicholson, or the £13.5 million calculated by Lord Wolseley.[109] Additional loans were obtained under the military works acts of 1899 and 1901 but improvements and renovations were still being executed in 1906 when it was decided to complete only those projects which had already been commenced.[110]

What then was the effect by 1900 of the previous forty-five years of improvements to army barracks? Army Medical Department reports and those of the Army Sanitary Committee provide undeniable evidence that considerable improvements had been made over the conditions of even forty years earlier. The effect of these measures in reducing the incidence of many of the infectious diseases which took such a heavy toll was an essential element in army health, especially during the first decade after 1856. Equally clear however is the fact that this was not carried far enough. The improvements which were introduced in army barracks were part of a public health movement which transformed the face of Britain after 1850. Whether the movement was more or less effective within the

the army than it was in civilian life is difficult to say. Its effects on the health of the army, however, were reinforced by other influences, some of them particular to the military forces.

3. Army Medical Services

Trained medical staff obviously made a substantial contribution to the health of the regular army throughout the whole of the period 1856-99, but more so in later years when significant reforms improved the extent and quality of medical care. The army's staff of doctors comprised a separate branch of the Service known as the Army Medical Department. The primary functions of this department were to care for and treat sick and wounded, to administer medical facilities, and to cooperate with military officers in the prevention of disease (by tendering advice on such matters as hygiene and sanitation in barracks and the choice of temporary camps). In 1856 the Department's performance of these functions was seriously hampered by its own disorganisation and its procedures of selection and training, by its position and influence in the army, and by the state of medical science and the profession in Britain as a whole.

At the outset of the period army doctors were for the most part the only medical personnel employed by the forces with any formal training. Although practising physicians and surgeons were sometimes taken, doctors were normally recruited directly from one of the leading medical schools. Qualification for general practice from either London, Edinburgh, Glasgow or Dublin was insisted upon, a requirement which ensured that army medical officers received training identical to that of civilian doctors, and that there would be close links between military and civilian medicine.[111] This procedure had its negative aspects as well. The education of the army doctors comprised no instruction either at school or upon joining the forces in the areas of medicine which were especially to be encountered in the Services such as matters relating to the selection of permanent and temporary camps, the supervision of sanitary measures and facilities in army barracks, the problems of water and food supply in foreign ports, and the treatment on a large scale of wounds and injuries. Rates of pay for medical officers were too low to attract the best men, and in the years immediately after the Crimean War there was great dissatisfaction among doctors with the administration of the foreign service roster, with the system of promotion, and with the question of their relative rank in the forces.[112]

Beneath the army doctor, there was a serious lack of trained personnel. A medical staff corps of specially volunteered enlisted men had been formed during the Crimean War to carry out the more elementary duties of nursing, dispensing of medicines and ambulance work, but the unit was disbanded when the forces left the East and its duties devolved as before the war on men seconded regimentally by commanding officers.[113] Privates and non-commissioned officers attached to the medical service remained responsible not necessarily to the medical officers, but to the senior officer present. Thus the administration of even the regimental hospital was out of the hands of the Army Medical Department and instead was the responsibility of regular combatant officers who had neither the skill nor the interest required for the job.

The framework within which medical services operated was the regimental system. All medical officers except those attached to the large general hospitals at Netley and Woolwich were assigned to a regiment and a regimental hospital. As such they were responsible to the commanding combatant officer upon whom depended the equipment, size and efficiency of the unit's medical service. The drawbacks of such a system were obvious: the army's medical facilities were organised into too many small units really to work under active conditions, no peacetime training was given in what would be wartime situations, overworked commanding officers tended to give medical questions too little time, and the multiplicity of small hospitals which were sometimes poorly equipped allowed no development of a uniform treatment of the sick or opportunity for medical officers to experience a wide enough variety of illnesses and injuries.[114]

Disorganisation within the Army Medical Department itself was another weak point in the system. The collection and preparation of medical statistics was haphazard, and there was a persistent lack of cooperation and of communication between military and medical officers which was frequently the undoing of sanitary and hygienic reforms. Surgeons testifying before the Army Sanitary Commission in 1857 recalled a number of instances where their efforts had been frustrated by administrative difficulties.[115]

Army reformers, anxious to improve the efficiency of medical services, were quick to pick out the trouble spots. During the Crimean War the Army Medical Department underwent a great deal of criticism as the inefficiencies of the campaign became known. Not a little of it came from the prolific pen of Florence Nightingale.[116] When peace was restored it was not unnatural that army medical services should still share the light of publicity. As with conditions in army barracks, reformers relied upon publicity and upon pressure exerted in private to force government action.[117] The appointment of committees of enquiry was the first major success. In 1856 a select committee was appointed to report on the state of the Army Medical Department. It confirmed charges that the administration of the service was disorganised and that there was serious dissatisfaction among doctors with their rank and prospects of promotion. The committee also recognised the need for a specially enlisted and carefully trained corps of soldiers to carry out the more elementary duties of the department.[118]

Little was done until the appointment of the Army Sanitary Commission one year later. It reported similar findings, but its recommendations were a little more explicit. Recognising the necessity, for instance, of providing new medical officers with some instruction in the special branches of their profession the Commission argued: 'It is in a military hospital alone, and from professors specially qualified to communicate it, that the probationer can acquire the knowledge which is indispensable to the proper exercise of his profession in the army.'[119]

Because the demands for reform in the training and organisation of army medical services coincided with public concern over the health of the army and the state of military barracks, a number of measures were taken which were to have an important effect. By the time public ardour had cooled, enough had been done to ensure that the initiative for reform lay with the medical services themselves.[120] The creation of an army medical school was agreed to by the War Office.[121] It was opened in the Fort Pitt Hospital, Chatham, in 1858 to provide four months of instruction in such subjects as the treatment of tropical diseases, and military hygiene and sanitation, for all new army doctors.[122] Its work of instructing in the special requirements of military medicine standardised medical techniques and procedures. In the 1860s the school was moved to Netley Military Hospital, as the facilities at Chatham proved to be inadequate. The site at Chatham had always been regarded as temporary, but the move to Netley aroused controversy.[123] Once there however the school quickly gained a European reputation. G.H. Porter, Thomas Longmore and Henry McCormac, leading nineteenth-century surgeons, each occupied the chair of surgery. Edmund Parkes, author of *A Manual of Practical Hygiene* (1864), was Professor of Military Hygiene for a number of years, and Sir David Bruce initiated Britain's first courses in bacteriology at Netley. Nevertheless, in the 1870s, the War Office proposed abolishing the school to make money available for higher rates of pay for army doctors. This was frustrated by Florence Nightingale and John Sutherland, who were able to convince the Secretary of State for War, Gathorne Hardy, that such a move would be unwise.[124]

Initial training was improved, but there was serious dissension over other problems. Despite a reform in the administration of the Medical Department, an apparent increase in cooperation between military and medical officers,[125] and the introduction in 1858 of the increase in pay which the Army Sanitary Commission had recommended,[126] army doctors remained unhappy with both their salary and position.[127] It is difficult to say what effect this had on the recruitment of doctors, but the number of applicants certainly dropped sharply. In 1868 thirty-seven candidates competed for twenty-one vacancies; in 1873 fifteen applied for eighteen positions. and in 1878 forty doctors were needed but there were only nineteen applicants.[128] This had a serious effect on medical care. In 1861 medical services made up 0.48 per cent of the officers and men in the army; by 1873 their proportion had fallen to 0.36 per cent.[129]

It was only in 1878, however, that a War Office enquiry accepted the need to make the medical service more attractive by giving army doctors higher pay and the rights and privileges normally accorded to combatant officers.[130] The War Office in the following year increased salaries but not until 1886 was full combatant rank conceded. In 1889 on the direction of another committee salaries were again increased and at long last made more competitive.[131] Finally in 1898 the creation of the Royal Army Medical Corps removed the last major grievance and stumbling-block to full recruitment.

The reorganisation of army medical statistics was carried out during these years. In 1857 the Army Sanitary Commission had called for the creation of a special statistical branch of the medical services,[132] and the following year with the assistance of the sub-commission appointed to oversee reform, medical statistics were reorganised. Much of the groundwork was done by Dr T.G. Balfour and Sir Alexander Tulloch.[133] In 1859 the completion of their efforts saw the setting up of a statistical branch of the AMD.[134] In 1860 the first statistical report on the health of the army was compiled by Balfour and presented to Parliament.[135] Because of their accuracy and completeness, British medical statistics became the most reliable of any army's in Europe.[136] Military medicine inspired few reforms which affected public health, but one of the closest connections between the two came with the realisation that the ill-health of the British people was mirrored in the physical condition of army recruits,[137] and this was outlined in detail in Army Medical Department statistics.

The value of reforms undertaken in the first few years after Sebastopol in the employment of auxiliary medical personnel was more doubtful. Despite the successes of female nursing during the Crimean War, for several years women were employed only in the army's two large general hospitals at Woolwich and Netley.[138] The Army Sanitary Commission had recommended the introduction of female nurses in army hospitals,[139] and Florence Nightingale, who by virtue of her vast experience was perhaps the leading authority in Britain on nursing, pressed the government to accept this measure.[140] A subsequent War Office enquiry however contended that a properly trained corps of male attendants was preferable to female nurses and reinforced opposition to the employment of women.[141] Strikingly similar objections were raised during these same years by doctors and hospital administrators to the use of trained female nurses in civilian hospitals. As Brian Abel-Smith has shown, the nursing profession provided a respectable outlet for the energies of middle and upper-class women,[142] and pressure for the employment of trained female nurses was eventually successful because it came from the top of the social spectrum. But army nursing was quite different. The army was a traditionally male enclave, and therefore difficult, if indeed desirable, to penetrate,[143] and nursing there had none of the attractions of service in the large voluntary hospital.[144] Florence Nightingale was unwilling to support the introduction of female nursing unless it be done in the proper manner, i.e. that nurses be women of character, well trained and adequately disciplined and housed. If this was not done, she argued, there was a danger that nursing could be permanently discredited.[145]

Male attendants continued to perform nursing and other duties in army hospitals. The creation of the Army Hospital Corps in 1857 was ultimately to have an important effect upon their efficiency. Such a measure had been urged by the Select Committee on the Army Medical Department a year before[146] and the government acted upon these recommendations. The AHC was formed of men who were enlisted especially for medical service and who received special training during a two-months course of instruction at Aldershot. By 1883 there were 2,000 men enrolled, three-quarters of them employed in Britain.[147]

Medical care improved considerably with the institution of this corps, yet for the first few years there were clear drawbacks in its management and training. the men of the Army Hospital Corps, like those detached for medical service before them, remained responsible to the senior officer present, and this seriously hindered the administration of military hospitals. Moreover the training they received was inadequate, and promotions tended to be given not in nursing, but out of nursing into clerical positions.[148] This detracted seriously from the professional competence of the Corps. In 1883 there was strong criticism over its performance on active service in Egypt. In that same year a committee of enquiry confirmed charges that NCOs and men were not sufficiently trained in nursing, the preparation of food, and in hospital administration.[149]

The first of the many reforms necessary to improve the efficiency of the Army Hospital Corps had already been taken in 1873. In that year, as part of a general organisation in administration, the Army Medical Department assumed full responsibility for the command, training and discipline of the AHC, and this was the first step in the unification of the two bodies which ultimately took place with the formation of the Royal Army Medical Corps in 1898.[150] In 1884, after the enquiry of the previous year, training was made more comprehensive and steps were taken to introduce female nursing in most of the larger station hospitals.[151] Florence Nightingale's influence can be seen. Although she ceased to be concerned so much with the living quarters of the home army after Herbert's death, she remained involved with nursing throughout the whole of her life. Through her many connections in the Army Medical Department and through Douglas Galton at the War Office, Nightingale furnished the authorities with a great deal of information outlining the principles to be involved in employing female nurses, their training and duties, and schemes of hospital management to be followed.[152] Even the question of the provision of adequate quarters was one to which she devoted attention.[153] She was also one of the first to see that there was a place for female nurses on active service and was able to influence a War Office decision to send nurses to Egypt in 1882.[154]

Medical science, especially bacteriology, made significant progress during the last decades of the century. With army doctors receiving their initial training in civilian establishments, there remained close ties between military and civilian medicine, each benefiting from new theories, techniques and facilities. Unfortunately the failure to attract the best candidates affected the quality and the quantity of medical care available in the army. In a free market civilian medicine was consistently able to attract most of the best doctors. In 1899 the army still lacked dentists and anaesthetics, and medical care in the field especially was rough, a weakness which was to be brought out in the South African War. Nevertheless in most respects, the medical care available to the rank and file of the regular army compares favourably with standards of civilian medicine. Civilian doctors and nurses were no better trained than their counterparts in the army, and public hospitals, although they certainly catered for the poor, at the same time often excluded those requiring long-term medical care. Any who were incapable of looking after themselves, who had no family to fall back upon and who were unable to afford private nursing care would normally end up in the workhouse infirmary or sick ward. There, even at the end of the century, the standards of care they received varied considerably. It is also true that general practitioner services varied greatly between districts, and in many areas were often poor.

Another factor which had an important bearing on the quality of army medical care was the type of facilities medical staff had at their disposal. In 1856 two different types of hospitals were in operation for the use of troops in the United Kingdom: the general hospital and the regimental hospital. General hospitals with accommodation for two or three hundred men were located at Chatham, Dublin and Cork. Their medical staff was more or less permanent and they were intended for the treatment of serious diseases and injuries and for long-term care. Smaller regimental hospitals with perhaps as few as thirty beds or less were maintained by each regiment and were separately administered, medical staff as well as medicine and other supplies travelling with the regiment in every transfer. At a number of the larger stations, Aldershot, Shorncliffe, Portsmouth and Dublin for instance, regimental hospitals combined to occupy the same buildings although they continued to be administered and to be staffed separately.[155]

The administrative difficulties and inefficient use of facilities that such a system entailed could ill be afforded. In 1861 the Barrack and Hospital Improvement Commission visited a set of regimental hospitals in Dublin organised on this basis. Although there was regulation accommodation for 208 sick, the Commission found that the wards were

> . . .divided into no fewer than eight separate and distinct hospitals,

> all exactly alike. . .There is nothing in common, not even a consulting room or operating theatre. Each hospital is as independent of its neighbour as if it were miles away. The space and attendance in one hospital may be taxed to the very utmost, while next door, and under the same roof the wards may be nearly empty and the medical officers and attendants with little or nothing to do.[156]

This was merely one of the difficulties. Enquiries into the health of the army after the Crimean War revealed that the condition of many of the army's regimental hospitals was on a par with that of some of the worst barracks. In 1857 the Army Sanitary Commission found many instances of hospitals with inadequate ventilation, lighting, toilets and washing facilities. The Commission had recommended accommodation in military hospitals be provided at the rate of 1,200 cubic feet of space for each patient,[157] but in spite of subsequent government agreement to this standard, the Army Sanitary Committee calculated in 1861 that should it be enforced immediately, available hospital space would be reduced by 2,900 beds or 42.5 per cent.[158] On this basis military hospitals compared unfavourably with London workhouses.[159] 'Of all parts of a barrack', the Committee argued,

> the hospital is planned with the smallest apparent amount of attention or consideration for the objects which the building is intended to fulfil. . .there has been no general recognition of the fact that the observance or non-observance of these principles exerts almost as great an influence as it exerted by the medical treatment on the final result of cases admitted into hospital whether as regards their duration or termination.[160]

It was recognised that these conditions reduced a patient's chance of recovery and prolonged his convalescence.[161]

Real and significant changes in army hospitals did not come about until after 1860. In 1857 the Army Sanitary Commission outlined fairly detailed proposals for better hygiene, water supplies, ventilation, heating and lighting and for more space and other improvements.[162] Three years later the Barrack and Hospital Improvement Commission set out principles upon which it was hoped the construction of hospitals in the future would be based.[163] Much of the current thinking favoured the pavilion system of construction with large airy wards housing from twenty to twenty-five patients in two rows, each bed with its head between two large windows.[164]

These measures were presented as part of the general package of reforms necessary to bring about a significant improvement in the health of the forces, and the government agreed to them as such. In addition, because they applied to a sphere of their own and came more under the wing of the AMD, which itself was undergoing reform, improvements to military hospitals, encountered little opposition within the army. Significant improvements seem to have come quite quickly. In 1857 military hospitals were contrasted unfavourably with naval hospitals because in comparison they were damp, dingy, cramped, and even dirty.[165] Within fifteen years, army hospitals were said to be better run, cleaner, and to provide the better facilities.[166] In 1861 military hospitals had accommodation in Britain for 8,800 patients, which if each man were to be allotted the regulation 1,200 cubic feet, was adequate only for 4,400.[167] Twenty years later with an average of 4,643 men in hospital there was accommodation for more than 8,500 patients.[168] In 1861, 500 wards in fifty-three of the fifty-nine hospitals which the Army Sanitary Committee inspected had undergone improvements in ventilation, and in many there were also baths and better water supplies, and better sewage disposal and sanitation.[169] In subsequent years, the annual reports of the principal medical officers in each of the military districts illustrate that improvements continued. Given the statistical evidence there is no doubt that the rate of physical improvement to hospital buildings was greater than that to army barracks. Nevertheless many of the same problems were encountered. The normal reluctance by successive governments to lay out large capital expenditures for improvements was encountered,[170] and there were higher standards of hygiene and sanitation which continually had to be met. This was all aggravated by the extent of the task at hand. Enquiries into the condition of military hospitals which were initiated after the outbreak of enteric fever in Dublin in 1886 revealed nowhere near the same state of neglect that had befallen many of the country's army barracks, but there were certainly cases where conditions were not all they should have been.[171]

The inefficiencies and lack of harmony of the regimental system of hospitals were checked in 1873 when regimental hospitals were replaced by larger garrison hospitals whenever two or more units were stationed together, and staff and facilities were combined. Medical officers were henceforth attached to either one of the two general hospitals or to a station hospital and no longer had to conform to a regimental tour of duty or to acquaint themselves with the medical problems of a new area each time a regiment was transferred. While regiments maintained small medical units or aid centres, the large well-equipped hospitals under the responsibility of officers of the Army Medical Department which were set up at the larger stations, permitted the establishment of better facilities, uniform methods of treatment and preparation for wartime conditions.[172] These advantages more than compensated for the loss of the regimental medical officer as personal friend and physician in his unit. Nor is there any evidence to support charges that improper supervision of the sick resulted from the change.[173]

A third and equally important feature of the post-Crimean reform of army hospitals was the construction of two new general hospitals, one at Netley near Southampton and the other at Woolwich. Defects in the general hospital at Fort Pitt and the inadequacies of accommodation at St Mary's, Chatham, prompted demands during the Crimean War for a new general hospital. The government agreed to a new hospital at Netley, but in construction a bitter and protracted conflict arose between medical reformers on one side and government and contractors on the other over the design and plans for the building. These had been approved by the government without first being submitted to any of the sanitary commissions and without being vetted by any of the drainage and ventilation experts recognised by the Herbert-Nightingale group.[174] An examination of the course this controversy followed illustrates the type of conflicts that often arose between sanitary reformers and their colleagues in the medical profession. The hospital was intended not for the treatment of contagious or infectious diseases, but specifically to receive and to hospitalise invalids from overseas, many of whom would be able to move about the hospital on their own. In the circumstances designs incorporating smaller wards were substituted for the pavilion system of large airy rooms preferred by many reformers. This in turn created a furore in both parliament and the press. Herbert, Florence Nightingale and others violently criticised the new hospital for its supposedly unhealthy location, inadequate ventilation and lighting, and faulty design.[175] Considerable pressure was put on the Secretary of State for War, Lord Panmure, to have the building either scrapped or redesigned but hospital facilities were urgently needed, and he successfully resisted.[176] For a time Florence Nightingale even convinced Lord Palmerston, the Prime Minister, that Netley was a liability.[177] In 1857 the Barrack and Hospital Improvement Commission raised objections to continuing construction. On the instigation of Nightingale and Sutherland a special committee was appointed by the government to examine the location and the plans for the hospital.[178] The Committee however rejected accusations that the proposed site was unhealthy, and denied that the design was unsuited for the purposes for which the building was intended.[179] Subsequent expert advice solicited by the government supported these findings. To satisfy critics a few minor modifications in design were approved,[180] but construction of the new hospital was proceeded with.[181]

By 1859 building at Netley was complete. The three general hospitals which had been in existence until that time, Dublin, Cork and Woolwich, were either beyond repair or inadequate for the needs of the army. These were closed and their patients sent to the new general hospital. That same year Sidney Herbert, as Secretary of State for War, initiated construction of a second general hospital at Woolwich. When it was discovered that the old general hospital at this station could not be brought up to requirements the buildings were converted into barracks and plans laid for a new hospital.[182] Still smarting at their defeat over Netley, but realising the necessity for a large general hospital for protracted treatment of injuries and disease, reformers, including influential officers of the Army Medical Department, were able to have designers of the new Herbert hospital incorporate the pavilion system and other advanced techniques. The principles of construction outlined by the Barrack and Hospital Improvement Commission were followed closely and current sanitary theories were put to use.[183] Both the Herbert and Netley hospitals were well equipped and were operated successfully throughout the nineteenth and well into the twentieth century. Together they provided accommodation for more than 1,600 patients.[184] Netley remained the home of the Army Medical School, and provided special facilities for the treatment of invalids, tropical diseases and psychological cases. There was criticism of its location and design for many years,[185] yet in the course of time the location was found to be excellent and its design and construction adequate.[186] In later years it was the establishment of the Herbert hospital that came to be questioned. Army health had improved to such an extent by 1876 that the Treasury at that time questioned whether the institution at Woolwich was really necessary.[187] Subsequent experience as well suggested that in a few cases the ventilation had been overdone. Medical officers reported that some of the wards were so breezy that patients were catching chills and were in danger of contracting pneumonia.[188]

It was the variety and scope of operation of army medical services that allowed them to play such a significant role in the health of the forces. By and large there was constant medical care for the soldier throughout the whole of his career. Medical care began at the time of enlistment when all recruits were inspected by a doctor before being passed for the Service. Until 1873 medical officers were attached to each regiment or battalion and a unit hospital or aid centre was maintained for every detachment of troops. After the reorganisation of the hospital service these were replaced by larger garrison hospitals and unit infirmaries. Daily sick parades, at which any illness could be reported, were commonly supplemented by frequent periodic examinations by army doctors with nothing to gain by keeping an ill man out of hospital. At the same time strong steps were taken to prevent soldiers from abusing medical facilities. To what extent they reduced the effectiveness of army medical care is difficult to estimate. To discourage what was felt to be a danger of malingering and to help pay for expenses, the sum of 9d, a sizable proportion of daily pay, was deducted from each man's wage for every day he spent in hospital for a disease or injury other than that resulting directly from his duties. This probably discouraged malingering but there is evidence that it tended to encourage concealment as well.[189] In cases where recovery from a severe illness or disability was unlikely and it was therefore doubtful that the soldier in question would be fit for further service, he was discharged, with, if he were fortunate, a permanent pension, and consigned in theory to the care of relatives or friends. The size of the award depended on the nature and the extent of his afflictions. The inadequacies of army pensions and the fact that after several years' military service many had no friends or relatives upon whom to depend, led them to destitution or the workhouse. Two veteran hospitals at Chelsea and Kilmainham provided care for a limited number of those on a permanent pension and who were willing to commute this for the status of in-pensioner.[190]

Medical care for the solder's family dates from the latter half of the nineteenth century. Initially there were Treasury objections to the increased expense of caring for wives and children and it was not until 1878 that full responsibility was accepted for their welfare. In 1880 a maternity and child care service was undertaken and women were for the first time admitted to hospital before confinement, a practice still not common in civilian hospitals as late as 1900.[191] The effects of better medical care and better accommodation were plainly felt and can be seen in the significant drop which took place in illness and mortality rates amongst soldiers' families.[192]

Looking at the period 1856 to 1899 as a whole, the benefits of medical care which the regular soldier enjoyed do not compare unfavourably with those which were available to the civilian working classes. The constant supervision which the army was able to provide was certainly lacking, although the public hospitals did cater specifically for the poorer classes.[193] In the end where disease or injury was chronic and protracted medical care was necessary, the discharged soldier and civilian might well end up together in the workhouse infirmary. Conditions there varied considerably despite the fact that there were vast improvements after the Poor Law Act of 1867. The smallpox epidemics of 1871 and 1876–7 led to the gradual extension of medical care to the whole community; nevertheless those who could afford private care in their own homes continued to steer clear of hospitals. This attitude rubbed off on the poorer sections of the community who did not always seek to enter a hospital or a workhouse infirmary whenever they became ill.[194] Unlike the soldier, a day off work sick for the civilian might mean that the head of the household would lose his job. In the circumstances only serious illness could be taken notice of.[195] Army pensions may have been meagre and not easily obtained, but the civilian working man received no compensation whatsoever for any illness he might contract in his employment.

4. The Particular Case of Venereal Disease

During the last fifty years of the nineteenth century there were circumstances where the problems of army health were felt to concern the nation as a whole. If special measures were necessary in cases of epidemics or the unhealthiness of certain areas to protect the army from society, society it is quite clear had in some cases to be protected from the army. Venereal disease in particular occasioned special efforts. It aroused a great deal of interest because it posed a serious threat and because it touched on the sensitive question of sex and morals. Venereal disease was a constant problem among the army in India, and in the early 1860s an especially large outbreak occurred in the home army as troops returned from overseas. Just as Gladstone was trying to prune the army estimates, hospital and medical expenses were on the increase. Medical reformers became especially concerned. The incidence of the disease in 1860 was 369 cases per 1,000 men. This compared with seventy-eight in the navy on home station, seventy in the French and thirty-four in the Prussian services. The loss of service was equivalent to the withdrawal of every soldier from the army for eight days or of two full battalions every year in Britain.[196]

Throughout the remainder of the century the incidence of the disease remained very high, although the threat it posed in 1899 was considerably less than in 1860. Never less than one man in ten, and for most of the period one in five or an even higher proportion, underwent treatment each year.

Military authorities reacted in a variety of ways to the threat of venereal disease in the army. Medical officers provided mercury treatment for those who had contracted VD; however special efforts were made towards prevention. Military officers, chaplains, and many others with influence endeavoured to persuade troops to avoid situations where the disease might be contacted. In India brothels were maintained for the use of the troops and prostitutes were checked by medical officers.[197] The large network of libraries, recreational centres, soldiers' homes and the like which sprang up in barracks during the latter half of the century through military and private initiative and financing had as one of its goals the prevention of venereal disease in the army. A goal of short-service enlistment introduced in 1870 was the alleviation of the evils of enforced celibacy in the forces, both at home and in India.[198] Certain efforts were made as well to coerce men into good behaviour although they met with little success. In 1873 it was decided to dock soldiers' pay if they were found to have venereal disease. The figures for 1873–4 show an enormous decrease, but in 1875 it was discovered that soldiers were skipping medical parades and were cauterising their sores with mercuric iodide and nitric acid bought from chemists near the large stations.[199] In spite of the concern for the prevention of venereal disease, persuasion, coercion and attempts to educate the troops themselves in its avoidance and in the undesirability of its contraction seems to have had no effect on many men. Spike Mays, a cavalry recruit in 1924, was informed by his seasoned and wiser comrades, 'You ain't a pukka soldier, boy, until you've had a nap-hand (syphilis and gonorrhoea twice each) an' got five reds on yer crime sheet.'[200]

More extreme attempts at prevention, and ones which involved reformers outside the army as well, were made in the field of preventive legislation.[201] 1862 was an especially bad year for venereal disease in the forces. In that year the number of men hospitalised rose

rose to 25,787 or 33.0 per cent of the forces in the United Kingdom.[202] The Secretary of State for War, Earl de Grey, became anxious that some sort of action be taken. The following year he agreed to the appointment of a committee to investigate the incidence of venereal disease in both the army and navy. Although a properly enforced system of coercion might have reduced the prevalence of disease, public opposition was feared and the committee advocated only that medical facilities be improved and extended and that women suspected of prostitution be induced to admit themselves voluntarily for treatment.[203]

Stronger measures were wanted by the War Office and others who were anxious to protect the soldier. The solution they sought to employ, the Contagious Diseases Acts, was designed to restrict not the troops but the women with whom they came in contact. Acts were passed in 1864, 1866 and 1869. They were based on the conviction that strict scientific laws of social improvement were discoverable and applicable. The terminology 'Contagious Diseases' was borrowed from the Contagious Diseases (Animals) Act and indeed many of the notions of venereal disease in prostitutes were influenced by opinions on the eradication of contagious diseases such as cattle plague and scab. The poisoning of innocent children was in a way akin to effects of food adulteration already being curbed by legislation.

The first of the Contagious Diseases Acts provided for compulsory hospitalisation of any woman accused by a policeman before a magistrate in closed court of being a prostitute and of acting within certain protected districts.[204] The second Act provided for compulsory examination at three-month intervals and for a more regular examination of suspected women within a ten-mile radius of a protected area. As in the earlier legislation prostitutes could be identified by the accusation of a single constable presented before a magistrate in closed court.[205] A committee assembled in 1867 to report on the pathology and treatment of venereal disease recommended weekly examination of prostitutes by medical police, the inclusion of a penal clause to punish violation, the periodic examination of all troops, and the extension of the Acts to all garrisons or seaport towns where troops or ships of war were stationed.[206] Government action was milder than this. The third and final Act introduced in 1869 extended the radii of protected areas to fifteen miles and made provision for the compulsory incarceration of women for five days before they were examined. This latter provision made the examinations more effective, but denied its victims the fundamental right of habeas corpus.[207]

The introduction and operation of the Contagious Diseases Acts aroused a great deal of controversy, and a campaign of considerable size was mounted to bring about their repeal. Some resentment was felt because the Acts had been slipped through Parliament before many members knew what they dealt with.[208] Most people however opposed the Acts on moral grounds. Florence Nightingale had been against even voluntary treatment of women, arguing that the introduction of more and better recreational facilities in the army was a surer way of dealing with the problem.[209] 'You cannot reclaim prostitutes,' she charged, 'you must prevent prostitution.'[210] John Sutherland argued that in spite of how vicious a woman was, she still had inalienable social rights.[211] Both sides in the campaign to repeal the Acts produced volumes of figures, most of which were of questionable accuracy. Some of the methods employed by the abolitionists particularly were open to criticism. For this reason noted reformers like Nightingale and Sutherland, although they favoured repeal, refused to become associated with any of the anti-Contagious Diseases Acts associations.[212] But even without their active assistance, the campaign for repeal had a strong enough case that in time it was successful. In 1886 Henry Campbell-Bannerman, then Secretary of State for War, circulated his cabinet colleagues and received their agreement to repeal on the grounds that such a move was necessary in the interests of the health of the army and the moral condition of the garrison towns.[213] The Acts were repealed that year, much to the regret of a number of officers who continued to argue their effectiveness and to wonder what measures could replace them.[214]

In their operation the Contagious Diseases Acts were both degrading and dehumanising. The examinations were physically painful and the women subjected to them were often housed in darkness or kept in chapels or prisons. In many places these examinations were conducted on a special day of the week in a hall with windows that were imperfectly screened. Their effectiveness in controlling venereal disease was questionable as well. The first of the Acts prescribed three months of treatment for women found to be diseased.[215] With modern drugs an effective cure may take up to two years depending on the type of venereal disease contracted. Failure to provide the money for the 'special lock' (i.e. compulsory isolation) hospitals that were required helped to render the first of the Acts virtually unoperative. The effect of the subsequent legislation was limited because many women tended to live outside the prescribed area and to commute, or were kept by army officers and were secure from police questioning.[216]

Nor is it certain that the Acts alone were successful in restricting venereal disease in the army. The claim that they contributed significantly to a decrease at the military stations under protection is dubious,[217] since figures supplied by the Army Medical Department tend to support this contention only with regard to syphilis.[218] If venereal disease was reported to be less virulent in the protected areas it may be because the women were driven elsewhere. Furthermore, in the absence of blood tests which were not introduced until 1908 by Wasserman, it is conceivable that patients who were considered cured were merely enjoying a natural remission in symptoms. The accuracy of the numbers of soldiers represented in statistics as being diseased may be questioned too. Some regiments were known to have vigorous medical inspections at sick parades while many others were much more lax. It may well be as some have suggested that venereal disease underwent a long-term decline in virulence during the latter half of the century which had more of an effect on statistics than any attempts to prevent its spreading.[219] Recruiting figures show at least a progressive decline in the percentage of men rejected on enlistment for venereal disease. This implies a decline in incidence among the civilian population as well.[220]

In fact there was a number of other influences which helped to contain venereal disease. In 1913 the Director-General of the Royal Army Medical Corps, Sir Alfred Keogh, ascribed the decline in incidence to higher public standards of sanitation and cleanliness.[221] Another factor certainly was the greater provision for recreation with more and better libraries, games rooms and sports programmes to occupy the soldier's time.[222] The introduction of short-term enlistment, by reducing the average age of the man in the ranks, may also have had something to do with lowering the incidence of the disease, but to what extent it is impossible to say.

The question of venereal disease is a case in point where extensive extra-medical efforts were made to eradicate one particular form of disease, but where the results of these precise efforts are at least open to interpretation. The general question of the health of the rank and file is less vague. In this case it is clear that army medical services exerted an important influence. Better trained and more capable staff, better hospitals and equipment, and more efficient and extensive services made valuable contributions towards improving the health of the forces. As in civilian medicine, without advances in medical science the role of medical services could not have been as effective as it was.

5. Physical Training

Gymnastic exercise and physical training, now so much a part of all military instruction, were lacking in the British army at the mid-point of the last century. During the campaign of 1854–6 the problem of providing reinforcements and replacements for the army in the East was particularly trying and occasioned the near breakdown of the recruiting system. In the circumstances a considerable number of the drafts sent overseas were unprepared for the strenuous tasks and harsh conditions that awaited them. Their suffering and hardship aroused grave concern over what was feared to be a deterioration in the physique of the recruit. In searching for a solution to the problem of maintaining the health and physical capabilities of the soldier, attention was drawn to the apparently successful programme of gymnastic instruction in use by the French army.[223]

In 1858 the Army Sanitary Commission strongly recommended that some form of physical training be considered.[224] Direct benefits in terms of the efficiency of the forces were expected, and within three years the decision was taken by the army command to institute a programme of gymnastics which was to be incorporated in the training of each recruit. An officer and twelve NCOs were sent to Oxford for six months' instruction and later that same year a school of gymnastics was opened at Aldershot. The Commandant, Major F. Hammersley, worked successfully to popularise gymnastics in the army and in 1862 orders were issued authorising the construction of a gymnasium at every garrison. In 1865, army regulations based on the recommendations of a War Office Committee of the previous year on gymnastic instruction required every recruit to undergo a course of at least three months along with his ordinary drill and all trained infantrymen of less than ten years' service to receive an hour of instruction every other day for three months annually. Medical superintendence of drill and Army Medical Department responsibility for the installation of proper ventilation and other sanitary facilities in gymnasia were stipulated as well. These regulations securely established the army's programme of gymnastics, however there were at the time only thirty-seven gymnasia in operation and instruction was by no means universal. Furthermore current training techniques and the equipment which was in use, i.e. weights, climbing ropes, horizontal bars and the vaulting horse, tended to produce muscular development of the upper body and not the all-round physical conditioning that would have been obtained from calisthenics or proper gymnastic exercises.[225]

Enthusiasm within the army for some sort of physical training which would help to increase the capabilities of the soldier was considerable and facilities were rapidly expanded. Medical and commanding officers were virtually unanimous in their praise of the beneficial effects produced by gymnastics and physical training.[226] In the *Journal of the Royal United Services Institution* of 1864 a medical officer, Dr M. Roth, claimed that three-fifths of those recruits who failed to pass their medical examination were rejected for a physical unfitness which could easily be cured by the proper exercises. He then went on to suggest a system of what he called 'rational gymnastics', more or less calisthenics and aerobic exercises, which would produce physical conditioning but not 'brute muscular strength'.[227]

In 1878 a gymnastic demonstration was presented at the Albert Hall and was so successful that the following year it was combined with a Volunteer Force display on Wimbledon Common. In 1880 the performance was given at London's Agricultural Hall where there were better facilities and this in turn developed into the annual 'Military' and later 'Royal Naval and Military Tournament' which was so valuable an advertisement for the Services in peacetime.

A system of drill to music patterned on the Danish system was introduced in 1882 but not until the last decade of the century was the full importance of physical training completely appreciated. 'Free gymnastics' was instituted in 1894–5 and lasted until a proper scheme of gymnastics and calisthenics based on a Swedish model was introduced in 1906. Regimental sports were common by the end of the century. Boxing in particular became very popular in the 1890s as more facilities were made available. The first army championships were held in 1893. Colonel J.S. Napier, who became Inspector of Gymnastics in 1897, supervised the erection of over eighty new gymnasia, almost doubling the staff employed, and opened the army's first swimming pool at Aldershot in 1900.[228]

The question of physical training was not merely one of health. As an article in *Colburn's United Services Magazine* of 1861 suggested, a properly organised system of gymnastic instruction would increase the army's physical capabilities and might be expected to reduce idleness and the tedium of army life.[229] In fact, the introduction of physical training clearly had a number of valuable and positive effects. For one thing, the capabilities of the soldier and therefore of the army could not help but be increased. Army training manuals observed that after three months of instruction, men who had made normal progress could be expected to execute ten pull-ups on a horizontal bar and fourteen dips on a parallel bar, to jump to a height of three feet and to run a mile in seven minutes without undue fatigue.[230] Physical training produced real improvements in the health of those who went through the courses of instruction. In 1869, for instance, the Director of Army Gymnasia reported that the classes at each of the gymnasia under his supervision without exception all improved their muscular development and general state of health and in the winter months especially showed significant weight-gains as a result of their training.[231]

Gymnastics provided not only opportunities for recreation and physical development which were then beyond the reach of most civilians, but also what was seen to be equally important, diversion from the unwholesome activities of drinking and whoring. How much it achieved in this line is impossible to say, though drinking did decline. Like improvements in barracks and hospitals and like other reforms which benefited the health of the army, physical training was introduced from above, not from the ranks, and this to some extent may have limited its effectiveness. Surgeon-Captain J.R. Forrest in 1896 wrote:

> The whole system of physical training in the Army is most carefully calculated to produce, and does produce, men of the greatest physical vigour, and it is not the fault of the system that the Army hospitals are so full as they are. Fifty per cent of the cases would not be there if soldiers would manfully determine not to allow themselves to be led into any excesses of ANY KIND. They would be better men physically and morally. The vicious man is never an athlete, and conversely the athlete is always a well conducted man.[232]

This seems to suggest that though gymnastics undoubtedly contributed a great deal to the health of the army, it was in conflict with deeply ingrained patterns of behaviour.

6. Clothing

The report of the Army Sanitary Commission in 1858 devoted a relatively small amount of space to the influence of clothing on the health of the soldier. It did stress however the importance of protection and freedom of movement. The basic uniform then consisted of tight-fitting and uncomfortable tunics and trousers, heavy ungainly helmets, high choking stocks, and cumbersome ill-designed accoutrements. Much of the extra equipment in a man's kit was of doubtful value, some of it through design or manufacture virtually useless. The army greatcoat for instance '. . .of very bad material, of little use against the cold, while it readily imbibes and retains wet'.[233] By 1900 the picture was only just changing despite occasional official enquiries and a great deal of public interest. In general the agitation for modification of the uniform centred around the question of utility, and not specifically health.

In 1851 an article by Lieutenant-Colonel E. Napier in *Colburn's United Services Magazine* advocated more modern and better quality clothing, lighter and less cumbersome belts, and a universal service dress. Infantry kit at that time weighed well over sixty eight pounds.[234] In 1855 Charles Hamley argued in *Blackwood's Magazine* that the clothing and equipment of the soldier restricted both movement and respiration, and gave no shelter from the elements. In the future, he urged, all clothing should be serviceable, adaptable, comfortable, and provide protection from the weather.[235] Three years later the views of the Army Sanitary Commission supporting these arguments were made known. But resistance to change and to the expense of re-equipment, not only on the part of the army but successive governments as well, shortened the pace of progress. In 1865 a War Office committee was drawn up to look into the relationship between heart and lung disease and the uniform and equipment of the soldier. Returns from Fort Pitt military hospital showed that one man in seven with under two years' service was discharged for heart disease, yet the average incidence of this ailment in the whole army was one in thirteen. Lung disease claimed one in three with under two years' service, one in five in the army as a whole.[236] These figures tend to indicate a larger proportion of infirmity in the younger age group as heart and lung disease claimed most of their victims among recruits and younger soldiers. The explanations the committee offered (and Professor E.A. Parkes and Dr T.G. Logan, the Inspector-General of Hospitals, were among its members) was not that military drill or duties were excessive, but that restrictive clothing and equipment and the uniform's poor protection from the weather were especially harmful to the younger soldier.

In spite of some very straightforward recommendations for the improvement of uniforms and equipment, supported by continued agitation in the military press over the next few years,[237] progress was slow. Flannel underclothing was introduced and the stock eventually abolished, but pipeclay, brass buttons and easily soiled uniforms persisted until the turn of the century.[238] A War Office enquiry in 1897 into the various patterns of headdress then in use in the army found the lightest helmet a weighty sixteen ounces, the heaviest, that of the Life Guards, nearly three pounds.[239] In 1908 another enquiry into the physiological effects of food, clothing and training charged that there was still too much stress placed by officers on show and smartness on the line of march, and that tightly buttoned tunics and heavy awkward equipment seriously reduced physical capabilities.[240]

Regulars at home and on active service continued to wear scarlet for most of these years.[241] After red had proved such a conspicuous target at Majuba Hill in 1881 the Adjutant-General, Garnet Wolseley, threw his weight behind efforts to modernise and improve the army uniform.[242] In 1883 a committee of which he was chairman suggested the adoption of grey for service dress.[243] But attachment in the army to the traditional scarlet was strong and not to be easily overcome. In April the Commander-in-Chief, speaking at a dinner at the Mansion House, stated:

> I should be sorry to see the day when the English Army is no longer in red. I am not one of those who think it at all desirable to hide ourselves too much. I must say I think the soldier had better be taught not to hide himself, but to go gallantly to the front. In action the man who does that has a much better chance of succeeding than the man who hides himself.[244]

Military thinking like this led of course to disaster in South Africa sixteen years later.

Khaki service dress was introduced in time for the Boer War and in 1900 a committee under the chairmanship of Major-General Vetch recommended that the uniform be restricted to working and full dress, and that working dress incorporate comfort, utility and protection.[245] The War guaranteed the adoption of these reforms, and by 1902 more sensible uniforms were at last in use. It was also only in 1899 that the War Office took steps to improve the army issue boot.[246]

A decrease in the weight of the equipment carried took place gradually. In 1871 the valise replaced the knapsack and by the late 1880s webbing was beginning to replace leather. In 1888 the weight of the infantry pack was reduced to forty-one pounds, or fifty-six including arms and ammunition. In transit eighteen pounds of this went into a separate valise for shipment. The tendency with arms and ammunition though was in the other direction. The weight of the infantry rifle and of each round of ammunition remained fairly constant but more was carried as the calibre of the rifles was reduced. The soldier equipped with the .45 calibre Martini-Henry packed seventy rounds in 1871; the Lee-Metford rifle, a .303 introduced in 1889, required ninety rounds; the .303 Lee-Enfield, the standard weapon of both world wars, 100 or more.[247]

There is ample evidence that enlisted men would have welcomed improvements to their dress,[248] yet the restrictions of military discipline prevented any advocacy on their part, at least while serving.[249] Another factor was the low standards of dress many seem to have been used to before enlistment. Working men were not forced to wear tight jackets and heavy hats or to carry useless equipment for the sake of fashion, yet financial restrictions bound them as effectively. For those who had to make do with what they could afford, the army might be a source of undreamt-of luxuries. Few of those who received their first pair of boots on enlistment would be likely to complain that they were uncomfortable.[250] When all is said and done inadequate clothing undoubtedly contributed to the statistics of poor health in the army, especially in circumstances of poor accommodation. Yet significant clothing reforms were not brought about much before 1900, and therefore did not figure more than marginally in the considerable improvement which took place in army health after 1857.

7. Diet

What and how the soldier eats determines to a certain extent the health he enjoys. How far was the quality of army food responsible for the ill-health of the forces in 1856; did the army diet change significantly over the subsequent forty years; and if so, what was the effect of these changes on the health and condition of the enlisted man?

The soldier's official ration was first fixed in 1813, and remained essentially unchanged for fifty years. It consisted simply of one pound of bread and three-quarters of a pound of meat per man per day. By 1857, when the Army Sanitary Commission looked into the diet of the army, this was frequently supplemented either on a regimental level by the addition of vegetables, spices, tea and butter, for which an extra charge was made on the soldier's pay, or by the soldiers themselves who might purchase extra prepared meals on their own.[251] Conditions varied considerably from regiment to regiment, but it was not uncommon for the staples of the day to be merely bread, meat and potatoes. This was normally served in three lots: an early breakfast of bread and a basin of tea, a twelve o'clock dinner of beef and potatoes, and a four o'clock supper of tea supplemented with whatever of his day's bread each man had left from the morning. Such a diet was neither nutritious nor was there enough of it to fill an empty stomach.[252] Because cooking facilities were limited–they usually consisted of merely a large copper boiler–boiled beef and potatoes were served with monotonous regularity.[253] Furthermore twelve ounces of meat, after boiling and with the bone removed, frequently cooked down to no more than seven ounces of tough stringy food which one needed the best of teeth to chew. Under such circumstances men sent their meals out to be baked at their own expense, supplemented them with food bought elsewhere, refused to eat army food altogether and either ate elsewhere, killed their appetite with tobacco and beer, or sometimes ate what there was and still went hungry.[254]

The question of the relationship between the soldier's diet and the state of his health concerned the Army Sanitary Commission in 1857. The soldier's legendary intemperance was considered as a possible cause of his high mortality, only to be dismissed because he probably drank no more than other members of his class, and because of the absence of a high incidence of those diseases which would have been due to excessive alcohol consumption. Nevertheless Commissioners were unequivocal about the inadequacy of the soldier's diet and the direction in which responsibility for improvement lay. 'It is clearly the duty of the Government', their report remarked,

> to see that the soldier is supplied with and consumes a diet so composed as to keep him, as far as possible, at all times and in all climates in health and efficiency. . .a mere bread and meat ration, even if increased in quantity, could never ensure health, even with the addition of vegetable food.[255]

The Commission had at their disposal medical evidence including chemical analysis. Although scientific dietary knowledge was not great and there was as yet no understanding of the importance of vitamins, they were unanimous about the necessity for greater variety in diet and the inclusion of vegetables and fats in the menu. Their report also made the point that 'the men will never secure the whole advantage to be derived from the supply of materials of a sufficient ration unless proper and sufficient means of cooking it are provided'.[256]

After 1858 varied cooking facilities and modern kitchens were installed in many army barracks in conjunction with the introduction of sanitary reforms.[257] In 1870 the army's School of Cooking opened its doors at Aldershot and within a few years the effect of trained cooks was being felt. But progress was halting and at best uneven. There was a reluctance by military authorities to exert too much control over the soldier's diet and there was a limit too to the expense to which the War Office was willing to go. The basic meat and bread ration in the army remained unchanged before 1900. After 1857 an extra threepence halfpenny per man was allotted for the inclusion of vegetables, spices and condiments in the daily menu, but it was left to regimental authorities to contract for and supply the food from this fund. The variation in diet from unit to unit was as a result extreme. Commanding officers with the ability and the interest to deal with supplies and to experiment with menus came up with a very substantial diet. A War Office enquiry under the chairmanship of Sir Stafford Northcote into army messing in 1889 was especially impressed for instance by the quantity and quality of the meals served in the Royal Irish Rifles.[258] At the same time the meals provided by many other regimental messes were uninspired and unappetising. An editorial article in *Colburn's United Services Magazine* in 1876 remarked that army food was as coarse, insipid and wearisome as that issued to criminals and in the circumstances it is not surprising that most of the soldier's pay went towards beer and food.[259] In 1884 Lieutenant-Colonel C. B. Tulloch delivered a lecture before the Royal United Services Institution in which he charged that the standard military diet was insufficient in quantity and that it contained many nutritional deficiencies. 'Unfortunately', he argued, 'an excess in one kind of nutriment required by the body will not make up for the deficiencies in another, any more than a deficiency in boots could be made good by a second pair of trousers.'[260] Those attending the lecture warmly supported Tulloch's conclusions. Colonel William Knollys for instance allowed 'I am quite certain, if the growing lads we have, had as much to eat as they wanted, they would drink very much less, they would smoke very much less strong tobacco'.[261]

A. F. Corbett, a regular soldier who enlisted in the late 1890s, recalled of his military service:'. . .sometimes I was so hungry at night. Fortunately the heavy drinkers were lighter eaters, and many times I have felt along the barrack shelves and found a dry crust for my supper.

To be poor and independent is nearly an impossibility'.[262] Horace Wyndham was in the Service at approximately the same time. He recollected that the quality of the food served in his regiment was adequate, but there just was not enough of it. The young recruits he remembered ate nearly all their bread for breakfast and had to do without for the rest of the day. By the time their meat ration had been cooked they were lucky to get seven or eight ounces. Uncommonly greasy tea, the result of boiling water in the potato pots, then allowing the tea to stew for an hour, was served with every meal.[263] 'Wullie' Robertson began his army career, which eventually led him to the position of Chief of the Imperial General Staff, in 1877. When he enlisted regulation meals consisted of coffee and bread, meat and potatoes with a soup or pudding once a week. If supper or something besides dry bread for breakfast was fancied, this had to be purchased from barrack hawkers or the canteen.[264] An official pamphlet issued for recruiting purposes and entitled *Life in the Ranks of the English Army* remarked in 1883 that men were free to 'buy some butter, cheese, or bacon, to help down the dry bread at breakfast and tea'.[265] Hardly the most attractive inducement to a career in the army.

In 1889 Dr J. Lane Notter, Professor of Military Hygiene at the Army Medical School, spoke to the Royal United Services Institution on 'The Soldier's Food, with Reference to Health and Efficiency for Service'. In his lecture he criticised the nutritional content of the army's normal diet, its monotony, and the refusal of military authorities to provide a late meal on the grounds that men off duty supposedly preferred instead to leave the barracks in the evening.[266] Notter's criticism focused on the poor quality of the rations, and other evidence supports his charge. William Douglas, an ex-soldier, wrote in 1865 '. . .a soldier's rations are seldom or ever even of an average quality. In towns the gentry get the best of the meat, so the contractor sends the worst to the barracks'.[267] Another serviceman, A.V. Palmer, charged in an article in *The Nineteenth Century* in 1890 that there were so many middle men in the contract system that weights were frequently short and the soldier cheated in his meals.[268] In 1866 the War Office was criticised in public for condoning the issue of bad bread and meat rations to troops in Canterbury.[269] Within three years, the Northcote Committee looking into the soldier's diet had confirmed charges that inspection was poor and that the quality and quantity of rations were inadequate.[270] A letter from an Oxford butcher addressed to Sir William Harcourt, the Under-Secretary of State, was appended to an original copy of the report, now in War Office files. It is illustrative of the carelessness with which military authorities received contracted supplies:

> I have long known that the beef supplied for the consumption of soldiers and sailors was not what it should be, consisting as it does of the boniest and most unprofitable beast we receive from abroad. . .it is evident that by purchasing a better class of animal our soldiers would have 2 or 3 ounces more to every pound supplied. Besides this the meat would be a better quality and more nourishing. With regard to the mutton supply–it is well known to consist of the oldest and worst description of ewes. There seems to be no way to secure a better supply except by the appointment of an experienced man as inspector.[271]

The enquiry and recommendations of the Northcote Committee undoubtedly improved army food and messing in general. The exposure of the normally inadequate inspection of contracted meat and other supplies led the War Office to agree to the introduction of special classes at London meat markets and subsequently at Aldershot to instruct regimental officers in the inspection of meat; and later to the appointment of three officers (one for Ireland, two for Britain) whose assignment it was to visit barracks and report on the quality of rations issued. Revisions were also made in the contract system to prevent tampering with carcasses in order to conceal age and sex, and provision was made for heavy fines to be imposed whenever improper meat was tendered. The enquiry also revealed complaints of bread being issued uncooked or sour. Because the customary four-pound loaves were in practice too large to be used immediately, soldiers had to throw away quantities of stale bread daily. Although the government refused to make what were considered unnecessary improvements in the flour and yeast that was used, it did agree to the baking of bread in more economical two-pound loaves.

By 1890 army cooking seems to have become notably better. Variety and care in preparation meant at least that food was more palatable, and perhaps that it was more nutritious as well. In the next decade efforts to better the contracting and supply of rations would begin to make army meals more attractive still. With the gradual assumption of the duties of contracting and supply of the newly formed Army Service Corps, greater attempts to vary and supplement basic rations with other foods were made after 1890. Army meals were more nutritional and more substantial and the importance of a well-balanced diet became generally accepted. In 1891 a lieutenant from the Royal Irish Rifles spoke to the

Royal United Services Institution on army cooking and messing. His implication that his regiment was the only one serving anywhere near decent meals was angrily received and disputed by fellow officers.[272]

All this amounted to a significant contribution to the health of the army. Yet because of the decentralised nature of army messing the improvements were far from uniform at least before 1890. Even so, army meals did not necessarily compare unfavourably with civilian food. One of the results of a better diet may be an increased resistance to disease; and it can be argued that army diets were in many respects superior to those enjoyed by the civilian working classes. Military authorities frequently observed that the health of recruits improved even on basic army meals. This was confirmed by the findings of both the Herbert and Northcote Commissions in 1857 and 1889.[273] The work of Charles Booth and Seebohm Rowntree and the findings of the Interdepartmental Committee on Physical Deterioration were testimony to the inadequacy of the diet among the poorest sections of the working class.[274] Some households were lucky to see meat once a week. Such was the relative effect of any army diet, that at least by the end of the period recruits on furlough frequently returned to their families not only heavier, but sometimes taller than when they enlisted.[275]

8. Conclusion

The forty or so years between 1856 and 1900 were remarkable because of advances in medical science and public health, which affected both soldier and civilian, but a number of special factors influenced the conditions of military service. Change within the army came partly from recruiting difficulties since there were claims from time to time that the state of army health and the condition of army barracks deterred enlistment. But there was a quite independent public concern about the health of the army and the marshalling of this opinion by reformers at times had an important influence. When interest in the forces lagged, reform too faltered unless it could be carried on routinely and at little expense. Much of the public was ready to believe at such times that the necessary reforms had been seen to, and that progress had been rapid. Others, underestimating the real extent of change, continued to associate the health of the army with the Crimea. But 1856–99 was a transition period, and the conditions of service were never as advanced nor as regressive as they were often thought to be.

Notes

1. The working classes did not regularly consult a physician when ill, nor was there compulsory notification of disease throughout Britain until 1899. The only comprehensive statistics available therefore are those showing rates of mortality.
2. *Report of the Royal Commission on the Regulations Affecting the Sanitary Condition of the Army, the Organisation of Military Hospitals, and the Treatment of the Sick and Wounded,* P.P., XVIII (c.2318), 1857–8, p.viii; cited hereafter as *Report of the Army Sanitary Commission* (1857–8).
3. *Report of the Army Sanitary Commission* (1857–8), pp.vii-xi, xxx.
4. Significant fluctuations in figures from year to year did not, in bodies of men like the Guards, necessarily represent a significant change in the health of the forces, since the number of men involved was often small. The tendency of statistics such as these to give a mistaken impression concerned their compilers, but no satisfactory remedy could be found. T. G. Balfour to Florence Nightingale, 4 March 1861, Nightingale MSS., 45772.
5. These figures would reflect 1,000 admissions to hospitals in a unit of 1,000 men as 100.0, similarly more than one visit by the same man may result in (say) 1,050 admissions or a proportion of 105.
6. Army medical services were extended between 1856 and 1899, and in the circumstances it is likely that the soldier made more use of them than he otherwise would have. Certainly improvements to the medical care provided under the Poor Law resulted in an increase in expenses and a greater use of available facilities. The drop in the proportion of soldiers admitted to hospital each year between 1860 and 1899 would therefore appear all that more significant.
7. The percentages of men invalided from the home army in these years were 1.8 and 2.2 respectively. *Report of the Army Medical Department,* P.P., XXXIII (c.3051), 1862, p.32; XXXIX (c.521), 1901, p.23.
8. Charles Booth, in his monumental study of the poor in London, noted that the death rate per capita was very much higher in the poorer districts than in middle or upper-class areas. He was unable to say however how much of this was due to high infantile mortality rates. Charles Booth, *Life and Labour of the People in London,* Final Volume (1903), p.26.
9. Minimum physical standards were progressively lowered and sometimes varied between 1856 and 1899. There was no definite standard of height at the beginning of the period as there was at the end, but recruiters may have enlisted only those whom they considered to be of adequate size. Because standards were specified but then were sometimes disregarded if a recruit seemly likely to grow, the responsibility for ruling upon a man's physical stature devolved more upon army medical authorities. See Appendix I, Table IA-1.
10. See Appendix I, Table IA-2.
11. Surgeon-General T. Longmore, *Manual of Instruction for the Guidance of Army Surgeons in Testing the Range and Quality of Vision of Recruits, and in Distinguishing the Causes of Defective Vision in Soldiers* (1875), p.61; *Memorandum of the Inspector-General of Recruiting,* P.P., XLII (c.57), 1870, p.2.
12. *Report of the Army Medical Department,* P.P., XXXIV (c.3233), 1863, p.28.
13. *Report of the Army Medical Department,* P.P., LIII (c.9453), 1899, p.38.
14. See for instance Major-General Sir Frederic Maurice, 'National Health,

a Soldier's Study', *The Contemporary Review,* LXXXIII (1903), pp.41–57; and Miles, 'Where to Get Men', *The Contemporary Review,* LXXXI (1902), pp.78–87.

15. *Report of the Interdepartmental Committee on Physical Deterioration,* P.P., XXXII (c.2175), 1904, pp.1–2, 16–21, 39–41; cited hereinafter as *Report of the Physical Deterioration Committee* (1904).
16. Throughout the 17th and 18th centuries, Parliament had been generally opposed to a large standing army and tended to look upon barrack construction as an excuse to increase the establishment. The current system of billeting troops on the civilian population was seen on the other hand to tend towards the reduction of the numbers under arms and to encourage a healthy dislike for soldiers. Colonel Sir Charles M. Watson, *History of the Corps of Royal Engineers,* III (Chatham, 1915), 133.
17. Troop Sergeant-Major Edwin Mole, *A King's Hussar* (1893), p.303.
18. John Ryder, *Four Years' Service in India* (Leicester, 1853), p.199.
19. *Report of the Committee on Barrack Accommodation for the Army,* P.P., XXXII (c.405), 1854–5, p.iii; cited hereafter as *Report of the Barrack Accommodation Committee* (1854–5).
20. A minimum of 400 to 500 cubic feet of space per man in temperate climates was specified. This regulation was laid down in *Orders and Regulations for the Guidance of the Corps of Royal Engineers and Royal Sappers and Miners at Home and Abroad* (1 January 1851).
21. *Report of the Barrack Accommodation Committee* (1854–5), p.iii; *Report of the Army Sanitary Commission* (1857–8), p.xvii.
22. *Report of the Barrack Accommodation Committee* (1854–5), pp.78–91.
23. *Report of the Army Sanitary Commission* (1857–8), pp.xvii-xix.
24. Robert Edmondson, *John Bull's Army from Within* (1907), p.30.
25. Pointed out to me by Mr W. F. Boag, M.A., Scottish United Services Museum, Edinburgh Castle. I have found no evidence to support this, but it seems likely that it may have happened occasionally.
26. *Report of the Army Sanitary Commission* (1857–8), p.295.
27. Ibid., p.xvii.
28. Ibid., p.194.
29. A.E. Sullivan, 'Married Quarters–a Retrospect', *Army Quarterly* (1951), pp.113–19; see also *Report of a Committee on the Married Establishment of the Army,* WO.33/38; Dr Rennie, 'Supplementary Remarks on the Army Reorganisation Question', *Colburn's* II (1867), pp.164–8; *Report of the Barrack Accommodation Committee* (1854–5), p.iv.
30. *Treatment of Soldiers' Families in Garrison Hospitals,* WO.43/75.
31. *Report of the Army Sanitary Commission* (1857–8), p.xviii.
32. Lt.-Col. Maule to Deputy Q.M. General, 21–6 July 1851, Panmure MSS., GD45/8/96. The War Office was criticised for the distress experienced by soldiers' wives who were left behind in England when regiments went overseas, and were urged to make some provision to advance them part of their husbands' pay immediately upon separation. This suggestion was rejected on the grounds that it would entail a change in book-keeping procedures. Florence Nightingale to Douglas Galton, 21 Sept. 1863, Nightingale MSS., 45761.
33. Rev. S.P.H. Stratham, 'Marriages in the Army without Leave', *The United Services Magazine,* VI (1892–3), pp.295–305; Horace Wyndham, *The Queen's Service* (1899), p.271.
34. *Lancet,* II (1853), p.393.
35. Royston Lambert, *Sir John Simon 1816–1904 and English Social Administration* (1963), p.49.

36. In 1893 for instance Florence Nightingale discussing a recent conference held in Buckinghamshire wrote to Sir Douglas Galton, 'God forbid that the Bucks. Sanitary Conference should come to the conclusion that Typhoid Fever, Diphtheria, etc. of which they have had a great deal are the direct consequence of Bacillus F, Bacillus D instead of bad drainage, cesspools instead of dry earth closets, fouled water supply, etc. etc.' Florence Nightingale to Douglas Galton, 24 May 1893, Nightingale MSS., 45766.
37. Suggestions for Executing Sanitary Works in Barracks and Hospitals, WO.33/19.
38. *Report of the Inquiry on the Deficient Warming of Barracks,* WO.32/6966.
39. This is amply shown by Sir Edward Cook in *The Life of Florence Nightingale,* I (1914), pp.311–415, and by Cecil Woodham-Smith in *Florence Nightingale, 1820–1910* (1950), pp.263–330. The many volumes of the Nightingale Papers now in the British Museum contain a mass of such information. The most important are those containing correspondence with Sidney Herbert, Douglas Galton, John Sutherland, T.G. Balfour, Lord de Grey and Lord Panmure. See BM.Add.MSS.43394–7, 45751–67, 45772–3, and 45824; also the Panmure Papers, GD45/8/327.
40. Herbert's influence is discussed in Lord Stanmore's *Sidney Herbert* (1906); and by Cook in *Life of Florence Nightingale,* I, pp.311–415, and Woodham-Smith in *Florence Nightingale,* pp.270–376.
41. While on the one hand there is no doubt that Nightingale's knowledge was immense and that she was widely respected for her technical expertise, there are a number of instances where material that went out under her signature was not in fact her own. The volumes of her correspondence reveal two such occasions in 1861 for instance, where she wrote to Douglas Galton offering him advice on materials to be used in hospital construction. In each case she had previously received letters from Sutherland outlining the same principles in precisely the same wording. In 1863 there was an instance where a letter from Nightingale to Douglas Galton about an India Office–War Office conjoint commission on Indian sanitation was matched by a note of the same date and in identical wording in Sutherland's writing. And there are other such examples. Florence Nightingale's biographers remark on her dependence on Sutherland in later years, but go no further. See John Sutherland to Florence Nightingale, 3 February 1861, 20 August 1861; Florence Nightingale to Douglas Galton, 3 February 1861, 4 March 1861, 20 August 1861. Nightingale MSS., 45759, 45761. See also Cook, *Nightingale,* II, pp.205–6, and Woodham-Smith, *Nightingale,* p.511.
42. J. H. Lefroy to Florence Nightingale, 26 August 1856, Nightingale MSS., 43397. Florence Nightingale too argued that the only way to influence Ministers was through the public.
43. Florence Nightingale to Sidney Herbert, 18 February 1858; Florence Nightingale to Douglas Galton, 6 June 1864, Nightingale MSS., 43394, 45762.
44. See for instance *The Times,* 1 February 1856; 9 May 1856; Hansard, CXLII (19 June 1856), cc.1706–1712; also Woodham-Smith, *Nightingale* pp.263–73.
45. Draft instructions were submitted to the government by Florence Nightingale and Sidney Herbert. The latter had reluctantly agreed to be chairman, and then only on his own terms, but was allowed to vet the final versions. Other members of the Commission included Andrew Smith, the much-criticised Director-General of the Army Medical Department; Thomas Alexander, an army doctor noted for his interest in sanitary reform; and Dr John Sutherland. Florence Nightingale exerted a considerable

influence from the background. She submitted statistics and other important written material, commented on the evidence of witnesses called, and even advised Herbert on the examination of witnesses and other procedures. There is a great deal of material about the Commission in the Nightingale papers. See especially the Nightingale-Herbert correspondence in BM.Add.MSS.43394, and Florence Nightingale's own notes in BM.Add.MSS.45823. See also Lord Panmure's correspondence with Sidney Herbert in the Panmure MSS., GD45/8/327.

46. *Report of the Army Sanitary Commission* (1857–8), pp.xvii, lxxvi.
47. Florence Nightingale to Sidney Herbert, 12 March 1858, Nightingale MSS., 43395; Cook, *Nightingale,* II, p.377.
48. Sidney Herbert to W.E. Gladstone, 17 February 1858, Gladstone MSS., 44211.
49. *The Times,* 6 February 1858.
50. Ibid., 9 February 1858.
51. *Punch,* 27 March 1858.
52. D. MacDougall, *The Sanitary Reform of the British Army* (1858), passim. See also some of the material in the collection of Parkes Pamphlets in the Royal Army Medical College.
53. Sidney Herbert, 'The Sanitary Condition of the Army', *The Westminster Review,* LXXI (1859), pp.52–98.
54. James T. Howell, 'The Health of the Army', *The Edinburgh Review,* CVIII (1858), pp.136–65; see also Andrew Wynter, 'The Lodging, Food, and Dress of Soldiers', *The Quarterly Review,* CV (1859), pp.155–76; J.H. Burton, 'The Soldier and the Surgeon', *Blackwood's Edinburgh Magazine* LXXXIV (1858), pp.1–24; Anon., 'The Sanitary Condition of the Army', *Dublin University Magazine,* LI (1858), pp.210–24; Anon., 'Organisation of the War Department', *The Westminster Review,* LIX (1858), p.537.
55. Evolutionist, 'Decentralisation', *Colburn's,* III (1889), p.129.
56. Separate day rooms as such were not to be introduced; however the need for them was obviated by the provision during the next forty years of extensive recreational facilities in barracks, including coffee bars, games rooms and auditoriums. This is discussed fully in Chapter 3 below.
57. *Report of the Barrack Accommodation Committee* (1854–5), pp.21–38.
58. Ibid., pp.38–49.
59. Hansard, CXLIX (26 March 1858), cc.802–803.
60. Ibid., c.798
61. During the winter of 1886–7, Field Marshall Sir Evelyn Wood, as Inspector-General of the Eastern Military District, was shocked to find one Commanding Officer who after six months at a particular station did not know upon what principle the camp latrines functioned, nor even where they were situated. Field Marshal Sir Evelyn Wood, *From Midshipman to Field Marshal,* II (1906), p.272.
62. Florence Nightingale to Douglas Galton, 1 February 1869, Nightingale MSS., 45763.
63. 'Last year there was a sentiment of danger at home which disposed people to wish for a strong army as well as a strong navy', Gladstone remarked in 1861. 'This year the sentiment of danger was materially abated; and a cry for economy has become audible.' W.E. Gladstone to Sidney Herbert, 26 January 1861. Gladstone MSS., 44211; see also Hansard, CLII (4 March 1859), cc.1311-38; CLVI (17 February 1860), cc.1278-1314.
64. Hansard (3 August 1866), CLXXXIV, cc.1999–2003; CXLIX (26 March 1858), cc.790–6; Sidney Herbert to W.E. Gladstone, 8 March 1857;

W.E. Gladstone to Sidney Herbert, 19 December 1859, 31 March 1860, Gladstone MSS., 44210–1.

65. In 1865 Lord Panmure, now the Earl of Dalhousie, launched an attack in the House of Lords on sanitary principles in general and sanitarians in particular. Woodham-Smith sees it as a mark of progress that his comments fell flat. Woodham-Smith, *Nightingale*, pp.402–3. See also Hansard, CLXXVII (6 March 1865), c.1099.
66. *Report of the Barrack and Hospital Improvement Commission*, P.P., XVI (c.2839), 1861, p.33; cited hereafter as *Report of the Army Sanitary Committee* (1861).
67. *Report of the Barrack Accommodation Committee* (1854–5), pp.v–xiii.
68. *Report of the Army Sanitary Commission* (1857–8), p.xvii.
69. Herbert promised Panmure that he would be the one to receive the credit for quick results. Sidney Herbert to Lord Panmure, 7 August 1857; Lord Panmure to Sidney Herbert, 8 August 1857, Panmure MSS., GD45/8/327.
70. Reformers also hoped that the appointment of the sub-commissions would save Herbert, who was not at this time a member of the government, from the invidious and untenable position of being asked to answer in the House of Commons for the spending of public funds. He was able to remain involved by obtaining a place on each. Florence Nightingale, Note on the Appointment of Sub-Commissions, circa August 1857; Sidney Herbert to Florence Nightingale, 7 August 1857, Nightingale MSS., 43394, 45823.
71. Florence Nightingale, Army Sanitary Administration and its Reform under the late Lord Herbert, 12 June 1862, Nightingale MSS., 43395.
72. The original instructions for the Army Sanitary Committee were submitted to the War Office in draft by Herbert and Nightingale; the latter acted in an advisory capacity, commenting extensively on its enquiries and the measures necessary to improve specific sanitary defects. See Florence Nightingale, Draft Instructions for the Guidance of the Barrack and Hospital Improvement Commission, 7–16 August 1857, Nightingale MSS., 45824. See also Florence Nightingale's correspondence with Sidney Herbert, Douglas Galton and John Sutherland in BM., Add.MSS.43394–5, 45751, 45759; Sidney Herbert to Lord Panmure, 22 November 1856, 16 August 1857, Panmure MSS., GD45/8/327.
73. *Interim Reports on Barracks*, WO.33/6a.
74. Florence Nightingale, Army Sanitary Administration and its Reform under the late Lord Herbert, 12 June 1862, Nightingale MSS., 43395.
75. *Correspondence Relating to Barrack Improvements, etc.*, P.P., XXXVII (c.300), 1857–8.
76. *Army Estimates 1859–60*, P.P., XLI (c.60), 1860.
77. Lord Stanley to W.H. Smith, 12 November 1886, Smith MSS., WO.110/6.
78. See for instance Lord Panmure's correspondence with the Queen on this matter in Panmure MSS., GD45/8/145.
79. *General Annual Return of the British Army*, P.P., LIII (c.9426), 1899, p.8.
80. An inquiry by the Army Sanitary Committee into the ventilation of cavalry stables in 1864 for instance showed that troop accommodation–the quartering of men above the horses–which had in an earlier era been found unobjectionable was now no longer acceptable. *Report of the Committee on the Ventilation of Cavalry Stables*, P.P., XVI (c.3290), 1864, p.5.
81. *Report of the Army Sanitary Committee* (1861), pp.155–6.

82. Florence Nightingale, Memorandum on the Army Sanitary Committee circa 1887, Nightingale MSS., 45824.
83. *Report of the Army Sanitary Committee* (1861), p.157.
84. Florence Nightingale to Lord de Grey and Ripon, 1 Feb. 1869, 28 Jan. 1870, Ripon MSS., 43546; Florence Nightingale to Edward Cardwell, 5 Feb. 1869; Florence Nightingale to The Barrack and Hospital Improvement Commission, 13 April 1877; Florence Nightingale to Douglas Galton, 17 June1888; Nightingale MSS., 45753, 45766, 45787.
85. See for instance *Report of the Barrack and Hospital Improvement Commission,* P.P., XIII (c.3084), 1863, pp.17, 24, 193; cited hereafter as *Report of the Army Sanitary Committee* (1863).
86. Even reformers seem to have regarded their task complete and to have concentrated their interests elsewhere. Florence Nightingale's correspondence shows that in later years she tended to concentrate principally on the questions of Indian and Indian army sanitation. See BM., Add.MSS.45758. See also her correspondence with the Earl de Grey and Ripon, Ripon MSS., 43546; and her correspondence with Edward Stanhope, Stanhope MSS., 1313.
87. *Report of an Inquiry by a Sub-Committee of the Army Sanitary Committee on Deficient Warming and Ventilation of Barrack Rooms at Certain Stations in the United Kingdom,* WO.32/6966; Anon., 'The Knightsbridge Barracks', *Colburn's* (1870), p.90; Major-General J.F.C. Fuller, *The Army In My Time* (1935), p.60; Robert Edmondson, *Is a Soldier's Life Worth Living?* (circa 1902), p.13; idem, *John Bull's Army From Within* (1907), p.30.
88. During the 1890s expenditure on army barracks was greater than indicated by the army estimates alone. See Appendix I, Table IA–3.
89. Significantly, the principal victims of the unhealthy quarters in this case were not rank and file, but commissioned officers. For this reason all that much more notice was taken.
90. *Report of the Army Sanitary Committee* (1861), p.15.
91. John Sutherland reported enthusiastically in 1871 on the state of Dublin barracks and the improvements that had been carried out since Sidney Herbert's first visit in 1859. He commented particularly on the excellent recreational facilities that had been installed. J. Sutherland to Florence Nightingale, 20 March 1871, Nightingale MSS., 45755.
92. *Interim Report on the Sanitary Condition of the Royal Barracks, Dublin,* P.P., XVII (c.5653), 1889, p.4; cited hereafter as *Interim Report on Dublin Barracks* (1889).
93. The Secretary of State for War, W.H. Smith, showed particular concern. A series of reports from the Adjutant-General and Principal Medical Officers highlighted the problem, and in November a report from Sir A. Orr-Ewing called attention to the state of cavalry barracks in the City. 'I have known many young men who have lost their lives by the shameful unhealthy condition of these barracks', wrote Ewing. 'It must be either the water or the drainage. Surely it is the duty of the government to protect the lives of their soldiers by giving them the best sanitary arrangements.' Reports by the Adjutant-General and Principal Medical Officers, circa 1886. Sir A. Orr-Ewing to W.H. Smith, 17 Nov. 1886, Smith MSS., WO.110/5. Smith did not leave matters lie at that, but sought further information and advice. When contacted, Florence Nightingale remarked, 'Dublin barracks lie like a nightmare on me and always have.' Florence Nightingale to Douglas Galton, 7 Dec. 1886, Nightingale MSS., 45764. Requests to Lord Stanley for confidential reports produced a

different result. Stanley freely admitted that army barracks in Dublin were in need of improvement, but doubted for military reasons if the troops could be moved. 'If they are needed in unhealthy areas,' he argued, 'then they must stay and die.' Lord Stanley to W.H. Smith, 12 Nov. 1886; W.H. Smith to Lord Stanley, 10 Dec. 1886, Smith MSS., WO.110/6.

94. *Report on the Prevalence of Enteric Fever in the Royal Barracks, Dublin*, P.P., XXV (c.5292), 1888, pp.19–20.
95. *Interim Report on Dublin Barracks* (1889), p.12.
96. Sir Henry Ponsonby to Edward Stanhope, 6 Jan., 20 Jan., 26 Jan. 1889, 28 Feb. 1892; Edward Stanhope to Queen Victoria, 8 Jan., 22 Jan. 1889; Stanhope MSS., 1367, 1396, 1407.
97. General Sir Lothian Nicholson to Edward Stanhope, 8 Feb. 1890; Lord Wolseley to Edward Stanhope, 27 Nov. 1891; Stanhope MSS., 1316, 1333.
98. Hansard, CCCX (17 February 1887), c.1763.
99. In 1886 W.H. Smith had begun to think hard about barrack accommodation in the army. He calculated that expenditures in excess of £1,660,000 were necessary to replace temporary huts erected in 1855–6, yet all he would propose to spend during 1886–7 was £70,800. W.H. Smith, Notes on Army Huts, Circa 1886, Smith MSS., WO.110/8. General Sir Lothian Nicholson, the Inspector-General of Fortifications, seriously doubted if the Treasury would agree to the funds necessary for barrack repairs. In 1887 he had estimated that £9 million was necessary for improvements alone. General Sir Lothian Nicholson to Edward Stanhope, 11 Nov. 1889, Stanhope MSS., 1316.
100. Hansard, CCCXXII (10 February 1888), c.154.
101. Hansard, CCCXXX (20 November 1888), c.1657.
102. Part of the problem with Aldershot was that it had originally been intended for use as temporary or seasonal accommodation, and there was therefore not as much effort spent as there should have been in constructing suitable permanent barracks. See the Duke of Cambridge to Lord Panmure, 12 Dec. 1856; Lord Panmure, Notes on Aldershot, no date; Panmure MSS., GD45/8/117, GD45/8/496.
103. Watson, *History of the Royal Engineers*, III, p.161.
104. B. Seebohm Rowntree, *Poverty, a Study of Town Life* (1900), p.144.
105. Robert Roberts, *The Classic Slum* (Manchester, 1971), p.19.
106. Hansard, CCCXXXIII (11 March 1889), c.1434.
107. Hansard, CCCXXXIII (11 March 1889), cc.1435, 1442–7; Florence Nightingale argued that Lothian Nicholson was chiefly responsible for persuading Stanhope to set the required funds aside. There is no doubt that his influence was an important one, but so too was that of Stanhope's colleagues in government and in Parliament. Florence Nightingale to Douglas Galton, 9 Aug. 1889, Nightingale MSS., 45766.
108. Florence Nightingale, Notes on the ASC, no date. Nightingale MSS., 45824; Douglas Galton to Edward Stanhope, 11 Dec. 1888, 20 Dec. 1889, Stanhope MSS., 1349; Edward Stanhope to Douglas Galton, 13 Dec. 1888; Florence Nightingale to Douglas Galton, 8 Feb. 1889; Nightingale MSS., 45766; Florence Nightingale to Edward Stanhope, 26 Aug. 1889, Stanhope MSS., 1313; Florence Nightingale, Report of Interview with Thomas Crawford, 6 Dec. 1889, Nightingale MSS., 45722.
109. Lord Wolseley to Edward Stanhope, 27 Nov. 1891, Stanhope MSS., 1333. Even with the large funds voted reformers found that the War Office was still attuned to the dictates of economy. Florence Nightingale to Douglas Galton, 24 Nov. 1895, Nightingale MSS., 45767.

110. Watson, *History of the Royal Engineers,* III, p.170.
111. In 1857 the Herbert Commission had expressed praise for the training and skill of medical officers. *Report of the Army Sanitary Commission* (1857–8), pp.lvi–lxiii. At this time some twenty-one different institutions (eleven universities, nine medical corporations, and the Archbishop of Canterbury) could admit candidates to medical practice. Not until 1878 was uniformity in qualifications for civilian practice ensured.
112. See Sidney Herbert to Lord Panmure, 19 Feb. 1857; Memorandum of Medical Officers, 22 Nov. 1857; Panmure MSS., GD45/8/327. Also *Report of the Army Sanitary Commission* (1857–8), pp.lvi et seq.
113. Alexander Smith to Florence Nightingale, 31 Jan. 1857, Nightingale MSS., 45772.
114. *Special Reports on the Working of the Mixed Regimental and Station Hospital System,* WO.33/33.
115. See *Report of the Army Sanitary Commission* (1857–8), p.341.
116. See the correspondence in the Panmure MSS, GD45/8/327–8; also Cook, *Nightingale,* I, pp.286–96; Woodham-Smith, *Nightingale,* pp.243–50.
117. See for instance Sidney Herbert, 'The Sanitary Condition of the Army', *The Westminster Review,* LXXV (1859), pp.52–98; also Woodham-Smith, *Nightingale,* pp.272 et seq.
118. *Report of the Select Committee on the Medical Department (Army),* P.P., XIII (c.331), 1856, p.iv.
119. *Report of the Army Sanitary Commission* (1857–8), p.lix.
120. Both Herbert and Nightingale exerted a great deal of influence in organisational matters and on a number of occasions were able to persuade the government to accept their recommendations on staffing. Florence Nightingale continued to give advice on these questions after Herbert's death in 1861. See Florence Nightingale, Notes on Systems of Inspection in Army Hospitals and the Reorganisation of the Army Medical Department, no date; Sidney Herbert to Florence Nightingale, Feb. 1861; Florence Nightingale to Thomas Crawford, 3 May 1888; Florence Nightingale to Douglas Galton, 21 March 1863, 17 June 1863, 30 July 1864, 9 July 1888; Nightingale MSS., 43394, 45751, 45760–2, 45772, 45824; Florence Nightingale to Earl de Grey and Ripon, 17 Dec. 1861, 21 March 1863, Ripon MSS., 43546.
121. A sub-commission appointed to oversee its organisation made certain that the plans drawn up by reformers would be incorporated. See Florence Nightingale, Army Sanitary Administration and its Reform under the Late Lord Herbert, 12 June 1862; J.H. Lefroy, Proposed Constitution of the School of Military Medicines and Surgery, with pencilled notes by Florence Nightingale, 19 Nov. 1856, Nightingale MSS., 43395, 43397.
122. Nightingale and Herbert were particularly involved with the course content at the School, and corresponded at length with instructors. See E.A. Parkes to Florence Nightingale, 4 Aug. 1860, 22 Dec. 1860, 17 Jan. 1861; Sidney Herbert to W.C. Maclean, 7 Oct. 1860; William Aitken to Florence Nightingale, 13 Oct. 1860; Sidney Herbert to Florence Nightingale, 24 Oct. 1860; Nightingale MSS., 43395, 45773.
123. Florence Nightingale and her group opposed the move to Netley arguing that the hospital was unsuited and the site unhealthy. Other government advisers however felt otherwise. See Report of a Committee to Inquire into and Report on the Removal of the Army Medical School from Chatham, and its Future Position and Arrangements,

22 April 1863. Florence Nightingale to Douglas Galton, 26 July 1860, 3 Sept. 1860, 26 March 1863, 4 Jan. 1866; William Aitken to Florence Nightingale, 31 Aug. 1860; Florence Nightingale to Lord de Grey and Ripon, 23 March 1863; Nightingale MSS., 43546, 45759–60, 45763, 45773, 45824.

124. John Sutherland to Florence Nightingale, 5 April 1876; Florence Nightingale to Douglas Galton, 21 April 1876, Nightingale MSS., 45758, 45763.
125. *Report of the Army Medical Department*, P.P., XXXIII (c.3051), 1862, pp.195–255, passim; XXXVIII (c.604), 1872, pp.25–33, passim; LIX (c.2960), 1881, pp.185–94, passim.
126. *Report of the Army Sanitary Commission* (1857–8), pp.lxiv–lxv.
127. Although civilian doctors employed by friendly societies were often under-paid, army doctors considered themselves worse off than the majority of other civilian colleagues. This dissatisfaction was reflected in the general correspondence in medical journals. Jeanne L. Brand, *Doctors and the State* (Baltimore, 1965), p.139; see also Sidney Herbert to Florence Nightingale, 21 Jan. 1859; Florence Nightingale to Douglas Galton, 5 Jan. 1863, 24 Dec. 1863, 20 Feb. 1864, Nightingale MSS., 43395, 45760–2.
128. *Report of the Committee on Candidature for the Army Medical Department*, P.P., XLIV (c.2213), 1878–9, p.3; cited hereafter as *Report on Candidates for the AMD* (1878–9).
129. *General Annual Return of the British Army*, P.P., XLII (c.1323), 1875, p.8.
130. *Report on Candidates for the AMD* (1878–9), p.3.
131. *Report of the Committee on the Pay, Status, and Conditions of Service of Medical Officers of the Army and Navy*, P.P., XVII (c.5810), 1889, pp.5–7.
132. *Report of the Army Sanitary Commission* (1857–8), p.lv.
133. Florence Nightingale to Douglas Galton, 28 July 1864, Nightingale MSS., 45762.
134. Florence Nightingale, *Notes on Army Statistics*, 20 June 1868, Nightingale MSS., 45823.
135. *Statistical Report on the Health of the Army*, P.P., XXXVII (c.2853), 1861.
136. Cook, *Nightingale*, II, p.389; Florence Nightingale, Army Sanitary Administration and its Reform under the late Lord Herbert, 12 June 1862, Nightingale MSS., 43395.
137. Bentley B. Gilbert, *The Evolution of National Insurance in Great Britain* (1966), pp.83–91; Brand, *Doctors and the State*, p.142.
138. *Report of the Committee on the Organisation of the Army Hospital Corps, Hospital Management, and Nursing in the Field, and the Sea Transport of Sick and Wounded*, P.P., XVI (c.3607), 1883, p.xxix; cited hereafter as *Report on the Army Hospital Corps* (1883).
139. *Report of the Army Sanitary Commission* (1857–8), p.xlvii.
140. Florence Nightingale to Lord Panmure, 3 May 1857, Nightingale MSS., 43397; Panmure MSS., GD45/8/337.
141. *Report on the Proposed Regulations for Army Hospitals*, WO.33/7.
142. Brian Abel-Smith, *A History of the Nursing Profession* (1960), p.36.
143. Patients were almost certain to be young men known for their rude habits. In the circumstances, military hospitals might well be looked upon as little suited for the employment of respectable young women.
144. Abel-Smith, op.cit., pp.40–3, 48.
145. Florence Nightingale, Memoranda on Nursing and Military Hospitals, May

1857, Panmure MSS., GD45/8/337; June-July 1866, Nightingale MSS., 45752; Florence Nightingale to John Sutherland, 1 Oct. 1869; Florence Nightingale to Douglas Galton, 1 June 1862; Florence Nightingale to Thomas Carford, 9 Aug. 1883, Nightingale MSS., 45754, 45764, 45772.

146. *Report of the Select Committee on the Medical Department (Army)*, P.P., XIII (c.331), 1856, p.iv.
147. *Report on the Army Hospital Corps* (1883), p.viii.
148. Florence Nightingale to Douglas Galton, 22 May 1882, 9 Sept. 1883, Nightingale MSS., 45764.
149. *Report on the Army Hospital Corps* (1883), p.xix.
150. *Report of the Committee on the Nursing Service of the Army*, WO.33/53.
151. Douglas Galton to Florence Nightingale, 5 Dec. 1882, Nightingale MSS., 45765.
152. Florence Nightingale at one point blocked a proposal by the National Aid Society to provide the funds for female nurses in the army, arguing that the financing of such a project was and must remain the responsibility of the War Office. Florence Nightingale to Douglas Galton, 25 Nov. 1880, Nighingale MSS., 45763.
153. Florence Nightingale to John Sutherland, 10 Oct. 1869, 11 July 1870, 31 Jan. 1871; John Sutherland to Florence Nightingale, 11 Oct. 1869, 29 July 1870, Nightingale MSS., 45754–5. 45764.
154. Florence Nightingale to John Sutherland, 24 Oct. 1873; Thomas Crawford to Florence Nightingale, 26 July 1882, 6 April 1883, Nightingale MSS., 45757, 45772.
155. *Report of the Army Sanitary Commission* (1857–8), p.xi.
156. *Report of the Army Sanitary Commission* (1861), p.129.
157. *Report of the Army Sanitary Commission* (1857–8), pp.xxxiii-xl, xlvi.
158. *Report of the Army Sanitary Committee* (1861), p.148.
159. Florence Nightingale to Douglas Galton, 31 Oct. 1866, Nightingale MSS., 45763.
160. *Report of the Army Sanitary Committee* (1861), p.123.
161. *Report of the Army Sanitary Commission* (1857–8), p.xxxvii; *Report of the Army Sanitary Committee* (1861), p.133.
162. *Report of the Army Sanitary Commission* (1857–8), pp.1xxvii-1xxviii.
163. *Report of the Army Sanitary Committee* (1861), p.133. There was a clear connection here between improvements to army and to civilian health. In 1857 Sidney Herbert argued that army hospitals must perforce be copies of civilian ones as far as their peculiarities would allow. A way to improve them therefore was to improve the models. Sidney Herbert to Florence Nightingale 27 Jan. 1857, Nightingale MSS., 43394.
164. Florence Nightingale's ideas were very much in the mainstream. See her *Notes of Matters Affecting the Health, Efficiency and Hospital Administration of the British Army* (1857). This was written as a guide for the ASC. Nightingale provided a great deal of information to both the Army Medical Department and to the government on the principles of hospital construction and management and the improvement of water supplies, sewerage and washing facilities. She frequently drew attention to the condition of particular hospitals, and on occasion was able to prompt direct action by the War Office. Her correspondence with Sutherland, Galton and Thomas Longmore contains a mass of information relating to these matters. See BM., Add.MSS.45751, 45757, 45759, 45766, 45773. Also Florence Nightingale, Notes on Principles for Constructing a Lunatic Asylum, circa 1861; and Plans for a Lying-In Hospital, 4 March 1869, Nightingale MSS., 45751, 45753; J. J. Frederick (Under-Secretary of State at the War

Office) to Florence Nightingale, 22 Dec. 1868, Nightingale MSS., 43397.
165. Sidney Herbert to Florence Nightingale, 19 May 1857, Nightingale MSS., 43394.
166. John Sutherland to Florence Nightingale, 24 Oct. 1871, Nightingale MSS., 45756.
167. *Report of the Army Sanitary Committee* (1861), pp.132–6, 288–9.
168. *Report of the Committee on the Army Hospital Corps* (1883), p.ix.
169. *Report of the Army Sanitary Committee* (1861), pp.155–6.
170. William Aitken to Florence Nightingale, 4 Sept. 1860; Florence Nightingale to Douglas Galton, 29 April 1862, Nightingale MSS., 45773, 45760.
171. The Arbour Hill Hospital in Dublin, for instance, which had earlier been singled out by the Barrack and Hospital Improvement Commission, was a particularly glaring example of neglect and cause for concern. So too it appears was the Guards Hospital at Aldershot. See Lord Sandhurst to Henry Campbell-Bannerman, circa 1892, Campbell-Bannerman MSS., 41227; *Report on the Sanitary Condition of Dublin Barracks*, P.P., XVII (c.5653), 1889, p.12.
172. *Special Reports on the Working of the Mixed Regimental and Station Hospital System*, WO.33/33.
173. As Florence Nightingale and others claimed, Florence Nightingale to Douglas Galton 6 April 1882, Nightingale MSS., 45764.
174. Lord Panmure, Notes on Netley Hospital, circa 1859, Panmure MSS., GD45/8/413. Nightingale claimed that this proved that army medical officers were insufficiently instructed in sanitary matters, since the plans for Netley hospital had received the approval of the AMD. Florence Nightingale, Notes on the Construction of Netley Hospital, 29 June 1857, Nightingale MSS., 45823.
175. John Sutherland, Notes on the Construction of Netley Hospital, June 1857; Sidney Herbert to Florence Nightingale, 13 Jan. 1858, 21 Jan. 1858, Nightingale MSS., 45751, 43394; William Tate MP, to Lord Palmerston, 15 Sept. 1857; Sir Harry Vernay to Lord Palmerston, 7 Dec. 1857, Panmure MSS., GD45/8/149, GD45/8/413.
176. Herbert and Nightingale wanted the building turned into an army barrack instead. Sidney Herbert to Florence Nightingale, 30 Jan. 1858, Nightingale MSS., 43394. James Clark to Lord Panmure, 12 May 1857, 21 Aug. 1857; Lord Panmure to Lord Palmerston, 19 Jan. 1857, 31 Dec. 1857, Panmure MSS., GD45/8/151, GD45/8/413.
177. Palmerston wrote that he would 'rather pay himself for throwing away every brick and stone laid there than be a party to completing a building likely to send thousands upon thousands to a premature grave'. Lord Palmerston to Lord Panmure, 5 Feb. 1857, Panmure MSS., GD45/8/150.
178. Florence Nightingale to Douglas Galton, 8 Oct. 1863, Nightingale MSS., 45760.
179. *Report of the Committee on the Site of the Royal Victoria Hospital, Netley*, P.P., XIX (c.2401), 1857–8, pp.5–11; cited hereafter as *Report on Netley* (1857–8).
180. *Report on Netley* (1857–8), p.14.
181. John Sutherland wisely argued that although Netley was not perfect, it was a better hospital than had ever been built before by the government, and that since it was probably the best that could be built for the money, it should be kept. John Sutherland to Florence Nightingale, 9 Sept. 1857, Nightingale MSS., 45751. Florence Nightingale however did not agree, and continued in vain to oppose construction. Florence Nightingale to

Lord Panmure, 1 July 1857; Lord Panmure to Florence Nightingale, 6 July 1857, Panmure MSS., GD45/8/337.

182. Report on Woolwich Garrison Hospital, 11 Jan. 1861, Nightingale MSS., 43395; *Report on the Herbert Hospital at Woolwich*, P.P. XXVI (c.3579), 1865, p.3; cited hereafter as *Report on the Herbert Hospital*, (1865).

183. Douglas Galton was closely involved with the design of the Herbert Hospital, and on a number of occasions consulted with Florence Nightingale on details. Florence Nightingale, Sir Douglas Galton at the War Office, circa 1896; Florence Nightingale to Douglas Galton, 14 Jan. 1861; Douglas Galton to Florence Nightingale, 3 March 1861, Nightingale MSS., 45759, 45767; *Report on the Herbert Hospital* (1865), p.3.

184. *Report on the Army Hospital Corps* (1883), p.vi.

185. See for instance A.L.A., 'A Visit to the Victoria Military Hospital', *Colburn's* III (1873), pp.83–93.

186. In 1865 the Earl of Dalhousie, who as Lord Panmure had been Secretary of State when the construction of Netley was finally begun, replied to criticism by reminding the Lords that the site and plans of the hospital had been carefully chosen, and that it was now one of the best institutions in the country. In spite of the prejudice against it and the attempts made to stop its construction, he asserted, the building had proved its own worth. Hansard, CLXXI (6 March 1865), c.1103.

187. Stafford Northcote to Gathorne Hardy, 20 March 1876, Hardy MSS., T501/271

188. *Report of the Army Medical Department* P.P. LI (c.1887), 1877, p.38.

189. Joseph Byrne, 'The Private Soldier's Wrongs–Boy Sergeants', *The Nineteenth Century*, XXVIII (1890), pp.835–9; Surgeon-Major Frederick Robinson, 'Hospital Stoppages', *Colburn's*, II (1871), pp.405–10.

190. The discharge and pensioning of troops is discussed more fully in Chapter 4.

191. Major D.D. Maitland, 'The Care of the Soldier's Family', *The Royal Army Medical Corps Journal* (1950), pp.107–25.

192. See *Annual Reports of the Army Medical Department*, P.P.

193. Brian Abel-Smith, *The Hospitals 1800–1948* (1964), p.102.

194. Ibid., pp.109, 133.

195. Seebohm Rowntree, *Poverty, a Study of Town Life* (1900), p.168.

196. *Report of the Committee on Venereal Disease in the Army and Navy*, WO.33/12.

197. Frank Richards, *Old Soldier Sahib* (1936), p. 198. These arrangements were strongly objected to by religious leaders on the grounds that prostitution, a recognised social evil, was patronised by and provided for by British authority. Such objections did not succeed however in ending them. The Baptist Missionary Society, Petition to the Hon. Edward Cardwell, Secretary of State for War, July 1873, Cardwell MSS., PRO.30/48/6/35.

198. Edward Cardwell to the Rev E. Underhill, 17 July 1873, Cardwell MSS., PRO.30/48/6/35.

199. On at least one occasion Cardwell was warned that this would be the result. In 1869 Sir E. Lugard suggested that fines would lead to concealment, and recalled that at one time there had been special stoppages which might be waived if men identified the woman responsible. Not even this worked satisfactorily since soldiers often named the wrong one. Sir E. Lugard to Edward Cardwell, 8 Sept. 1869, Cardwell MSS., PRO.30/48/6/38; F.B. Smith 'Ethics and Disease', *Historical Studies*, XV (1971), p.131.

200. Spike Mays, *Fall Out The Officers* (1969), pp.6–7.

201. The medical profession began increasingly to turn its attention to the possibilities of diminishing the rates of contraction by some form of

legislated control partly because of the inadequacy of known specifics in the attempted treatment of venereal disease. E.M. Sigsworth and T.J. Wyke, 'A Study of Victorian Prostitution and Venereal Disease', in Martha Vicinus, ed., *Suffer and Be Still : Women in the Victorian Age* (1973), p.91.

202. *Report of the Army Medical Department*, P.P., XXXVI (c.3404), 1864, p.6.
203. *Report of the Committee on Venereal Disease in the Army and Navy*, WO.33/12.
204. Fourteen large naval and military stations and the surrounding communities were designated 'protected areas' under the Acts.
205. *An Act for the Better Prevention of Contagious Diseases at Certain Naval and Military Stations*, 29 and 30 Vict. (11 June 1866).
206. *Report of the Committee on the Pathology and Treatment of Venereal Disease, with the View to Diminishing Its Injurious Effect on the Men of the Army and Navy*, P.P., XXXVII (c.4031), 1867–8.
207. *An Act to Amend the Contagious Diseases Act, 1866*, 32 and 33 Vict. (11 Aug. 1869).
208. Gladstone, for instance thought that the second Act referred to animals. See Smith, *Historical Studies*, XV (1971), p.120.
209. Florence Nightingale to T.G. Balfour, 10 Dec. 1862; Florence Nightingale to Douglas Galton, 22 April 1862; Florence Nightingale to John Sutherland, June 1877, Nightingale MSS., 45758, 45760, 45772.
210. Florence Nightingale to Douglas Galton, 25 June 1861, Nightingale MSS., 45759.
211. John Sutherland to Florence Nightingale, 3 May 1871, Nightingale MSS., 45755.
212. Florence Nightingale to John Sutherland, 22 Aug. 1870, 27 Nov. 1871; John Sutherland to Florence Nightingale, 12 Sept. 1870, 27 Nov. 1871, Nightingale MSS., 45755–6.
213. Henry Campbell-Bannerman to Lord de Grey and Ripon, W.E. Gladstone and H.C.E. Childers, 12 Dec. 1886; W.E. Gladstone to Henry Campbell-Bannerman, 13 Dec. 1886; Campbell-Bannerman MSS., 41215.
214. Lord George Hamilton to W.E. Smith, 26 Aug. 1886; Lt./Col. de Mesurier to W.E. Smith, 16 Oct. 1886, Smith MSS., WO.110/4–5; Dr Edgehill to R. Knox, circa 1890, Stanhope MSS., 1350.
215. *An Act for the Prevention of Contagious Diseases at Certain Naval and Military Stations*, 27 and 28 Vict. (29 July, 1867).
216. Smith, *Historical Studies*, XV (1971), p.120.
217. See Richard L. Blanco, 'The Attempted Control of Venereal Disease in the Army of Mid-Victorian England', *JSAHR*, XLV (1967), pp.234–41.
218. *Evidence Taken by the Select Committee on the Contagious Diseases, (Animals) Acts*, P.P., VIII (c.323), 1878–9; *Return on Hospital Admissions re Contagious Diseases*, P.P., LIV (c.217), 1897, p.3.
219. Smith, *Historical Studies*, XV (1971), p.132.
220. Major H.C. French, *Syphilis in the Army* (1907), p.64.
221. Brevet Colonel C.H. Melville et al., *A Manual of Venereal Diseases* (1913), p.l.
222. See Chapter 3.
223. The establishment of gymnasia for the use of the army had been suggested before the war, and some attempts had been made, but for want of proper instruction and adequate facilities, results were minimal. Lord Dalmeny to Fox Maule, 12 July 1847, Panmure MSS., GD45/8/28.
224. *Report of the Army Sanitary Commission* (1857–8), p.xiv.
225. *Report of the Committee on Gymnastic Instruction for the Army*, WO.33/14.

226. *Report of the Director of Gymnastics on the Gymnastic Instruction of the Army for the year 1869,* P.P., XLII (c.265), 1870, pp.8–10; cited hereafter as *Report on Gymnastic Instruction* (1870).
227. M. Roth, 'On Scientific Physical Training and Rational Gymnastics', *JRUSI,* VII (1864), pp.176–87.
228. Lieutenant-Colonel E.A.L. Oldfield, *History of the Army Physical Training Corps* (Aldershot, 1955), passim. Sports are discussed further in Chapter 3 below.
229. 'M', 'Idle Soldiers', *Colburn's* (1861), pp.171–5.
230. *Instructions for the Physical Training of Recruits at Regimental Districts* (1896), p.7. These standards are beyond the capabilities of most civilians today, and as far as they go are certainly as difficult as those of the modern army. The current programme is more varied, and its emphasis lies in other directions in that it stresses physical fitness rather than muscular strength *per se.* See *Recruits' Physical Training* (1969), pp.3–5; *Army Physical Fitness Assessment* (1975), pp.2–3.
231. In a class of sixteen at Aldershot in 1869, the average gain in weight was reported to be 1¼ pounds, while men on the average put 3⅞ inches, ¾ inches, and 1⅛ inches on their chest, forearms and upper arms respectively. *Report on Gymnastic Instruction* (1870), pp.1–2.
232. Surgeon-Captain J.R. Forrest, *The Soldier's Health and How to Preserve It* (Aldershot, 1896), pp.19–20.
233. *Report of the Army Sanitary Commission* (1857–8), p.xxviii.
234. Lieutenant-Colonel E. Napier, 'Proposed Alterations in our Military Dress, Arms, and Equipments', *Colburn's* (1851), I, pp.1–19, 199–207.
235. Charles Hamley, 'How to Dress Him', *Blackwood's Edinburgh Magazine,* LXXII (1855), pp.379–401.
236. *Report of the Committee on the Effect on Health of the Present System of Carrying the Accoutrements, Ammunition, and Kit of Infantry Soldiers,* WO.33/15.
237. See for instance Anon., 'The Dress and Accoutrements of Our Soldiers', Parkes Pamphlets, V (1871); An Old Infantryman, 'Suggestions Respecting Infantry Costume', *Colburn's* III (1873), pp.488–99; Red Coat, 'A Voice From The Ranks', *Colburn's,* II (1884), pp.1–10; Evolutionist, 'Our Infantry Uniforms', *Colburn's,* III (1889), pp.447–57.
238. Major-General J.F.C. Fuller, recalling his military service, wrote, 'A Frenchman likes a soldier to look like a soldier, we like him to look like a pantomime artist. If we cannot dress him in a uniform which would stampede a bull a mile off, we hang every imaginable thing about him, so that people may exclaim: "Oh my! Look at that! What is it?" Consequently most of our gunners appear as if they had looted an optician's store, and the infantry have funny little pockets and pouches all over them, whilst the cavalry–they look like mounted pedlars. If through lack of money we are forbidden to invent a shako three feet high, we go to the other extreme, yet design something the people *must* look at–a hat which no sober rat-catcher would go out in at midnight. It is all a matter of show." Major-General J.F.C. Fuller, *The Army in My Time* (1935), p.7.
239. *Report of the Committee on the Various Patterns of Headdresses Now in Use in the Army,* WO.33/68.
240. *Second Report on the Physiological Effects of Food, Clothing and Training on the Soldier,* WO.32/4768.
241. Khaki had first been developed in India to be cool, inconspicuous, and not to show dust, but was not generally accepted even there until the Afghan War of 1878–80.

242. Reports of the Committee on Infantry Equipment, Official W.O. Papers of General Viscount Wolseley, W.45 (1883), Central and Army Library.
243. *Report of the Colour Committee,* P.P., XV (c.3536), 1883, p.5.
244. *The Times,* 3 April 1883.
245. *Report of the Committee on Clothing for British Soldiers in Peace and War,* WO.33/210
246. In the Egyptian campaign of 1898, issue boots fell apart during long marches while better quality footwear worn by officers did not. Heavily criticised for this, the War Office was forced to take steps to develop and introduce an improved pattern of footwear. See Philip Warner, *Dervish* (1973), pp.201–2.
247. Major G. Tylden, 'The Accoutrements of the British Infantryman, 1640–1940', *JSAHR,* XLVII (1969), pp.5–22.
248. *Report of the Army Sanitary Commission* (1857–8), pp.xvii-xviii; see also An Old Infantryman, 'Suggestions Respecting Infantry Costume', *Colburn's,* III (1872), pp.488–493; Red Coat, 'Voice From the Ranks', *Colburn's,* II (1884), pp.1–10.
249. In 1895, more than a decade after he left the Service, Robert Blatchford recalled the unsuitability of army uniforms: 'A Fusilier, buckled and belted up tight in a scarlet tunic, with straps under his armpits, a knapsack, folded coat, and canteen on his back, with a stiff band of slippery buff in the way of his rifle-butt, and with a great fur balloon on his head, was a noble mark for an enemy's fire; and could not have shot straight himself if he had been an angel.' Yet when he and others had the impertinence to complain just to their fellow-soldiers, they were treated with hostility. 'You ought to be jolly well birched, you impudent young cub!' was a typical reply. Robert Blatchford, *My Life in the Army* (circa 1895), pp.148–9.
250. John Williamson, *The Narrative of a Commuted Pensioner* (Montreal, 1938).
251. *Report of the Army Sanitary Commission* (1857–8), pp.xxi-xxvii.
252. As many a recruit found out. See A.F. Corbett, *Service Through Six Reigns* (1953), p.10.
253. Army cooks had a reputation for being chosen for their unsoldierly-like appearance, military incompetence and insanitary habits so there is little likelihood that much care was taken with the preparation of meals. See Troop Sergeant-Major Edwin Mole, *A King's Hussar* (1893), p.28.
254. *Report of the Army Sanitary Commission* (1857–8), pp.123, 161.
255. Ibid., pp.xxii-xxiii.
256. Ibid., pp.xxvii, 431.
257. *Report of the Army Sanitary Committee* (1861), passim.
258. The accounts of this regiment show that the standard cooked meat and potatoes were daily supplemented by coffee, tea, sugar, cheese, butter, jam, marmalade, golden syrup, brawn, corned beef, vegetables, onions, salt, pepper, mustard, herrings, split peas, lentils, barley, curries, flour, celery, milk, oatmeal, bacon, and eggs; *Report of the Committee on The Soldier's Dietary,* P.P., XVII (c.5742), 1889, p.20; cited hereafter as *Report on the Soldier's Diet* (1889).
259. Anon., 'The Health of the Army and Navy', *Colburn's,* I (1876), pp.225–38.
260. Lieutenant Colonel C.B. Tulloch, 'Soldier's Food', *JRUSI,* XXVIII (1884), p.886.
261. Ibid., p.904.
262. A.F. Corbett, *Service through Six Reigns* (1953), p.10.
263. Horace Wyndham, *The Queen's Service* (1899), p.30.
264. Field-Marshal Sir William Robertson, *From Private to Field-Marshal* (1921), p.4.
265. Anon., *Life in the Ranks of the English Army* (1886), p.12.

266. J. Lane Notter, 'The Soldier's Food, with Reference to Health and Efficiency for Service', *JRUSI,* XXXIII (1889), pp.537–65.
267. William Douglas, *Soldiering in Sunshine and Storm* (Edinburgh, 1865), p.316.
268. A.V. Palmer, 'A Private Soldier on the Private Soldier's Wrongs', *The Nineteenth Century,* XXVIII (1890), pp.325–36.
269. W.H. Smith to L.G., 4 Sept. 1886, Smith MSS., WO.110/3.
270. *Report on the Soldier's Diet* (1889), p.7.
271. *Report of the Committee on the Soldier's Dietary,* WO.32/6969.
272. Lieutenant P.J. Thorpe, 'Army Cooking and Messing', *JRUSI,* XXXV, 1891, pp.239–79.
273. *Report of the Army Sanitary Commission* (1857–8), pp.xii-xxiii; *Report on the Soldier's Diet* (1889), p.8.
274. Charles Booth, *Life and Labour of the People in London,* IX (1897), p.421; Rowntree, *Poverty,* pp.227–43; Albert Fried and Richard M. Elman, ed., *Charles Booth's London* (1969), pp.95–6; *Report of the Physical Deterioration Committee* (1904), pp.39–44.
275. 'The change wrought by the Army life among the recruits was astonishing', wrote Robert Blatchford. 'In four months louts became soldiers; were transformed into men. . .There was one frail little fellow, who certainly was not fifteen years of age, and was too weak to pull himself up on the horizontal bar, and in a dozen weeks or so he was a tall, smart, young man, who could throw his rifle about like a walking stick. I met this youngster three years later, and he was a big drummer in a line regiment, stood six feet two inches in his stockings, and weighed nearly fifteen stone.' Blatchford, *My Life in the Army,* p.136.

2 ARMY EDUCATION

> I think that all compulsory education is an impossibility. . .there are circumstances which require the Commanding Officer to promote a non-commissioned officer or private who has perhaps not the information which will qualify him for a certificate. . .it would be very disadvantageous to the service if you made such a certificate absolutely necessary. . .
>
> The Duke of Cambridge

> The instruction given in our regimental schools rarely proceeds beyond the most elementary stage, and instances are numerous of non-commissioned officers and men who have profited little by years of nominal attendance. . .Nearly every regiment in the service includes among its corporals, and even sergeants, a proportion of non-commissioned officers who. . .may be most devoted and gallant soldiers, but it may be safely affirmed that they would be yet better soldiers, and better fitted for Her Majesty's service, if they were more educated men. . .
>
> J. H. Lefroy

A close parallel can be drawn between army education and army health during the years 1856 to 1899. During the forty-five years after the siege of Sebastopol, Britain moved only very slowly towards a national system of free compulsory education, hindered in part by a disregard in some quarters for universal education. In sharp contrast to this, extensive provisions were made by the army for the education of the soldier and his children and facilities were developed which were to standardise army education throughout Britain and the Empire. Surprisingly perhaps there seems to have been no corresponding fear that such a programme would have an adverse effect on discipline. Important steps were taken in the areas of adult education, technical instruction for the serviceman in trades and skilled crafts, the provisions which were made to educate army children, and school-teachers and the quality of teaching in army schools.

1. Literacy and the Education of the Rank and File, 1856–99

At the midpoint of the nineteenth century British society reflected very much the class distinctions and class barriers within it. Because the army was a microcosm of this society, these notions were deeply engrained within it. Yet while the background and outlook of the officer corps mirrored the education and habits of the upper and upper-middle classes, because of the provisions which the army made for educating the rank and file, the level of literacy they achieved depended only partly on that of the civilian working classes.

Responsibility for army education changed hands several times between 1856 and 1899. During most of the 1850s the Inspector-General of Army Schools was the Chaplain-General, G.R. Gleig. This was not an arrangement which proved altogether workable; certainly by 1857 Lord Panmure, the Secretary of State for War, felt Gleig was performing the duties of Inspector-General of Army Schools neither discreetly nor satisfactorily.[1] Gleig resigned in 1857 and was replaced as Inspector-General by Colonel J. H. Lefroy, but his stay was brief and controversial. Lefroy's appointment raised the question of civilian control of army education. Panmure argued that ultimate control should rest with the Secretary of State for War,[2] and intended that Lefroy should assume responsibility for Sandhurst as well. Superintendence of officers' education was a jealously guarded prerogative of the Horse Guards, and one which was inevitably to result in a trial of strength between the Secretary of State and the Commander-in-Chief. From the point of view of civilian control, however, the time for such a contest was not yet ripe. With the Queen's support and by strenuous objections on his part, the Duke of Cambridge was able to have Lefroy's appointment terminated, and to retain in his own office responsibility for officer education and training.[3]

In 1860 the Council of Military Education, a supervisory body first appointed in 1857 to deal with the organisation of the Senior and Junior Departments at Sandhurst, the system of examination for direct appointments in the army, and examinations for the promotion of officers, absorbed the Inspector-General's duties—control over army schools and libraries, and responsibility for the selection, promotion and discipline of army schoolmasters.[4] Before his office was abolished Lefroy was able to prepare a detailed report on the army's regimental and garrison schools which was the first major document of its kind and set a precedent for subsequent work.[5] In some respects the change in 1860 was not a good one. A fatal weak point of the Council was its lack of executive and financial power and its shortage of agents in the field, shortcomings which were underscored by the Royal Commission appointed in 1870 to examine all facets of military education.[6] On their recommendation the government replaced the Council with a Director-General, a step which centralised the administration of army education and markedly improved its efficiency.

In 1857 20,000 NCOs and men were on the school books, but daily attendance averaged only slightly better than 7,500,[7] in spite of a remarkable proportion of illiterate men within the army. As the following table shows, less than 5 per cent of the rank and file had anything even approaching what was in fact an elementary level of education, but within the different arms of the Service the percentage of literacy varied considerably. The infantry, into which the mass of recruits were taken, had the highest proportion of uneducated men in the ranks. In the Royal Engineers, where particular efforts were made to enlist tradesmen and skilled workers, the number of men who were totally illiterate was insignificant.

Table 2–1 Literacy in the Rank and File of the Regular Army, 1857

Percentage unable to read or write	20.5
Percentage able to read but not write, and barely able to sign their own names	18.8
Percentage able to read and write a little	56.0
Percentage with a 'superior degree' of education	4.7

Literacy in the Army by Arm of Service, 1857

	Percentage Unable to Read or Write and Percentage Able to Read Only	Percentage Able to Read and Write
Cavalry	24.8	75.2
Foot Guards	20.4	79.6
Infantry	44.6	55.4
Royal Artillery	40.4	59.6
Royal Engineers	3.0	97.0

Source: Brevet Colonel J.H. Lefroy, *Report on the Regimental and Garrison Schools of the Army* (1859), pp.6–7.

These figures invite comparison with what indications there are of basic levels of literacy among the civilian working-class population. Here standards varied greatly from area to area, yet except in isolated localities rarely more than 50 per cent were not minimally literate and illiteracy fell significantly by 1900. By the middle of the century, there were large networks of schools in Britain, yet education was not free, and it was far from universal. Precedents for compulsory elementary education existed, but the number of children involved was small.[8] In England education spread quickly during the 1850s, but there were many who did not attend school and for those who did what little instruction they received was very often defective.[9] The Newcastle Commission in 1861 led to the introduction of the disastrous system of 'payment by results' which deprived education of the means to develop, while relations between teachers, parents and educational authorities worsened. Forster's Education Act in 1870 created local education authorities empowered to enforce compulsory school attendance, but the steps taken and the success they achieved varied greatly from locality to locality. At the beginning of the 1880s school attendance in many parts of the country still depended on indirect compulsion only, and that half-heartedly or intermittently enforced. The central government did not take steps to enact compulsory attendance until 1880, and even then regulations were not easy to enforce. Free elementary education was not fully established until 1891, and the last remnants of payment by results were not removed until 1893–5. The development of comprehensive secondary education was equally as halting.

With few exceptions, the extension of primary education in Scotland was as laborious. The tradition that clever students from any background should have a right to education plus the closer connection that had always existed between primary and secondary schooling meant that the probabilities of working-class and pauper children obtaining some sort of an education were in the last century higher than in the rest of Britain;[10] nevertheless, as the Argyll Commission was to reveal in 1867, primary education was hopelessly inadequate in many areas.[11] Not until the Education Act of 1872 was provision made for state control of education by school boards, and only in 1893 was elementary education at last made free. Fees for secondary education were not dropped until 1918. Although minimal literacy rose from 53 per cent of those over five years of age in 1851 to 85 per cent in 1911, education in Ireland was even more desperate during the nineteenth century. The national school system established in 1831 made little contribution towards reducing illiteracy before 1880. Compulsory school attendance was not enacted until 1892, teacher training was neglected, and poverty excluded 90 per cent of Irish children from obtaining any secondary education.[12]

Between 1856 and 1899 literacy in the army rose considerably. Yet statistics compiled by educational authorities can be misleading since clear desire existed to present as favourable a picture as possible and educators tended therefore to overstate their case. They do seem to indicate solid improvement but their interpretation needs a great deal of care. Table 2–2 shows what was reported to be the state of education of the rank and file of the regular army between 1860 and 1899.

Table 2–2 The Educational Attainments of the Rank and File of the Regular Army, 1860–99

Year	Percentage Unable to Read or Write	Percentage Able to Read Only	Percentage Able to Read and Write	Percentage Possessing a Superior Education
1861	19.0	19.7	53.9	7.4
1864	13.4	17.3	64.1	5.2
1866	12.2	16.1	65.5	6.2
1868	9.5	10.6	73.8	6.1
1870	7.8	7.9	78.3	6.0
1872	6.9	6.4	73.0	13.7
1874	5.4	4.6	49.9	40.1
1876	5.0	4.4	45.6	45.0
1878	4.7	3.8	42.7	48.8
1880	4.2	4.0	34.2	57.6
1882	3.7	3.2	21.6	71.5
1884	3.2	2.3	16.2	78.3
1886	2.9	3.5	14.2	79.4
1888	2.2	2.6	9.9	85.3
1889	1.9	2.2	10.5	85.4

Year	Percentage Illiterate or Barely Literate	Percentage Educated
1890	61.9	38.1
1892	62.9	37.1
1894	64.0	36.0
1896	61.7	38.3
1898	61.5	38.5
1899	60.8	39.2

Source: *General Annual Return of the British Army,* P.P., XLIV (c.1323), 1875, p.58; XLII (c.6196), 1890, p.85; LIII (c.9426), 1899, p.96; *Reports of the Council of Military Education,* P.P.; *Reports of the Director-General of Military Education,* P.P.

The conclusion that a dramatic but progressive improvement took place is clearly modified by the figures for 1890 to 1899. The level of achievement of many of those who apparently possessed a 'superior education' in earlier years was in fact meagre. Army educational certificates were introduced in 1861, and despite the fact that the standards required for the first certificate were very low, every man who achieved the minimum qualification was deemed to possess a 'superior education'. In 1873 the Director-General of Military Education enthusiastically reported that 32.61 per cent of the rank and file had a superior degree of education and that 56.02 per cent were fully able to read and write. In this same year, however, 73 per cent possessed no certification of education whatsoever, and 8.4 per cent had only elementary fourth-class certificates.[13] In 1876 44.95 per cent were reputed to be well educated and 45.68 per cent to be able to read and write, yet in 1877 less than 50 per cent of all troops had obtained any class of certificate, and 22 per cent had reached only fourth-class standing.[14] The absurdity of this situation was finally realised in 1889. In that year army returns reported 84.5 per cent of all troops with a high level of education,[15] yet just one year previously the Director-General of Military Education had shown in his report that in excess of 60 per cent of all rank and file had not obtained even the minimum educational certificate.[16]

Henceforth army statistics began to represent more accurately the state of education in the forces. Looked at realistically they do show what progress had been made. In 1860 less than 8 per cent of the rank and file were able to do much more than read a little and write their own name. Within forty years, illiteracy as defined in this way had been virtually banished and nearly 40 per cent of the rank and file had a degree of education.[17] However, there is another side to this. In 1899, nearly thirty years after the passage of Forster's 1870 Education Act and the 1872 Scottish Education Act, fewer than 40 per cent of the rank and file of the regular army had gone beyond the barest level of literacy, and the standard reached by the majority of those in the ranks was elementary at best. Not only was the national system of education ineffective, therefore, but so too it appears were the provisions made by the army.

Army Medical Department figures, showing the literacy of recruits approved for the regular army, illustrate that enlistment of better educated men increased after 1860.[18] But again these figures need careful interpretation. The benefits expected by the army from Forster's Education Act of 1870 and from other improvements in civilian education were considerable. Many officers, like Garnet Wolseley, predicted that the army would soon be able to do away with its schoolmasters entirely. Yet the statistics are significant only in showing a continuation in the gradual rate of improvement in the literacy of army recruits, and here again the accuracy of official figures is suspect. Recruits shown in Medical Department reports as able to read and write must clearly be regarded, in later years especially, as minimally literate. A War Office Committee on army schools and schoolmasters in 1887 allowed that the results of the Education Act of 1870 were visible but remarked that the standard of literacy of recruits was not as marked as was generally supposed.[19] The Chairman, Lord Harris, argued that there were still large numbers who were unable to achieve even the minimum standards required by the lowest of the army education certificates.[20] In 1886, 86.6 per cent of that year's recruits were reported by the Army Medical Department as being able to read and write,[21] yet 36.5 per cent of the men enlisted failed to qualify for even the elementary fourth-class education certificate.[22] In 1893 the Director-General of Military Education remarked that the level of education of the adult civilian population was so low that education within the army for the rank and file was a vital necessity.[23]

Regular schools in the army dated back to the late seventeenth century. Since military tactics made few demands on individual thought and initiative, schooling at first was rarely more than an elementary rendition of the '3Rs'; enough to make military drill intelligible to the untutored recruit and to give NCOs the basis for reading and transcribing orders, for arranging the billet of men under their charge, and for keeping such accounts as were required. By 1856 schools were operating with virtually every permanent detachment of troops and tuition was available in reading, writing, arithmetic, English history and geography. Army regulations specified a minimum school attendance of four hours per week for each recruit, but in 1861, because of doubts about the legal right to enforce this compulsory attendance was discontinued.[24]

The goals of military education were diverse. Tactics required complicated mass-movements and concerted action for effectiveness, while improvements to firearms made them progressively more sophisticated. In 1854 the Enfield rifle, the first rifled musket to be adopted for general service, came into use with the British army. In 1865 the Snider breech-loading conversion was introduced. Although drill was still learned largely by repetition, the necessity of instructing troops in the use of this more complicated weaponry, of gathering precise information on their state and position, and of issuing instructions to them through non-commissioned officers made education important. Education in the army also reflected a moral concern and a sense of duty 'Education', promised an article in *Fraser's Magazine*,

> . . .will indeed contribute to the soldier's respectability as well as to his comforts. . .will cause him to respect himself. . .[and] will create in him tastes for higher pleasures than those which spring out of mere animal gratifications. . .[it] will save him from many an act of folly, and its necessary result of suffering; and above all, will provide for him resources against the time when his country shall have dispensed with his services.[25]

Many of those with a hand in the management of the army felt particularly strongly about the value of education, and policy reflected these views. 'It is scarcely less essential to the soldier', remarked army regulations in 1857, 'to be able to read and write, and keep even his own accounts, than to be acquainted with his drill.'[26] Most senior officers favoured some form of compulsory education. In 1870 Lieutenant-General Sir J. Yorke Scarlett argued that the attendance of all recruits at school should be made compulsory again and that a degree of learning be required for promotion. Lord Strathnairn, then commanding the army in Ireland, felt that '. . .it would be a benefit to the soldier and an advantage to the service to render his instruction compulsory when off duty'.[27]

Despite the enthusiasm with which education was regarded in these quarters, however, there was considerable disagreement in the forces as to how much education was necessary or even wise. Compulsory schooling especially was questioned. Regimental officers and on occasion senior officers as well frequently saw little point in efforts devoted to educating the soldier. Many tended to feel that the recruit's time was best spent learning his drill, and that compulsory education was an unwelcome interference in regimental affairs. Others doubted whether it was possible or even desirable to give the soldier anything beyond a very elementary level of education.[28]

Official army policy which favoured the encouragement of education was at times frustrated by this opposition and forced to oscillate between compulsory schooling and voluntary attendance. When compulsory attendance was abandoned in 1861, hopes of compensation were placed in increasing the use of existing regimental libraries and reading rooms, and programmes of special lectures and courses.

The value of libraries had been recognised early in the nineteenth century. In 1840 their establishment for the rank and file was authorised at each of the large barracks in the United Kingdom and throughout the colonies. By 1857 army regulations noted that the purpose of libraries and reading rooms was: '. . .to encourage the soldiery to employ their leisure hours in a manner that shall combine amusement with the attainment of useful knowledge, and teach them the value of sober, regular, and moral habits.'[29] Within three years, virtually every major station in Britain had a library in operation, although facilities were sparse at first, and there was a real shortage of books and magazines of a nature that would appeal to soldiers. A War Office Committee in 1861 reported that the library at Woolwich for instance contained such works as *Sketches of the Irish Bar, Divorce Cases, Foxe's Martyrs,* and *Recollections of Parliament.*[30] Its recommendations proved the basis for the organisation and operation of army libraries until well after the turn of the century. On its suggestion more provision was made for magazines, for books for general reading, and for the texts and reference works related to the curriculum in army schools, and there were efforts to make surroundings more comfortable and to integrate libraries with dayrooms, games rooms, soldiers' institutes and other recreational facilities in barracks.[31] After 1861 the use of libraries increased considerably. In 1864 there were 85 in Britain and the Colonies, in 1870 there were over 120, by 1876 the number had risen to 150. In 1871 210,000 volumes were in store, within five years nearly 230,000 were in the catalogues and over 600,000 separate circulations a year were being made.[32]

Lectures and illustrated talks first came into their own after the Crimean War. Lectures were normally given on winter evenings at the larger stations and attendance was voluntary. A wide range of topics might be dealt with. In 1859 for instance the Lefroy report on army schools and libraries listed twenty-seven different lectures that had recently been given at Aldershot on subjects ranging from the 'Composition of Gunpowder with Chemical Experiments' to 'Indian Dress and Customs'.[33] In 1866 lectures given to troops in Britain ranged from 'Natural Magic', 'Electricity', and 'The Use of Iron in Fortifications' to 'Wit and Humour of Different Nations', 'Self-Improvement' and 'The Results of Intemperance'. In 1860 461 different lectures were given to the troops at home and abroad and in 1866 more than 1,730 were presented.[34] The skill of speakers and the quality of lectures varied, regiments tended to compete with each other in the number and variety they could provide, and army schoolmasters gained favour with their superiors by increasing the number of talks they were prepared to give. In the circumstances presentation often suffered. On the advice of the Royal Commission on Military Education in 1870, quality rather than quantity began to be stressed, and figures were no longer published quoting the number of lectures given at any one time.[35]

In 1861 a new inducement towards learning was the army certificate of education. On the recommendation of the Council of Military Education three levels or standards were set out and were linked with promotion in the ranks. The third-class certificate specified the standard for promotion to the rank of corporal: the candidate was to read aloud and to write from dictation passages from an easy narrative, and to work examples in the four compound rules of arithmetic and the reduction of money. A second-class certificate, necessary for promotion to sergeant, entailed writing and dictation from a more difficult work, familiarity with all forms of regimental accounting, and facility with proportions and interest, fractions and averages. First-class certificates were a great deal more difficult and were required for commissions from the ranks. Successful candidates had to read and take dictation from any standard author; make a fair copy of a manuscript; demonstrate their familiarity with more complicated mathematics, except cube and square root and stocks and discount; and as well prepare for examination in at least one of a number of additional subjects. After 1887 candidates were examined in British history and geography in place of a special subject. First-class certificates were awarded on the results of periodic examinations held by the Council (later Director-General) of Military Education. Second and third-class certificates were presented on the recommendation of the Army schoolmaster.[36]

Authorities were optimistic about the results of educational certificates; however these were not at first encouraging. School attendance dropped significantly when compulsion was withdrawn thus reviving arguments for a return to the pre-1861 situation. Between 1862 and 1870 every report of the Council of Military Education on regimental and garrison schools stressed the unsatisfactory figures of school attendance and called strongly for revisions in the Mutiny Act to provide compulsory schooling for all recruits.[37] A Royal Commission appointed in 1868 to enquire into provisions for educating officers and officer cadets found that its jurisdiction extended to cover the provisions which were made to instruct the rank and file. It too felt that the inability to compel men to attend school was an unnecessary stumbling-block. The third-class certificate of education was considered to be too high given the level of literacy of many army recruits, and the Commission urged the introduction of a fourth (minimum) standard.[38]

1870 had witnessed the first major step towards a national scheme of compulsory elementary education, and it is not surprising that action resulted from this advice. In 1871 compulsory school attendance of five hours per week for recruits and a new fourth-class certificate of education designed as a minimum to be achieved by all were introduced.[39] Official policy once more began to reflect the enthusiasm with which the promise of education was regarded. Annual reports by the Inspector-General of Recruiting which were first presented in 1870 frequently cited the increasing level of education in the army as being indicative of the improved condition of the British soldier and as a positive inducement to enlistment.[40] Army regulations were another indication of this type of thinking. In 1870 General Orders remarked:

> It is important that the soldier should be able to read and write and keep his own accounts, as well as be acquainted with his drill. Without such acquirements the soldier cannot look for promotion, and he is deprived of the interest and improvement derivable from the libraries placed within his reach.[41]

Unfortunately for all concerned, the fourth-class certificate was to prove unsuccessful. Its requirements, simple reading and a few easy sums, the level an eight-year-old child might be expected to obtain, were so low as to be almost meaningless, and as Colonel A.C. Gleig, the Inspector of Army Schools in Britain perceived, its introduction encouraged men to go no further and to delude themselves into believing they had attained a fair standard of education.[42] Moreover large numbers of men failed even to reach this level. In 1882 for instance nearly 40 per cent of the rank and file were unable or perhaps unwilling to pass the examination for this certificate.[43] This led to demands for its discontinuance and gave additional weight to the arguments of those who opposed compulsory education on the grounds of its failure to have any effect.[44] These viewpoints were echoed in 1887 by a War Office Committee under the chairmanship of Lord Harris which recommended that both compulsory education and the lower class of educational certificate be discontinued.[45]

The report of the Harris Committee resulted in a number of different measures being taken. Faced with the obvious unsuitability of present regulations and the apparent inadequacy of steps to encourage education in the ranks, the government discontinued the fourth-class certificate in 1888. Compulsory school attendance was a casualty since the average recruit could not reasonably be expected to achieve a third class with just a few weeks of schooling. The abolition of compulsory schooling for recruits was greeted with particular dismay by the Director-General of Military Education and others who stressed the value both to the army and to society in educating even those who appeared not to want to learn.[46]

To compensate for ending compulsory schooling, authorities once more turned to persuasion and inducement. In 1889 the first and second-class certificates of education were made a condition for promotion to sergeant and to corporal respectively, thus increasing the numbers who would be forced to try for these qualifications. A centralisation of army schools to increase their efficiency was begun in this year as well. The Harris Committee had pointed out the difficulty with the present system, and on their recommendation larger garrison schools, able to accommodate adults and children from several units, were substituted wherever possible for the smaller regimental schools. In time this measure economised on teaching and teaching staff, and permitted the introduction of better facilities.[47]

There can be no doubt that this oscillation between compulsory and voluntary school attendances severely limited the effectiveness of army education. In the absence of compulsion, the emphasis placed on education in the army varied a great deal from regiment to regiment. While some units on their own tied promotion to educational standards and offered pecuniary awards to induce men to attend school, a great deal less care was shown in other cases.[48] The result of this lack of concern was paralysing. As 'a private soldier' wrote in 1864, 'the support both moral and practical which the officers should give to it [school attendance], is *withheld;* and while such is the case, army education can never prosper'.[49] In 1896 the Director-General's report singled out and criticised the lack of interest shown by some commanding officers.[50]

An additional but closely-linked reason for the failure of army education to produce results much faster than it did was the lack of importance placed on it by many of the troops. When compulsory schooling was discontinued, attendance at regimental and garrison schools fell markedly. In 1858 Lefroy had reported over 20,000 NCOs and men on the school books,[51] by 1865 average daily school attendance was only 14,843.[52] As late as 1896 the Director-General's report on military education stressed the irregularity of school attendance.[53]

Attendance figures do not tell the whole story. Among those who attended many looked upon schooling merely as a release from more onerous duties. In 1859 Colonel Lefroy observed that '. . .instances are numerous of non-commissioned officers and men who have profited little by years of nominal attendance'.[54] Private Grenville Murray recalled in 1882 men in his regiment who had spent ten years in the ranks and had done perhaps 2,000 hours of schooling without even learning how to read and write.[55] An ex-soldier writing in 1864 remarked that 'in the British service, corporals unable to write are not uncommon, and I know sergeants who cannot read their own writing after it is written, far less that of anybody else'.[56] The Harris Committee in 1887 reported similar findings, remarking that it was not uncommon for men to prefer to sit in school for six months regardless of the purpose for which they attended and heedless of the instructions of the schoolmaster rather than try to obtain an education certificate.[57]

The presence of slow learners only exacerbated the problem, for even when their interest could be maintained, progress was limited. Personal recollections provide a vivid illustration. 'Imagine the large school room filled with about a hundred soldiers, divided into six classes', recalled an ex-serviceman.

> Here were the forms for beginners who could neither read nor write – fearful dolts some of them, who bleated through their spelling most ruefully; further on, some recruits were tracing pot-hooks and hangers with clumsy fingers. Then came a class which contained several middle-aged corporals who had got third-class certificates, but were trying to qualify for sergeantships by getting second classes. . .Some of these unfortunates, who were splendid soldiers, fairly sweated over the difficulties of compound interest and rule of three. The big drops stood on their foreheads, and there was a dazed frown between their eyes, as they tried to comprehend the patient demonstrations of their teacher expounding to them that ½ and $^6/_{12}$ meant the same thing.[58]

Libraries and special lectures were a potentially valuable solution, and certainly there is evidence that they were important.[59] In many cases men were encouraged to read but Grenville Murray recalled of his military service that only 20 per cent of the rank and file at the most ever used the regimental library and that many borrowed books intending to read them but never actually did so. Novels, books of travel and adventure, and Samuel Smiles' *Self Help* were most popular in his recollection; religious works were hardly touched at all.[60]

Several years earlier Lefroy had been able to show that the use of books in a 'typical' military library was not much different.[61]

In the circumstances it is not surprising that incentive schemes met with only limited success. Given the state of public education and the educational needs of the forces, the levels set for the first three certificates of education were realistic and useful. Between 1870 and 1896 alone there was a positive increase of nearly 30 per cent in the proportion of rank and file who had achieved a third-class certificate or better. Considering that recruitment was running at 30,000 to 40,000 per year and that the establishment of the army was increased from 170,817 in 1870 to 209,701 in 1899,[62] this was a definite achievement. Yet it appears that a formal education was of little importance to the majority of soldiers. The percentage of men with a first-class certificate of education remained consistently small throughout the period.[63] The lack of prospect for a commission, and even the unattractiveness of such prospects, encouraged very few men to try for the top standard.[64]

In the end army education achieved limited success because it was not enough merely to teach men to read a few simple passages. If the soldier was to make full use of his leisure time and of the facilities at his disposal, he needed not only to acquire a certain proficiency but to be taught to enjoy and to see the value in both reading and learning. These were habits best acquired when young, but to which few recruits can have been exposed before the last few years of the century. In the circumstances compulsory schooling coupled with enthusiasm for education at the regimental level may have been part of the solution; it is unfortunate that for so many years neither could be enforced.

2. Technical Education

Technical training was an area of education from which the army stood potentially to gain a great deal. As the hardware and logistical needs of the army increased and became more technical, with for instance the introduction of improved weaponry and of communications systems such as telegraphy and heliography, the need for men trained in these fields increased yearly. Equally important was the problem of resettling the ex-soldier in society. In the modern voluntary-service army, the opportunity for soldiers to learn a trade is an important inducement to recruitment. In the nineteenth century the paltry efforts that were made to help the ex-soldier to find employment and the consequent spectacle of veterans in uniform destitute and begging for money was a serious hindrance to recruitment. Technical training which would answer some of the army's supply problems and technical needs and which could give the ex-soldier a start in civilian life might well have proved a solution.

Although the army made considerable efforts between 1856 and 1900 to enable and even to encourage its men to acquire an ordinary basic education, surprisingly little was done to provide an opportunity for any technical training aside from purely military duties. The several technical corps all provided occupational training, but this affected only a small percentage of enlisted men. The reasons for the general lack of such educational provisions for the majority of soldiers were twofold: (1) a reluctance on the part of military authorities and those controlling the purse-strings to provide the facilities necessary for any ambitious programme, and (2) the failure to realise the potential value of this type of instruction for the army in terms of recruiting, and for the soldier himself in respect to his eventual resettlement in civilian life.

The idea of technical education did attract considerable support. Instruction in simple trades, not requiring much in the line of machinery or expenditure but which would benefit both the soldier and the army, was a central goal. While there was a campaign in print for action, in Parliament individual MPs at times strongly pressed the government.[65] A debate in 1862 led to the appointment the following year of a select committee under Major-General J.R. Crauford to consider the instruction and employment of soldiers and their children in trades. The Crauford Committee fully recognised the value a number of skilled craftsmen would bring to the army since dependence upon the hiring of outside craftsmen for military works was still very large.[66] On the other hand the extent to which vocational training would have bettered conditions for the soldier both during his active service and after discharge, and would have acted as a stimulus to recruiting was not fully appreciated even though most of the officers who were questioned replied enthusiastically to suggestions for technical instruction and employment.[67] The Crauford recommendations called for instruction to be given by the Royal Engineers to first-class soldiers and their sons who could then be employed in military and public works. Tools, supplies and other equipment were to be provided by the government and any earnings in excess of cost were to go to the men. If all went as planned, soldiers could expect to supplement their incomes by from 6d to 1s 3d per day.[68]

At no time before 1900, however, did the government come under intense pressure to act. General Sir George Brown, the commander of the forces in Dublin, argued that soldiers did not have enough time for additional instruction or work, and that if employed as tradesmen they would cease to become good soldiers. He also insisted that the tradespeople of a town should be allowed to gain from the presence of troops.[69] The most effective opposition came from the Commander-in-Chief, the Duke of Cambridge, who asserted that workshops and materials would be hard to produce, that the soldier's legitimate duties occupied too much of his time for attention to be given to other matters, and expressed the fear that fully-trained soldiers would want to leave the army as soon as possible.[70]

Virtually nothing therefore came of the recommendations of the Crauford Committee. In 1871 a committee constituted to frame regulations for the employment of soldiers at trades found the average number of craftsmen and potential instructors per battalion still sadly inadequate.[71] The efforts of this second committee were no more successful. It had been constituted in 1870 after demands in Parliament the previous year for a reconsideration of the problem. The War Office under Edward Cardwell was anxious to find an inexpensive solution to recruiting difficulties and with short service in prospect, a means of smoothly passing men through the ranks. Signs at first seemed promising. The committee drew up proposals for the instruction by the Royal Engineers of a number of men from each battalion in various trades and for their employment in military and public works. A few workshops were constructed and initial efforts were made to replace the old pioneers with skilled artisans who would train men in their respective trades, but the effect of these measures was minimal.[72] On the whole the necessary workshops were lacking and opposition to the instruction and employment of soldiers in any but military duties was too deep-seated. With the failure of these last efforts no other attempts were made to institute any form of technical or vocational instruction for troops until well after the end of the century. As late as 1904 a War Office enquiry into army schools stated that their main purpose was to impart a general education and rejected any suggestion that they should teach a trade.[73] Another three years were to lapse before any comprehensive programme of instruction was initiated.[74]

Nineteenth-century plans for the resettlement of ex-soldiers on the whole went no further than positions of trust with government departments, such as postmen, warders, messengers or grounds keepers. In the field of technical and vocational training for servicemen virtually no progress was made but this is not surprising given that precedents in civilian life were few. For the most part apprenticeship remained the chief method of learning a trade before 1900. Little was done to foster technical education on a large scale in secondary institutions until the 1880s, and even then results were patchy. Nevertheless the advantages to be gained by the army through independent action were clear. Nor was there any trade union opposition to the army providing instruction. A variety of trades could have conveniently been taught, which would have benefited the army and the soldier. Book-keeping and clerical work, carpentry and plumbing, blacksmithing, tailoring, saddlery and butchery would have given the army a valuable corps of tradesmen and craftsmen, would have helped to alleviate the tedium of army routine, and would have given the ex-soldier a fresh start in civilian life.[75] Yet in an era of improvements in education and of conscious efforts to make the army more attractive, conservatism and considerations of economy were allowed to prevail.

3. Children's Education

The tuition of the soldier, whether recruit or veteran of several years' service, was not the sole concern of army education. The education provided for soldiers' children played a particularly important role for two reasons: (1) considerable time, effort and resources were involved, and (2) a significant proportion of each year's recruits were army children.[76] The army made no provision at any time during our period for the offspring of unofficial marriages, but there were two main avenues open to the children of those families that were 'on the strength': the normal regimental and garrison schools of the army and two large boarding schools, the Royal Military Asylum at Chelsea and the Royal Hibernian Military School in Dublin. A third alternative was schooling for a number of children in institutions maintained by the Royal Victoria Patriotic Fund, a charity founded after the Crimean War for the relief of the families of servicemen.

The army had two major goals in educating the soldier's children. These did not change throughout the whole of our period. There was first of all a desire for humanitarian reasons to provide children in its care with a useful elementary education. This in turn could prove a benefit to the army by assuring the Service of a proportion of educated recruits each year. Secondly, by minding and educating his children, authorities hoped to enhance the attractions to the soldier of military service. With these aims in view, army regulations remarked:

> . . .the main purposes for which the regimental schools are established are, to give soldiers the comfort of being assured that the education and welfare of their children are objects of the sovereign's paternal solicitude and attention, and to raise from their offspring a succession of loyal subjects, brave soldiers, and good Christians.[77]

How successful were these efforts? Military authorities clearly understood that the advantages to be expected from schooling soldiers' children could only be realised if education were made compulsory. For this reason the regular attendance of all children between the ages of four and fourteen was effectively enforced by the authority of the commanding officer. By 1857 army regulations specified:

> All soldier's children are to attend the regimental school, and, a morning report, specifying by name any that are absent, or prevented from attending by sickness will be sent daily to the regimental orderly room. The parents of the children are held responsible for their cleanliness and regular attendance at school, and should they neglect their children, they will be deprived of all indulgences which they might otherwise receive as married people.[78]

Fees of 2d per month for one child plus 1d for each additional one were levied so schooling was not at first free, but it was universal and compulsory, a step that was not to be taken for civilian children until the last decades of the century. The report of a Royal Commission on military education in 1870 recognised that fees discouraged education while contributing little in the way of revenue,[79] and on its recommendation they were withdrawn the following year; another twenty years were to lapse before public education took the same step.

The number of children attending regimental and garrison schools varied considerably between 1856 and 1899. From 1857 to 1870 enrolment nearly doubled, then between 1870 and 1900 it all but halved. In 1858 Colonel J. H. Lefroy reported there were in excess of 12,000 children in army schools.[80] By 1870, when the Royal Commission on Military Education reported, more than 20,000 were attending regularly.[81] From an establishment of 212,295 in 1861, the army fell by nearly 44,000 men to 174,198 rank and file in 1870 so an increase in the size of the forces was not the cause of this rise.[82] More likely an answer was the enforcement of compulsory attendance. In 1896 only 12,000 children were on the school books,[83] yet the strength of the forces had by this time been increased by 39,000 men to 213,500.[84] Soldiers had permission to send their children to national schools after 1870 but because army schools were free by this time it is doubtful if many did so. The Director-General of Military Education frequently remarked after 1870 that attendance at the children's schools was poor because of sickness, children moving with parents on a regimental transfer, or the school being closed for one reason or another.[85] There is no evidence however that the same criticism would not have been equally valid before 1870. The two most likely causes of the reduction in the number of children attending army schools by 1896 were a recommendation of the Royal Commission of 1870 which excluded from schooling the children of non-military personnel, who at that time numbered approximately 3,000,[86] and the fact that there were probably fewer married men hence fewer families in the forces after the introduction of short-service enlistment in 1870.

When children's education was first introduced, instruction was provided by the schoolmaster in reading, writing, arithmetic and English grammar. In addition, the boys were often taught tailoring and shoemaking by a regimental tradesman, and the girls needlework by one of the soldiers' wives. In 1850 the provisions for education were broadened considerably. Two new types of classes, i.e. infant and 'industrial' schools under the care of a schoolmistress were introduced. Younger children, boys under the age of eight and girls until they could read words of two syllables, spent their mornings in the infant school where they were taught spelling, reading and singing. As before older children attended grown children's classes in the morning where there was instruction in reading, writing, singing, dictation, grammar, English history, geography, arithmetic, and in some cases algebra. In the afternoon girls and infants normally received lessons in needlework while the elder boys remained with the schoolmaster for further study and for some training in trades.[87] These afternoon sessions were what was meant by 'industrial schools'.

Until 1870 at least standards of comparable civilian schools were none too high. The revised code of 1861 cut the funds available for education and encouraged teachers to concentrate on meeting government examinations but to teach as little as possible. For the majority of children, especially those in industrial areas, there was still little real schooling available. Army education, universal, compulsory and free after 1871 had a limited curriculum, but succeeded none the less in providing a general education acceptable for its day to all army children everywhere. Observers in the earlier period who had the opportunity to compare army schools with the national schools believed the army system as good as or better than the civil one. In spite of the movement entailed by army life, the Council of Military Education remarked in 1861 that army children were every bit as well-instructed as children attending a national school.[88] The Newcastle Commission in 1861 reported favourably on army schools, expressing satisfaction especially with the curriculum for older students and the industrial schools.[89] In 1870 the Royal Commission on Military Education observed that army schools:

> . . .are on the whole such as to provide the means of sound and useful elementary education. . .the results of the schools are decidedly successful, as compared with those of civil schools of a similar class. . . The regularity of attendance, which is enforced by the authority of commanding officers, gives the instructors a distinct advantage over those of the National Schools of the country, and contributes greatly to the satisfactory progress of the pupils. The subjects taught appear. . .well adapted to the social condition and future wants of the children, and the system of instruction seems to be well devised and practically successful in its results.[90]

Others were equally enthusiastic in their praise encouraging as a result a certain dangerous complacency. G.R. Gleig remarked in 1870:

> In my opinion there is no comparison between the moral and intellectual condition of army schools and schools in civil life. The army schools are very superior to those in civil life. I have had many opportunities of examining schools both in London and in the country, and I think nothing approaches the generality of our military schools.[91]

That same year a schoolmaster at Aldershot argued:

> . . .the best scholars in our schools can beat all comers from the civilian school in the district in open competition in the examinations under the Society of Arts. . .The children receive a good plain education, and they are able to compete successfully with schools of a similar class in civil life.[92]

But army schools had a number of serious faults which comparison with the civilian school system tended only to obscure. When, after 1870, there were marked improvements in the curricula, quality of teaching and facilities offered by the latter, the faults of the army schools were brought sharply into focus.

There had been warnings even before this. In 1858 Colonel J.H. Lefroy had had a great deal of praise for the working of the regimental schools, yet pointed out a too prevalent tendency for children to learn their lessons by rote without really thinking, an aspect at this time of both military and civilian schooling.[93] On at least two occasions, in 1866 and again in 1868, the Council of Military Education remarked that the standard of achievement in children's schools was declining somewhat.[94] The Royal Commission on Military Education two years later pointed out that aside from needlework there was virtually no technical training of any sort given to army children. Their recommendations that there be greater opportunity for instruction of this nature met with little favour because of a lack of facilities and competent instructors, and anticipated difficulties with apprenticeship.[95]

By the end of the 1880s it was becoming increasingly clear that army schools were falling behind. In 1886 efforts were made to assimilate their curriculum to that of the public elementary schools. However the flexibility given to the latter by the civil codes of 1890–1 in the choice of subjects taught could not be copied since the mobility of soldiers and their families who were often on the move due to transfers and unit rotations required strict uniformity of curricula in all army schools. In the circumstances reading, writing, arithmetic, singing, recreation, physical drill, English grammar, geography and history, and for the more advanced students algebra, Euclid or mensuration were made compulsory, but most of the other subjects authorised in the civil codes, i.e. chemistry, physics, animal physiology, botany, French and Latin, could not be taught because of financial and other limitations. This meant of course severe restrictions on the scope of education army schools could provide. As early as 1887 the advantages to be gained by sending army children to large civil schools had been realised, however the obvious lack of such schools abroad and the necessity for uniformity of instruction throughout the army precluded any such action.[96] The Army Schools Act of 1891 attempted to get around these difficulties by classifying military schools as public schools and permitting students to take advantage of scholarships and other aids to continue their education at other institutions. Only occasionally was advantage taken of these provisions; it was so difficult for army children to do so, and in any case many boys intended enlisting in the forces at an early age.[97]

A lack of adequate facilities comparable to those in newer civilian schools was another of the problems encountered by the army. With the limited funds at their disposal, military authorities had difficulty in even maintaining minimum standards, not to mention providing new equipment and facilities. The report in 1896 of the Director-General of Military Education showed how slowly progress was being made in bringing school buildings up to the standards required by the Education Department for public schools, and stressed that large numbers of younger children were risking deformity by sitting in chairs and desks constructed for adults.[98]

Although the shortcomings of army children's education was accentuated by the progress that had been made in public elementary education, the military schools succeeded, for the most part, in their principal goal, the provision of a useful general education. There are indications too that the children's education, especially when civilian standards were low, may well have added to the attractions of military service. It would be going too far to argue that they were a consideration in recruiting, but it is clear that the opportunity to have their children educated at very little expense was a matter of some importance to married soldiers and was looked upon as one of the advantages of a career in the forces. In 1887 the Harris Committee on Army Schools and Schoolmasters observed that the very existence of army schools was '. . .appreciated by the married men as a reward for their long and faithful service, by the children as tending to encourage in their minds, the feeling that the army is their home, and by the service in general as in many ways raising its tone.'[99]

The central role in army education played by the regimental and garrison schools must not be allowed to totally overshadow that of the other schools which were involved in the same field. These were the Royal Military Asylum, Chelsea, and the Royal Hibernian Military School, Dublin, large boarding schools run by the army for soldiers' children, and two smaller schools managed by the Royal Victoria Patriotic Fund. The influence which these institutions together exerted on children's education was a major one.

The Royal Victoria Patriotic Fund was founded by public subscription during the Crimean War for the relief of the widows and orphans of men killed on active service. Shortly after it became operational two children's boarding schools known collectively as the Royal Victoria Patriotic Asylum were set up at Wandsworth. Education and support for orphans whose father had once served in either the army or navy was free, and acceptance was based on need and on the resources of the fund. Both schools were run along similar lines. A standard primary curriculum consisting of reading, writing, arithmetic, English grammar, geography and history was followed. In the boys' school there was also some instruction in military drill and in trades; girls had additional tuition in sewing and in domestic work.[100]

By 1865 there were 180 boys and over 260 girls being cared for at Wandsworth. The school leaving age was fourteen or fifteen, at which time boys were either encouraged to enlist in the forces or if unwilling to do so were apprenticed or left in the care of friends. Girls were placed in domestic positions or sent to friends or relations. After 1860 the Royal Victoria Patriotic Fund expanded the range of its services and took on the administration of a number of other charities and funds. It extended its functions by supporting the education of children of servicemen enrolled in civilian boarding schools. By 1872 a total of 725 children attending boarding institutions in Britain were being supported; 322 of these were girls and 224 boys at the Patriotic Fund's own schools at Wandsworth.[101] The school for girls was in operation until the turn of the century, but a controversy over unequal treatment of Roman Catholic students resulted in the closure and sale in 1880 of the boy's school.[102] The money received was used thereafter to support the education of army orphans, both Roman Catholics and Protestants, in public elementary schools.

Although army children were educated at the schools financed by the Royal Victoria Patriotic Fund, there was no army involvement in the curriculum or the administration of the schools themselves. Furthermore it is not known how many students enlisted in the forces, and although it seems that most were army children, it is not known how many students were the sons or daughters of seamen killed in action. A more central role in army children's education, for the Patriotic Fund schools were essentially civilian schools, and certainly one which involved the army a great deal more, was played by its own military boarding schools, the Royal Military Asylum in Chelsea and the Royal Hibernian Military School in Dublin.

The importance of these two schools to the army and to the state of education in the forces lay largely in the number of recruits they furnished annually. The student body consisted of soldiers' children with preference being given to orphans. Initially both sexes had been taken, but by 1850 boys only were admitted. Each school operated on a fixed establishment regulated according to the institution's physical capabilities. The enrolment at the RHMS Dublin remained a steady 410 throughout our period, but the numbers attending Chelsea fluctuated considerably. In 1860 there were 496 boys enrolled at the RMA; in ten years the numbers had fallen to 457.[103] By 1896 enrolment had risen to 545.[104]

Enlistment in the army was not compulsory but the education was designed to train boys for the forces, and there was a great deal of pressure put on them to follow such a course. In 1884 regulations made it clear that if a student refused to go into the army no other children from his family would be permitted to attend either school. Not every applicant of course could pass the medical examination,[105] yet the percentages who did enlist each year were quite high.[106] The highest point came during the late 1860s and early 1870s when percentages were in the eighties. There was no official explanation given for this, but the peak at this time may have been due to the initial attractions of short-service enlistment introduced in 1870, and the subsequent decline may have resulted either from disillusionment with the terms of service or from stiffer medical examinations for all recruits. When compared with the number of enlistments from total sources annually, which were 9,998 in 1856 and 29,583 in 1895 alone,[107] the numbers involved here were small. If they are added to the unknown but certainly significant number of recruits who as children had previously attended regimental or garrison schools, however, they provided an important nucleus of each year's enlistment. The army attached considerable value to recruits from RMA and RHMS.[108] Most of those who had attended either one of the schools did exceptionally well in the forces (though, as we shall see, their education was in some ways defective). Figures for 1883 for instance show that the character of former students was very much better than the general grading. The ranks these men had obtained in the forces depended to some extent on length of service, nevertheless figures do indicate as well that a higher proportion than average achieved positions of authority.[109]

Although the Royal Military Asylum and the Hibernian School together fed, clothed and housed free of charge quite a number of boys annually between 1856 and 1899, the quality of education they provided was inconsistent. The schools attempted only to supplement education received elsewhere, and a child's residence in either institution might be limited to only two or three years. Unlike regimental schools which took children at a very early age, RMA admitted boys between the ages of ten and twelve, and RHMS between the ages of seven and twelve. Both institutions enforced a compulsory leaving age of fourteen.[110]

At the time of the Lefroy report on army schools in 1858 the curriculum at RMA and RHMS comprised instruction in a number of academic subjects[111] plus training in music, tailoring, shoemaking or carpentry with a view to future military service. Altogether there were six and one-half hours of tuition each day except Sunday, two hours of this devoted to either music or industrial training. Military drill, gunnery, gymnastics and swimming were taught as well and were an integral part of the daily routine.[112] There was considerable satisfaction in the army with the educational system of the two military schools, and early inquiries testified enthusiastically to its effectiveness. J.H. Lefroy found the students generally intelligent, quick, cheerful and healthy.[113] In 1862 and again in 1866 the Council of Military Education expressed similar praise.[114] The Royal Commission on Military Education observed in 1870 that the system of teaching and subjects taught seemed 'well adapted to boys of the age and class of life of the pupils. . .we believe that the results of the method pursued may be regarded as highly satisfactory'.[115] Army officers and those engaged in teaching at either RMA or RHMS were quick to testify to the value of the education provided and its usefulness to prospective army recruits.[116] Each offered the basics of a good general education, but again some at least of the enthusiasm was due indirectly to the fact that civilian standards were as low as they were. In1866 the Council of Military Education estimated that most of the students at the Royal Military Asylum each year came away with a better education than was provided by the national schools.[117] In 1870 an infantry officer told the Military Education Commission:

> We have now eight men who have come from the Duke of York's school [the Royal Military Asylum] one of whom is the band

> master, another the trumpet major, and they are all very well behaved except one, who is an excellent musician, and who has very great temptations. On the whole they are better educated than the average number of men whom we get.[118]

In fact both the administration and the curriculum of the two schools left a great deal to be desired. For one thing, conditions for students were crude. Living quarters were far from healthy, there was little provision for recreation, diets were poor, discipline very strict, and long hours were demanded. This was the situation in the 1850s and it had changed little by the report of the Military Education Commission in 1870.[119] For another, although technical instruction was considered an important part of the curriculum since RMA and RHMS graduates were frequently taken into the army as qualified musicians, shoemakers or tailors, instruction in these skills was deficient, and in 1858 of a total enrolment of 821, half were receiving no industrial training whatsoever.[120] In 1869, again, the Council of Military Education found this situation little changed.[121] Yet demands that conditions at the schools be improved and that technical training be increased without any detriment to academic instruction were largely ignored.[122] Instead of improving facilities and increasing the amount of technical instruction available, a 'half-time' system was introduced at Chelsea in 1876 and at Dublin in 1879. This scheme provided for six hours of instruction per day, equally divided between academic subjects and trades. Classes in algebra, drawing, mensuration and elementary mechanics were discontinued while the remainder of the academic curriculum was curtailed. At the same time regulations were introduced requiring students to perform many of the arduous domestic and other duties associated with the running of the two schools. The health of many began to suffer, and educational standards dropped seriously. In 1883 a committee of enquiry was able to show that one-quarter of the boys who left the Royal Military Asylum during the previous year after four years of instruction and who enlisted in the forces, were unable to obtain even an elementary fourth-class education certificate.[123] In 1889 80 per cent of the boys were below the standards for their age in the elementary subjects, 63 per cent were more than one standard below. Some boys were leaving the institution almost illiterate and with no instruction in any trade.[124]

Only in the last decades of the century as the achievements of the national school system became increasingly apparent was the situation retrieved to any extent. Colonel A.C. Gleig, the Inspector of Army Schools, had praised the introduction of the 'half-time system' for its efficiency and allotment of more time to industrial training.[125] This attitude stood in the path of any change. It was his retirement in 1889 that paved the way for a return to a full-time system and a reorganisation of the curriculum to comply with the standards of civilian schools.[126] These steps went far towards restoring the quality of education that the schools had once boasted of. By 1893 the curriculum of the Royal Military Asylum and the Hibernian School had begun to compare more favourably with civilian institutions,[127] and by 1896 nearly one-half out of the total enrolment of 957 had reached standards up to or above those attained by children of the same age in national schools.[128]

Throughout the period 1856–99 as a whole, the Royal Military Asylum and the Royal Hibernian Military School were not as successful in educating army children as were the regimental or garrison schools or even the institutions supported by the Patriotic Fund. For one thing the number of students involved were fewer, for another there were serious weaknesses in the curriculum which limited its effectiveness. Yet their influence on army education was by no means negligible. When standards of civilian education were low, the military schools made a major contribution to the education of army children and indirectly to the state of education in the forces. As civilian education improved however they failed to follow its lead. The half-time system from 1870 to 1889 came roughly at the time when the proportion of recruits from the schools into the army was at its peak. The last decade of the century saw the gap between army and national schools become increasingly visible, but at the same time progress was made in improving the curriculum at the Royal Military Asylum and the Hibernian School, and greater success was achieved in providing the basics of both a general education and technical training.

4. Army School Teachers

Up to this point little has been said about the schoolmasters and schoolmistresses upon whom so much of the success of army education ultimately depended. Trained enlisted schoolmasters were normally in charge of the instruction in unit schools and were responsible for seeing that the curriculum laid down by the central education authority was followed. During the day they were employed in teaching the children of the regiment; in the late afternoon and evening they held classes for recruits and for others studying on their own or for educational certificates. A schoolmistress usually assisted the schoolmaster and was responsible for teaching the younger children and for instructing girls in needlework and domestic work. Where there was a shortage of trained staff regular soldiers might be seconded to assist and soldiers' wives or daughters asked to fill in as acting schoolmistresses.

Trained schoolmistresses were hired on a contract basis and remained civilians throughout their period of employment with the army. Prospective schoolmasters, who might be either civilians or regular soldiers, were required to enlist in the Corps of Army Schoolmasters, a branch of the Service founded in 1846. A normal school for teachers had been attached to the Royal Military Asylum, Chelsea, since that time. The course of instruction was two years and comprised a varied curriculum.[129] All male school teachers, even qualified civilians, were required to enrol and attend for the full period. Professional training for army teachers was based on civilian precedents. In the 1840s Sir James Kay-Shuttleworth founded the first teacher-training establishment in Britain in an effort to cope with the nation's drastic shortage of trained teachers. So successful were his efforts that other institutions sprang up in imitation, among them the army school. An additional source of teachers were the pupils of the Royal Military Asylum. A monitorial system based on Bell's model provided for the training of pupil-teachers, many of whom later went on to enrol in the normal school and to join the Corps of Army Schoolmasters.[130]

The existence of a trained body of school teachers to staff regimental and garrison schools was important in promoting education in the army. Between 1846 and 1858, 178 teachers were trained, 37 of whom had been civilians, 48 NCOs, and 93 monitors or pupil-teachers at the RMA who had stayed on to obtain teaching qualifications.[131] By 1860 there were 244 trained schoolmasters and 242 trained schoolmistresses in positions in army schools. Their numbers increased only slightly during the next forty years. In 1896 there were 265 schoolmasters and 285 schoolmistresses employed in the army school system.[132]

Initially army teachers were as well prepared as their civilian colleagues, and the quality of instruction they imparted was probably as high. However, they ran foul of many of the same difficulties which confronted all teachers during the latter half of the century, and in addition were faced with the peculiarities of army service to be overcome. At times dissatisfaction with their position was widespread, and the quality of army education was adversely affected. After 1861, the philosophy of payment by results in English education inaugurated a disastrous system which was to hamstring the efforts of the teaching profession for nearly forty years, but it did not affect army teachers who remained unfettered by any need to maintain attendance or to have pupils reach certain standards each year. Yet for the success of army schools, a great deal depended on the cooperation and encouragement given to education by regimental officers. An obstructive or uninterested CO might well make the task of the schoolmaster virtually impossible. Irregularity of attendance, especially by the adult soldiers, clearly led to frustration and dissatisfaction. Moreover duties which required the army teacher to tutor children in the daytime, and then to return in the late afternoon and evening for adult classes could prove an exhausting workload. A schoolmaster who signed on with the forces in 1897 recalled:

> I thought I had done a very good day's work at 4.45 p.m. and in my polite civilian way I bade 'Good-day' to the Schoolmaster in charge, only to be informed that he would see me after tea, as the Second Attendance for men who had been prevented from being present at the First, was due at 6 p.m. and lasted until 7.15 p.m. I was immensely surprised but I learned on further explanation that this was the ordinary routine on every night except Wednesday, when there was no Second Attendance. I pondered this deeply and very nearly concluded that one such day in the Army was enough for me.[133]

Like their civilian opposite numbers, army schoolmasters suffered from poor relations with their superiors and from being forced to occupy an ambiguous social position. As part of the regiment to which they were attached, teachers were liable to transfer or move, even overseas, on short notice. Being neither an officer nor enlisted man but a non-combatant NCO often led to friction and misunderstanding as well. Distrusted by the troops and regarded as radical by many officers, the status of the army schoolmaster was never secure. 'By Jove!, the Old Duke of Wellington is reported to have once exclaimed, 'if ever there is a mutiny in the army—and in all probability we shall see one—you'll see that these new fangled schoolmasters are at the bottom of it.'[134] In 1864 a journal article remarked:

> Many commanding officers have a deep-rooted objection to the Normal Schoolmasters, for being, as it were, in a kind of indefinite position; they are neither officers nor sergeants, but a sort of mixture of the two; disliked, and termed upstarts by one party, while looked down upon and snubbed by the other.[135]

Army wages in no way compensated for the shortcoming of military service. All schoolteachers enjoyed job security and the prospect of an army pension, but these were more than offset by low salaries. In 1859 schoolmasters received from 3s to 6s 6d per day (£55–£118 per annum), schoolmistresses £24 to £36 per annum.[136] The Newcastle Commission reported in 1861 that the average salary of a random sample of certificated masters in civilian schools was £94 3s 7d per year, that of a similar group of certificated schoolmistresses £62 13s 10d.[137] On the recommendation of the Royal Commission on Military Education in 1870 the salaries of army schoolmasters were raised to 4s–7s per day (£73–£128 per year) and that of schoolmistresses was increased to £30–£44 per annum.[138] But the late 1870s and 1880s saw a strong growth of professionalism in the teaching profession in Britain and an increase in real wages, and the disparity between army and civilian salaries continued. In 1889 when the maximum salary of trained schoolmistresses was increased to £76 11s 9d, the starting salary of the London School Board was £85 per annum, there was an opportunity of secure posts worth up to £140 per year, and the prospects for promotion were better than the army could offer.

Disenchantment with the prospects of army teaching and with army life was widespread and was reflected in fewer applications for positions and in a falling enrolment at the Normal School at Chelsea. In 1859 forty-one students were attending classes there, sixteen civilians, thirteen NCOs and twelve monitors.[139] In 1869 applications for training for the Corps of Army Schoolmasters fell to three.[140] By 1877 only twenty-four students were enrolled in the Normal School. In 1896 the Director-General of Military Education reported that because army salaries were so low he was unable to recruit enough candidates to fill vacant positions for teachers.[141]

The shortage of trained personnel was further exacerbated by attempts to wring economies out of military expenditures. The Normal

School at Chelsea was one of the first to suffer. In 1870 the Military Education Commission had attacked it for not providing enough instruction in teaching and recommended its discontinuation in favour of open competition between qualified civilians and soldiers trained in civilian institutions for teaching positions.[142] A number of senior officers still wary of the results of education in the army supported such a move by arguing that schoolmasters were needlessly over-educated. The Duke of Cambridge for instance remarked:

> I have very great doubts whether it [the maintenance of the School] would be necessary. I think that men who are intended for schoolmasters must pass examinations, and that they ought to have an opportunity of obtaining a certain amount of experience in instruction at a school. I think that you might do that by having such a class attached to the Duke of York's School; but I do not see the advantage of the Normal School, it is an entirely separate establishment.[143]

The Normal School weathered out this storm, but in 1883 a committee enquiring into the working of the Royal Military Asylum revealed that the quality of instruction was suffering from a shortage of properly trained staff. A larger budget might have cured this, but with the need for economies the writing was already on the wall. The Committee's recommendations echoed those of 1870 in calling for the discontinuation of the School and the training of teachers in civilian establishments.[144] In 1887 the Harris Committee raised the points again.[145] They argued that vacancies for teaching positions were not being filled, partly because compulsory attendance for two years at the Chelsea Normal School deterred civilian applicants, and that in any case this training was deficient since it offered no experience in teaching adults. The following year the Normal School was finally closed and applicants for teaching positions, soldiers and civilians alike, were sent to garrison schools as assistants for a limited period of training.[146] Although the way was now open for better trained civilians, a substantial amount of control over the preparation of teachers had been lost in the process.

In another effort towards economy the War Office discontinued the hiring of trained schoolmistresses after 1888 on the advice of the Harris Committee, explaining that they were an 'unnecessary expense'. In their place acting schoolmistresses, such as soldiers' wives, were appointed on a small salary with no allowance or pension. In less than a year it was evident that not enough acting schoolmistresses could be found and that the quality of instruction in infant and industrial schools had begun to suffer. The administration was forced to retrace its steps in this instance, and on the recommendation of the Director-General of Military Education in 1889 trained schoolmistresses were rehired and at an increased salary.[147]

What influence through all this did army teachers have on education in the forces between 1856 and 1899? It is not easily documented; but it can nevertheless be shown that their role was an important one. For one thing, a large percentage of teachers were recruited from within the system. Many instructors had themselves been brought up in army schools and so spent most of their life in the Service. Similarly a large proportion of the students enrolled in the Normal School each year had either been pupil-teachers at the Royal Military Asylum or the Royal Hibernian Military School or were serving soldiers. In some respects this may have bred a narrowness and unawareness of civilian techniques and innovations, but equally it assisted the standardisation of procedures and of curricula which was necessary to an ever-changing body of students in an army that was constantly on the move between home stations, colonial duty and active service overseas. If in later years the training of schoolmasters was not up to that given in civilian institutions, this was alleviated after 1886 with the closing of the Normal School and the direct recruitment of trained civilian teachers for the Corps of Army Schoolmasters. The shortage of trained personnel which was experienced throughout the period was another matter however. A reflection of both official reluctance to spend adequately to cover the needs of education and of the discouragements of military service, shortages forced reliance on untrained assistants, a practice which cannot in the long run have had beneficial results.

5. Conclusion

There were many different sides to army education between 1856 and 1899, each with its own story to tell. There was a particular lack of progress in the field of technical education, although other areas enjoyed real if modest success. A great deal more might have been achieved had education received more encouragement at the regimental level and if the private soldier had taken more advantage of existing facilities. Nevertheless the increase in both literacy and in the number of soldiers with a creditable education was significant evidence that the army was changing with society.

Authorities within the army and without consistently placed a high value on education. More was done in this area than in any other for the dependants of the enlisted man. The necessity of educating the rank and file and their children was accepted not only because it would increase their value to the army, but because the influential classes felt an obligation towards all levels of the society of which the army was more than ever a part. Education was an important aspect of the army's transition from an earlier uncaring, fiercely-disciplined body to a more humane organisation with greater provision for the welfare of its men. During the First World War the Director-General of the Royal Army Medical Corps emphasised the new spirit of education and in a way summed up a half century of progress. 'It is not enough to mend their bodies', he wrote, '. . .it is a national obligation to do all possible to mend their minds and their later lives as well.'[148]

Notes

1. Lord Panmure to Queen Victoria, 16 Feb. 1857, Panmure MSS., GD45/8/143.
2. These were views shared firmly by both Gleig and Lefroy as well. See G.R. Gleig to Lord Panmure, 4 Dec. 1856, 5 Feb. 1857; J.H. Lefroy to Lord Panmure, 19 Sept. 1856; J.H. Lefroy, Paper on the Organisation of the Department of Military Education, Oct. 1856; Lord Panmure to Lord Palmerston, 19 Jan. 1857; Lord Panmure to the Duke of Cambridge, 5 Dec. 1857; Panmure MSS., GD45/8/151, 45/8/322, 45/8/389.
3. Queen Victoria to Lord Panmure, 14 Feb. 1857, 17 Feb. 1857; The Duke of Cambridge to Lord Panmure, 12 Dec. 1856, 15 April 1857; Panmure MSS., GD45/8/143, 45/8/152, 45/8/398.
4. *Report of the Council of Military Education,* P.P., XXIV (c.2603), 1860, p.3.
5. Brevet-Colonel J.H. Lefroy, *Report on the Regimental and Garrison Schools of the Army* (1859).
6. *Second Report of the Royal Commission on Military Education,* P.P., XXIV (c.214), 1870, pp.13, 31; cited hereafter as *Report of the Military Education Commission* (1870).
7. Lefroy, *Report on Army Schools,* p.27.
8. The opportunities that working-class children had for an education depended on there being a school in their neighbourhood and on their parents having the inclination and the money to send them. R.K. Webb, *The British Working Class Reader 1799–1848* (1955), pp.21–2; Gillian Sutherland, *Policy-Making in Elementary Education, 1870–1895* (Oxford, 1975), pp.117–18.
9. The Newcastle Commission in 1861 reported that a high percentage of children were going to school, but that attendance was often irregular and too short. 20 per cent (100,000) of all pauper children received no

education whatsoever, while 80 per cent of those who were being educated were being taught in workhouses. *Report of the Royal Commission on the State of Popular Education in England*, P.P., XXI (c.2794), 1861, pp.373, 381; cited hereafter as *Report of the Commission on English Education* (1861).

10. R.K. Webb, 'Literacy among the Working Class in Nineteenth Century Scotland', *Scottish Historical Review*, XXXIII (1954), p.100. It may well be that the renown of the Scottish regiments in battle was due less to actual prowess than to the fact that the Scottish soldier was better educated and wrote more letters home. This has been suggested by Mr. W.F. Boag MA, Scottish United Services Museum, Edinburgh. I have found no evidence to either substantiate or refute such an argument.
11. See *Report of the Royal Commission on Education in Scotland*, P.P., XXV (c.3845), 1867.
12. Joseph Lee, *The Modernisation of Irish Society, 1848–1918* (Dublin, 1973), pp.13, 27–31.
13. *Report of the Director-General of Military Education*, P.P., XII (c.1085), 1874, pp.vii–ix.
14. *Report of the Director-General of Military Education*, P.P., XXX (c.1885), 1877, pp.x–xii.
15. *General Annual Return of the British Army*, P.P., XLIII (c.6196), 1890, p.85.
16. *Report of the Director-General of Military Education*, P.P. XVII (c.5805), 1889, p.21.
17. Moreover recruitment, which between 1885 and 1899 averaged 35,000–40,000 young men per year, and discharges, which amounted to approximately 11,000 annually, most of them older men who had received an army education, must have had a negative effect on the statistics of literacy in the forces by tending to increase each year the proportion of uneducated men in the ranks. The influence of army education was therefore even somewhat greater than available figures would indicate.
18. There is no evidence to suggest that the army was able to tap a different pool of recruits in later years. See Appendix II, Table IIA–1.
19. *Report of the Committee on Army Schools and Schoolmasters*, WO.33/47, p.1082.
20. Lord Harris to Edward Stanhope, 25 May 1890, Stanhope MSS., 1327.
21. *Report of the Army Medical Department*, P.P., LXVII (c.5447), 1888, p.30.
22. *Report of the Director-General of Military Education*, P.P., XVII (c.5805), 1889, p.16.
23. *Report of the Director-General of Military Education*, P.P., XVI (c.7017), 1893–4, p.8.
24. In 1858 a test case involving compulsory education was put before the law officers of the Crown, who ruled that it was inconsistent with military discipline to require recruits to attend school. Unwilling to press for remedial legislation, the War Office withdrew the regulations enacting compulsory attendance in 1861. Lefroy, *Report on Army Schools*, p.178; *Report of the Military Education Commission* (1870), pp.xii–xiii.
25. Anon., 'Education in the Army', *Fraser's Magazine*, XXXIII (1846), pp.719–20.
26. *Queen's Regulations and Orders for the Army* (1857), p.17.
27. *Report of the Military Education Commission* (1870), pp.xvii, 97.
28. Lord William Paulet, the Adjutant-General, opposed compulsory schooling on grounds of the difficulty to be encountered in carrying it out.

The Duke of Cambridge argued in a similar vein before the Royal Commission on Military Education in 1870, and in 1881 was to testify before a parliamentary committee that examinations for army education certificates were too difficult for NCOs, and that only elementary writing and reading was necessary. See for instance *Report of the Military Education Commission* (1870), pp.35, 40, 90, 99; Anon. 'The Education of our Troops', *Colburn's* (1868), pp.1–7, 235–41; *Report of the Committee on Army Reorganisation,* P.P., XXI (c.2791), 1881, p.321; cited hereafter as *Report of the Army Reorganisation Committee* (1881).

29. *The Queen's Regulations and Orders for the Army* (1857), p.245.
30. *Report of a Committee on the Present State and on the Improvement of Libraries, Reading Rooms, and Day Rooms,* WO.33/10.
31. *Report of the Military Education Commission.* (1870), pp.xxiii–xxiv.
32. *Report of the Council of Military Education,* P.P., XXXIV (c.3422), 1865, p.237; *Report of the Military Education Commission* (1870), p.xxiv.
33. Lefroy, *Report on Army Schools,* p.63.
34. *Report of the Council of Military Education,* P.P., XXXII (c.2957), 1862, p.xxv; XLIV (c.3737), 1860, p.xlv.
35. *Report of the Military Education Commission* (1870), p.xxv.
36. See *Report of the Council of Military Education,* P.P., XXXII (c.2957), 1862, pp.vi–xi; *Report of the Director-General of Military Education,* P.P., XVI (c.7017), 1893–4, pp.6–8; *Guide to Obtaining a First Class Certificate of Army Education* (Chatham, 1886), pp.4–7; *Guide to Obtaining a Second Class Certificate of Education* (Chatham, 1884), pp.4–7, 10; *The Third Class Army School Certificate Made Easy* (Chatham, 1889), pp,7–11.
37. *Report of the Council of Military Education,* P.P., XXXII (c.2957), 1862, pp.iv–vi; XXXIV (c.3422), 1865, pp.xii–xiii; XLIV (c.3604), 1866, pp.xi–xii; XXII (c.4108), 1868–9, p.xii; XXV (c.131), 1870, pp.x–xi.
38. *Report of the Military Education Commission* (1870), pp.xii–xiii.
39. Edward Cardwell, The Army in 1872, Gladstone MSS., 44120.
40. There is no evidence to suggest however that recruiting needs had anything to do with the passage of measures to improve educational standards, or indeed that army education was an inducement to enlistment. See for example *Report of the Inspector General of Recruiting,* P.P., XV (c.3503), 1883, pp.9–10; XIII (c.4677), 1886, p.15; XX (c.6597), 1892, p.5; XVIII (c.7659), 1895, pp.6–7.
41. *General Order LXX* (1871).
42. *Report of the Director-General of Military Education,* P.P., XXX (c.1885), 1877, p.25.
43. *Report of the Committee on Army Schools and Schoolmasters,* WO.33/47, p.1082.
44. For instance *Report of the Director-General of Military Education,* P.P., XXX (c.1885), 1877, pp.25–6.
45. *Report of the Committee on Army Schools and Schoolmasters,* WO.33/47.
46. *Report of the Director-General of Military Education,* P.P., XVI (c.7017), 1893–4, p.5. It was not until 1913 that action was taken and recruits were required to attend school either during their first six months of service or until they attained a third-class certificate.
47. *Report of the Director-General of Military Education,* P.P., XVII (c.5805), 1889, p.6.
48. *Report of the Military Education Commission* (1870), pp.xii–xiii.
49. A Private Soldier, 'Education in the Army', *Good Words and Sunday*

Magazine, IV (1864), p.393.

50. *Report of the Director-General of Military Education*, P.P., XVIII (c.8421), 1896, pp.33–4.
51. Lefroy, *Report on Army Schools*, p.27.
52. *Report of the Council of Military Education*, P.P., XLIV (c.3604), 1866, p.xiii.
53. *Report of the Director-General of Military Education*, P.P., XVIII (c.8421), 1896, pp.33–4.
54. Lefroy, op.cit., p.28.
55. E.C. Grenville Murray, *Six Months in the Ranks* (Leipzig, 1882), p.86.
56. Private Soldier, *Good Words and Sunday Magazine*, IV (1864), p.398.
57. *Report of the Committee on Army Schools and Schoolmasters*, WO.33/47, p.1083.
58. Grenville Murray, *Six Months in the Ranks*, p.169.
59. *Report of the Council of Military Education*, P.P., XLIV (c.3604), 1866, p.xlvi; XXII (c.4108), 1868–9, p.xxxiii; Field-Marshal Sir William Robertson, *From Private to Field-Marshal* (1921), p.30.
60. Grenville Murray, *Six Months in the Ranks*, p.327.
61. See Lefroy, *Report on Army Schools*, p.43.
62. *General Annual Return of the British Army*, P.P., XLIII (c.1323), 1875, p.7; LIII (c.9426), 1899, p.26.
63. See Appendix II, Table IIA–5.
64. Robertson, *From Private to Field-Marshal*, pp.29–33; see also Chapter 4 below.
65. Hansard, CLXV (13 March 1862), c.1461; CXCVI (4 May 1869), c.90.
66. *Report of a Committee on the Proper Means for the Instruction and Employment of Soldiers and Their Children in Trades*, P.P., XXXII (c.3133), 1863, pp.5–6.
67. Ibid., pp.v–x.
68. Ibid., pp.viii–ix.
69. Ibid., p.48.
70. *Copy of the Correspondence on the Subject of the Employment of Soldiers in Trades*, P.P., XXXII (c.181), 1863.
71. *Report of a Committee Appointed for the Purpose of Framing Regulations for the Employment of Soldiers at Trades*, P.P., XXXIX (c.62), 1871, p.2.
72. The Army in 1872, Official War Office Papers of General Viscount Wolseley, W.39.
73. *Report of the Committee on Army Schools*, WO.32/6956.
74. *Report of the Steps Taken to Provide Technical Instruction to Soldiers*, P.P., XLIX (c.3511), 1907, p.8.
75. Instruction in these trades was introduced in 1907. See *War Office Report on the Steps Taken during 1907 to Provide Technical Instruction to Soldiers to Fit Them for Civilian Life*, P.P., XI (c.4059), 1908.
76. There are no precise figures to indicate what proportion of recruits had relatives in the Service, but contemporaries very often remarked that a large number of those in the ranks had followed fathers or brothers into the army. Officials maintained as well that recruits of this type who joined the Service out of a desire for an army life usually proved the most reliable and valuable of soldiers. See Chapter 5 below.
77. Quoted in *Report of the Committee on Army Schools and Schoolmasters*, WO.33/47, p.1081.
78. *The Regulations and Orders of the 48th Regiment* (1857), p.65.
79. *Report of the Military Education Commission* (1870), p.x; Edward

Cardwell to Robert Lowe, 10 Mar. 1871, Cardwell MSS., PRO.30/48/5/23.
80. Lefroy, *Report on Army Schools,* p.34.
81. *Report of the Military Education Commission* (1870), p.43.
82. *Report of the Inspector-General of Recruiting,* P.P., XIII (c.4677), 1886, p.43.
83. *Report of the Director-General of Military Education,* P.P., XVIII (c.8421), 1896, p.16.
84. *Report of the Inspector-General of Recruiting,* P.P., XI (c.9185), 1899, p.36.
85. See for instance *Report of the Director-General of Military Education,* P.P., XVI (c.7107), 1893–4, pp.14–15.
86. The children of civilians employed at the Royal Arsenal for instance. *Report of the Military Education Commission* (1870), p.ix.
87. Ibid., pp.viii–ix.
88. *Report of the Council of Military Education,* P.P., XXXII (c.2957), 1862, pp.xv–xvi.
89. *Report of the Commission on English Education* (1861), pp.420–3.
90. *Report of the Military Education Commission* (1870), p.ix.
91. Ibid., p.52.
92. Ibid., p.15.
93. Lefroy, *Report on Army Schools,* p.36.
94. *Report of the Council of Military Education,* P.P., XLIV (c.3609), 1866, pp.xvi–xix; XXII (c.4108), 1868–9, pp.xii–xiii.
95. *Report of the Military Education Commission* (1870), p.xi.
96. *Report of the Committee on Army Schools and Schoolmasters,* WO.33/47, p.1081.
97. *Report of the Director-General of Military Education,* P.P., XVI (c.7017), 1893–4, pp.12–15.
98. *Report of the Director-General of Military Education,* P.P., XVIII (c.8421), 1896, p.16.
99. *Report of the Committee on Army Schools and Schoolmasters,* WO.33/47, p.1081.
100. *Report of the Royal Commissioners of the Patriotic Fund,* P.P., XXIX (c.69), 1865, pp.6–7.
101. *Report of the Royal Commissioners of the Patriotic Fund,* P.P., XVIII (c.847), 1873, p.8.
102. *Report of the Royal Commissioners of the Patriotic Fund,* P.P., XX (c.2922), 1881, p.7.
103. *Report of the Council of Military Education,* P.P., XXXII (c.2957), 1862, pp.xxv, xxvii; XXV (c.131), 1870, pp.xix, xxiii.
104. *Report of the Director-General of Military Education,* P.P., XVIII (c.8421), 1896, pp.24, 50.
105. In 1862–3 for instance, every boy who left the RHMS volunteered for the army, yet only 85 per cent were accepted. *Report of the Council of Military Education,* P.P., XXXIV (c.3422), 1865, p.xxviii.
106. See Appendix II, Table IIA–3.
107. *General Annual Return of the British Army,* P.P., LIII (c.9426), 1899, p.26; *Report of the Royal Commission on Recruiting in the Army,* P.P., XV (c.2762), 1861, p.326, cited hereafter as *Report of the Commission on Recruiting* (1861).
108. See for instance the Duke of Cambridge to Edward Cardwell, 31 Dec. 1870, Cardwell MSS., PRO.30/48/3/14.
109. *Report of the Committee on the Royal Hospitals at Chelsea and Kilmainham, and on the Educational Establishments at The Royal*

Military Asylum, Chelsea, and the Royal Hibernian Military School, Dublin, P.P., XV (c.3679), 1883, p.25; cited hereafter as *Report on RMA and RHMS* (1883).

110. Except band boys for whom it was fifteen, and monitors for whom it was seventeen. *Report on RMA and RHMS* (1883), p.20.
111. These were reading, writing, dictation, arithmetic, algebra, mensuration, elementary mechanics, geography, English grammar and history, singing, drawing and religious history.
112. *Report of the Military Education Commission* (1870), p.xxxii; Lefroy, *Report on Army Schools,* pp.70–82.
113. Lefroy, *Report on Army Schools,* p.82.
114. *Report of the Council of Military Education,* P.P., XXXII (c.2957), 1862, pp.xxii–xxviii; XLIV (c.3604), 1866, pp.xxiii–xxvi.
115. *Report of the Military Education Commission* (1870), p.xxxviii.
116. The Duke of Cambridge to Edward Cardwell, 31 Dec. 1870, Cardwell MSS., PRO.30/48/3/14; *Report of the Military Education Commission* (1870), pp.177, 185.
117. *Report of the Council of Military Education,* P.P., XLIV (c.3604), 1866, p.xxxvii.
118. *Report of the Military Education Commission* (1870), p.37.
119. Ibid., pp.xxiv, 172.
120. Lefroy, *Report on Army Schools,* pp.69, 82.
121. *Report of the Council of Military Education,* P.P., XXV (c.131), 1870, pp.xiii, xix.
122. *Report on RMA and RHMS* (1883), pp.20–3.
123. Ibid., pp.21, 31.
124. *Report of the Director-General of Military Education,* P.P., XVII (c.5805), 1889, p.17.
125. *Report of the Director-General of Military Education,* P.P., XXX (c.1885), 1877, p.xix.
126. *Report of the Director-General of Military Education,* P.P., XVII (c.5805), 1889, p.18; XVI (c.7017), 1893–4, p.25.
127. *Report of the Director-General of Military Education,* P.P., XVI (c.7017), 1893–4, p.25.
128. *Report of the Director-General of Military Education,* P.P., XVIII (c.8421), 1896, pp.46, 50.
129. The curriculum included arithmetic and mensuration, algebra, geometry, trigonometry and logarithms, industrial mechanics, English and colonial history, grammar, geography, penmanship, chemistry and physics, fortification, drawing, singing, reading and religious knowledge.
130. *Report of the Council of Military Education,* XXXII (c.2957), 1862, p.xix; *Report of the Military Education Commission* (1870), pp.xxviii–xxxi.
131. Lefroy, *Report on Army Schools,* p.69.
132. *Report of the Director-General of Military Education,* P.P., XVIII (c.8421), 1896, pp.19, 23.
133. W. Blackman, 'Reminiscences of the Retired', *Army Education* (September 1946), p.12.
134. Colonel H. de Watteville, *The British Soldier, His Life from Tudor to Modern Times* (1954), p.147.
135. Anon., 'Education in the Army', *Good Words and Sunday Magazine,* IV (1864), p.397.
136. *Report of the Military Education Commission* (1870), p.xviii.
137. *Report of the Commission on English Education* (1861), pp.64–5.
138. *Report of the Military Education Commission* (1870), p.xxi.

139. Lefroy, *Report on Army Schools,* p.69.
140. *Report of the Military Education Commission* (1870), p.xviii.
141. *Report of the Director-General of Military Education,* P.P., XXX (c.1885), 1877, p.xvii; XVIII (c.8421), 1896, p.19.
142. *Report of the Military Education Commission* (1870), pp.xxviii–xxxi.
143. Ibid., p.93.
144. *Report of the Committee on RMA And RHMS* (1883), pp.25–8.
145. *Report of the Committee on Army Schools and Schoolmasters,* WO.33/47, passim.
146. *Report of the Director-General of Military Education,* P.P., XVII (c.5805), 1889, pp.4–5.
147. Ibid., pp.11–13.
148. Lieutenant-General T.H. Goodwin, quoted in Colonel Lord Gorell, *Education and the Army* (1921), p.129.

3 DISCIPLINE AND CRIME IN THE ARMY

There is too much punishment in the Army; discipline does not require it.

Robert Blatchford

Soldiers only require to be treated like reasonable beings, and to be given proper opportunities, to become as steady and as respectable members of society as civilians of the same classes from which they are usually drawn.

Lord Roberts

For the due maintenance of discipline in an army raised as ours is by voluntary enlistment, a more drastic code of laws is required than for one raised. . .on the principle of universal service. The greatest ruffians in the three kingdoms enlist in our army.

Lord Wolseley

I never knew an instance of any man suffering any subsequent ill effects from receiving fifty lashes.

Lt.-Col. W.G. Alexander

Historians, sociologists and criminologists are generally agreed that the many changes undertaken in Scots and English criminal law, criminal procedures and penology during the second half of the nineteenth century resulted in a considerable lessening in the rate of detectable crime. To support these contentions, some have made wide use of criminal statistics,[1] while others, on grounds of their unreliability, have instead chosen to base their arguments on literary evidence.[2] These same years witnessed comparable changes in military law and punishment and, in a wider context, considerable efforts to prevent crime through other means than deterrence.

While statistics tracing the event of crime in the forces between 1856 and 1899 seem to indicate that the incidence of crime increased significantly between 1856 and 1899, it must be appreciated that there are certain limitations to their use which must qualify such an assertion. In general nineteenth-century British criminal statistics are open to a number of criticisms. New laws, changes in the administration of particular laws, and varying notions of which constituted a particular crime were rarely taken into consideration in their preparation. They normally list information about the unsuccessful criminals, unlucky or unskilful enough to be caught, and tend to reflect variations in the enforcement of the law. Neither conviction, prosecutions nor even reported crimes define the total amount of criminal behaviour. As Leon Radzinowicz has noted, at every stage 'offences go unnoticed or unreported, offenders go undetected, unprosecuted or unconvicted'.[3] Variations in the compilation of figures add to their unreliability. Moreover, there is little basis of comparison between civil and military crime quite apart from the unreliability of the statistics, since what constituted an offence under military law would not in most cases have been regarded as an offence by the civil judiciary. It is therefore not possible to compare in detail the incidence of crime in the army and that among the civilian population, though certain general points can be made. For example, the influence of recruitment on the incidence of crime in the army is impossible to define. It may be that the decline in the army crime rate partly reflected recruitment from a better behaved civilian population but whether this is true or not is uncertain.

Military statistics seem more reliable than civilian ones, although they are open to some of the same general criticisms. They are based on the numbers court-martialled, imprisoned or otherwise punished, and therefore, except for deserters, cannot take account of those offenders who went unapprehended. Moreover, it is difficult to detect in them variances in the interpretation of the nature of particular offences, though interpretations must have varied, for example, on the borderline between insubordination and disobedience. Against this it must be pointed out that on the whole military law remained fairly consistent in its definition of disciplinary offences. Furthermore the potential for enforcement of discipline in the army was greater since the soldier's every movement was monitored by his superiors and powers of arrest were considerable. The nature of an offence against discipline was such that virtually every infraction had to be noted in order to exist.[4] Logically therefore, for many disciplinary offences, there is no possibility of unreported crime.

Some major reservations arise with regard to the methods employed in the compilation and expression of military statistics. Figures relating to disobedience and to the length of prison sentences are particularly open to doubts about accuracy and consistency. Violence to superiors and insubordination, and disobedience, were classified as two separate offences until 1881. In that year they were reclassified as violence and disobedience to superiors, and minor insubordination and neglect of orders respectively. Between 1856 and 1870 the average length of sentences served by prisoners was given annually; afterwards prison sentences were given in categories according to their length. This can only be dealt with by expressing these figures as far as possible in such a manner as to minimise complications. There are difficulties as well with attempts to calculate recidivism. Statistics do not exist in the case of every military offence although they do for a range of important offences, and by bringing these together, a reasonable picture of recidivism can be obtained. In general there is more information on certain types of crimes than others, and more is known of those punished by imprisonment than by other means. Confinement in barrack cells or provost prisons was described as a summary punishment, and therefore figures for imprisonment relate to those confined in military prisons only. Prison statistics provide useful information on the character of inmates but men were sent to prison for serious offences only. There is not similar information on those who committed minor offences. The common-sense assumption is that there may have been proportionally fewer older men committing minor offences because they would be more accustomed to military service. But apart from this there is no indication that the minor offender differed from the major one significantly. Information on prisoners, therefore, probably is relevant in any general discussion of all soldiers who ran foul of military law.

Statistics do show that throughout the second half of the nineteenth century crime proved to be one of the chief problems facing military authorities. At no time between 1856 and 1899 was there an average of less than 500 soldiers confined in military prisons in Britain; not infrequently the figure was twice this amount, a number equal in size to two regiments of cavalry. In the same period courts-martial involved ten to twenty thousand men each year, the equivalent of fifteen or twenty full-sized infantry regiments. In terms of just the quantity of men withdrawn from active service therefore, the problem was a major one, and it was relieved only slightly by a reduction in the incidence of crime after 1856.

Nevertheless, it is important to get the balance right. The years between 1856 and 1899 were marked by a drop in the number of courts-martial and by a lessening of punishments, both in number and in severity. In the 1880s some officers might nostalgically complain that the army was no longer what it used to be,[5] but as others emphasised, the change for the better was to be seen in the declining incidence of crime.[6] For the most part the soldier was no longer looked upon by his officers as a drunken brawling fool, and their changed outlook was seen in their willingness to defend his conduct in public.[7] The surest indication, however, of this new attitude towards the soldier and of an improvement in his own behaviour is the reduction in the amount and severity of punishments enforced by the military penal system.

1. The Statistics of Crime in the Army, 1856-99

Punishments were inflicted summarily by commanding officers, and more formally by courts-martial. They principally consisted of minor summary punishments, capital and corporal punishment, and imprisonment.

Statistics indicate that the number of minor punishments awarded by commanding officers, and the proportion of men so punished, declined significantly between 1868, when the first figures are available, and 1898. Moreover, more use was made of summary punishments after 1865, and the summary jurisdiction of commanding officers to deal with minor offences was increased. It appears, therefore, that there was a real drop in the number of offences committed. It is also clear that the proportion of men who received minor punishments was consistently greater in the home army. No doubt the temptations to and the opportunities for misbehaviour were greater on home station than they were overseas, a posting which frequently involved conditions of active service. In addition, because there was a minimum age below which a man could not be posted overseas, the home army contained a larger proportion of younger soldiers who committed the majority of crimes.

A major part of the summary jurisdiction of commanding officers was the authority to inflict fines for drunkenness. The scheme providing for such fines was introduced after 1868. As Table 3–2 indicates, the number of fines imposed reached a peak around 1872 by which time their imposition was a common practice throughout the whole of the army. Drunkenness did not go unpunished thereafter, nor was there any detectable alteration in its definition, yet the number and proportion of men fined declined progressively between 1872 and 1899. Drunkenness, supposedly the mark of a 'licentious soldiery' and an offence which particularly galled critics of a standing army, was by the later decade of the century of much less frequent occurrence.

Statistics of the number of men tried by courts-martial illustrate the declining proportion of more serious crime in the forces. The proportion court-martialled dropped considerably between 1865 and

1898. Moreover, although it is not the only evidence on recidivism, it is significant that the proportion of soldiers tried more than once by court-martial decreased as well.

Table 3–1 Minor Punishments Awarded by COs and the Proportion of Men So Punished, 1868–98

Year	No. Punishments Home Army	No. per 100 Effectives	No. Punishments Whole Army	No. per 100 Effectives
1868	150,771	177.4	------ not reported	-----
1872	159,405	160.5	249,179	136.1
1876	163,538	176.3	255,231	144.8
1880	127,176	144.8	216,033	119.2
1884	148,946	173.2	250,725	147.3
1888	120,541	117.4	236,201	116.3
1892	113,919	112.1	207,384	101.1
1896	102,245	100.9	206,857	97.5
1898	113,987	116.5	217,236	100.5

Source: *General Annual Return of the British Army*, P.P., XLIII (c.1323), 1875, p.37; XLIII (c.6196), 1890, p.53; LIII (c.9426), 1899, p.59.

Greater use was made of imprisonment during the second half of the nineteenth century than previously, partly because of the progressive abolition of corporal punishment between 1867 and 1881. It also gradually became the policy of the last decades of the century to discharge habitual offenders from the Service on the expiration of their sentence and to award short-term imprisonment for less serious offences which earlier would have merited other forms of punishment. In these circumstances, a long-term trend can be seen. Looking at this period as a whole more men were sent to military prisons, but because sentences were shorter the average numbers confined dropped significantly. This can be seen in Tables 3–4 and 3–5. These figures also indicate that over the whole period recidivism among (a) prisoners and (b) the army as a whole was reduced as well. This was partly a result, of course, of both the deliberate discharge of hardened offenders. and of the introduction in 1870 of short-service enlistment. The drop in recidivism among military offenders occurred at a time when there is evidence to suggest a marked increase in the number of civilian habitual offenders.[8]

Table 3–2 The Number of Fines Inflicted for Drunkenness and the Proportions of Men So Punished, 1869–98

Year	No. of Fines	Per 100 Men of Whole Army
1869	28,374	16.1
1872	51,501	28.1
1876	49,442	28.0
1880	40,684	22.5
1884	41,505	24.2
1888	39,598	19.5
1892	25,776	12.6
1896	27,953	13.2
1898	26,243	12.1

Source: *General Annual Return of the British Army,* P.P. XLIII (c.1323), 1875, p.36; XLIII (c.6196), 1890, p.58; LIII (c.9426), 1899, p.50.

Aside from indicating general rates of crime and of punishment in the forces, penal statistics give particular insight into the commission of specific offences. With the exception of fines for drunkenness there are no figures to distinguish the offences for which minor summary punishments were awarded in the army, but after 1865 there are precise records of the offences for which men were court-martialled and for which they were sent to military prisons. The records of courts-martial are the most complete and revealing, showing the numbers of men who were court-martialled and the crimes for which they were tried.[9] These figures indicate clearly that trials for drunkenness and for miscellaneous offences registered the greatest decrease between 1865 and 1898. The increasing use made of summary punishments may account for this to some extent, but how much it is impossible to say. A lower incidence of these crimes is certainly suggested. Charges for theft of equipment and for quitting or sleeping on post diminished significantly, another indication of a decrease in serious crime. The number and proportion of offences of absence without leave were also less in later years, however there was no apparent decline in the number of fraudulent enlistments. Disobedience and insubordination definitely increased, and neither disgraceful conduct nor desertion declined to any significant extent.

Somewhere between 1,500 and 2,000 men might be tried for desertion in a single year, a number equivalent to perhaps two or three battalions of infantry, and these figures take account only of those deserters who were recaptured or who gave themselves up. Desertion was a relatively easy offence to get away with and one whose incidence varied substantially from state to station. It was not so common in India but presented serious problems in both Britain and North America.[10] Recruiters were given rewards for apprehending deserters and spotting fraudulent enlistments,[11] but since they also collected a commission for every man enlisted, they tended often to smuggle men into the army. The primary method of vetting recruits was one of relying on referees and character checks. Fingerprinting all recruits was considered, as well as proposals for tattooing and for special vaccination as a means of identification, but all were discarded for fear of public opposition.[12]

Table 3–3 Number of Courts-Martial, Number and Proportion of Men Court-Martialled, 1865–98

Year	No. of Men Court-Martialled	As Percentage of Total Force	No. of Courts-Martial	As Percentage of Total Force	Percentage of Those Tried Who Had Been Previously Court-Martialled at Least Once
1865	18,590	9.1	21,612	10.9	16.3
1872	12,024	6.6	14,290	7.8	18.8
1876	12,187	6.9	13,657	7.7	12.1
1880	13,711	7.6	15,242	8.4	11.2
1884	11,100	6.3	12,493	7.3	12.5
1888	10,625	5.2	12,188	5.9	14.7
1892	9,874	4.8	11,267	5.5	14.1
1896	8,069	3.8	9,167	4.3	13.6
1898	8,704	4.0	9,676	4.5	11.2

Source: *General Annual Return of the British Army,* P.P., XLIII (c.1323), 1875, p.37; XLIII (c.6196), 1890, p.53; LIII (c.9426), 1899, p.55.

The actual number of cases of desertion each year and the number of deserters who were recaptured or who rejoined were recorded. These statistics indicate that the gross loss was in fact two or three times higher than court-martial statistics alone would indicate.

Desertion, like drunkenness, was extremely visible to the public. Deserters were often well known in their own neighbourhood, the *Police Gazette* frequently contained advertisements for men who had absconded from the Services, and very often the only occasion local newspapers took to comment on the state of the army was to report the capture of a local boy who had deserted from the ranks.[13] Desertion not only helped to spread the belief that the army was extremely unpopular amongst the rank and file and hindered recruitment, but also was a source of great expense to the public purse. In 1881 a committee calculated that the cost to the Crown of an infantryman during his first year of service was £56 17s 8d, while that of an engineer was as much as £115 4s 6d.[14] The majority of deserters were young soldiers within their first year or two of service unable to reconcile themselves to the demands of military life. Between 1868 and 1898, the proportion of those who had served less than two years increased considerably. To this extent at least the attempts which were made to make the army more attractive to the younger soldier were not entirely successful.[15] The very large number of recruits who absconded or deserted each year before joining their regiments is also a comment on the methods of recruitment, despite the success of efforts to do away with forms of trickery and deception in the recruiting process.[16]

Table 3–4 Total Soldiers Sent to Military Prisons and Their Proportions of the Whole Army, 1856–98

Year	Total Confined	As Percentage of Army	Total Convicted of Crime(s) Previously	As Percentage of Prisoners	As Percentage of Army
1856	6,376	2.6	1,491	23.4	0.6
1860	6,719	3.1	2,380	35.4	1.1
1865	6,390	3.2	2,927	45.8	1.5
1872	4,273	2.6	2,836	60.0	1.6
1876	4,707	2.7	2,242	47.6	1.2
1880	3,447	1.9	1,654	47.9	0.9
1884	5,804	3.3	1,244	21.4	0.7
1888	6,772	3.3	1,255	18.5	0.6
1892	7,393	3.6	1,363	18.4	0.7
1896	6,665	3.1	1,120	16.8	0.5
1898	8,672	4.0	1,305	15.0	0.6

Source: *Reports on the Discipline and Management of Military Prisons,* P.P.

More is known of the length of service of deserters than of those who committed other offences, but there is a wealth of detail about all the inmates of military prisons. Records accurately noted the length of service, the age, nationality and religion of prisoners between 1856 and

1898. Comparisons can be made with the regular army as a whole, and in this way the character of the serious offender can be defined. More particularly, it is possible to discuss at least tentatively whether the soldiers who were confined to prison were representative or typical of the average soldier and the soldier who committed less serious infractions of discipline.

Table 3–5 Average Numbers and Proportions of the Home Army Confined in Military Prisons in the UK, 1856–98

Year	Average Number in Prison	As Percentage of Home Army
1856	896	1.24
1859	837	0.79
1862	972	1.14
1865	1,051	1.24
1868	1,241	1.47
1872	1,033	1.0
1876	1,018	1.2
1880	514	0.6
1884	1,159	1.3
1888	807	0.8
1892	535	0.5
1896	515	0.5
1898	624	0.6

Source: ***Reports on the Discipline and Management of Military Prisons,*** P.P.

Statistics of this sort reveal that proportionally there was a greater number of young men in prison than in the ranks of the army.[17] This suggests that younger soldiers were more prone to commit offences, or at least were more likely to be caught for doing so, than older, more experienced men who by the time that they had served six or seven years would have become accustomed to the demands of military life, would have the maturity to cope with such demands, and might have achieved greater responsibility and greater freedom with promotion. There is a sharp contrast with the figures on the inmates of civilian prisons, since these seem to indicate a significant increase in the proportion of older and more hardened offenders confined as the century wore on.[18]

Several trends are indicated by an analysis of the nationality and religion of prisoners. The numbers of Irish soldiers sent to military prison declined significantly between 1856 and 1899 because of falling enlistments, yet in comparison with the army as a whole, there was a slightly greater proportion of Irish in prison in most years. The number of Scots remained fairly consistent with their relative proportion in the ranks while proportionally there were fewer English troops behind bars. The number of Roman Catholics in prison was greater than the percentage of the forces who were of that denomination, and is not fully accounted for even by the total number of Irish soldiers confined, unless 'Irish' is taken to include soldiers born in Britain from families of Irish origin. Also, of course, some Irish were certainly Protestants.

Table 3–6 Numbers and Proportions of Deserters from the Regular Army, 1862–98

Year	No. of Cases of Desertion	As Percentage of Army	Numbers of Deserters Recaptured/Rejoined	Net Loss from Desertion	As Percentage of Army
1862	2,895	1.4	1,215	1,680	0.8
1865	3,519	1.8	1,010	2,509	1.3
1868	3,011	1.6	1,221	1,790	1.0
1872	5,861	3.2	1,855	4,006	2.2
1876	4,835	2.7	2,063	2,772	1.6
1880	4,833	2.6	1,557	3,276	1.8
1884	4,478	2.5	1,803	2,675	1.5
1888	4,330	2.1	2,008	2,322	1.1
1892	4,962	2.4	2,178	2,784	1.4
1896	3,367	1.6	1,538	1,829	0.9
1898	4,074	1.9	1,934	2,140	1.0

Source: *General Annual Return of the British Army,* P.P., XLIII (c.1323), 1875, p.26; XLIII (c.6196), 1890, p.33; LIII (c.9426), 1899, p.35.

The level of education of prisoners is more difficult to ascertain, nevertheless a reasonable indication can be obtained. Between 1856 and 1866 the standard of literacy only of soldiers recommitted to prison was noted, but in spite of this limitation it is clear that there was a very high significant increase during the years 1856 to 1899 in the proportion of prisoners who could read and write; more than one-half those confined in prison in 1856 were illiterate, but by 1898 the proportion of men in this category was minimal. This change was no doubt brought about by the educational factors discussed in the previous chapter. It was only in 1895 that instruction in the subjects required for certificates of education was introduced into prisons.[19]

Civilian prison statistics would seem to suggest that prisoners were more poorly educated *vis à vis* the rest of the population at the end of the century than they had been earlier.[20] Allowing for the difficulty of comparing levels of literacy it does seem that those confined in military prisons were not markedly any less literate than their comrades. This is not surprising given the drop in recidivism between 1856 and 1899 and the fact that those sent to prison tended more to be younger men.[21]

2. Military Law and Military Courts

Military law is the system of rules and regulations by which an armed force governs and conducts itself. The Victorian army defined it as '. . .the law relating to and administered by military courts, and which concerns itself with the trial and punishment of offences committed by officers, soldiers, and other persons who are from circumstances subjected, for the time being, to the same law as soldiers'.[22] The object of military law was the inculcation and the maintenance of discipline, that special purpose of will without which armed forces seemingly cannot function. Discipline in turn may be said to have two principal aims: obedience and high morale. The Victorian army placed great emphasis on the importance of the unhesitating and unquestioning reaction to orders. In 1871 army regulations intoned:

> Every order given by a superior must be obeyed at once, and without hesitation. Its propriety must not be disputed, or questioned at the moment. If any individual feels himself aggrieved by any order he receives, redress is always open to him afterwards, but not at the time of execution.[23]

In battle when men wear out like clothes it is often discipline alone that prevents them from giving way in time of danger. Much of the Victorian army's mystique and its reputation for steadiness came from the unswerving obedience it demanded. 'Those corps in which the strictest discipline has been maintained in times of peace', argued a staff officer in 1870, 'will always be found to be the most efficient in times of war or on occasions of emergency.'[24] This was a favourite thesis of the regular army. In 1899 the author of the Royal United Services Institution prize essay argued:

> In the actual stress of battle the all-absorbing struggle for life will keep men braced up to their task, but when the blood is warmed with no keen excitement, when the frame is wearied with long marches, and the mind with uncertainty as to what may happen, then it is that a good discipline makes itself evident more than at other times, and then must a leader feel that on the existence of it all depends.[25]

Similar viewpoints were commonplace.[26] 'War', wrote Spenser Wilkinson, 'is essentially a conflict between two wills. . .For this reason discipline–the training of the will–is always, and will always be, the foundation-stone of an army.'[27]

Morale, the second principal goal of discipline, is closely tied to and to some extent dependent upon obedience. The British regimental system infused in its proper functioning a high degree of morale and of *esprit de corps.* In the earliest edition of *The Soldier's Pocket Book* Lord Wolseley argued: 'The soldier is a peculiar animal that can alone be brought to the highest efficiency by inducing him to believe that he belongs to a regiment which is infinitely superior to the others around him.'[28] 'High Morale', John Baynes has observed,

> is the most important quality of a soldier. It is a quality of mind and spirit which combines courage, self-discipline and endurance. It springs from infinitely varying and sometimes contradictory sources, but is easily recognisable, having as its hallmarks cheerfulness and unselfishness. In time of peace good morale is developed by sound training and the fostering of *esprit de corps.* In time of war it manifests itself in the soldier's absolute determination to do his duty to the best of his ability in any circumstances.[29]

In this way *esprit de corps* played an important role in fostering discipline. Stephen Graham, a private in one of the Guards regiments, was to remark, 'The sterner the discipline the better the soldier, the better the army.'[30]

However, discipline had another side to it and that was to secure the soldier's conformity to the multitude of regulations considered necessary for the normal functioning of the army. The laws and regulations of nineteenth-century society were designed primarily to preserve order and to protect property. As a British citizen the soldier was subject to virtually all of them. Where he infringed upon or broke the law, he could be tried and sentenced in a civilian court.[31] Yet unlike the civilian, he was also bound by a mass of army regulations.

From the time of his enlistment until the date of his eventual discharge, the soldier's every movement was regulated and strict obedience was expected to regulations concerned with the minutest details of conduct. In 1868 for instance regulations specified that 'the hair is to be neatly cut, and kept short. Moustaches are to be worn, and the chin is to be shaved (except by pioneers, who will wear beards)'.[32] Forty years later standing orders still insisted: 'No soldier is permitted to shave his upper lip. Any contravention of this order will be severely dealt with.'[33]

Leisure activities were very closely monitored. Writing around 1895, Robert Blatchford recalled procedures in his regiment:

> After Retreat, the main gate was closed, and all soldiers returning to barracks had to pass through a small gate. Here they had to run the gauntlet of the sergeant or corporal on gate duty, two men of the military police, [and] the sentry on the main guard... Let a man waiver in his walk or stumble over the awkward step in the dark and his doom was sealed. He was instantly pounced upon, run into the guardroom, and confronted with the sergeant of the guard. 'Drunk,' said the sergeant; and the man was thrown or hustled into the prisoners' room, and the door banged behind him.[34]

Strict regimen such as this was no means exceptional. In all branches of the Service, dress, conduct and the duties of the rank and file were set down specifically. As Brigadier-General J.H.A. MacDonald was to observe, drill was 'brought to the condition of appearing to have for its object "precision and stiffness alone, in exercises not having any real object in war", and so forced in a hundred minute little points on the rank and file until they responded to the word of command as the machine answers to the pressing of the button'.[35] An unfortunate concomitant of this was that virtually no room was left for initiative, a lack of which could be overlooked in small colonial wars with untrained and native armies, but which was to have dire consequencies by the end of the century.[36]

Military discipline had another effect as well: it prevented agitation from the ranks in support of virtually any cause whether a political movement or a campaign to improve the terms and conditions of service. For this reason impetus for reform came from the higher ranks or from without the Service and changes were imposed from above. In

1883 regulations maintained:

> Deliberations or discussions among any class of military men, having the object of conveying praise, censure, or any mark of approbation towards their superiors or any others in Her Majesty's service are strictly prohibited, as being subversive of discipline. . .Officers, non-commissioned officers, and private soldiers are forbidden to institute, or take part in, any meetings, demonstrations, or processions for party or political purposes in barracks, quarters, camp or elsewhere.[37]

Infringement of these regulations was regarded with seriousness, and unhesitatingly punished. In 1872, for example, there were seventeen soldiers serving prison sentences for what were termed Fenian activities.[38]

To deal with disciplinary offences there existed a separate military judicial system which administered the Mutiny Act, the Articles of War and army regulations on which military law was based. The major offences with which it was concerned included mutiny, desertion, fraudulent enlistment, absence without leave, murder and assault, drunkenness, disgraceful conduct, theft and embezzlement. Military courts also had jurisdiction to try ordinary civil crimes including murder if committed by persons subject to military law. In practice, unless military personnel only were involved, these cases were normally handled by the civilian courts.[39]

Judicial procedure within the army followed a well-established routine. Every offence was treated as a crime and offenders were detained and placed under custody in guardrooms or barrack cells until their case could be heard. There was no guarantee of writ of habeas corpus against indeterminate confinement, nevertheless military regulations specified clearly the circumstances in which confinement could be resorted to, and it is unlikely that these were more than infrequently overstepped. The exception to this, the case of RSM Lilley, was infamous.[40] Prisoners remained in cells or the guardroom until they could be seen by the commanding officer, however, and several days might well elapse before their case could be heard.[41] Simple disciplinary offences could be dealt with almost immediately, but for more serious offences men were brought forward for court-martial. Three different levels of tribunals existed: the regimental, the district, and the general court-martial. Regimental courts-martial were convened by the commanding officer and normally dealt with offences committed within the regiment. District courts-martial were convened by general officers commanding military districts to deal with offences of a larger nature. The most serious cases were tried by a general court-martial. As each tribunal had a different jurisdiction, so each had different powers of punishment as well.

The system of courts-martial was said to be well spoken of by all ranks.[42] Army regulations guaranteed proper judicial procedure, defendants were allowed the services of counsel and to call witnesses if they so desired, and ample time was given to prepare a defence. Acquittals were promulgated immediately; convictions had to be confirmed by a superior authority, usually a high-ranking officer.[43]

Nevertheless it is easy to see how the judicial system could be abused. There was little recourse against summary punishment awarded by a commanding officer regardless of the injustice of the charges upon which it was based. Few men could complain to their CO with much hope of success; those that failed were liable to court-martial or punishment for making frivolous complaints.[44] The formality of a court-martial and the presence of ranking officers would be more than enough to overawe the average enlisted man, whose testimony (where it was controversial), was unlikely to be accepted over the conflicting evidence of an NCO or officer. In 1864, for instance, a soldier with a record of good character was court-martialled for protesting against the charge made by a sergeant that he had appeared dirty on parade. Such an accusation could well have been spurious, an attempt to punish the soldier for any reason. The court-martial brought in a verdict of guilty, and awarded a sentence of four years' penal servitude.[45] Sergeant Robert Edmondson, who was twice court-martialled, labelled the exercise a farce and the officers who sat in judgement '. . .poorer in natural intelligence, less educated, and more full of themselves and of their own importance than any other class of persons I have had any personal knowledge of'.[46] 'Heads we win, tails you lose', he argued, seem to be the governing maxim of military law.[47] One must, of course, allow for some element of bias in these remarks.

In some respects the civil judicial system was no fairer. Most members of the working class would be easily overawed in court where the evidence of a police officer would probably be accepted over their own. Yet there were three major differences in the system as provided for by military law, and these were as true in 1899 as in 1856. Firstly, to repeat a point which has already been made, army regulations were all-embracing and governed a larger sphere of each man's daily conduct since military crimes included actions or misdemeanours which under civilian law would not be regarded as an offence. Secondly, although trial by a magistrate was commonly resorted to in the civil courts for routine offences, there was in the case of more serious crimes provision for trial by jury, an element of justice which was lacking in military courts-martial.[48] Finally, the punishments which were awarded in the army either summarily or by court-martial seemed frequently to bear little proportion to the offences committed. Records were kept of even the most minor misdemeanour and not only dogged the soldier for the remainder of his career in the army, but followed him into civilian life as well.[49]

The most common punishments, since the majority of offences were minor infractions of discipline, were those awarded summarily by commanding officers. These extended to imprisonment, fines, and stoppages of pay, confinement to barracks, deprivation of rank and privileges, punishment drill and extra duties.[50] The punishment most frequently awarded was confinement to barracks with punishment drill or extra duties included. In general the tendency for much of the second half of the century was to extend the army officer's authority to mete out punishments of this nature.[51] A similar process extended the summary jurisdiction of civilian magistrates, and the reasons in both cases were similar. Summary powers were increased to ease the burden on military courts, to speed the process of justice, and to provide alternative methods of punishment to imprisonment.[52]

A first milestone was the 1868 report of the Royal Commission on the constitution and practice of courts-martial. It recommended that the powers of summary imprisonment possessed by commanding officers should be increased from fourteen to twenty-one days' confinement, and that a system of fines for drunkenness should be instituted.[53] On the whole, however, law makers were reluctant to give too much power to regimental officers and the first recommendation was not implemented. In 1878 a Select Committee considered the revision and consolidation of military law, and the following year, as a result of its labours, the Army Discipline and Regulation Bill passed through Parliament.[54] In the course of the debates on this bill the question of extending the commanding officer's jurisdiction was repeatedly raised, but once more there was opposition to delegating too much power.[55] In 1881 another Select Committee urged the extension of summary jurisdiction.[56] However, this did not materialise until 1893, when a committee under Lord Sandhurst, the Under-Secretary of State for War, again proposed it with the strong support of Redvers Buller, the Adjutant-General at the War

Office who was an opponent of regimental courts-martial because of the time and effort they consumed in dealing with minor offences. Impressed by the need to deal more quickly with minor offences, and under these pressures, the government agreed to allow commanding officers to imprison for up to twenty-one days without trial. Regulations which put this into effect preserved a safeguard, however, by requiring that a court-martial must be convened should one be requested by the accused.[57]

The institution in 1868 of the new scheme to fine men for drunkenness was a major increase to the summary jurisdiction of commanding officers. Under the terms of the powers provided, COs could impose a fine up to 10s for any case of drunkenness not involving dereliction of duty. The usual fine for a first offence within a six-month period was 2s 6d; 5s for a second, and for habitual drunkenness (a fourth offence) the maximum penalty was 10s.[58]

In general, whether as a result of legal changes or not, there was an increasing use of summary powers.[59] However, the move from courts-martial to summary punishment was not consistently one towards leniency. Summary punishment could be and was resorted to for the most minor of offences. Seven days' confinement to barracks for leaving a brush out of a kit display was not uncommon.[60] Punishment drill involved four separate hours of exercise on the parade square in heavy equipment every day except Sunday. It could destroy any shred of self-respect and frequently led men to commit a second crime in order to avoid it by being sent to a military prison.[61] Nevertheless, while there is no indication of any change in what was held to constitute an offence or misdemeanour during the course of the period, there is evidence to suggest that the amount and the harshness of the summary punishments awarded decreased during the later half of the century. In the 1840s for example, Private Waterfield remarked that for going AWOL men were forced to go on a 28-mile march, often returning to barracks with their boots full of blood to collapse on their cot too tired even to eat.[62] By the 1880s at least the common punishment for absences without leave was either deprivation of pay or short-term confinement.[63]

3. Contemporary Explanations of Crime

In the later nineteenth century criminologists tended to interpret the causes of crime in a variety of ways. This was true of those concerned with the offender in uniform as well as those with the civilian criminal. The neo-classical school of criminology, a child of the early nineteenth century, was already being superseded, but its basic principle, that man is a rational being responsible for his acts and receptive to a fear of punishment, continued to hold much sway. The two most widely-held theories were those which saw the causes of crime as constitutional or inherited, and those which sought to explain crime by stressing the effect of environmental conditions. Both sets of theories had points of validity, neither necessarily excluded the other, and indeed criminologists have now come to realise that there can be no one single theory applied universally. Both of the above types of approach seem to have been used by those seeking to understand and to obviate the causes of crime in the army and, as often as not, several variations of the same argument were advanced at once.

The individual or constitutional theory posited the existence of a distinct criminal class believed by phrenologists and others to be distinguishable through a series of precise physical measurements. While there is no evidence of any use of phrenology or other such technique to monitor criminals in the army, there certainly were many who laid much of the blame for crime in the forces at the feet of a professional criminal class. In 1868 for instance, the governor of one of the military prisons observed:

> Men of loose and unstable principles must constitute a very large element in our army. Poverty forces these characters to enlist, and exposed to the low temptations of our garrison towns they naturally revert to their former habits; and thus become inmates of a military prison.[64]

Similar opinions were expressed by colleagues[65] and by others concerned about the recruitment of such a class into the forces.[66] Through phrenology has now been discredited, some criminologists still put great store in the theory of a distinct criminal class, and when such theories were applied to the Victorian army they were not entirely without foundation: certainly some soldiers would not have been able to behave themselves regardless of the rules of the game.[67] Robert Blatchford describes in his memoirs a man of this kind in his regiment who had spent ten years in the army, nine of them in gaol.[68]

Environmental theories of crime are more widely accepted today; they gained great favour during the second half of the last century and were used most frequently in one form or another to explain the incidence of crime in the forces. Their basic thesis is that individuals commit offences because of their inability to adjust to or because of the demands placed on them by the environment in which they find themselves. This type of argument lent itself to examinations of crime in the forces from several different angles. Many soldiers and civilians agreed that rigid discipline and the restrictions of military life were too exacting and that soldiers used to a less demanding civilian life were thereby driven to hasty action.[69] The army's high rate of insubordination and desertion among younger soldiers especially was largely explained in this way.[70] As we have seen most of those sent to military prison were young men in their first year of service. Edward Cardwell for one argued that desertion varied directly with the number of recruits enlisted each year, and that the incidence of this particular offence was the highest in Britain where the chances to desert successfully were the greatest and temptations in the form of high wages in industry or of emigration to America or the colonies higher.[71] A variation in this theme maintained that men were sometimes encouraged to commit offences or to desert by the treatment they received from young inexperienced NCOs and officers.[72] As one soldier observed, '. . .it is the pin-prick smallness of the annoyances that aggravate great bearded men who are sometimes treated as if they were babies rather than soldiers'.[73] This argument was particularly stressed after the introduction of short service in 1871. Others meanwhile charged that men were cheated on enlistment or at least were led to believe that the army held more in store for them than they ultimately were to receive.[74]

All of these arguments had their detractors,[75] yet for the most part they were widely accepted. A wealth of soldiers' memoirs confirm the accuracy of these assumptions. Many soldiers complained of the harshness of discipline and of the overbearing vindictiveness of NCOs that was a part of their daily lives and that drove their comrades to insubordination or desertion.[76] Others were disillusioned on enlistment with their pay[77] or their surroundings,[78] or sometimes were actually taken advantage of.[79] In some instances for example, recruits were deliberately given defective equipment, and then charged for damaging it. After their pay had been stopped, the same equipment was issued to other new men.[80]

Environmentalists also held that drunkenness was a root cause of much crime, and that the lack of amenities and recreation provided for the use of the soldier drove him to the canteens.[81] As late as 1887 it was argued that alcohol was responsible for 75 per cent of the crime in the army.[82] This was probably true. For example, as the Inspector-General of Military Prisons recognised, there was a close relationship between it and desertion. A drunken spree frequently led to a man going

AWOL involuntarily, and in the clear light of day many were then forced to desert to avoid the consequences of their actions.[83] Others voiced the same argument.[84] Paydays in the forces were not infrequently marked by indiscriminate and excessive drinking, and at such times insubordination and other crimes increased almost inevitably.[85] Army Temperance Association figures show that the incidence of crime and of disease among non-abstainers was rarely less than four of five times as high as it was among abstainers, frequently much higher,[86] though this is a biased source and it is not clear how these calculations were reached.

The final set of explanations for the prevalence of drunkenness in the Service applied equally to the civilian population. Drinking was a main outlet of many civilians, and not unnaturally the habit was continued in the forces.[87] As in civilian life, the absence of adequate recreational facilities and sufficient comforts led men to seek the conviviality and comfort in the diversion of beer and spirits.[88] 'After all,' one old veteran has written,

> what else was there for the soldier to do but drink? He had no sorrows to drown, but he had a good deal of spare time and practically nothing to do with it, and not being a particularly imaginative fellow, he spent most of his time in the canteen. Drunkenness was rather the fault of the authorities, who provided no alternative recreation for the Tommy in those days.[89]

Sir William Robertson was one of the many who agreed that responsibility lay with the authorities, who 'neglected to provide them [the rank and file] with congenial means of recreation, to place greater trust in their self-respect, and generally, to call forth the better part of their nature'.[90] The dietary misconceptions which Brian Harrison points out as common in the first half of the century,[91] persisted if anything longer in the army. In India men often drank to escape the sun, the flies and disease,[92] and as late as 1910, veteran soldiers swore that a regular drink would keep a man healthy while his comrades were dropping from cholera or fever.[93]

4. Punishment and Deterrence

The multiplicity of criminological theories and explanations naturally led to numbers of different approaches to the problem of crime in the army. Military authorities tended to react in several ways. They required punishment to be meted out for every misdemeanour, but they also wanted to attract better recruits, to expel habitual offenders from the ranks rather than deal with them by very hard sentences, and to encourage good behaviour by improving conditions and providing recreational facilities.

However, a belief in punishment was always strong. It was seen as necessary to establish a cause-effect relationship and so deter potential offenders.[94] The certainty of punishment, many asserted, was the only effective deterrent to crime. If punishment followed the commission of an offence as a matter of course, the soldier would be happier and there would be no inconsistencies in his behaviour.[95]

One of the mildest punishments was the fine. Did it have a deterrent effect? The most obvious instance to single out in any attempt to answer this question is drunkenness, for which summary fines became the main punishment in 1868. However the effect which the new system of 1868 had upon the incidence of drunkenness in the army was mixed. As we have seen earlier, the number fined for drunkenness dropped significantly each year during the 1870s, yet as Table 3–7 shows, a high proportion of fines annually continued to be levied for repeated drunkenness. If as a preventive measure fines were effective (and there is no way of calculating separately the effect of the introduction of short-service enlistment in 1870), they certainly made disappointingly less progress in attacking specifically habitual drunkenness. The most palatable rationalisation for recidivism is that the criminal returns to crime again, not because the treatment was inappropriate or ineffective, but because when released he again comes under the influence of a crime breeding environment. This, however, overlooks the fact that treatment may bear no real relation to the cause of the criminal behaviour in question, and that many of those involved in crime may be non-reformable. The 'human sponge' may well have been disappearing from the ranks as contemporaries argued,[96] but there is no doubt that in 1898 there were still quite a few of this genre left. On the evidence fines did little to reduce their number. Nor can it be argued that these men were alcoholics who were not amenable to treatment or discipline since the offence with which they were charged was drunkenness, not drunkenness on duty, and this would imply that they were able to control, to some extent at least, their drinking habits.

In general punishments became milder. The military penal system made a transition between 1856 and 1899 from severe, even brutal punishments, towards those which were more lenient and humane. This move reflected an increasing sense of humanity and of concern for the individual soldier within the army, a response to public pressure and the

Table 3–7 Men Fined for Drunkenness, 1869–98

Year	Once	2–4 Times	5–9 Times	10 Times or More	Total No. Fined	Total Fines
1869	----------	Not Reported	----------		20,680	28,374
1870	----------	Not Reported	----------		35, 267	54,398
1872	13,785 (52.8%)	10,709 (41.0%)	1,589 (6.1%)	28 (.1%)	26,111	51,501
1875	12,352 (51.5%)	10,083 (42.0%)	1,539 (6.4%)	34 (.1%)	24,008	47,880
1880	12,332 (56.0%)	8,607 (39.1%)	1,084 (4.9%)	6 (.02%)	22,029	40,684
1885	11,671 (50.1%)	10,000 (42.9%)	1,619 (6.9%)	34 (.1%)	23,324	47,699
1890	8,728 (51.4%)	7,196 (42.3%)	1,069 (6.3%)	7 (.04%)	17,000	33,677
1895	7,519 (53.5%)	5,699 (40.6%)	822 (5.9%)	10 (.07%)	14,050	26,914
1898	7,770 (54.9%)	5,708 (40.3%)	680 (4.8%)	7 (.04%)	14,165	26,243

Source: *General Annual Return of the British Army*, P.P., XLIII (c.1323), 1875, p.36; XLIII (c.6196), 1890, p.58; LIII (c.9426), 1899, p.60.

exigencies of voluntary recruitment. In 1861 the number of civilian capital offences was reduced to four (which remained unchanged until 1957). In the army, capital punishment, awarded by court-martial, covered offences so punishable under civilian criminal law, and offences commited on active service, such as desertion, mutiny, or violence to a superior officer.[97] The latter remained unchanged before 1900.[98] The normal means of execution in the forces was by hanging or by firing squad, with the victim's comrades looking on. Earlier the prisoner was forced to march round the barrack square while his comrades followed him with his coffin and the band played the death march; he was then forced to kneel on the coffin to be executed, and the regiment then marched past to view the body.[99] Such barbaric methods of execution do not seem to have been used in this period,[100] and indeed capital punishment was infrequently resorted to after 1856. Between 1865 and 1898 thirty-seven men were executed.[101] In contrast, the resort to corporal punishment was more common, and its form changed considerably.

Corporal punishment, especially whipping, was provided for by civilian criminal law during the later nineteenth century, but because it was resorted to for the more trivial offences, it is impossible to ascertain the frequency with which it was used or to gauge its effect.[102] In the forces, corporal punishment, that is tattooing (or branding as it was called), and flogging had been sharply curtailed by 1856 and was all but discontinued by 1900. This move was made under the public pressure of humanitarian concern with the welfare of the soldier, but there was also dissatisfaction within the army with the results of corporal punishment and some appreciation that an easing of the severity of punishments awarded by criminal courts had not resulted in an increase in crime.

Branding was resorted to for desertion or for serious misbehaviour. It was a relic of the practice of marking vagrants and other miscreants in the past and was a particularly humiliating experience.[103] Nevertheless it was justified by the army as a cheap quick method of identifying deserters and unmanageable characters and hence of preventing fraudulent enlistments and of protecting the public from criminals.[104] Critics attacked it on the grounds that it deterred decent men from enlistment. Military insistence upon its necessity remained firm, however,[105] until 1871 when the War Office to help popularise the army had branding abolished.[106] Even then, in some quarters its loss was lamented for years afterwards.[107]

The debate over flogging or whipping aroused many more passions than did that over branding. The practice sprang from a brutal past when fierce punishments were deemed necessary to intimidate and to control the rank and file who had no possessions of which they could be deprived. A variety of instruments and of engines of torture were used to maintain discipline in the ranks, but by the beginning of the nineteenth century flogging with a cat-o'-nine tails was most common. At its peak flogging was employed for nearly every serious crime not involving the death penalty and for many offences that were hardly serious at all. It is with flogging that corporal punishment in the British Army is usually associated.[108]

By the outbreak of the Crimean War in 1854 the number of strokes that could be inflicted in any one punishment had been limited to fifty.[109] Beyond this, however, reform was difficult, for the War Office and many of the army's most influential officers firmly believed in flogging as a necessary form of punishment and refused to contemplate its abolition. Lord Wolseley, normally a champion of army reform, argued in 1881 that the army would be forced to rely heavily on the death penalty should flogging be abolished. 'For the due maintenance of discipline in an army raised as ours is by voluntary enlistment,' he wrote, 'a more drastic code of laws is required than for one raised as in France, Germany, etc. on the principle of universal service. The greatest ruffians and criminals in the three kingdoms enlist in our army and we cannot prevent serious cases than by resorting to the penalty of death. . .'[110] Foreign armies did indeed use other methods of punishment, chiefly imprisonment for less serious offences,[111] but the argument that Britain recruited from the lowest levels of society was self-defeating, for that was exactly the type of recruit reformers wished to discourage. However, much the same sort of argument was expressed by others with influence in the War Office.[112] Redvers Buller and Lord Chelmsford, who commanded the expedition in Zululand in 1879, both believed as Wolseley did, that there could be no substitute for flogging. Sir William Harcourt, the Commander-in-Chief of the forces in India, argued, 'I do not believe that order and discipline can be maintained in an army exposed to the temptations of war if the Commander has no other effective means of enforcing his authority in serious cases than by resorting to the penalty of death.'[113]

Flogging was defended on other grounds as well. Some argued that it was quick and did not remove men from duty as did lengthy imprisonment. This of course is to ignore the amount of time a man might spend in hospital recovering. After fifty strokes of the cat a soldier's back could be jelly and an inexperienced man wielding the whip could blind or maim. As late as 1867 a young private given fifty lashes and 168 days' imprisonment died in hospital from the beating he had received.[114] Still others argued that a flogging reformed the offender and by its example had a salutary effect on those looking on.[115] There is no doubt that in many cases it served to do neither. To be tied up and whipped in front of one's comrades was a humiliating, brutalising experience and not infrequently drove men to commit further crime.[116] As one private soldier recalled at the outset of the period,

> The number of men I have seen flogged during my career of 23 years and 8 months in the Service would not be less than 100. I have closely watched the career of many of the recipients of this degrading punishment, and I can safely say that I never knew not even one that it made any improvement in, either in his moral character or as a soldier. But on the other hand, many a good and brave soldier has been lost to the Army through the brutal punishment of the lash, inflicted for some offence committed at the commencement of his career as a soldier.[117]

The effect that a flogging had upon those required to watch was not entirely what the authorities expected. Undoubtedly many were deterred for a while at least from committing any offences which might lead them to the cat,[118] but on the whole the spectacle of a flogging sickened and angered those in the ranks.[119] General Sir Bindon Blood recalled over 100 men fainting in the ranks when watching two of their comrades being flogged.[120] Another soldier who witnessed a friend given fifty lashes wished himself out of the army with every stroke.[121] Repeated watchings clearly limited the deterrent effect and only bred an animosity for authority.[122]

Nothing did more to bring corporal punishment into disrepute than the fact that its use depended to a great extent on the whims and caprices of each commanding officer. In 1856 corporal punishment was resorted to in the home army for what were on the surface regarded as serious offences: mutiny, insubordination, sale of equipment, theft from comrades, drunkenness on duty, or 'other disgraceful' conduct.[123] This left a great deal open to interpretation and the CO's influence in a regimental court-martial was considerable. Officers became accustomed to the sight of a flogging and could easily imagine that men's backs had become accustomed as well. Thus floggings might be awarded for offences which would be regarded by civilian courts as being of a trivial nature.[124] An examination of the records of the Judge Advocate-General's department reveals many such cases. Courts-martial regularly awarded fifty lashes for drunkenness on duty and even mere insubordinate language.[125] Perhaps no other form of punishment was so open to the charge of bearing no proportion to the offences for which it was awarded. Moreover, as Table 3–8 shows, if in the decade of the Crimean War the number of lashes which could be given was limited, the extent to which flogging was used seemed to be as great as ever. The rapid decrease in the number of corporal punishments awarded after 1865 resulted from reforms limiting its use. A staggering increase occurred in 1878–9 and was due almost entirely to the resort to corporal punishment by the forces employed on active service in Zululand. In an age of humanity in which civilian courts on the whole were meting out softer punishment, flogging in the army stood out as brutal, dehumanising, and paradoxically, largely ineffective.

The campaign for the abolition of flogging was mostly waged in Parliament. Criticism of corporal punishment was an inevitable result of reforms that had been brought about in British criminal law reducing the number of capital offences and the severity of punishments. In the interests of humanity and if the forces were to be anywhere near successful in recruitment, it was argued that the soldier could not be seen to be brutally punished for offences which in civilian life might lead only to short-term imprisonment.[126] Public horror of a crime was limited to the offence as defined by the law, and they could not in an age of increasing equality regard with equanimity a situation which countenanced especially severe punishments for one group of citizens. Another factor was that it was feasible to devise other forms of punishment than those inflicting physical pain.

The debate on flogging revived each year with the passage of the Mutiny Act through Parliament. Opposition to its use was led by Arthur Otway and William Williams who consistently argued, firstly that the maintenance of flogging in the army was a major hindrance to recruitment,[127] secondly that as a punishment it was ineffective,[128] and thirdly that it was brutal and over-severe.[129] Recruitment was a vulnerable and touchy area and the negative influence that flogging had upon enlistment was especially stressed. The support of newspapers and journals strengthened this parliamentary campaign.[130]

As a result of military conservatism[131] it was not until 1881 that flogging was finally abolished. Strict limits were put on its use before this, however. In 1859 the Horse Guards agreed to some concessions in disciplinary methods, and classified all troops into two categories: the

Table 3–8 Corporal Punishment in the Army, 1847–81

Year	Corporal Punishments	Corporal Punishments Plus Imprisonment
1847	42 (2,200 lashes)	
1857	45 (2,250 lashes)	
1858	218 (9,338 lashes)	
1860	651	
1863	367	
1865	233	631
1867	54	210
1869	1	–
1872	–	–
1876	2	–
1878	29	4
1879	545	50
1880	25	13
1881	14	1

Source: Hansard, CLVI (16 Feb. 1860), cc.1162–3; *Report on the Discipline and Management of Military Prisons*, P.P., XXXV (c.4075), 1867–8, p.11; *General Annual Return of the British Army*, P.P., XLIII (c.1323), 1875, p.40; XLIII (c.6196), 1890, p.56.

90 per cent of the army who had good characters and could henceforth be flogged in peacetime for mutiny only, and the remaining 'Bad Characters' who were liable to corporal punishment in peace and war.[132] These gains were more illusory than real, for the number of corporal punishments inflicted in the forces continued to rise. In 1867 a young soldier died after being flogged[133] and General Peel, who was then Secretary of State for War, was able to offer only inept excuses in the Commons.[134] More concessions were then made which meant that in peacetime Class II soldiers would be flogged only for mutiny, aggravated insubordination or disgraceful conduct. Flogging seemed about to die out, but in 1878 it was revived in all its former vigour to maintain discipline among the forces in South Africa. Corporal punishment this time raised its head as a party issue with Hartington, Gladstone and the Liberals arguing for its abolition.[135] Support for the arguments advanced by the military authorities faltered. In 1879 the maximum number of lashes that could be inflicted was reduced to twenty-five, but the government hoped to forestall total abolition by ruling that corporal

punishment might be applied whenever the penalty at present was death. 'This includes every grave offence against military discipline,' Lord Beaconsfield wrote, 'but it stops agitation, for it will be difficult to stir the multitude by advocating the bullet against the lash.'[136] This last-ditch attempt failed, however, and in 1881 corporal punishment was abolished completely.

The army accepted the decision that was forced upon it, but many within it considered a serious mistake had been made. The Duke of Cambridge continued to argue that flogging was not a deterent to enlistment and that it was necessary to maintain discipline.[137] In 1882 the Queen expressed anxiety that no substitute punishment could be found.[138] A year earlier Lord Chelmsford voiced similar fears.[139] while another officer remarked that abolition was the foolish act of 'enthusiastic old women in trousers'.[140] These arguments persisted until the turn of the century[141] and a common complaint in later years was that the various stages of abolition had resulted in an increase in crime, especially insubordination.[142]

These claims were in the main unsupported by those authorities especially involved with military offences.[143] In 1869 only one governor of a military prison reported an increase in insubordination with a restricted use of the lash;[144] in 1873 the Inspector-General of Military Prisons reported a definite decrease in insubordination.[145] Six years after the abolition of corporal punishment a Commons select committee observed that the amount of crime as a whole had fallen.[146] Yet as we have seen, army statistics clearly indicate that there was an increase after 1876 in the proportion of men court-martialled for insubordination, although it is impossible to say how much of this was caused by discontinuing corporal punishment. The Inspector-General of Military Prisons may not have been far wrong in arguing that the larger proportion of young soldiers in the ranks after 1870 tended to offset what would have been a normal decrease since they were more likely to commit this type of misdemeanour than any other.[147] Outwardly the discipline of the army did not suffer through the easing and gradual withdrawal of corporal punishment. Gradually the army had to concentrate on other forms of correction, and by no means all officers were wedded to flogging and unwilling to consider alternatives.[148] Increasingly a principal alternative was imprisonment.

There were different levels of imprisonment in the forces. For short sentences men were confined in provost prisons or gaols, i.e. cells located within the barracks or the garrison. Lengthier terms were served in separate military prisons. These were a creation of the 1840s, and before this the normal practice was to confine soldiers in civil gaols. However, during the early 1840s magistrates in London and centres near other military barracks protested against the crowding of the gaols with soldiers[149] and a number of military prisons were created in which provisions were made for both solitary confinement and for hard labour.[150] By 1856 there were ten military prisons in Britain; five in England, one in Scotland, and four in Ireland; and ten prisons at military bases overseas.[151]

Close connections were preserved between military and civilian penal systems. The chaotic state of the old public gaols which John Howard had underlined in his *State of the Prisons* in 1777 were well on the way to disappearing by the early part of the nineteenth century. The Gaols Act of 1823 required justices to classify prisoners and submit regular reports to the Home Secretary and in 1856 the government adopted the Irish or progressive stage system which provided for a series of four stages of imprisonment beginning with solitary confinement and ending almost in probation. Authorities recognised that prisons were breeding grounds and schools for criminals but classification gave rise to conflict over the merits of two schemes imported from America, the separate system and the silent system, each aimed at preventing bad prisoners from corrupting others. The Prison Act of 1865 settled the controversy by requiring prisons to give inmates separate cells and to prevent the association of prisoners. The ending of transportation in 1867 provided an opportunity for the penal system to improve its effectiveness. Henceforth the emphasis began to shift from general prevention to individual prevention with some attention paid to rehabilitation through education, training and the execution of useful tasks while in confinement. These tendencies were confirmed in the Prison Act of 1898.[152]

Military prisons followed very closely this lead. The choice in 1844 of Captain J. Jebb, the surveyor-general of civil prisons, as inspector-general of military prisons was a deliberate effort to secure uniformity of treatment and discipline for military offenders.[153] Jebb was succeeded in both positions by Lieutenant-Colonel Henderson, and he was followed in 1869 by Captain E.F. DuCane. DuCane's years as Chairman of the Prison Commission, 1878–95, saw an increase in the severity of imprisonment in public gaols, and a 'uniform application of cellular isolation, absolute nonintercourse among the prisoners, the rule of silence, oakum-picking, and the tread wheel'.[154]

The tendency throughout the nineteenth century was towards shorter sentences for a given crime. This was consistent with the transition towards lighter punishments.[155] Well-defined connections between the civil and the military judicial systems encouraged a similar trend in the army. This can be illustrated by statistics, although they are imprecise to the extent that there is no way of calculating the frequency with which imprisonment was resorted to.[156] Table 3–9 indicates the average length of prison sentences handed down by courts-martial between 1856 and 1898. Figures for the two periods 1856–68 and 1872–98 do not exist in a form which allows strict comparisons, but they do show that during the latter period there was clearly a change in emphasis from longer to shorter periods of confinement.

Table 3–9 Prison Sentences, 1856–98

Year	Average Length of Sentence (Home Army) in Days
1856	53
1860	60
1865	60
1868	59

Year	Percentage Sentences 60 days or less	Whole Army 60–90 days	90+ days
1872*	39.2	28.4	32.4
1876	31.8	23.6	44.6
1880	43.2	19.2	37.6
1884	44.6	14.6	40.8
1888	54.0	21.7	24.3
1892	62.2	22.3	15.5
1896	63.7	18.6	17.7
1898	68.3	18.8	12.9

*Home Army only

Source: *Annual Reports on the Discipline and Management of Military Prisons, P.P.*

Court-martial records are difficult to interpret because each case tends to have its peculiarities which are not fully described in the reports of proceedings. Nevertheless some comparisons of records from 1873, among the most recent available, with those of 1857, the first full year of peace after the Crimea, again suggest that for the same offence military courts were awarding shorter periods of imprisonment. In 1857 minor theft, drunkenness, desertion and insubordination all normally met with sentences of four years' or more penal servitude. In 1873 imprisonment and hard labour for up to three months was more common.[157]

In both public and military prisons, shorter periods of confinement were accompanied at first by severer conditions. As imprisonment came to be relied upon increasingly as punishment for all levels of offences, public prisons came under criticism for supposed laxity and for conditions of confinement which were no deterrent.[158] This led not only, as has been mentioned, to the implementation of the separate system, but also to efforts to make imprisonment more severe. Military prisons too were initially charged with being ineffective[159] and, in view of the normal barracks and the army diet, of being relatively comfortable and attractive.[160] There was little truth in these charges. Although inmates were not separated, punishments were commonly employed either as part of a sentence (i.e. one involving hard labour) or as retribution for an infraction of prison discipline.[161] Oakum-picking was the normal employment of most military prisoners who had their heads shaven and were required to wear prison uniforms.[162] The diet consisted largely of oatmeal, Indian meal and bread.[163] So unpleasant was the regime in fact that men likely to be sent to military prison frequently committed additional offences in order that they should instead be discharged from the forces.[164] Others are known to have feigned sickness or even to have maimed themselves in an effort to escape imprisonment.[165]

However, criticism of the supposed lack of severity in military prisons persisted until the 1880s at least,[166] particularly of their failure to separate prisoners because of their haphazard and ill-suited buildings.[167] Prison officials strongly advocated a toughening-up procedure and the assimilation of the techniques used in civilian prisons.[168] Colonel Joshua Jebb, for example, wrote, 'I am satisfied of the necessity of preserving, under all circumstances, the general prestige of a severe punishment, either by the *length of the period of confinement or the stringency of the discipline.*'[169] In 1868 the War Office was forced to take action because of the curtailment in the previous year of the use of corporal punishment,[170] and the criticisms of the Royal Commission on the judicial system of the forces. The Commission underscored the disparity between conditions of imprisonment in military and public institutions, and recommended the construction of a central military prison in Britain capable of housing all prisoners and of employing the techniques approved in public penitentiaries. Until such a prison was complete, the existing military prisons were to be closed and military prisoners confined to civil institutions.[171] With encouragement from within the army the War Office closed the military prisons in 1869 and sent their charges to public institutions.[172] Imprisonment in barrack cells and provost prisons, used for shorter terms of confinement up to three months, was where possible made more severe. In 1876 cornmeal and gruel became the staple prison diet.[173]

The new regime of severity was not universally acclaimed. In some quarters critics stressed the value of leniency and emphasised the liberalisation that had affected the army and the new worth that was being placed on the value of the soldier.[174] It is notable too that whereas in 1844 magistrates had complained of their cells being packed with common soldiers, objections were now raised to forcing soldiers into confinement with common criminals.[175] Neither military authorities nor the War Office were entirely unreceptive to criticism of this nature. Enquiries were held in 1879[176] and 1880,[177] with the absolute abolition of corporal punishment imminent, to consider the most suitable type of imprisonment for military offences. They led to the establishment of separate military prisons in more suitably constructed buldings, and steps were taken to copy more closely the prison regime in public institutions.

It was a failing which remained in the military judicial system that while recruiting officers argued that crime was decreasing in the forces, and that a better type of recruit was being attracted, hardened offenders were kept in confinement for lengthy periods and then released back into the ranks to detract from the army by their presence.[178] If military service were to be as attractive as many thought it could be, efforts would have to be made to discharge forcibly habitual offenders. This solution had been stressed repeatedly for years,[179] and indeed deserters and some other bad characters were regularly discharged from the Service. Renewed emphasis was placed upon the ignominious discharge after 1880,[180] however, as the forces saw the weapon of corporal punishment being taken from their hands and as the need to make the career of a soldier more attractive became increasingly apparent.[181] In 1881 the War Office directed that habitual offenders, and men sentenced to discharge after a period of imprisonment or penal servitude, should serve their sentences in public prisons, after which ignominious discharge would follow.[182] This effectively separated soldiers who had committed minor offences of discipline from more hardened offenders. The following table shows the number of men ignominiously discharged in certain years between 1867 and 1898. It contains a degree of imprecision for there is no way of ascertaining the extent to which the variation in the figures represents an increase or decrease in the crime rate, a heavier reliance on ignominious discharge, or both. Yet army reports certainly indicate a greater emphasis on the use of discharge during the later decades of the century;[183] for example, between 1879 and 1898 eighteen men were discharged with ignominy without previous punishment, but there were no similar discharges prior to this.[184]

Table 3–10 Ignominous Discharge from the Forces, 1867–98

Year	Number	Percentage of Total Force
1867	2,470	1.3
1870	1,616	0.9
1875	1,667	0.9
1880	1,826	1.0
1885	1,008	0.5
1890	1,603	0.8
1895	1,758	0.8
1898	1,945	0.9

Source: *Reports on the Discipline and Management of Military Prisons, P.P.*

Ignominious discharge and the removal of habitual offenders to civilian gaols permitted an easing of the severity of other types of punishment. Increasingly towards the close of the century military prisons came to be used solely for the punishment of breaches of discipline. In the circumstances authorities realised that if the prisons were to enhance their rehabilitative function and that if men were to return to the ranks 'in every sense improved and better fitted to take their place', attempts must be made to ease the severity of the prison regime.[185] Considerable progress was made towards these goals in the last decade of the century. In 1893 the report of a War Office committee brought about improvements in the prison diet. In 1895 a second committee led to an easing of prison regulations and a less frequent imposition of punishment.[186] On one hand the aim of imprisonment as a deterrent was reaffirmed; on the other, it was argued that imprisonment must also attempt to reform the offender, to improve him mentally and physically, and to carry on his military training.[187] In 1896 a reformed system similar to that adopted earlier in civilian institutions was put into effect. This allowed prisoners to progress within ten weeks from a first stage involving solitary confinement, hard labour and an unattractive diet, to a final stage in which men were employed at industrial work, received schooling and physical training, and were allowed visitors, library books and other privileges.[188]

Important rehabilitative steps were taken particularly in two areas: schooling and industrial employment. Some schooling had been given in military prisons before 1854,[189] but many prisoners were illiterate[190] and the instruction scarcely achieved much effectively.[191] It was limited to men who were serving lengthy sentences and who had been enrolled in an army school when imprisoned, and affected only few.[192] In 1895, however, military prisons undertook to provide elementary instruction to all men who had been unable to obtain a third-class certificate of education. Enthusiastic reports were received on the results of this instruction,[193] and by 1899 it was available to all prisoners not restricted to hard labour.[194]

The introduction of industrial employment came about equally as slowly, as a part of the trend towards shorter sentences and a concern with the purposes of imprisonment.[195] It was introduced on the initiative of individual prison administrations, and supported and further encouraged in 1887 by a War Office committee. In 1866 only a third of military prisoners were employed in this type of work, and as late as 1885 an average of nearly 700 men (57 per cent) in military prisons were still occupied on nothing more constructive than picking oakum.[196] In 1887 a War Office committee encouraged prisoners to be put to manufacturing goods needed by the army. This may have lightened the tedium of the prison regime, but the skills which were taught were of little use elsewhere. In general, of course, the army educational authorities had rejected any need for the technical training of soldiers.

The principles of retribution, deterrence and rehabilitation can all be detected in military policy. There can scarcely be much doubt that in general the punishments meted out were adequate retribution for the offences committed, and although it probably cannot be proved conclusively were also a forceful warning to others against the commission of similar offences. The translation towards lighter punishment did not lessen this effect. The decrease in the incidence of crime in the army was probably due more to an effective system of deterrence than to the enlistment of a progressively better-behaved civilian population. For one thing, the army was getting younger, and the higher proportion of younger men increased disciplinary problems. For another, recidivism declined remarkably during the period, and this is the best indication of the effectiveness of the judicial and penal systems in discouraging crime and in redeeming offenders.[197]

Clearly one of the most important achievements of the army penal system after 1856 was the awareness of the danger and futility of over-punishment. Hence the accent on abolishing corporal offenders from the forces, and in easing the severity of other forms of punishment. 'Obedience', manuals were to observe by the outbreak of the Great War, is

> . . .not the product of fear, but of understanding, and understanding is based on knowledge. . .As obedience is a moral quality, so must punishment be the same, for it is resorted to to foster and nurture it. Punishment of a vindictive nature is a crime, of a useless nature an immoral act, the act of a fool.[198]

Another facet of this spread of humanitarianism was the increasing emphasis after 1856 not on deterrence, but on prevention.

5. Organised Leisure and Other Preventive Influences

The arguments that a great deal of crime in the army was endemic among the type of men who enlisted, and that it was occasioned by the restrictions of the Service and its lack of amenities for recreation led the army to devote considerable efforts to altering the basis of recruitment and to improving leisure activities. Traditional army policy had been to get men at the cheapest cost to the state, and in times of emergency criminals had been released from gaol on condition that they agreed to serve in the army. To overcome this debasement of the rank and file authorities recognised the necessity of encouraging the enlistment of a better class of recruit,[199] and one of the aims of the introduction of short service in 1870 was to reach in greater numbers the mature well-behaved man.[200] What effect it was to have on the incidence of crime in the forces is difficult to say. All that statistics suggest clearly is that recruits were on the whole better educated in 1899 than they had been in 1856, and this may well have made them more amenable to discipline and more ready to use their spare time for constructive purposes.

The need to ease the restrictions of military service was stressed by some soldiers and civilians.[201] There is evidence that senior officers acting on their own initiative occasionally did so,[202] and on an official level the award of good conduct pay, which had been introduced in 1832, was an inducement to good behaviour. In 1860, 1870, and again in 1876, its attraction was increased when the qualifying periods of service were sharply reduced.[203] A comparison of training manuals from the beginning and end of our period shows that by the late 1890s regulations were less minute (it was no longer considered necessary to specify the exact length of the infantryman's pace, for example) but that there were still a great many petty regulations outlining drill, movements, and other procedures.[204] With regard to the interpretation of these regulations, there is little indication that on the whole NCOs and officers loosened their authority in order to make the soldier's life any easier. On balance the irksome nature of military discipline changed little.

Insubordination and desertion, an outcome of this situation, remained high especially because little was done to make it easier for men to get out of the service if they felt that they had made a wrong choice in enlisting. There were provisions to allow men to purchase a discharge, but the cost (£100 within the first three months of service, and £18 thereafter), was beyond the reach of the average soldier.[205] At times proposals were considered which would have modified the scale of payments,[206] but these came to nothing. As Table 3–11 shows, the number of discharges purchased each year actually declined in the long run after 1860. This situation only served to encourage acts of desperation. In some cases soldiers were known to mutilate themselves in order to procure a medical discharge.[207] More frequently they deserted when the opportunity arose. Short-service enlistment in theory provided an escape valve by shortening the minimum period of colour service, but the first stint with the colours, six years originally, later raised to seven, was in fact too long to do so.

Improvements to barracks, by making surroundings more agreeable, must have removed some of the temptation to heavy drinking, desertion, and other offences;[208] how much is impossible to say, for this was only a fringe benefit of reforms aimed at improving army health. A more central problem, and one which was fixed upon by reformers within the Service and without, was the inadequacy of recreational opportunities, and the lack of profitable employment for the soldier's considerable leisure time.

Many urged fuller provisions for education,[209] others underscored the necessity of improving the management and the functions of the ubiquitous canteen.[210] Considerable stress was placed on wholesome

Table 3–11 Discharges from the Army by Purchase, 1861–98

Year	No. of Discharges Purchased	Year	No. of Discharges Purchased
1861	2,217	1880	2,645
1862	1,614	1882	2,209
1864	1,662	1884	1,853
1866	2,399	1886	1,770
1868	2,031	1888	1,339
1870	1,493	1890	1,584
1872	2,839	1892	1,467
1874	2,653	1894	1,236
1876	2,853	1896	1,430
1878	2,058	1898	1,574

Source: *General Annual Return of the British Army,* P.P., XLIII (c.1323), 1875, p.25; XLIII (c.6196), 1890, p.32; LIII (c.9426), 1899, p.34.

diversions for the soldier's leisure time and the greatest number by far called for the establishment of games rooms, recreation rooms, enlisted men's clubs, and gardens.[211] *The Times* observed '. . . though we can no longer inspire our recruits with so powerful a motive of good conduct as Puritan fanaticism, we ought at least to protect them as far as we can against acquiring habits which make them worse soldiers as well as worse men'.[212] Better organised recreation it was felt would lead to less drunkenness and in turn to less crime. Less crime would mean fewer hospitals and prisons and more effectiveness. In moral character-building harmless amusement was an important first link in the chain. Captain E.S. Jervais, the commandant of a military convalescent home at Great Yarmouth, confidently expected,

> The men will become more rational, and expert, simply from not having imbibed the usual amount of bad liquor, and from having employed their time in thinking how they could play their next domino, draught, or chessman; which would also lead them to reflect before they wasted a rifle-ball in the air.[213]

Many of these ideas were taken up by military authorities. Some progress was made first of all in improving the state of canteens. The guiding principle was a sound one: even though a fair proportion of enlisted men might by voluntary restraint or the absence of vending facilities in barracks be prevented from drinking spirits and even beer, a large percentage would drink regardless and if there was no army canteen available, they would (they might anyway) frequent the ginshops, public houses and low haunts of the nearby town. 'Men who go out of barracks will eat and drink, as young men do, somewhere,' Major-General Montgomery Moore pointed out in 1891, 'and giving them a place where good food and drink can be had under civilised conditions, instead of remorsely driving them to the public house teaches them temperance in its broadest sense, and undoubtedly tends to the decrease of drunkenness and the increase of self-respect.[214]

The basic canteen had come into existence with the building of new barracks after Waterloo. Initially premises were let out to private contractors, who in exchange for the highest rent the government could exact, were licensed to sell beer, wines and spirits. As might be expected the chief beneficiary was often the canteen tenant who charged exorbitant prices and adulterated the liquor he sold in order to assure himself a handsome profit.[215] In 1863 regimental management was substituted and profits from the running of the canteen henceforth went to the regiment. A board of officers was normally chosen to run the business and senior sergeants were appointed as canteen stewards.

The regimental system was probably fairer than the tenant system, but dishonest stewards were frequent and adulterated beer was commonplace. Canteen stewards were frequently able to purchase their discharge with the money they had accumulated from these activities.[216] Nor were the items offered for sale as inexpensive or of as high a quality as they might have been. Inexperienced or careless officers frequently failed to obtain the best quality supplies at the most favourable prices.[217] This situation was improved somewhat in 1894 when a group of officers formed the Canteen and Mess Cooperative Society which undertook volume purchase of canteen supplies. Regimental canteens were invited to join and several took the opportunity of doing so. The remainder continued to manage themselves independently until 1900, when the army reintroduced a modified form of the tenant contract system.[218]

The proliferation between 1856 and 1899 of other facilities besides the liquor bar was a more significant development, because, as medical and legal opinion testified, better health and a lower crime rate could only be expected if the soldier were induced to spend less of his time engaged in heavy drinking.[219] Better managed canteens could only contribute a little to this. At night for the ordinary soldier the attractions of the nearby civilian town were very powerful. In 1860 at Aldershot, for instance, there were eighteen canteens in barracks, twenty-five public houses and forty-seven beer houses (the latter all reputed to be brothels) in the town.[220] The proper way of correcting this situation was not by declaring civilian establishments out of bounds, but rather by adding to the number of attractive amusements in barracks.[221] The initiative in establishing these facilities was taken at first by regimental officers,[222] although by 1860 higher authorities were aware of their value, and were beginning to undertake their construction with government funds.[223] The report in 1862 of a committee on soldiers' dayrooms in particular argued strongly that crime could be reduced by greater provision for recreation.[224] Within the next ten years, as the Army Sanitary Committee remarked, substantial progress had been made.[225] By 1900 regimental and garrison institutes comprising games rooms, grocery shops, luncheon rooms, canteens, and in some cases even theatres and halls had grown up around the solitary canteen of earlier days.[226]

The extension of education after 1856 played a complementary part. The schools, libraries and special lectures and slide shows and the higher rate of literacy encouraged soldiers to take part in other forms of amusement than drinking.[227] As one commanding officer reported in 1870, 'The number of men who pass their evenings in the recreation rooms, or in reading a book in their barracks, instead of in public-houses, increases steadily, and is a source of much gratification.'[228]

Music was another important diversion. In 1856 the Military School of Music was founded and the training of musicians in the army improved.[229] This led to greater scope for men to pursue musical interest and in the long run improved the quality of performance.[230]

Perhaps the most popular of all forms of recreation, particularly during the last decades of the century, were regimental sports, especially football, boxing, and to a lesser extent gymnastics. Enthusiasm, notably for football, spread quickly in the army as it did outside. The equipment required was relatively inexpensive and there was plenty of encouragement from authorities at regimental and higher levels for organised athletes. Army teams took many prizes in local and national competitions, and were entered regularly in Football Association matches. They were to prove instrumental in encouraging the growth of the sport in Britain.[231]

The proliferation of these recreational facilities was paralleled and encouraged by the efforts of private individuals and religious institutions, which had their source in missionary work. At at time when missions to the poor were also becoming popular the concept of missions to the armed forces received support among religious circles in

Britain.[232] One result was the establishment near many of the large garrisons and stations of 'Soldiers' Homes' or mission centres—institutions offering baths, sleeping quarters, meeting halls, smoking and games rooms, a tea and coffee bar, and other comforts. For the most part, this was done with private funds, since the War Office normally refused to contribute to any proposal where a particular religious denomination was involved.[233]

The first Soldiers' Home was inaugurated at Chatham by the Wesleyan Charles Henry Kelly in 1861. Miss Louisa Daniell, a civilian evangelist, founded a large home at Aldershot in 1862, and from then the movement spread rapidly.[234] In Ireland Soldiers' Homes got under way in 1877 when Elise Sandes founded her first home at Tralee.[235] The examples set by these individuals was shortly followed by some of the churches.[236] At Aldershot the first Wesleyan Soldiers' Home was built in 1869, in 1883 a Church of England Home, boasting among other things a fine billiard room, was built, and in the 1890s Salvation Army and Primitive Methodist homes were constructed on a modest scale. What happened at Aldershot took place at other stations, and indeed it was not until the end of the century with the construction of more new barracks that army provisions could match the private Soldiers' Home.[237]

The regimental or garrison institute and the Soldiers' Home were both well patronised, and were believed to have contributed largely to the falling incidence of crime between 1856 and 1899.[238] Each had peculiar advantages and disadvantages and probably appealed to different types of men. The private Homes were probably more comfortable and there are many soldiers' testimonials to their enjoyment of them.[239] Yet equally it is clear, despite claims to the contrary, that many men were driven away by the religion that was forced on them or by the strict prohibition of alcoholic beverages.[240] Government institutions were free from proselytising; however, as late as 1900 they could be criticised for a general roughness and lack of refinement not conducive to good conduct, for frequently being housed in unsuitable buildings, and for a tendency to promote the sale of liquor rather than soft drinks.[241]

Outside the armed forces recreational facilities on the scale available to the soldier were scarce. This was particularly so during the 1870s and 1880s. The development of regimental and garrison institutes and Soldiers' Homes was paralleled to an extent by the growth of working men's clubs towards the end of the century, and enthusiasm for organised sports gripped soldier and civilian alike, but civilian working hours were very long, and the six-day week common. With limited transport, very little money to spend, and with only evenings free, it was not until the close of the century that any major change came in civilian life. In contrast the soldier, as the period wore on, had a great deal found for him and a widening choice of diversions.[242] 'There were many ways open to men,' a cavalry sergeant was to recall in 1893, 'according to their individual inclinations, of occupying or amusing themselves. There was really no excuse for a man to soak in order to kill time.'[243] These advantages were clearly appreciated by the men in the ranks[244] and made a career in the army more attractive.[245]

The close involvement of religious bodies with the establishment of soldiers' institutes was but one form in which missionary zeal towards the army was expressed. A second and more direct way was through a straightforward participation in the religious life of the forces, and the use of moral suasion to prevent crime. The traditional military view of religion was an instrumental one: chaplains were useful for comforting the sick and wounded and for keeping an eye on the rank and file and doctrine did not matter as much as the fact that religious services contributed to morale and church parades kept men tidy.[246] However, the Crimean War and the Indian Mutiny inspired a new level of religicus enthusiasm. This was typified by William Hare, an army chaplain who wrote in 1855 that the army was a 'field in which a rich harvest, with proper culture, may be reaped to the glory of God's grace'.[247] Its practical expression was the missionary efforts of the principal religious denominations and of organisations such as the Army Scripture Readers and Soldiers' Friend Society.[248] Methodism was not officially recognised in the forces, but by 1856 its missionaries were no longer excluded from barracks and camps, in spite of protests from the established Episcopal church.[249]

Since the 1820s the policy had been to reduce the number of military chaplains and to leave ministration to the troops to the parochial clergy. After 1844, when G.R. Gleig became Chaplain-General, this policy was reversed gradually. The early 1850s witnessed considerable concern in the army over a number of incidents in which Roman Catholic priests in Ireland particularly, were accused of preaching sedition to the troops.[250] Recognising that it would be impossible to prevent men from attending church, however, the War Office was prompted to regularise and therefore to control religious activities by the appointment of army chaplains. In 1858 it was decided that Church of England, Presbyterian and Roman Catholic chaplains should be engaged according to the proportions of men of each religion in the forces; the following year chaplains were commissioned and in 1860 they were uniformed. Secretaries of State, such as Sidney Herbert and Lord Panmure, were clearly hopeful that a spread of religion in the ranks would benefit discipline and perhaps reduce the amount of crime. By the mid-1860s there was more provision being made for the spiritual welfare of the army than for either the town or country population in general.[251]

There was close correlation between nationalities and religion in the forces, but this does not mean that many soldiers were devout. Every recruit was required to declare a religious affiliation and was given a choice only of one of the above three.[252] Many had no preference, but because church parades were compulsory and the band went to services with the Anglicans, tended to elect to belong to the Church of England. Recruiting sergeants too often made arbitrary choices on their behalf.[253] The indications are that only a small percentage of men ever became devoutly religious. The compulsory church parade, which required half of Sunday to prepare for, made that particular day the most hated of the week.[254] Soldiers on the whole seem to have detested having religion forced upon them[255] and those who were visibly devout were frequently ridiculed by their comrades, especially if hypocrisy was suspected.[256]

Yet the influence of religion in the army was by no means entirely negative. Churchmen certainly claimed to have influenced many soldiers for the better although these claims are impossible to confirm.[257] Churches and religious societies were involved in temperance reform, and drinking did become less of a problem in the forces. From the beginning of the period separate religious organisations were active in this area and in 1893 joined forces to form the Army Temperance Association. The ATA received support from military authorities[258] and membership grew quickly. By 1895 it boasted 8,641 members,[259] and within a few years 2,000.[260] It is likely that the Association's influence was greater than its nominal membership would suggest, although this is impossible to estimate. As the name implied, a principal goal was temperance, not necessarily abstinence.

6. Conclusion

Criminologists were correct in arguing that there was no one single cause of crime in the army, yet it is likely that most offences were a reaction to the sudden harshness of military discipline, the strangeness of army life, and the lack of anything to do in spare time but drink. The significant decrease in the rate of crime in the army after 1856 was a measure of the success not only of efforts to deter offences by punishment but of preventive attempts to strike at these causes.

The criminal statistics describe the nature of the fall in the incidence of crime. They also point out the areas of failure of both deterrence and prevention. The increasing proportion of young men in the army, particularly after 1870, coincided with a rise in the incidence of disobedience and insubordination and a continued high rate of desertion and disgraceful conduct. The two events are clearly related, inasmuch as there was a disproportionately high number of young soldiers involved in these serious offences. Not only had the majority of deserters served less than two years in the army, but the proportion with two years' service or less rose from slightly over 50 per cent in 1868 to more than 85 per cent within thirty years.

In general, conditions of service improved between 1856 and 1899, and the incidence of crime in the army as a whole declined significantly. At the same time there was a signal failure to improve adequately those aspects of military service that were objectionable to younger soldiers particularly. As well as with restrictions of discipline, part of this blame lay with recruiting methods, since at the end of the period many young men were as disillusioned as ever upon discovering what army life held in store for them. Rates of pay bore a share of responsibility, and are one of the subjects of the chapter which follows.

Notes

1. See V.A.C. Gatrell and T.B. Hadden, 'Criminal Statistics and their Interpretation', in E.A. Wrigley, ed., *Nineteenth Century Society, Essays in the Use of Quantative Methods for the Study of Social Data* (Cambridge, 1972), pp.336–96.
2. See J.J. Tobias, *Crime and Industrial Society in the Nineteenth Century* (1967).
3. Leon Radzinowicz, *Ideology and Crime* (1966), p.64.
4. *Manual of Military Law* (1899), pp.19–30.
5. Lieutenant-Colonel W.W. Knollys, 'The Position of the British Soldier', *Colburn's,* (1881), pp.42–9.
6. Staff Surgeon Frederic Roberts, 'On the Development of Military Offences in Camp and Quarters', Parkes Pamphlets, II (1853); Mole, *A King's Hussar,* p.352; 'G', Views on Army Reform: an Answer', *Colburn's,* VI (1892–3), pp.469–75; *Report of the Inspector-General of Recruiting,* P.P., XX (c.6597), 1892, p.4.
7. When in 1879 for instance the military correspondent with the *Daily Telegraph* criticised the troops on active service in Zululand for disgracing themselves and the army by their misbehaviour, he was strongly taken to task and his accusations disproved by no less eminent an officer than Lord Wolseley. A year later isolated incidences of misbehaviour among troops serving in Afghanistan were defended as 'only natural' by superior officers.

Suum Cuique, 'The Daily Telegraph's Correspondent and the Army in South Africa', *Colburn's* II (1880), pp.1–6; *Reports by Sir Garnet Wolseley on the Conduct of the Troops in South Africa,* P.P., XLII (c.74), 1880, pp.433 et seq.; General Sir H. Norman to Edward Stanhope, 9 Nov. 1878, Stanhope MSS., 1320.

8. Gatrell and Hadden, in Wrigley, ed., *Nineteenth Century Society,* pp.382–3.
9. See Appendix III, Table IIIA–1.
10. *Report on the Discipline and Management of Military Prisons,* P.P., XXXIII (c.846), 1873, p.4; see also the exchange of letters between the Horse Guards and the GOC Canada, circa 1854–7, in the Panmure MSS., GD45/8/88, 45/8/452.
11. *Report of a Committee on Rewards for Apprehending Deserters and for Detecting Cases of Fraudulent Enlistment* (1878), WO.33/32.
12. Methods of Preventing Fraudulent Enlistment, WO.32/8708.
13. See for instance *The Border Advertiser,* 26 Feb. 1876, 14 Nov. 1888; *The Scottish Border Record,* 22 Sept. 1883, 29 May, 23 Oct. 1886.
14. *Report of the Army Reorganisation Committee* (1881), p.525.
15. Colonel W.W. Knollys, 'The British Army in 1885', *Colburn's,* II (1885), pp.483–96.
16. See Appendix III, Table IIIA–2.
17. See Appendix III, Table IIIA–3.
18. Gatrell and Hadden, in Wrigley, ed., *Nineteenth Century Society,* p.384.
19. See Appendix III, Table IIIA–4.
20. Gatrell and Hadden, in Wrigley, ed., *Nineteenth Century Society,* p.380.
21. Studies of the post-World War II army have shown, however, that there was a higher proportion of dullards among service criminals than in the rank and file as a whole. See John C. Spencer, *Crime and the Services* (1954), p.42.
22. *Manual of Military Law* (1899), p.7.
23. *Standing Orders of the 73rd or Perthshire Regiment* (1871), p.66.
24. Colonel Robert Carey, *Military Law and Discipline,* Official War Office Papers of General Viscount Wolseley, W.1 (1871), p.3.
25. R.M. Daniell, 'Discipline: Its Importance to an Armed Force and the Best Means of Promoting and Maintaining it', *JRUSI,* XXXIII (1889), p.295.
26. See for instance Captain E. Telfer, 'Discipline: Its Importance to an Armed Force and the Best Means of Promoting and Maintaining it', *JRUSI,* XXXIII (1889), p.334.
27. Henry Spenser Wilkinson, *War and Policy* (1900), p.142.
28. General Viscount Wolseley, *The Soldier's Pocket Book* (1869), p.4.
29. John Baynes, *Morale* (1967), p.108.
30. Stephen Graham, *A Private in the Guards* (1919), p.1.
31. This was true throughout the United Kingdom, although all debts under £30 were remitted on enlistment. See *Manual of Military Law* (1899), pp.107, 267; Horace Wyndham, *Following the Drum* (1914), p.224. No comprehensive figures were ever compiled of the number of soldiers dealt with in civilian courts.
32. *The Queen's Regulations and Orders for the Army* (1868), p.358.
33. *Standing Orders and Regulations for the 1st Battalion, The Black Watch* (1906), p.51.
34. Blatchford, *My Life in the Army,* pp.41–2.
35. Brigadier-General J.H.A. MacDonald, *Fifty Years of It* (Edinburgh, 1909), pp.75–6.
36. In South Africa it was discovered too late that soldiers were unable to think

and had never been trained to take advantage of even the most obvious situations. A young officer writing to his wife in 1900 notes, 'If there is no word of command he [the soldier] does nothing at all; if all his officers are killed or wounded; he is helpless.' Sir Reginald Rankin, *A Subaltern's Letters to his Wife,* (1901), p.72; see also *Report of the Royal Commission on the war in South Africa,* P.P., XL (c. 1789), 1904, pp.45–6; cited hereafter as *Report of the Commission on the War in South Africa* (1904); Deneys Reitz, *Commando* (1929), p.57.

37. *The Queen's Regulations and Order for the Army* (1883), pp.89–90.
38. E. Faversham to W. Gordon, 10 Sept. 1872, Cardwell MSS., PRO. 30/48/2/9.
39. *Manual of Military Law* (1899), pp.19, 107.
40. The confinement and subsequent death of RSM Lilley in 1861 resulted in the celebrated court-martial of Lieutenant-Colonel T.R. Crawley of the 6th Inniskilling Dragoons. See A.H. Halley, *The Crawley Affair* (1972); the Duke of Cambridge to Earl de Grey and Ripon, 31 Dec. 1862, Ripon MSS., 43511.
41. Field-Marshall Sir William Robertson, *From Private to Field-Marshal* (1921), p.11.
42. *Second Report of the Royal Commission on the Constitution and Practice of Courts-Martial and the Present System of Punishment for Military Offences,* P.P., XII (c.4114–I), 1868–9, p.iii; cited hereafter as *Second Report of the Commission on Courts-Martial* (1868–9).
43. *Manual of Military Law* (1899), p.65.
44. J. MacMullen, *Camp and Barrack-Room, or the British Army as It Is,* (1846), p.24. Men could of course complain to a visiting General Officer, but this too might lead to more trouble than it was worth.
45. Report of the Judge Advocate-General, WO.91/43.
46. Robert Edmondson, *John Bull's Army from Within* (1907), p.81.
47. Robert Edmondson, *Is a Soldier's Life Worth Living?* (circa 1902), pp.3–4.
48. Edmondson, *John Bull's Army,* p.75; anon., 'Military Laws', *Colburn's,* I (1878), pp.75–87.
49. Major H.W. Pearse, 'Defaulter Sheets', *Colburn's,* XI (1895), pp.74–7.
50. *Rules for Summary Punishment under the Army Discipline and Regulation (Annual) Act, 1881,* P.P., LVIII (c.368), 1881, p.1.
51. The nineteenth century saw a progressive extension of the summary jurisdiction of civilian magistrates in order to ease the burden on the courts, a process which began in 1827–8, and which was accelerated after the mid-point of the century. See Tobias, *Crime and Industrial Society,* pp.264–7.
52. *Report of the Committee on the Conditions of Service as Affected by the Short Service System,* P.P., XX (c.2617), 1881, p.3; cited hereafter as *Report of the Committee on Short Service Conditions,* (1881).
53. *Second Report of the Commission on Courts-Martial,* (1868–9), p.xi.
54. *Report of the Select Committee on the Mutiny and Marine Mutiny Acts,* P.P., X (c.316), 1878.
55. Hansard, CCXLIII (27 February 1879), cc.1917–20; CCXLV (7 April 1879), cc.477, 489–90.
56. *Report of the Committee on Short Service Conditions,* (1881), p.3.
57. *Manual of Military Law* (1899), p.40; A Lieutenant-Colonel, *The British Army* (1899), p.209.
58. *The Queen's Regulations and Orders for the Army* (1883), p.104, (1899), p.93; Cairnes, *The Army from Within,* p.124. Monies collected were applied to a general fund used to provide bursaries for men with good

conduct records upon their being discharged. See *Report of the Committee on Fines for Drunkenness,* P.P., XII (c.199), 1870, pp.1–12; WO.32/6249.

59. See Appendix III, Table IIIA–5.
60. A Voice from the Ranks, *The British Army*, p.11.
61. Robertson, *From Private to Field-Marshal,* pp.12–13.
62. Arthur Swinson and Donald Scott, *The Memoirs of Private Waterfield* (1968), p.16.
63. *The Queen's Regulations and Orders for the Army* (1883), p.99.
64. *Report on the Discipline and Management of Military Prisons,* P.P., XXX (c.4209), 1868–9, p.18.
65. *Report on the Discipline and Management of Military Prisons,* P.P., XXXIII (c.846), 1873, pp.11–12.
66. Anon., 'Our Military Reforms of Late Years and What They Have Done for Us', *Colburn's,* III (1860), pp.475–86; Florence Nightingale, Memorandum of Interview with Sir J. Lawrence, 3 April 1869, Nightingale MSS., 45753.
67. To some extent the enlistment of doubtful characters was encouraged by the provisions of the Mutiny Act which forgave all debts up to £30.
68. Blatchford, *My Life in the Army,* p.74.
69. Paul B. Bull, *God and our Soldiers* (1904), p.8; Anon., 'Discipline', *Colburn's,* II (1876), pp.101–5; Roberts, 'On the Development of Military Offences', Parkes Pamphlets; Note on the Discharge and Branding of Soldiers, WO.33/22; The Times, 12 Feb. 1876.
70. James F. Fuller, 'The Army: By a (Late) Common Soldier', *The Fortnightly Review,* VI (1866), pp.435–45; Anon., 'Desertion and Recruiting', *Colburn's*, I (1874), pp.296–307; *Report on the Discipline and Management of Military Prisons,* P.P., XXXIII (c.846), 1873, p.4.
71. Edward Cardwell to Earl Granville, 7 Dec. 1872, Cardwell MSS., PRO. 30/48/5/30.
72. Anon., 'Education and Crime in the Army', *Colburn's* III (1874), pp.525–39; Anon., 'The Discipline of Armies, Past and Present', *Colburn's* II (1876), pp.31–8; Wilfred Gore-Browne, 'The Private Soldier's Wrongs, Life in a Cavalry Regiment', *The Nineteenth Century,* XXVIII (1890), pp.840–53; C.B., 'Short Service Discipline', *Colburn's, I* (1881), pp.393–405.
73. A Voice from the Ranks, *The British Army and What We Think of it* (1871), p.11.
74. Bull, *God and our Soldiers,* pp.7–8.
75. 'H', A Late Sergeant in the Line, 'Desertion: its Causes and Prevention', *Colburn's*, V (1892), pp.375–9; Major T.S. Baldock, 'The Private Soldier's Wrongs ; an Officer's Reply', *The Nineteenth Century,* XXVIII (1890), pp.831–4.
76. An Old Crimean, 'Boy Soldiers in the Field', *Colburn's,* I (1880), pp.478–82; Macmullen, *Camp and Barrack-Room,* p.26.
77. MacMullen, op.cit., p.22; Wyndham, *Following the Drum,* p.56.
78. David Reid, *Memorials of the Life of a Soldier* (Edinburgh, 1864), p.4.
79. Wyndham, op.cit., p.30
80. Anon., Experiences of a Soldier, Unpublished MS. (circa 1890), NAM., 7008–13; Edmondson, *John Bull's Army,* p.52.
81. J.A. Stocqueler, *The British Soldier* (1857); Bull, *God and Our Soldiers,* pp.13–14; *The Times,* 22 Nov. 1861.
82. Dr Edgehill to Edward Stanhope, 9 Nov. 1887, Stanhope MSS., 1350.
83. *Report on the Discipline and Management of Military Prisons,* P.P., XXX (c.4209), 1868–9, p.4.

84. W.W. (A Company Officer), 'Desertion, its Cause and Prevention', *United Services Magazine,* V (1892), pp.296–307.
85. Robertson, *From Private to Field-Marshal,* p.29.
86. Army Temperance Association, WO.32/3998.
87. Baynes, *Morale,* p.42; Brian Harrison, *Drink and the Victorians* (1972), p.20.
88. John Williamson, *The Narrative of a Commuted Pensioner* (Montreal, 1938); Wyndham, *Following the Drum,* p.84.
89. John Fraser, *Sixty Years in Uniform* (1939), p.84.
90. Robertson, *From Private to Field-Marshal,* p.29.
91. Harrison, *Drink and the Victorians,* pp.39–41.
92. Swinson and Scott, *Memoirs of Private Waterfield,* pp.26–31; John Ryder, *Four Years' Service in India* (Leicester, 1853), p.13; A.H.D. Ackland-Troyte, *Through the Ranks to a Commission* (1881), p.70.
93. Frank Richards, *Old Soldier Sahib* (1936), p.248.
94. Daniell, *JRUSI,* XXXIII (1899), pp.287–332, passim.
95. An Officer, 'A Few Remarks on Discipline in the Army', *Colburn's,* II (1867), pp.187–92. These feelings persisted throughout the whole of our period. Writing of the First World War, a recent author has remarked, 'As soon as the private soldier realised the power of the organisation to which, body and soul, he now belonged, he realised also that, while he might learn certain ways of outwitting it, outwardly he had no choice but to submit. Any form of direct defiance was worse than useless.' John Brophy, in John Brophy and Eric Partridge, ed., *The Long Trail* (1965), p.14.
96. Reverend E.J. Hardy, *Mr Thomas Atkins* (1900), pp.178–9; John Fortescue, *A Short Account of Canteens in the British Army* (Cambridge, 1928), p.31.
97. Captain Thomas Frederic Simmons, *Remarks on the Constitution and Practice of Courts-Martial* (1863).
98. *Manual of Military Law* (1899), pp.318 et seq.
99. Swinson and Scott, *Memoirs of Private Waterfield,* p.31.
100. See Papers of the Judge-Advocate-General on Capital Punishment, WO.81/118, passim.
101. *General Annual Return of the British Army,* P.P., XLIII (c.1323), 1875, p.40; XLIII (c.6196), 1890, p.56; LIII (c.9426), 1899, p.58.
102. Tobias, *Crime and Industrial Society,* p.236.
103. A spring-loaded instrument either in the shape of the letters 'BC' or 'D' (for Bad Character and Deserter) was applied to the arm, hand or chest and a series of skin punctures one-quarter inch deep and in the shape of a one-inch letter were made. Either gunpowder or a mixture of crushed indigo and Indian ink were then rubbed into the wound to produce a permanent mark.
104. *Second Report of the Commission on Courts-Martial* (1868–9), p.x.
105. General Edwards, Memorandum on Army Reform, 21 Jan. 1869, Cardwell MSS., PRO.30/48/3/11; Edward Cardwell to the Duke of Cambridge, 3 April 1869, Cardwell MSS., PRO.30/48/3/11.
106. The Discharge and Branding of Soldiers, WO.33/32.
107. See for instance, *Report of the Inspector-General of Recruiting,* P.P., XIII (c.4677), 1886, pp. 9–10.
108. The cat usually had nine lashes of whipcord or rawhide sixteen to twenty-four inches long with three knots in each lash which together cut a man a total of twenty-seven times with each stroke. To receive a flogging soldiers were tied to halberds or to triangles on the parade square. If these collapsed in the course of the whipping, the sentence might well be completed with the victim lying on the ground. The entire regiment was

normally paraded to witness the event and one of the soldier's comrades wielded the cat. Floggings were supervised by medical officers whose duty it was to halt the whipping if they felt the soldier was unable to endure more punishment. In such a case the man would be removed to hospital until he had recovered, at which time the remainder of the sentence would be completed. See John de Morgan, 'Barbaric Military Punishments', *The Green Bag,* X (1898), pp.34–5; *The Queen's Regulations and Orders for the Army* (1859), p.227.

109. Abolition of Flogging, WO.32/6045, p.3. See also the Panmure MSS., GD45/8/12.
110. Abolition of Flogging, WO.32/6045, p.7.
111. Memorandum on the Various Methods for Punishment Adopted for Foreign Armies in the Field, WO.33/33.
112. G.R. Elsmie, *Field-Marshal Sir Donald Stewart* (1903), p.404; Donald Dalgetty, 'Rough Notes about the Army and its Punishments, Past, Present, and Future', *Colburn's,* II (1868), pp.336–50; Hansard, CLVI, (16 Feb. 1860), c.1167; CLXXV (15 March 1867), cc.1970–3; CCXLVI (15 May 1879), cc.421–2.
113. Abolition of Flogging, WO.32/6045, p.9.
114. *Dispositions of Witnesses and Verdict of the Jury upon the Inquest Held into the Death of Private Robert Slim by Flogging,* P.P., XLI (c.202), 1867.
115. General Sir Bindon Blood, *Four Score Years and Ten* (1933), pp.29–30.
116. Swinson and Scott, *Memoirs of Private Waterfield,* p.103; Joseph Donaldson, *The Eventful Life of a Soldier* (1863), p.131.
117. B. Adams, *The Narrative of Private Buck Adams* (Cape Town, 1941), p.22. The most outstanding personal account of a flogging is Alexander Somerville's. As a private in the Scots Greys, Somerville was court-martialled and awarded 200 lashes for involvement in political agitation and urging his fellow soldiers to disobey orders. He remembered his flogging the whole of his life and it never ceased to arouse in him feelings of shock and anger. Even at the time however he was neither repentant nor contrite. Alexander Somerville, *Autobiography of a Working Man* (1848), pp.187–90.
118. Archibald Forbes, 'Flogging in the Army', *The Nineteenth Century,* VI (1879), p.609.
119. Field-Marshal Lord Grenfell, *Memoirs of Field-Marshal Lord Grenfell* (1925), p.17; H.J. Wale, *Sword and Surplice* (1880), p.99; J.C. Ives, *Six Years with the Colours* (Canterbury, 1891), p.21.
120. Blood, *Four Score and Ten,* p.29.
121. Anon., *Recollections of an Old Soldier* (1886), p.107.
102. MacMullen, *Camp and Barrack-Room,* p.21–2; John Shipp, *Flogging and Its Substitutes* (1831), pp.20 et seq.
123. *The Queen's Regulations and Orders for the Army* (1859), pp.226–8.
124. Hansard, CLXXVIII (27 March 1865), c.367.
125. Records of the Judge Advocate-General, WO.86/9, WO.86/15.
126. See Hansard, CLXXVIII (27 March 1865), c.367.
127. Hansard, CLVI (16 Feb. 1860), cc.1161–66; CLXXXV (15 March 1867), cc.1951–6; CXCV (12 April 1869), cc.660–1; CCLI (11 March 1880), cc.847–9.
128. Hansard, CLXXXV (15 March 1867), cc.1967–70; CCXLVII (17 June 1879), cc.54, 69–70.
129. Hansard, CLVI (16 Feb. 1860), cc.1169–70; CLXXXV (15 March 1867), c.1957; CCXLVII (17 June 1879), cc.44, 73–4.
130. *The Times* particularly underscored the argument that the maintenance of

flogging hindered recruitment. Other papers stressed the humanitarian question that was involved. *The Glasgow Sentinel* wondered how flogging could be reconciled with Britain's 'much vaunted progress in civilisation'. *The Times* 16 Nov. 1859, 30 March 1867, 8 April, 1870; *The Examiner*, 17 Sept. 1859; *The Manchester Guardian*, 5 Sept. 1859; *The Glasgow Sentinel*, 10 April 1858. See also *The National Review*, X (1857), p.280; *The Lancet*, II (1859), p.546; I (1867), p.365.

131. The War Office answer in Parliament echoed the military view that the army could not do without the lash, a line of reasoning that swayed many critics. Hansard, CLXXXVI (18 March 1867), c.3 (1 April 1867), cc.903–4: *The Times*, 16 July, 1879. Sidney Herbert, who had immense prestige from his efforts to improve the health of the army and who normally bore the interests of the soldier at heart, was a particularly effective proponent of flogging. See Hansard, CLVI (16 Feb. 1860), cc.1181–8.
132. Any soldier in the first class who committed a serious offence would be reclassified and liable for corporal punishment on another occasion.
133. *Inquest into the Death of Private Robert Slim by Flogging*, P.P., XLI (c.202), 1867.
134. Hansard, CLXXXV (18 Feb. 1867), cc.464–5.
135. Hansard, CCXLVIII (17 July 1879), cc.634–41, 652–60.
136. Lord Beaconsfield to Queen Victoria, 7 July 1879, CAB.41/13/2.
137. Hansard, CCLX (7 April 1881), c.853.
138. Queen Victoria to Earl Granville, 26 July 1882, George Earl Buckle, ed., *The Letters of Queen Victoria, 1862–1885*, I (1881), pp.393–405.
139. Hansard, CCLX (5 April 1881), c.854.
140. C.V., 'Short Service Discipline', *Colburn's*, I (1881), pp.393–405.
141. Lieutenant-Colonel W. Gordon Alexander, *Recollections of a Highland Subaltern* (1898), p.6; G.R. Elsmie, *Field-Marshal Sir Donald Stewart* (1903), p.404.
142. *Report of the Royal Commission on the Constitution and Practice of Courts-Martial*, WO.33/22; Dalgetty, *Colburn's*, II (1868), pp.336–50; Hansard, CXCV (12 April 1869), cc.664–5; CCLXXIX (24 May 1883), c.810.
143. Anon., 'Military Prisons', *Colburn's*, II (1871), pp.75–87.
144. *Report on the Discipline and Management of Military Prisons*, P.P., XXXI (c.450), 1871, p.33.
145. *Report on the Discipline and Management of Military Prisons*, P.P., XXX (c.1074), 1874, p.7.
146. *Second Report of the Select Committee on the Army Estimates*, P.P., VIII (c.212), 1888, pp.v–vi.
147. *Report on the Discipline and Management of Military Prisons*, P.P., XXXVII (c.6154), 1890, p.35.
148. Colonel Robert Carey, *Military Law and Discipline*, Official War Office Papers of General Viscount Wolseley, W.1, p.3.
149. *Report on the Discipline and Management of Military Prisons*, P.P., XXV (c.2316), 1856, p.5.
150. *Report on the Discipline and Management of Military Prisons*, P.P., XLVII (c.7175), 1893–4, p.9.
151. *Report on the Discipline and Management of Military Prisons*, P.P., XXX (c.2900), 1861, p.3.
152. *An Act to Amend the Prison Acts*, 61 and 62 Vict. (12 Aug. 1898).
153. *First Report of the Royal Commission on the Constitution and Practice of Courts-Martial in the Army and the Present System of Punishment for Military Offenders*, P.P., X (c.4114), 1868–9, p.viii. Hereafter cited as *First Report of the Commission on Courts-Martial* (1868–9).

154 S. and B. Webb, *English Prisons under Local Government* (reprinted 1963), p.207; Tobias, op.cit., p.238.

155. In 1856 for instance, 64.5 per cent of those convicted of burglary in England and Wales were sentenced to a term of imprisonment greater than one year. In 1886 only 28.8 per cent of those convicted were awarded such a sentence. See Tobias, *Crime and Industrial Society*, p.253.

156. Robert Blatchford remarked that men often went to prison for the slightest offence; one of his comrades received two years' imprisonment with hard labour for attempting to hit an NCO. See Blatchford, *My Life in the Army*, pp.44–5, 261.

157. Records of the Judge Advocate-General, WO.91/37; WO.86/21.

158. In 1865 for instance Thomas Archer wrote: 'The health and physical comfort of the British felon is better cared for than that of the ordinary British pauper, and receives far more attention than that of the British soldier or the British sailor.' T. Archer, *The Pauper, the Thief, and the Convert* (1865), cited in Tobias, *Crime and Industrial Society*, p.242.

159. A Medical Staff Officer, 'Suppression of Crime', *Colburn's*, I (1853), pp.440–4; *Report on the Discipline and Management of Military Prisons*, P.P., XLIII (c.9416), 1899, pp.14–15.

160. *Report on the Discipline and Management of Military Prisons*, P.P., XLVII (c.6723), 1898, pp.9–10.

161. Prison punishments included loss of privileges (for minor offences), confinement in a dark cell, or confinement in irons. Heavy shot drill, stone breaking and the crank were normally awarded with sentences of hard labour. Shots weighted thirty-two pounds each, and they had to be lifted and carried a distance of five feet from one socket to another; the resistance at the crank handle was ten to fourteen pounds and men were required to perform up to 14,500 revolutions in eight hours. Extra spells at hard labour were sometimes awarded for breaches of prison discipline, and until 1881 flogging was inflicted as well although the number of cases of its being used was never very great. In 1877, for instance, when the average number in prison was 1,309, there were only twenty incidents of corporal punishment being awarded. See John Millar, 'Life in a Military Prison', *The Cornhill Magazine*, XV (1867), p.500; *Report on the Discipline and Management of Military Prisons*, P.P., XXXII (c.648), 1872, p.7; XLII (c.2171), 1878, p.7.

162. Robertson, *From Private to Field-Marshal*, pp.12–13.

163. Between 1856 and 1861 for instance only 6,119 men gained weight in prison, while 28,482 lost weight. *Report on the Discipline and Management of Military Prisons*, P.P., XXVI (c.3052), 1862, p.17.

164. Hon. S. Carr Glyn, 'Discharge with Ignominy', *Colburn's*, III (1872), pp.37–40.

165. *Report on the Discipline and Management of Military Prisons*, P.P., XXX (c.2900), 1861, p.19.

166. C.B., 'Short Service Discipline', *Colburn's*, I (1888), pp.393–405.

167. *First Report of the Commission on Courts-Martial* (1868–9), p.vii.

168. *Report on the Discipline and Management of Military Prisons*, P.P., XXV (c.2004), 1854–5, pp.18–28; XIX (c.2299), 1857–8, pp.23–35; XXXV (c.4075), 1867–8, p.3.

169. *Report on the Discipline and Management of Military Prisons*, P.P., XXV (c.2004), 1854–5, p.19.

170. *Report on the Discipline and Management of Military Prisons*, P.P., XLVII (c.7175), 1893–4, p.11.

171. *First Report of the Commission on Courts-Martial* (1868–9), p.viii.

172. *Report of the Royal Commission on the Constitution and Practice of Courts-Martial*, WO.32/6248; Robert Lowe to Edward Cardwell, 28 July 1869, Cardwell MSS;. PRO.30/48/5/22.
173. *Report on the Discipline and Management of Military Prisons*, P.P., XLVII (c.7175), 1893–4, pp.9–15.
174. Anon., 'Military Prisons', *Colburn's*, III (1876), pp.459–67; Anon., 'Army Crime in 1875', *Colburn's*, III (1876), pp.365–75; Anon., 'Army Crime in 1878', *Colburn's*, III (1879), pp.317–26; Hansard, CCXXXVIII (25 March 1878), cc.2024–5.
175. Anon., 'Military Prisons', *Colburn's*, II (1872), pp.75–87; Anon., 'Discipline in the Army', *Colburn's*, III (1861), pp.528–36; Anon., 'Army Crime in 1875', *Colburn's*, III (1875), pp.365–75.
176. *Proceedings of a Committee on Prison Accommodation*, Official War Office Papers of General Viscount Wolseley, W.45.
177. *Report of the Committee on Prisons for Military Offenders*, WO.33/35.
178. See for instance, *Report of the Inspector General of Recruiting*, P.P., XVIII (c.7659), 1895, pp.6–7; X (c.110), 1900, p.4.
179. *Report on the Discipline and Management of Military Prisons*, P.P., XXV (c.2004), 1854–5, p.19; XXX (c.4209), 1868–9, p.4; *Second Report of the Commission on Courts-Martial* (1868–9), p.xi; Anon., 'Desertion–The True Method for Eventually Checking It', *Colburn's*, III (1859), pp.94–102.
180. Hansard, CCCXXXIV (26 March 1889), cc.827–30; CCCXXXIV (5 April 1889), cc.1692–6; CCCXXXVII (17 June 1889), cc.37–40.
181. More than 44,000 recruits were initially examined by recruiters in 1880 alone. *General Annual Return of the British Army*, P.P., LIII (c.9426), 1899, p.30.
182. *Report on the Discipline and Management of Military Prisons*, P.P., XLII (c.398), 1900, p.38; XLVII (c.7175), 1893–4, p.14.
183. *Report on the Discipline and Management of Military Prisons*, P.P., XLII (c.398), 1900, p.38; XXXVII (c.6154), 1890, p.6; *Report of the Committee on Short Service Conditions* (1881), pp.12–13; *Report of the Committee on Prisons for Military Offenders*, WO.33/35.
184. *General Annual Return of the British Army*, P.P., LIII (c.9426), 1899, p.58.
185. *Report on the Discipline and Management of Military Prisons*, P.P., XLIII (c.9416), 1899, p.18.
186. Hansard, LXXI (8 May 1899), c.18.
187. *Report on the Discipline and Management of Military Prisons*, P.P., XLII (c.398), 1900, pp.37–9.
188. Hansard, LXXI (8 May 1899), cc.18–21.
189. *Report on the Discipline and Management of Military Prisons*, P.P., XXV (c.2004), 1854–5, pp.19–26.
190. *Report on the Discipline and Management of Military Prisons*, P.P., XXV (c.3567), 1865, p.12; XXXVI (c.3925), 1867, p.10.
191. Anon., 'Army Crime in 1875', *Colburn's*, III (1878), pp.365–75.
192. *Report on the Discipline and Management of Military Prisons*, P.P., XLVII (c.8983), 1898, p.10
193. *Report on the Discipline and Management of Military Prisons*, P.P., XL (c.8526), 1897, p.9.
194. *Report on the Discipline and Management of Military Prisons*, P.P., XLII (c.398), 1900, p.17. Government institutions by comparison offered instruction and lessons to civilian prisoners, but on a modest scale only; until the 1880s one-third of all prisoners in England were illiterate. The Prison Act of 1898, which placed greater stress on the rehabilitation of the prisoner followed the example of the military penal system by making

greater provision for the educational training of young offenders. This had been foreshadowed forty years earlier with the development of the reformatory school system and its emphasis on the importance of education in reducing crime. Max Grünhut, *Penal Reform* (Oxford, 1948), pp.97, 231; Tobias, *Crime and Industrial Society,* pp.249–52; *An Act to Amend the Prison Acts,* 61 and 62 Vict. (12 Aug. 1898).

195. Industrial employment therefore involved the simple manufacture of articles useful to the army such as bedding, sacking, tents, harness and equipment. The quantity of goods manufactured for the War Department was impressive. By 1899, 44,400 articles of bedding, 14,214 beds and 38,685 bags, mats, brushes and halters had been produced. It was not exciting or even interesting work, but it was better than heavy labour or oakum-picking. Another argument in its favour was that it saved expenditure and reduced reliance on civilian suppliers. *Report of the Committee on the Employment of Military Prisoners,* WO.33/47, passim; *Report on the Discipline and Management of Military Prisons,* P.P., XLII (c.398), 1900, p.14. Useful employments for prisoners in civilian institutions were introduced at an earlier date, nevertheless the progress in this particular reform was as slow and agonising as it was for military prisoners, and a great deal of time was to elapse before adequate schemes for rehabilitation were introduced.

196. *Report of the Committee on the Employment of Military Prisoners,* WO.33/47; *Report on the Discipline and Management of Military Prisoners,* P.P., XXXV (c.4828), 1886, p.6.

197. Table IIIA–6 in Appendix III provides a compendum of information on recidivism in the army.

198. Captain J.F.C. Fuller, *Training Soldiers for War* (1914), p.89.

199. Note on the Discharge and Branding of Soldiers, WO.33/22; Anon., 'Discipline in the Army', *Colburn's,* III (1861), pp.528–36.

200. W.E. Gladstone to Edward Cardwell, 23 Oct. 1873, Cardwell MSS., PRO.30/48/2/10.

201. See for instance Anon., 'Military Reform and Military Efficiency', *Colburn's,* II (1859), pp.317–28; An Old Dragoon, 'Suggestions for Preventing Desertion from the Army', *Colburn's,* I (1860), pp.272–4; Fuller, *The Fortnightly Review,* VI (1866), pp.435–45; W.W. (A Company Officer), 'Desertion: Its Cause and Prevention', *Colburn's,* V (1892), p.42; A Voice from the Ranks, *The British Army and What We Think on the Subject* (1871), pp.27 et seq.

202. Robertson, *From Private to Field-Marshal,* p.29; General Sir Horace Smith-Dorrien, *Memoirs of Forty-Eight Years' Service* (1925), pp.348, 355–7; Wood, *Midshipman to Field-Marshal,* II, 184, 208–10.

203. Good conduct pay and good conduct badges were first introduced in 1832. Badges, up to a maximum of five, could be earned by keeping clear of serious disciplinary offences for a specified period of years. Extra pay of 1d per day was awarded with each badge. These questions are discussed in Chapter 4 below and qualifying periods of service are set out. See also *Report of the Committee on Short Service Conditions* (1881), p.4.

204. Captain William D. Malton, *Company and Battalion Drill* (1862); *Infantry Drill* (1897); *Cavalry Training* (1904).

205. *Report of the Committee on Short Service Conditions* (1881), pp.9–10.

206. *The Queen's Regulations and Orders for the Army* (1883), p.475; *Report of the Inspector-General of Recruiting,* P.P., XV (c.3503), 1883, p.11; Lieutenant-General W.H. Goodenough and Lieutenant-Colonel J.C. Dalton, *The Army Book for the British Empire* (1893), p.327.

207. Charles M. Clode, *The Military Forces of the Crown* (1869), II, 46; The Marquess of Anglesey, *A History of British Cavalry 1816–1919,* I (1973), p.122.
208. Hansard, CCCXXXVII (18 June 1889), c.201.
209. An Old Dragoon, 'Suggestions for Preventing Desertion from the Army', *Colburn's,* I (1860), pp.272–4; Captain Cloane, 'Utilisation of the Soldier's Unemployed Time–a Proposed Scheme of Independent Government Supply; also a Plan for Regimental Canteens', *JRUSI,* XII (1868), pp.1–15; General Sir Richard Harrison, 'The Employment of the British Soldier in Peace–Can It Be Improved?', *Colburn's,* XVII (1898), pp.3–12; *Report on the Discipline and Management of Military Prisons,* P.P., XXVI, (c.3052), 1862, p.4.
210. Anon., 'Military Reform and Military Efficiency', *Colburn's,* III (1859), pp.317–28; Vinculum, 'Canteen Profits', *Colburn's,* XIII (1896), pp.571–80; Nemo, 'Canteen Profits', *Colburn's,* XV (1897), pp.598–601; Vinculum, 'Canteen Profits, Advantages of the Tenant System', *Colburn's,* XV (1867), pp.337–48.
211. Anon., 'Military Reform and Military Efficiency', *Colburn's,* II (1859), pp.317–28; Captain W.W. Knollys, 'The Soldier Off Duty', *Colburn's,* I (1864), pp.317–26; Anon., 'Soldiers' Garden Grounds', *Colburn's,* III (1865), pp.113–45; Captain F.G. Stone, 'Discipline: its Importance to an Armed Force and the Best Means of Promoting and Maintaining It', *JRUSI,* XXXIII (1889), pp.375–429; W.W. (A Company Officer), 'Desertion, its Cause and Prevention', *Colburn's,* V (1892), p.44; General Sir Richard Harrison, 'The Employment of the British Soldier in Peace–Can It Be Improved?', *Colburn's,* XVII (1898), pp.3–12; *The Times,* 22 Nov. 1861; Hansard, CCCXXXVII (18 June 1889), c.201.
212. *The Times,* 31 March 1862.
213. Captain E.S. Jervais, 'Recreation with Reference to the Sanitary Condition of the Army', *JRUSI,* IV (1860–1), p.385.
214. Major-General A. Montgomery Moore, 'Soldiers' Institutes', *The United Services Magazine,* IV (1891–2), p.169.
215. *Report of the Committee on the Existing Conditions under which Canteens and Regimental Institutes are Conducted,* P.P., X (c.1424), 1903, pp.vii–xi; cited hereafter as *Report on Canteens and Institutes* (1903).
216. Edmondson, *John Bull's Army,* p.150; Fortescue, *A Short Account of Canteens in the British Army,* pp.29–30.
217. Wyndham, *Following the Drum,* pp.45–6.
218. *Report on Canteens and Institutes* (1903), p.xiii.
219. Florence Nightingale to Douglas Galton, 28 Dec. 1859, 7 Oct., 5 Dec. 1860, 30 Jan. 1861, 14 Aug. 1862; Douglas Galton to Florence Nightingale, 14 Aug. 1861; Florence Nightingale to Thomas Longmore, 9 June, 26 June 1861, Nightingale MSS., 45759–60, 45773; Florence Nightingale to Earl de Grey and Ripon, 5 June, 19 Aug. 1862, Ripon MSS., 43546; *Papers Relating to Soldiers' Institutes,* P.P., XXXIII (c.332), 1863; cited hereafter as *Papers re Soldiers' Institutes* (1863); Staff Surgeon Frederick Roberts, *Cursory Remarks on Recruiting and Recruits* (1852).
220. *Report on the Soldiers' Institutes at Aldershot and Portsmouth,* P.P., XXXII (c.126), 1862, p.2.
221. Florence Nightingale to T.G. Balfour, 10 Dec. 1860; Florence Nightingale to Douglas Galton, 25 June 1861, Nightingale MSS., 45759, 45772; *Report of a Committee on the Present State and on the Improvement of Libraries, Reading Rooms, and Day Rooms,* P.P., XXXII (c.2920), 1862, pp.5–13; *Report of a Committee on the Present State and on the*

Improvement of Libraries, Reading Rooms, and Day Rooms, WO.33/10.

222. General Sir George Higginson, *Seventy-One Years of a Guards-man's Life* (1916), pp.67–70; Wood, *Midshipman to Field-Marshal,* I, pp.184 et seq; Major-General Sir George Bell, *Soldier's Glory* (1956), p.177; Erection of a Soldiers' Institute at Chatham, WO.32/6212.
223. *Papers re Soldiers' Institutes* (1863); *The Times,* 31 March 1862.
224. Florence Nightingale, Army Sanitary Administration and its Reform under the late Lord Herbert, 12 June 1862, Nightingale MSS., 43395.
225. John Sutherland to Florence Nightingale, 20 March 1871, 16 Jan. 1872, Nightingale MSS., 45755–6.
226. *Report on Canteens and Institutes* (1903), passim.
227. The importance of education in helping men to adapt to military life is underscored in studies of the post-World War II army. See Spencer, *Crime and the Services,* pp.17–18.
228. *Report of the Council of Military Education,* P.P., XXV (c.131), 1870, p.xxvii.
229. *Papers Relating to Military Bands, etc.,* P.P., XXXVII (c.128), 1857–8, pp.113–22.
230. R.J.T. Hills, *Something about a Soldier* (1934), p.143; the Duke of Cambridge, Memorandum, 20 Oct. 1887, Stanhope MSS., 1368.
231. Hardy, *Thomas Atkins,* pp.126–36. Outside the army football quickly took hold as a popular sport after 1870 and attendances at league matches rose from 2,000 to some 110,000 in thirty years. See Percy M. Young, *A History of British Football* (1968), pp.89–107, 111; John Cottrell, *A Century of Great Soccer Drama* (1970), p.23.
232. Anderson, *English Historical Review,* LXXXVI (1971), p.52.
233. John Sutherland to Florence Nightingale, 3 Sept. 1872, Nightingale MSS., 45756; W.H. Smith to the Rev George Litten, 23 Sept. 1886, Smith MSS., WO.110/5.
234. G.F.S. Daniell, *Aldershot: A Record of Mrs Daniell's Work Amongst Soldiers, and its Sequel* (1879), pp.21–38.
235. Elise Sandes, *Enlisted: or My Story* (1896), pp.51–6.
236. The Rev George Litten to W.H. Smith, 21 Sept. 1886, Smith MSS., WO.110/5.
237. Hanham, in Foot, ed., *War and Society,* p.170.
238. Hansard, CLII (4 March 1859), c.1317; WO.32/6212; Robertson, *From Private to Field-Marshal,* p.29.
239. Daniell, *Aldershot,* pp.89–114; Sandes, *Enlisted,* pp.54–6.
240. The accent on religion was strong. Elise Sandes for instance saw the goal of her institutions as providing 'A Home full of light, and gladness, and music, and free from the blasphemies and horrible songs which were polluting the air around me; a Home where these men would find warm, human hearts always ready to welcome, to help, and befriend them; a Home where they would hear of the Only One who could free them from sin, and make their lives glad, and useful, and victorious.' Sandes, op.cit., p.69. Many soldiers found the religious tone and the atmosphere of these Homes stultifying. See Horace Wyndham, *The Queen's Service* (1899), p.85; Moore, *United Services Magazine,* IV (1891–2), pp.165–9.
241. *Report on Canteens and Institutes* (1903), p.vii.
242. Hardy, *Thomas Atkins,* pp.115–25; Captain A. Hilliard Atteridge, *The British Army of Today* (1915), pp.38–9; H.S., 'The Young Soldier in India: His Life and Prospects', *Colburn's,* II (1888), pp.61–73; Whittington, *Colburn's,* IX (1894–5), pp.353–6; Colonel Henry Knollys, 'The English Soldier–As He Was and As He Is', *Blackwoods Edinburgh Magazine,*

CLVIII (1895), pp.850–65.
243. Mole, *King's Hussar,* p.179.
244. Grenville Murray, *Six Months in the Ranks;* J. Brunlees Patterson, *Life in the Ranks of the British Army* (1883), pp.134–44; Fraser, *Service Through Six Reigns,* pp.50, 95–101; Robertson, *From Private to Field-Marshal,* p.155; A.H.D. Acland-Troyte, *Through the Ranks to a Commission* (1881), Mole, op.cit., p.353; Blatchford, *My Life in the Army,* pp.100–1.
245. The potential of recreation as a drawing card for recruitment was repeatedly stressed. In 1883, for instance, recruiting pamphlets argued '. . .it may safely be said hardly in any place where young men live in ordinary employments can they have so many conveniences so easily within reach, and with so little to pay for the use of them, as they will find in barracks'. *Life in the Ranks of the English Army* (1883), p.11.
246. Hanham, in Foot, ed., *War and Society,* p.152.
247. G.R. Gleig, *Religion in the Ranks* (1855), p.7.
248. The society employed scripture readers, many of them ex-soldiers, who with official permission distributed tracts and periodicals and read bible lessons to the troops. The messages they delivered emphasised Christian behaviour, obedience to superiors, and strict abstention from alcohol. See Army Scripture Readers and Soldiers' Friend Society, *Annual Reports* (1876–80); *The British Flag and Christian Sentinel* (1871–80); *The Soldiers' and Sailors' Almanack* (1873).
249. William Harris Rule, *An Account of the Establishment of Wesleyan Methodism in the British Army* (1883), pp.72–6.
250. Colonel I. Campbell to Adjutant-General, 1 December 1850; Adjutant-General to General Fitz-Clarence, 5 December 1850; the Duke of Wellington to Fox Maule, 30 November 1850; Fox Maule to the Duke of Wellington, 1 December 1850; Panmure MSS., GD45/8/12, 45/8/20.
251. Anderson, *English Historical Review,* LXXXVI (1971), p.61–3.
252. Sir John Hay MP to W.H. Smith, 13 July 1885, Smith MSS., WO.110/1.
253. Robertson, *From Private to Field-Marshal,* p.9; Hardy, *Thomas Atkins,* p.226.
254. Robertson, op.cit., p.8.
255. Wyndham, *Queen's Service,* p.66.
256. Ackland-Troyte, *Through the Ranks,* p.39; Hardy, *Thomas Atkins,* pp.237–41; Bull, *God and our Soldiers,* pp.15, 29–34; Wyndham, *Queen's Service,* p.68.
257. The Reverend George Litten to W.H. Smith, 31 Sept. 1886, Smith MSS., WO.110/5; Reverend Maurice Jones, 'Church Parade', *Colburn's,* XV (1897), pp.651–5; Hardy, op.cit., pp.212–29.
258. The Army Temperance Association, WO.32/3998.
259. Army Temperance Association, *Report and Statement of Accounts from 6 November 1893 to 31 March 1895* (1895).
260. Hanham, in Foot, ed., *War and Society,* p.171.

4 RATE OF PAY, PENSIONS AND PROSPECTS OF POST-SERVICE EMPLOYMENT

> I think the pay is ridiculously small, it is impossible to get good or fully grown men for the pay we offer. . .Under [voluntary service] the only healthy basis upon which you can have an army is by making a man's involvements of such a nature that he will serve you willingly, any other system must be a fatal one. I think the question of recruiting for the Army turns upon money to a very large extent, and it is a very great national question, a far larger question than we in the army generally imagine it to be.
>
> Lord Wolseley

> You must not look upon the soldier as a responsible agent, for he is not able to take care of himself, he must be fed, clothed, looked after like a child and given only just enough to make him efficient as part of the great machine for War. Give him one farthing more than he really wants, and he gives way to his brutal propensities and immediately gets 'drunk'.
>
> Henry Clifford, VC

Any consideration of the manpower problems faced by the Victorian army needs to take account of the extent to which pay promised or seemed to promise financial reward or security. There were many stimuli to recruitment, nevertheless in all probability prospective recruits most immediately judged the attractions of military service in these terms. For the regular soldier the extent to which earnings could compensate for the less pleasant aspects of military service was important, and therefore it had also a bearing on the problem of discipline. The questions of army pay, career prospects, benefits for him and his family, pensions, and civilian re-employment were thus central issues both in recruitment and morale.

It is difficult to make valid comparisons between civilian and military life in regard to any other matters. For one thing there were major local wage variations in almost all civilian occupations.[1] Nevertheless it seems that even if the full value of the military wage is considered,[2] throughout the whole of the period 1856 to 1899 the army was consistently able to compete in financial terms with only the very lowest paid of civilian occupations.

1. Rank and File Pay and Perquisites

The military wage was substantially increased between 1856 and 1899, although the standard rate of army pay remained virtually unchanged. In 1856 the infantry private received 1s 1d per day, or 7s 7d per week, basic pay; in other corps wages were slightly higher.[3] In all units a few men could earn extra pay through employment as officers' servants and mess waiters, and in the artillery and engineers there was the additional opportunity of supplementing basic wages with what was known as working pay. This was essentially extra duty pay and was provided at rates up to two shillings per day for men employed at tasks which were outside normal duties, such as bridge and road construction, surveying and telegraphy.[4] Gratuities for distinguished service and special awards, such as those often given in musketry competition, were also awarded to a limited number.[5] But for the majority of rank and file good conduct pay was the principal means of supplementing their meagre stipend.

In 1856 a first good conduct badge could be earned after five years' service and each subsequent badge to a maximum of five might be awarded after further periods of five years.[6] An infantry private with twenty-five years' unblemished conduct to his record then could expect to earn, on paper at least, 1s 6d per day or 10s 6d per week. This was the best prospect most had of supplementing their wages, and between 1856 and 1899 a considerable proportion of the forces drew extra allowances for good conduct. It is clear that from 1870 on, when the first comprehensive figures are available, the proportion of men in receipt of good conduct pay varied only slightly, but there was a substantial increase in the number possessing one badge and a corresponding decrease in those possessing two or more. The periods of qualifying service were shortened several times between 1856 and 1899, but this was offset by the introduction of short-service enlistment in 1870 and the consequent decrease in the proportion of older men in the ranks.[7]

Throughout the period between 1856 and 1899, those engaged in recruitment tended to imply that minimum army pay was a clear one shilling per day.[8] Although this was true on paper, it was in reality a deception since every soldier's pay was subject to a large number of stoppages or deductions. By means of an immensely complicated book-keeping system the rank and file were credited with their basic pay plus extra emoluments, and from this the cost of goods and services was deducted. There are two explanations for this. The army's simplistic view of accounting was a carry-over from the time when regiments were contracted for separately, and were individually fitted out and maintained by their officers who claimed expenses from the government. In addition, there were considerations of recruitment; it was more appealing to advertise a daily rate of pay of one shilling and then to deduct quietly eightpence than it would have been to offer only a minimum fourpence.[9]

In the circumstances the frequency with which soldiers were disappointed and angered at receiving less than they had been led to expect was inordinately high.[10] As the century wore on army book-keeping became even more complicated with the calculation of working pay, deferred pay and messing allowances. By 1870 pressure to end any deception in enlistment had made it compulsory for potential recruits to be told clearly that the terms of service included stoppages from pay (though many recruits seem still to have believed they would get a clear shilling). Nevertheless it was not until 1902 and the report of a War Office enquiry into the subject that salary scales of the different branches of the Service were consolidated.[11] Several more years were to pass before regular stoppages for such items as messing were totally abolished.[12]

In 1856 the main stoppages were made for messing expenses, clothing and equipment replacement, washing, hair-cutting and barrack damages. If medical treatment in hospital were required or if fines were exacted for a particular disciplinary offence, further stoppages would be incurred. The weight of these regulations fell most heavily on soldiers in their first few years of military service before good conduct pay could be earned, and before the intricacies of caring for equipment and avoiding infractions of discipline could be mastered. The daily stoppage for the bread, meat and potatoes ration was fixed by 1856 at 4½d.[13] Washing and hair-cutting were normally another ½d to 1d per day and 3d per month respectively; charges for barrack damages, a considerable source of grievance since few men ever had any indication of what damages they were paying for,[14] might amount to 4d to 6d per month.[15] A few of the amenities of military service, use of the library or membership in a shooting club for instance, could run to another 3d per month each.[16] No deductions were made for rations while a man was in hospital, but a flat stoppage of 9d per day was exacted for medical expenses and this included whatever food was issued in the infirmary.

The initial clothing and equipment issue was free and at regular intervals there were subsequent issues without charge of certain uniform items such as tunics, trousers, boots and helmets, but every man was expected to maintain his own supply of underclothing, socks and cleaning materials, and to replace all other items lost, damaged or worn out before the date when they were due to be reissued.[17] At all times the uniform remained the property of the state and not of the individual wearing it. The original purpose of this rule was to prevent veterans or vagrants who might otherwise come by an old tunic from begging in uniform. In fact the authorised sale of uniforms from second-hand shops and the lack of any prohibition on the sale of militia uniforms largely circumvented these efforts.[18]

The system by which uniforms were issued was unpopular for a number of reasons. For one thing the clerical labour involved in accounting alone was enormous. Soldiers objected because under regulations they could be forced to return clothing to regimental stores and to purchase a new item when in many cases the existing item still seemed serviceable. Items of clothing of which there were free issues often did not last the required time. No credit was given for care in making uniforms last longer than required. Manoeuvres or other military exercises penalised the soldier since clothing received heavy wear which drastically shortened the life of boots, tunics, trousers and other items.[19] Although there was no lack of attention drawn to these injustices, most of the evils of the clothing issuance system persisted until beyond the end of the century.[20]

As if regulation stoppages were not enough, soldiers frequently had to contend with illegitimate charges as well. Not infrequently recruits were issued their kit with several items missing, then were placed under a heavy stoppage from their first day in the ranks to supply items for the loss of which they were not responsible.[21] Complicated book-keeping procedures placed a great deal of power in the hands of regimental paymasters, some of whom were vigilant of any opportunity to take advantage of the unwary recruit.[22]

Clearly a system which countenanced stoppages for whatever reason belied claims that the soldier was paid a clear shilling a day. At no time did the soldier see much of his daily shilling. Army regulations specified that a minimum of 1d per day was to be left after stoppages[23] and except for this many would have received nothing at all. For years after 1856 even experienced men were lucky to see 3d a day.[24] Out of this had to come any extra food, tobacco, beer, or other luxuries required. The following table serves as an illustration. In 1890 a record was kept of the stoppages paid by a group of 696 privates stationed at Aldershot; it shows the effect of legitimate stoppages alone, and their effect on the soldier's £18 5s per year.

Because it so closely involved questions of government expenditure and of recruitment, few matters concerning conditions in the army aroused as much controversy as did the issue of pay. Activated by interest in improving the lot of the rank and file, as well as by a conviction that higher pay would have a direct and beneficial effect on recruitment,[25] a strong body of opinion both within the army and without eagerly pushed for substantially more money for the soldier. A variety of schemes were put forward. A simple approach was a basic increase to the rate at which soldiers were paid. 'All reading-rooms, coffee-rooms, and bath-rooms that may be thrown open to the soldier', argued a writer in 1862, 'will not be considered equivalent to six pence a day additional pay.'[26] This view was repeatedly echoed in print[27] and in Parliament[28] during the next forty years by both soldiers and civilians, and influential officers frequently argued for a direct increase in army pay before official enquiries. In 1867 Colonel Hope Graham, Inspecting Field Officer of the London recruiting district, told the Royal Commission on Recruiting that the army was unable to compete for men because of the relatively low wages paid to soldiers.[29] In 1892 a committee on the terms and conditions of military service elicited similar views from many of the officers questioned.[30]

However, for several reasons there was a reluctance to place more money directly in the hands of the soldier. Many felt that only a very large increase in pay, entailing large public expenditure, would have any effect on recruitment.[31] Others doubtful of the soldier's abilities of self-discipline were unwilling to give him more than a few pence per day in hard cash, far less what was seen as a large amount.[32] In the circumstances alternative schemes for indirectly improving the soldier's financial position received the greatest support.

The most popular was the proposition that stoppages either be reduced or abolished altogether, thereby not only adding to the soldier's wages but eliminating as well a chief grievance and a serious bar to recruitment.[33] Lord Roberts was one of the most influential officers to take up this argument. In 1884 he had published an article in *The Nineteenth Century* in which he particularly criticised the system of stoppages as unfairly deceiving men on enlistment.[34] Eight years later when the Wantage Committee was looking into the terms and conditions of military service, Roberts wrote directly to the Secretary of State for War, Edward Stanhope, arguing for better pay and an end to all stoppages.[35] Similar views were repeatedly stressed in Parliament[36] and in the daily press.[37] Much of the evidence taken by official enquiries that touched upon the matter was equally unequivocal. Samuel Haden, Secretary of the Army and Navy Pensioners' Employment Society told the Royal Commission on Recruitment in 1866 that stoppages were one of the chief grievances in the forces and that they should be abolished as soon as possible.[38] In 1892 the majority of officers questioned by the Wantage Committee argued that a reduction in or the abolition of stoppages was essential.

Table 4–1 Stoppages from Pay at Aldershot, 1890

Average Pay £18 5d

Stoppage Item	Total Amount for 696 Men				Average Amount per Man		
Tailor's bill	£	213	17s	3d		5s	10d
Shoemaker	£	174	12s	11½d		4s	1d
Regimental necessaries	£	487	4s	8½d		14s	0d
Barrack damages	£	156	18s	7½d		4s	6d
Deficiencies in old clothing	£	92	11s	8½d		2s	8d
Washing	£	414	9s	5½d		11s	11d
Hair cutting	£	31	4s	11d			11d
Library	£	58	1s	0d		1s	8d
Fines	£	14	12s	6d			5d
Repair of arms and accoutrements	£	7	1s	2½d			2d
Other		£3,366	19s	7½d	£4	16s	13d
Total		£5,017	10s	11½d	£7	3s	13d

Source: *Return on the Total Amount of Stoppages from the Pay of Privates Stationed at Aldershot, 1890,* P.P., L (c.209), 1890–1, p.1.

A second alternative to a direct, across-the-board increase in army wages was to augment the pay of special groups of soldiers only, the men who for good behaviour, long service or the acquirement of special skills made themselves more valuable. This proposal attracted wide support. An increase in pay to veterans not only put money in the hands of more experienced and reliable and hence more useful men, but was felt to offer a considerable inducement to older soldiers to prolong their colour service and thus ease some of the army's recruiting difficulties.[39] Similarly higher pay for those who became proficient in such skills as signalling or musketry was an inducement not only for the older soldier to remain with the colours but for younger men to acquire skills necessary to the army.[40] A great effort was also aimed at reducing the amount of time required to earn good conduct pay.[41] Lieutenant-General Sir Evelyn Wood and others indicated considerable support for such reforms or for carrying them further in giving evidence before the Wantage Committee in 1892.[42]

A final scheme for indirectly improving army wages was a system of deferred payments. This called for each man's daily pay to be increased by 2d to 3d and for this amount to be held back and paid to him in a lump sum on discharge. This would discourage desertion, and give ex-servicemen a stake with which to begin a career outside the army. Destitution among ex-soldiers was often acknowledged to be a discouragement to enlistment.[43]

The financial position of the rank and file improved somewhat between 1856 and 1899, but for the most part the measures which were taken were inadequate. In the hearts of governments and politicians was an unshakeable reluctance to incur any increased military expenditure.[44] An MP discussing the virtues of deferred pay versus an overall increase to service pay before a military audience in 1891 succinctly phrased the mood of Parliament. 'Having some knowledge of the present tone and temper of the House of Commons,' he argued, 'I do not believe that any Minister, except under the pressure of a very great and threatening national emergency, would venture to propose any large addition to the army estimates.'[45] Within the army itself there was also some reluctance to trust the soldier with more money,[46] some conviction that an increase in the amount of available money of the size which might reasonably be expected would be insufficient to do any good,[47] that an increase in pay of any size was not in any case the solution to the army's difficulties, and a certain degree of complacency.[48] The Duke of Cambridge's objections were typical of those of many senior officers. 'It would not be wise to add to the soldier's pay,' he argued in 1892, 'it is a very doubtful benefit and it is better to avoid it if we can.'[49]

The first step in increasing army pay was small and indirect. In 1860 the regulations for good conduct pay were revised so that a first badge could be earned after three years with subsequent badges up to a maximum of eight available on good behaviour every five years thereafter.[50] While this measure was of some benefit to the enlisted man, it had little effect on recruitment, and continued shortages of men forced a reappraisal of all the conditions of service within a few years. The Royal Commission appointed in 1866 was presented with a splendid opportunity to reform all aspects of service pay. It recommended a not very bold pay increase of 2d per day, an extra 1d per day for all men on re-enlistment, and the elimination of all stoppages.[51] When a War Office Committee later that same year cut down these recommendations reaction was limited.[52] Extra pay of 2d daily plus 1d on re-enlistment was enacted in 1867, but the ruinous system of stoppages was left untouched.[53] What was offered, complained *The Saturday Review,* 'was not radical improvement so much as a mere tightening of the screws'.[54] *Fraser's Magazine* warned that in the light of the recent successes of the Prussian army much broader changes were imperative.[55] *Colburn's United Services Magazine* also protested that 'the question in reality is one of remuneration. . .of money; and as long as the position of the classes from which recruits are drawn continues to improve, so it will remain'.[56]

In 1870 one aspect of Cardwell's deal for the regular soldier was an increase in daily pay. Both Cardwell and Gladstone recognised the connection between the state of the labour market and recruitment, and each appreciated the importance of attractive financial inducements.[57] Gladstone promised that 'the wages of the day would pay the work of the day',[58] but believed that large expenditure was out of the question, and that funds allocated in one direction had to be compensated for if possible by savings in another.[59] In the end the basic bread, meat and potatoes ration became free, thus abolishing the 4½d daily stoppage; the requirements for good conduct badges were again revised so they might be earned after two, six, twelve, eighteen, twenty-three and twenty-eight years' service;[60] and the amount stopped for medical care was reduced from 9d to 7d daily. Some compensatory saving was achieved by abolishing the soldier's allowance for beer and by removing the extra 2d per day granted in 1867.[61] Attempts to cancel the re-engagement penny, that is the increase in pay given upon re-enlistment for a second term, were only thwarted by opposition from Northbrook and others at the War Office.[62]

The extent of these reforms was not considered satisfactory. Pressure for more concessions mounted, and in 1875 a War Office committee, to ease predicted recruiting difficulties, urged deferred pay as one means of making the army more attractive.[63] Gathorne Hardy, who had succeeded Cardwell at the War Office, seized upon this recommendation and in 1876 it was introduced. Twopence deferred pay per day was credited for up to twelve years of service.[64] It was calculated that this offered the soldier the prospect of a lump sum of £21 after seven years' service, enough to make a start in civilian life.[65] There was yet another revision downward of the requirements for good conduct pay at this time.[66]

As a result of all these changes net pay (what was left after regulation deductions) had been more than doubled in the twenty years from 1856, but it was still manifestly insufficient to attract enough good recruits, and in the last decades of the century this was repeatedly emphasised by senior army officers.[67] 'The only true method of maintaining an army by voluntary enlistment', General Sir Lintorn Simmons argued, 'is to make it popular. . .It is neither fair nor right to expect young men to make such sacrifices while giving them less wages than they can earn in civil life coupled with perfect freedom and the power to change their employers whenever they like.'[68] To compare the soldier's pay '. . .with that of the ordinary labourer', charged Lord Wolseley, 'is to compare two things which have absolutely no relevance to each other. . .As long as we pay men as badly as we do, we must take anybody we can get'.[69]

However, in 1885 the War Office turned down proposals to assist soldiers by sponsoring cheaper railway fares.[70] In 1890, the existing clothing regulations were maintained unchanged in the face of proposals that all clothing should become the property of the soldier, and that there might be a special clothing allowance.[71] These were signs of the growing strength of conservatism.

About this time deferred pay, which had been adopted in 1876, became a centre of controversy. It had attracted considerable support,[72] and it had proved very popular among soldiers of all ranks, but many senior officers began to argue that the promise of a large sum of money on completion of the first term of service acted to discourage men from re-engaging for a further period,[73] that it had failed to prevent desertion, and that once they had received it, many ex-soldiers contrived to spend it on a spree and in no time at all were left destitute.[74] The Wantage Committee in 1892 helped to polarise the debate, and it was clear that even many of those who supported increasing the soldier's wages were becoming opposed to deferred pay.[75]

The Committee had again to grapple with the whole problem of pay. It recommended the substitution of gratuities of £1 for each year of service in place of deferred pay; the abolition of all stoppages; the raising of service pay to the market rate for unskilled labour; a further downward revision of the requirements for good conduct badges and the modification of clothing regulations to ensure that all uniform items lasted the required period and that used clothing became the property of the soldier.[76] The War Office representative on the Committee, Under-Secretary of State Sir Arthur Haliburton, issued a minority report every bit as lengthy, which opposed these recommendations. When the Report was published, Stanhope, the Secretary of State for War, was angered by many of the opinions expressed, and a number of the senior officers who had testified, under some pressure, either retracted or qualified their evidence.[77] In the end only the recommendations for the issue of clothing were acted upon.[78]

Until the end of our period therefore the soldier's financial position remained precarious and very little changed. In 1898 deferred pay was abolished in favour of a messing allowance and a gratuity of £1 per year of service. This brought the infantry private's basic pay to 1s 3d daily before stoppages. The army took the opportunity in 1902 to simplify its rates of pay,[79] but it was not unil 1904 with the report of the Royal Commission on the War in South Africa that real efforts were begun to increase pay and to eliminate finally regular stoppages.[80] Autumn manoeuvres of 1896 brought complaints about the excessive wear and tear on uniforms which soldiers were required to bear, and arguments favouring the more frequent issue of clothing and the introduction of clothing allowances were repeated.[81] Not until the introduction of a working dress and the standardisation of the uniform after 1900, however, was there any progress made towards a more equitable system of clothing the army.[82]

Comparison of military and civilian wage rates highlights the relatively poor position in which the soldier was placed before 1900. In general, while army pay was rising, national prosperity, industrial expansion, action by trade unions and the scarcity of labour in rural areas due to massive migration to the cities helped to produce a significant rise in working-class incomes. Furthermore, a substantial fall in retail prices throughout the whole of the country boosted real wages. As A.L. Bowley has shown, consumer prices peaked around 1874, by 1889 had dropped to the pre-Crimean War level, and by 1900 had sunk even lower.[83] Though, of course, in making these generalisations, allowances must be made for the fact that gains in real wages were not evenly distributed among different income groups and occupations, and that there were large regional variations in incomes, rents and retail prices.

Unlike the civilian, the soldier could not readily change his profession short of deserting or completing his term of service, nor was he able to influence to any great extent the conditions of his service. The fall in retail prices left him largely unaffected since food, clothing and lodging were all provided by the forces. The graph in Figure I compares the rise or fall in prices and wages in Britain and in the cash

Figure I Comparison between the Increase in Civilian and Military Wage Rates and the Drop in Retail Prices, 1850–1900*

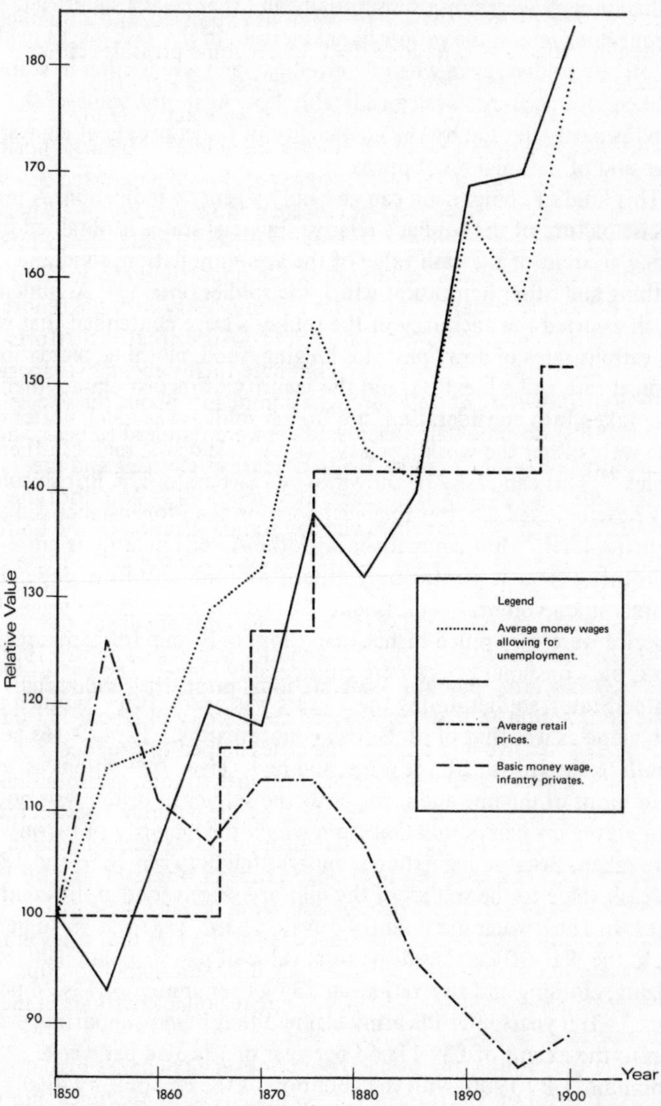

* Military and civilian wages were not equal in 1850, but are pegged at 100 for the purpose of plotting relative changes.

Source: B.R. Mitchell, *Abstract of British Historical Statistics* (1971), pp.343–4.

wages of the private soldier, 1850 to 1900. The relative increase over fifty years in each case is most important. The graph shows that while civilian money wages rose substantially and there was a significant drop in consumer prices, the proportional increase in the cash wages paid to the private soldier, even when deferred pay and a reduction in stoppages is taken into account, was considerably less. Again the value of the graph is partly limited by the artificiality of the concepts of an average wage and of national retail prices.

This kind of comparison can give only a general indication. A more precise picture of the soldier's relative financial status is obtained by taking account of the cash value of the accommodation, food and clothing and other perquisites which the soldier obtained. Arguments which asserted the adequacy of the soldier's wage contended that when the various rates of army pay plus lodging, food, clothing, recreation, medical care and education, and the security of regular employment were taken into consideration, the British soldier was much better off than were either the working classes as a whole or the men of other armies.[84] This can easily be shown to be inaccurate. The British soldier may have enjoyed a better financial position than for instance did the French soldier,[85] but comparison with the American army is more appropriate since it was the only other major military force dependent entirely upon voluntary enlistment. On the whole industrial wages in America were very much higher than those in Britain for comparable work, but consumer prices were considerably higher. The pay of the United States' soldier during these years was nearly twice as much in cash alone as was that of his British counterpart, £2 12s–£2 16s per month to the British £1 15s gross, and he received free rations as well.[86]

In terms of income and living costs the soldier in Britain was poor *vis à vis* the civilian population from which the majority of recruits were taken. Because regulation stoppages fell between 1856 and 1899, the cash value to the soldier of the military wage varied at different times. In 1867 when the infantry private's basic wage was 7s 7d per week, the War Office placed the total value of pay, fuel and light, lodging, clothing and free rations at £34 4s per annum or 13s 2d per week.[87] Ten years later the army claimed that it was supporting each man to the extent of £39 11s 6d per year or 13s 3¼d per week minimum.[88] By 1900, with the abolition of the compulsory 4½d stoppage for groceries this amount would be at the most £41 9s 1d per annum or 15s 10¾d per week.[89]

We have only the army's word for it that their contribution was as much as claimed. In 1867 for example, at least 2s 2d of the 13s 2d per week was fixed as clothing, rations and medical costs. Since the soldier had to pay for many of these items himself, it is questionable how much of this was actually borne by the army. The same criticism must apply to later estimates of the value of the military wage.

Even if army calculations are accepted as approximately true, there is a second problem which arises from the difficulty in accurately estimating comparable civilian wages and the effect of price increases or decreases. Wages varied considerably from area to area at any given time, and within each area there were major variations as well. Neither did the cost of living vary enough to offset these differences. Since most soldiers were unskilled or at best semi-skilled labourers by occupation, it is with them that comparison should be made. The army recruited heavily from both rural and urban areas and since conditions in each were different, they must be treated separately. Valid comparisons can be made as well with the police, whose terms of service closely resembled those of the army.

The army had firm ideas as to what constituted a comparable civilian wage. In 1867 its claim that the soldier was better off than the civilian worker was based on the calculation that the yearly wage of the lowest paid agricultural labourer in England, Scotland and Ireland was £30, £33 14s and £18 9s respectively.[90] Allowing for regional variations, this is approximately confirmed by what is known of wages at the time.[91] However, the military wage was not significantly greater than rural wages paid in England and Scotland, and it can be argued, therefore, that only the Irish farm worker was worse off financially. Between 1867 and 1900 average farm wages in Britain varied but on the whole they kept pace with or even overtook army salaries.[92] Perquisites in kind rather than in cash continued to be an important source of income.[93] Only the wages paid to Irish farm labourers continued to lag, although as we shall see, even this reservoir was drying up due to the attractions of immigration and the prospect of higher salaries in Britain and America.

Comparison between the military wage and industrial wages in Britain between 1856 and 1899 make it even clearer how poor was the soldier's relative financial position. This is especially significant given, as we shall see, that during these years the army was attracting recruits from urban areas in increasing proportions. In 1867 the War Office calculated that wages for unskilled labourers in the major cities varied from £39 3s to £49 per annum.[94] Even by their own admission, therefore, the military wage was outclassed. This same argument holds true throughout the remainder of the century. The army might claim to be supporting the infantry private to the amount of at the most 16s-17s per week (including some good conduct pay) between 1856 and 1900, but the wages of the urban working class rose significantly during these years and at no time were army salaries competitive. The average weekly wage of unskilled labourers in London rose from 21s 2d in 1861 to 29s 2d in 1899. During the same period, the average weekly wage paid to bricklayers (semi-skilled workers), rose from 33s to 41s 8d.[95] There were of course considerable variations in wages from region to region at any time and wages may have been slightly lower in the provinces, but these figures were not abnormal.

Many of the conditions of service experienced by policemen were similar to those of soldiers, and their respective financial positions were often compared by contemporaries. Like the soldier, the policeman enlisted for a long period, unless married lived in barracks, and was part of a uniformed disciplined body.[96] The wages paid to police constables varied considerably from county to borough and from area to area,[97] however it is clear from Parliamentary returns, from the reports of inspectors of constabulary, and from the evidence given by police officers before committees of enquiry, that the police constable was on the whole very much better paid than the soldier between 1856 and 1899. In 1857 constables in England and Wales received 16s to 21s per week depending on their length of service and the forces with which they were employed.[98] By 1876 the lowest minimum pay for a trained policeman in any part of Britain seems to have been 20s per week.[99] In 1899, minimum pay in some cases was no higher, but in most instances it reached 23s per week or more.[100]

In addition to basic salaries, it was common throughout the period to provide a certain number of allowances, and this in many areas like Scotland and Ireland may have helped to compensate for lower wages. Perquisites often included free uniforms or a clothing allowance, free accommodation, fuel and lighting, and in some cases food allowances.[101] With this taken into account, it is clear, as contemporaries were aware, that at no time between 1856 and 1899 did the soldier's financial position compare at all favourably with that of the British policeman.

In spite of its apparent inadequacy, the value of the military wage was heavily stressed in recruiting advertisements.[102] A pamphlet published in 1901 optimistically argued 'If every ambitious young man really knew all that life in the Army offered him, there would be no need for the recruiting sergeant'.[103] Yet clearly for those who could hope for regular employment there could be no attraction to army wages. 'You cannot get, or expect to get, respectable men to enter the service upon the wages of a shilling a day', a colonel argued in 1874, 'when a common mechanic can earn from three to five shillings. . .Let the country and the authorities stave it off as long as they may, the increase must ultimately come, and the day is not far off.'[104] By 1900 no significant increase had come, and without exaggeration reformers could claim that the relative position of the soldier had only declined since the time of Cromwell.[105] When regular employment was available, they asked who would 'give up their liberty' and subject themselves to rigid military discipline for 15s a week? Only those to whom the army appealed for other than financial reasons.[106]

This was certainly true, although it ignores one of the realities of recruitment, and a sobering fact about British society. A large proportion of each year's recruits signed on for the money and the security the army offered. The reason for this was that not all nor even the majority of the men whom the army attracted could have reasonably hoped for permanent employment elsewhere. In fact a significant proportion of the lower social classes were either temporarily or irregularly employed. In 1891 Charles Booth estimated that over 30 per cent of the people in the working-class areas he visited in London were living below the poverty line as he defined this, many of them unskilled labourers, and their families, in irregular work.[107] Seebohm Rowntree calculated that of a population of 75,812 in York in 1899, nearly 50 per cent of all families were living on a combined income of 30s or less a week. He also estimated that 15.5 per cent of the working class in that city were living in a state of 'primary poverty' in which earnings were insufficient to provide the food, shelter and clothing to maintain 'physical efficiency' – these people's calorific intake was below what was required to perform the tasks of their work and daily lives.[108] In rural areas, seasonal employment and low wages could mean poverty just as severe.[109] For men in such circumstances the army offered secure employment, and to them the pay, food, clothing and accommodation must have been attractive.[110] This assured the army of a limited pool of recruits, but no more. Any attempts to broaden the bases of recruitment would be cut short by the army's inability to compete with civilian wages.

2. Promotion and Its Advantages

The limited pay which the soldier received was somewhat compensated for by opportunities for promotion within the lower ranks of the army. There was a number of conditions for advancement. Enlisted men had first of all to satisfy superior officers of their abilities to perform the duties required. Judgements in these instances were normally based on length of prior service, conduct and estimates of ability. A second criterion was introduced in 1861 when, as we have seen, educational qualifications for promotion beyond lance-corporal were instituted. In the last decade of the century professional examinations requiring a knowledge of drill, weaponry and other procedures were introduced. The institution of these formal requirements was objected to by officers because of the restrictions they placed on their choice of NCOs.[111] However, selection remained with the officers of the regiment, and standards were low enough to be achieved by most soldiers willing to make the effort.[112] The prospects of advancement were such that it was reckoned that a well-behaved man could take his first step upward in five years, and within ten years reach the rank of sergeant,[113] but after the introduction of short-service enlistment in 1870 the turnover among NCOs became so much more rapid that in fact a first promotion could be expected after just two years.[114]

The chances of those actively seeking promotion were also boosted by the refusal of others to accept it. Few demands were made upon the private soldier, and although his pay was certainly meagre, his expenses were limited and his position was secure. In the circumstances it often happened that men shied away from a promotion which meant added responsibility and expense. Short-service enlistment also encouraged men to look upon military service as a temporary career, and many were thus unwilling to alter their uncomplicated status as a private soldier.[115] Finally, it is clear that the frequent tinkering by the War Office with the terms of service made soldiers unsure of what their pension rights were; of their right to re-engage if this was what they wanted, and of their duty as regards reserve service. All this uncertainty produced some reluctance to give up comparative security for the indefinite consequences of accepting a stripe.[116]

The necessity of a strong cadre of good NCOs was a concern of those involved with the welfare and the functioning of the army. Not only was the non-commissioned officer the link between officer and rank and file and the man upon whom much of the functioning of discipline depended, but the degree of attractiveness of his position could be an inducement or a discouragement to recruitment.[117] The pay and position of the NCO therefore became something of a *cause célèbre* after 1856. Concern to improve these was expressed in Parliament, the press, and in many of the committees of enquiry into army matters.[118]

Rates of pay varied with rank and branch of service and NCOs were subject to the same stoppages as rank and file. Between 1856 and 1899, their net pay increased as stoppages were reduced.[119] In addition basic pay was augmented. In 1856 corporals earned 1s 4d per day; sergeants 2s–3s 2d.[120] By 1900, daily pay had risen to 1s 8d–2s 8d and to 2s–5s respectively.[121] A special problem existed for the ranks of the lance-corporals and lance-sergeants.[122] Until 1892 men appointed to these positions drew the same pay as the rank below them, although they were of course required to perform extra duties.

In addition to facing the normal regulation stoppages covering such items as food and clothing, NCOs often found it necessary to pay men to clean their equipment and to carry out other duties for them.[123] Lance-sergeants were expected to join the sergeants' mess and to meet the expenses this entailed.[124] Non-commissioned officers were granted deferred pay with the rest of the army in 1876, but ranks above lance-corporal were not given good conduct pay,[125] and the soldier with several good conduct badges therefore often faced a loss in accepting promotion.

Secondment to special duties in a military department at the War Office allowed a few NCOs to supplement their pay each year. Approximately one thousand men annually were employed in this capacity on salaries ranging up to 7s per day. In 1881 the rank of warrant officer with a salary of 5s to 5s 10d per day was created after repeated pressure for an improvement in the position of the non-commissioned officer[126] and specific recommendations by a parliamentary committee on army reorganisation.[127] Attention was also drawn at this time to the matter of extra pay for lance-corporals and lance-sergeants,[128] but it was not until after the Wantage Committee in 1892 that extra pay of 2d or more daily was granted.[129]

In spite of the financial losses which could be incurred at least initially, promotion appealed to many enlisted men. NCOs not only drew higher wages but occupied a position of responsibility and prestige in the regiment and enjoyed the advantage of a comfortable life and the luxury of private messing facilities.[130] In addition, while permission to marry was restricted in the lower ranks, it was a privilege open to all warrant officers and staff sergeants and to 50 per cent of all other sergeants.[131] The opportunities for advancement within a particular line of work were rarely as high in civilian life, where chances to rise high in the economic scale and to transcend even class barriers came very infrequently to working-class men. Civilians could become geographically if not socially mobile, and could change occupations for higher wages and better working conditions, but there was not much vertical social and economic mobility within a trade or type of work.

If the opportunities for promotion within the lower ranks of the army were considerable, there was nevertheless a limit to how far a man could reasonably expect to rise. The chances of securing a commission from the ranks were slim, and remained so throughout the whole of our period. It was claimed at times that deserving NCOs were being commissioned at a high rate but in fact this was far from the truth.[132] Troop Sergeant-Major Edwin Mole after twenty years of service knew of only seven men in his regiment who received a commission and even then usually in unusual circumstances in which they had been favoured by luck and chance.[133] Other accounts of military service convey the same impression. 'Rising from the ranks can scarcely be called an attraction', an officer wrote in 1906, 'The prospect is too remote, and is probably not considered by one in 10,000 who enlist.'[134] Several years earlier another soldier remarked:

> There are hundreds of well-educated and intelligent non-commissioned officers who have perhaps ventured life and limb in their country's service, and who have a practical knowledge of their profession, yet they have about as much chance of getting a commission as Count Bismarck has of being elected President of the French Republic.[135]

There were two different types of first commissions available: as riding-master or quarter-master, and as second lieutenant (subaltern). The former were normally reserved for deserving NCOs and were the most common, although they were in fact an end-of-the-line promotion offering little prospect of any further advancement.[136] The available statistics of the number of NCOs commissioned do not cover the whole period from 1856 to 1899 systematically, but they indicate how restricted were opportunities, and how few actually did obtain a regular commission, especially as a lieutenant rather than a riding- or quarter-master. The following table shows the total number commissioned from the ranks during certain years between 1854 and 1898. The years 1854 to 1856 were somewhat exceptional because of the large number of active service commissions granted during the Crimean War.

These figures need to be placed in the context of the total number of commissions granted. Table 4–3 compares the number of NCOs and others commissioned as second lieutenants in the infantry and cavalry cavalry between 1871 and 1893. Table 4–4 breaks down some of these figures even further, and contrasts the number and type of commissions from the ranks with those from other sources.

Table 4–2 The Number of Men Commissioned from the Ranks During Selected Years, 1854–98

Year	Number of Men Commissioned from the Ranks
1854–6	252
1860–3	94
1880–4	58
1886–8	149
1889–90	119
1891–2	146
1893–4	143
1895–6	167
1897–8	127

Source: *Return of the Names of All NCOs of the Army Who Were Promoted to Commissions While Serving in the Field With the Army of the East, 1 May 1854–1 August 1856,* P.P., XXVII (c.188), 1857–8; *Return of All NCOs Who Received Commissions in the Army 1861–1863,* P.P., XXXII (c.495), 1863; *Return of All Officers Commissioned from the Ranks since 31 January 1880,* P.P., XLIV (c.90), 1884–5; *Return of Commissions from the Ranks, 1886–1888,* Official War Office Papers of General Viscount Wolseley, W. 18; *Return of the Commissions Granted During Each of the Years 1885 to 1898 Inclusive,* P.P., LII (c.281), 1899.

These statistics show clearly that the opportunities open to NCOs to obtain a commission, especially one which would offer prospect of future advancement, were seriously limited throughout the whole of the period. Neither the 6 per cent commissioned as second lieutenants in 1886–7 nor the 13.9 per cent commissioned in 1894 are significant given that other armies, such as the French, obtained one-third or more of their officers from the ranks.[137]

What were the reasons for this lack of opportunity? Since it is unlikely that there was any shortage of NCOs capable of performing the duties required,[138] explanations must lie in the other criteria by which officers were chosen. Throughout the whole of the nineteenth century and up until the South African War at least commissioned rank remained almost exclusively the preserve of the upper levels of society. Good family, a public school education and financial independence continued even after the abolition of purchase in 1871 to be stressed as the requisite qualities of an officer.[139] The social gap between officer and enlisted man was one of the widest in Britain.[140] Promotion from the ranks was actively discouraged on grounds that the men concerned would be unable to transcend the social gulf and to operate effectively in a new social milieu,[141] and that they would be unable to afford the personal and family expenses that such a move would entail.[142] It was frequently argued as well that the working classes lacked the moral training and experience necessary for a commissioned officer.[143] 'In twenty years regimental service with the army', wrote Lieutenant-General Gray, aide-de-camp to Queen Victoria, 'I never knew an officer who had come up from the ranks who was not a mistake.'[144] Others claimed that the soldier preferred officers who were true gentlemen, unacquainted incidentally with all the tricks and dodges that were the stock and trade of the rank and file.[145] Promotion of men from the ranks, continued this argument, resulted only in jealousy, discord, and discontent among the lower ranks.[146]

Table 4–3 The Number of Men Commissioned from the Ranks as Second Lieutenants and the Number of Commissions from other Sources, 1871–93

	Number Commissions from the Ranks		Number Commissions to Gentlemen from Other Sources				
Year	Cavalry	Infantry	Cavalry	Infantry	Unattached	Total	Percent from the Rank
1871–2	–	–	41	113	–	144	–
1874–5	4	5	32	209	197	447	2.0
1877–8	1	5	31	237	–	274	2.2
1880–1	9	4	48	444	–	505	2.6
1883–4	3	7	48	300	–	358	2.8
1886–7	8	22	59	409	–	498	6.0
1889–90	2	16	57	396	–	471	3.8
1892–3	4	11	77	447	–	539	2.8
Total 1871–93	98	195	1,183	7,594	532	9,602	3.1

Source: *Return of the Number of First Commissions (Exclusive of Quarter-Masters and Riding-Masters)*, P.P., LII (c.189), 1893–4.

The argument that the rank and file preferred gentlemen as their officers is difficult to substantiate, though certainly wide sectors of British society up until the First World War, at least, exhibited a traditional respect for the upper classes. In the army, A.H.D. Ackland-Troyte, a gentleman ranker, experienced preferential treatment from

Table 4–4 The Number and Type of Commissions from the Ranks and of Commissions From Other Sources, 1885–98.

Year	Number Commissions from the Ranks as				Number Commissions to Gentlemen from Other Sources	Total Commissions Awarded	Percent from the Ranks
	Second Lieutenant	Quarter-Master	Riding-Master	Total			
1885	32	63	6	101	754	855	11.8
1888	41	20	5	66	622	688	9.6
1891	21	46	2	69	584	653	10.6
1894	28	49	5	82	507	589	13.9
1897	9	41	7	57	663	720	7.9
1898	14	53	3	70	744	814	8.6
Total 1885–98	343	597	56	996	8,584	9,580	10.4

Source: *Return of the Number of Commissions Granted During Each of the Years 1885 to 1898 Inclusive,* P.P., LIII (c.281), 1899.

officers and men because of his background.[147] Slightly before the beginning of our period Rifleman Harris wrote, 'I know from experience that in *our* army the men like best to be officered by gentlemen, men whose education has rendered them more kind in manners than your coarse officer, sprung from obscure origin, and whose style is brutal and overbearing.'[148] Others expressed similar views. Recalling his experiences in the Boer War, another soldier remarked, 'What officers we had then, gentlemen a soldier could look up to with respect and admiration.'[149] There may therefore have been some basis to this argument, but how much it is impossible to say. It is clear that at the same time much of the army was coming increasingly to recognise the value of ability and professional skill in its officers, and this was reflected in the same views of the rank and file. Ex-sergeant Horace Wyndham argued, 'When he is facing the enemy the average private would much rather follow an intelligent lance-corporal than somebody who is all blue blood and no brains.'[150]

It was not too uncommon for men to enlist with the intention of gaining a commission, but few succeeded.[151] Many of those who did were Kipling's 'gentlemen-rankers', with the money and the social position to back their aspirations and thus frequently obtained their first commission within two years of enlistment.[152] No precise figures are available, but a fair proportion of NCOs commissioned each year must have been of this type.[153]

The path to commissioned rank for the man with neither the funds nor the social position to support him was a much more difficult one. Without special recommendation from his commanding officer, his case could not even be considered.[154] Even then he had to have a first-class certificate of education and demonstrate more skill and ability than possessed by the average officer who came into the army directly from public school.[155]

If successful in gaining a commission, the ex-NCO faced a difficult life ahead. Promotional examinations within commissioned rank often required the type of education acquired at a public school and not infrequently money and connections.[156] In the circumstances few promoted NCOs rose beyond the rank of captain.[157] The exigencies of military service were such that private means were almost essential. Only by extreme economy could an officer exist on his army salary, and even then the sole alternative to financial embarrassment might be to transfer to Indian service where expenses were less.[158] If he were unlucky he might be completely ostracised by his fellow officers because of the social gap that existed between them and his inability to conform fully to the customs of the regiment.[159] Even his family could be made to feel such restrictions, and if the worst came to the worst, he might be driven from the battalion. A regular officer, B. de Sales la Terriere, recalled

> If a chap wasn't wanted, and didn't suit, he was generally told so, politely but firmly, and also that he'd better make arrangements to go to another regiment. . .but if he took no notice, life in the regiment was made so hot for him that he was glad to clear out to save his skin. He was never allowed to go to sleep, except in a wet bed; everything he possessed was broken up; and he sometimes found himself in the horse-trough to cool his brain. I remember one chap who wouldn't go, and he was shut up in a room full of hay, which got alight, and he was then put in a horse-trough to put the fire out. He was a very bad case, a shocking cad, who joined with a wife off the streets, and with whom, it would have been impossible to live.[160]

Because he rose to such a high position in the army and played such an important role during the First World War, Field-Marshal Sir William Robertson's account of service through the ranks is the most widely known and perhaps the most frequently quoted. He was extremely fortunate in being openly accepted by his brother officers, but as his biographer notes,

> Social barriers. . .were the real crux, because they were intangible and spiritually overwhelming. A true ranker could never disguise his origin. He was continually being given away by his accent, tastes, habits, jokes, relations, friends (or lack of them), enforced parsimony, or whatever.[161]

Robertson himself wrote,

> For some years. . .I had cherished the hope of obtaining a commission, but. . .there seemed no more chance of this hope being realised than of obtaining the moon. Apart from riding-masters and quarter-masters it was very seldom that anyone was promoted from the ranks. . .I had no private means and without some £300 a year in addition to army pay it was impossible to live as an officer in a cavalry regiment at home. . .The ranker was not as welcome to the officers of a regiment as before, and the financial obstacle seemed

insurmountable.[162]

On their part, many NCOs were either aware that they could not handle the demands of a new life or were unwilling because of the difficulties involved and the meagre reward promised to go any further.[163] Troop Sergeant-Major Edwin Mole for instance, after weighing the advantages and disadvantages, strongly advised enlisted men to stop at the sergeants' mess.[164]

However, a substantial number of influential soldiers and civilians advocated increasing promotion from the ranks as an inducement to recruitment[165] and as a reward for ability.[166] Some, like Sir Charles Trevelyan, who was involved in establishing competitive examinations for the civil service, saw the army as a last major institution with its doors barred to the middle class.[167] In spite of these pressures, however, the War Office was unwilling to take much action. Nothing was done to augment the career prospects of the quarter-master and the riding-master or more than minimally to improve their financial position.[168] Repeated appeals for an increase in officers' pay to assist less wealthy men in obtaining a commission fell on deaf ears.[169] Military service continued to be regarded as an upper-class profession and keeping salaries low was a method of discouraging those without private means. As Brian Bond has noted, although

> . . .the British Army in the second half of the nineteenth century reduced the influence of wealth and social position and substituted objective educational tests for entry and a regularised system for professional advancement, at the same time it succeeded to a remarkable degree in preserving an essentially eighteenth century mode of life and in excluding all but a handful of officers from the lower-middle and working classes.[170]

3. The Problems of Discharge

One of the advantages of military service was security of tenure. Unless discharged for misbehaviour or for illness, soldiers could look forward to the full period of service for which they had enlisted. Engagements could be extended under certain circumstances, but twenty-one years was the normal maximum. In 1847 regulations permitted minimum service of eleven years and in 1870 this was shortened further to six (later seven) years. Large numbers of course left the forces every year, some after the full period of colour service, others after considerably less. Military records show that between 1861 and 1898 a total of

511,673 men were discharged from the army, an average of 13,465 per year. In addition 288,188 men (8,153 per year) were sent to the reserve.[171]

There was a number of circumstances under which soldiers were released from the army. These were on completion of an agreed term of service; as invalids no longer fit for duty; after having purchased a discharge or having been granted a free one;[172] and finally for misconduct. No attempts were made to help men in these latter two categories, but there was a number of provisions to assist both the man who had completed his term of service and the invalid to return to civilian life. One was deferred pay which, as we have seen, was introduced in 1876. Another was reserve pay. The Limited Enlistment Act of 1870 provided for a short period of colour service supplemented by a period of duty with the reserve. While under obligation for reserve service, each ex-serviceman was paid a retaining fee of 4d per day. Those who were invalided from the forces or who had completed the maximum period with the colours were not liable to serve with the reserve, but for this category of men some medical and institutional care and temporary and permanent pensions were provided. A final contribution to resettlement was in assistance in re-employment. Limited efforts were made by government and by a number of private agencies to help all those discharged with a good character regardless of length of service to find employment either in government departments or in the private sector.

Institutional care was provided for a limited number of ageing ex-servicemen in two large military hospitals located in Chelsea and in Dublin. Any ex-soldier in receipt of a permanent pension might apply for residence if he had no dependants.[173] The two institutions had facilities for approximately 500 and 150 in-pensioners respectively, and together were prepared to admit about 200 annually. Their restrictive military regimes created a certain amount of unpopularity, and most ex-servicemen preferred if possible to look after themselves.[174] Applications for admission each year exceeded the number of vacancies only slightly, and this gave rise to suggestions that the hospitals might be closed. This was avoided because it was argued closure would mean either setting up some other system of medical care or sending hundreds of men into workhouses.[175]

Pensions originated in the seventeenth century as compensation for illness or injury contracted in the line of duty (an alternative to hospitalisation) and a reward for long and valuable service. Disability pensions were awarded on the discretion of the Board of Commissioners of the Royal Hospital, Chelsea.[176] Throughout the nineteenth century they were granted either to soldiers invalided for sickness or injury caused directly by their military service, or to men with a minimum of fourteen years' service who were discharged for medical reasons not attributable to the exigencies of their duty. It was the practice to give permanent pensions only to those who had spent fourteen or more years with the colours and whose invalidity was a result of their military service. In other cases the Chelsea Commissioners determined the duration of the pension as well as its size. The normal rates for invalidity incurred as a result of service varied from 8d to 2s per day for privates and up to 3s per day for sergeants, depending on the nature and extent of the disability. For illness which was not a result of military duties, and if the minimum fourteen years had been served, pensions of 7d to 9d per day (9d–1s 3d for sergeants) might be awarded.[177]

The inadequacies of such a system are obvious. One of the principal reasons for the procedure of medical discharge was to get rid as soon as possible of the men unable to perform their duties. In many instances disability due to military service could not be proved and soldiers were invalided from the forces unable to look after themselves and without a penny a day to help them in civilian life. Between 1893 and 1898 for instance, nearly one-third of the more than 3,000 men who received a medical discharge from the army were left with no compensation for their military service.[178] Even where pensions were awarded they were often inadequate, in many cases insufficient to support a semi-invalid, let alone a man with a family to care for. In other instances pensions were only temporary. There is little evidence on the whole of much improvement between 1856 and 1899. Before the beginning of the period Rifleman Harris was discharged half-blind from the Service on 6d a day. A.F. Corbett, a veteran of the South African War, left the army blind in one eye from fever with a pension 'from a grateful country' of only 9d per day. There are many other instances of similar treatment in War Office files and in official correspondence. In 1871 a soldier who had served ten years and had earned two good conduct badges was discharged with ulcers on a pension of 8d per day for two and a half years. In 1875 a sergeant discharged for ill health after nearly nineteen years' service received the small sum of 1s 2d per day for three years.[179]

Permanent long service pensions were awarded to every soldier who had completed the maximum period of service with the colours. The size of the pension varied with the length of service over twenty-one years and with the soldier's rank. As was the case with disability pensions, service pensions were often inadequate. Many servicemen had difficulty finding employment after leaving the army, and with a family to provide for, a small pension could hardly be expected to meet their needs.[180] Normal rates started at 8d to 1s 6d per day for a private and ran to as high as 3s per day for a top sergeant.[181] Complicated army regulations limited the effectiveness of pensions even further. The warrant providing for service pensions was so complex that few men knew accurately where they stood.[182] Although a minimum of twenty-one years' service was required, the qualifying service for a pension was reckoned after re-engagement for a second term (privates) or by the number of years served as a non-commissioned officer. Service towards pensions was lost by desertion, fraudulent enlistment, a court-martial conviction, or forfeiture of pay due to imprisonment.[183]

For the most part, pensions were paid quarterly in advance, a procedure which, by placing a large sum of money in the hands of those unused to having more than a few shillings at once, encouraged the intemperate to waste their allowances.[184] There were also provisions for pensions to be commuted for a lump sum and these were frequently taken advantage of. Every soldier discharged with good conduct was given free transport to his place of enlistment or, if this was not farther, to his home; those who completed their engagement while in India or the colonies were allowed to remain where they were or to claim free transport to Britain or another colony.[185]

Between 1856 and 1899 the importance of increasing army pensions was repeatedly emphasised, and in particular the necessity of providing more funds to help those discharged after twenty-one years' service.[186] 'The Soldier is not only depressed in the social scale while serving, as being a poorer man,' an article in 1865 argued, 'but when discharged into private life is thrust into one so closely allied to poverty, that, as age creeps on, he sinks into its seething stream, or is borne away to that haven of humiliation, the Paupers' Union.'[187] Those who were reluctant to place more money directly in the hands of the serving soldier saw an increase in pensions as an alternative means of improving his financial position. In addition the argument for higher pensions was tied to the question of recruitment. The prospect of an adequate pension for life was not only an inducement to enlistment;[188] but the sight of ex-soldiers destitute and begging for hand-outs, or dependent upon parish assistance, was felt to be a serious discouragement to prospective recruits.[189]

The weight of authority behind such arguments was considerable. Lord Roberts for instance strongly urged more and better pensions as a means of bolstering recruitment,[190] and several influential War Office and Parliamentary enquiries stressed the same line of reasoning. The Wantage Committee in 1892 emphasised the number of men discharged from the Service each year without a pension and the disparity between pensions and the rates of daily pay the soldier had previously had in the army. Lord Wolseley, then Commander-in-Chief in Ireland, submitted a memorandum to the Committee which especially stressed the inadequacy of military pensions.[191]

The treatment of ex-servicemen brought the army a great deal of adverse publicity. National and local newspapers, including those with a working-class readership, frequently devoted space to discussing the plight of one veteran or another.[192] In May of 1868 for instance *The Glasgow Sentinel and Scottish Banner* carried a story of a soldier discharged with a bad heart on a pension of 7d per day for 17 months. Unable to work and support himself he eventually committed suicide.[193] In March 1894 the columns of *The Labour Leader* argued:

> The Chelsea Guardians have decided that old soldiers who go to their institution shall have their pensions confiscated, except a penny a day, which will be allowed as pocket money. This is called encouraging our military heroes to be independent and self-reliant. Does the Duke of Cambridge forfeit his pension when he lives in a state palace?[194]

These and similar revelations must have harmed recruitment.

After the Wantage Committee report in 1892, the ceiling on long-service pensions for NCOs was raised to 5s per day,[195] but not until after the South African War was action taken to raise the minimum for privates to 1s per day.[196] Nothing else was done to increase the rates and nothing at all to lower the requirements for pensions. Until just prior to the First World War, there was no consideration given to providing long-term medical care aside from that available at Chelsea and Kilmainham.[197] The need for a revision in existing regulations, both in the interests of the soldier and as an encouragement to recruitment, were admitted, yet budgetary restrictions and inertia precluded any significant action.[198]

Table 4–5 shows the number of men discharged in five-year periods from the forces between 1861 and 1898 either on medical grounds or

Table 4.5 Discharges Granted and Pensions Awarded, 1861–98

Year	Number Discharged after Completion of Service	Number Invalided	Total	Pensions Granted			Percentage of Invalids Pensioned	Percentage of Total Pensions Per Total Discharges
				Permanent	Temporary	Total		
1861–5	15,335*	26,132	41,467	14,434	18,086	32,520	84.8**	47.7
1866–71	28,947*	25,760	54,707	18,825	20,179	39,004	62.3**	44.5
1872–5	7,532	14,913	22,445	12,090	6,891	18,981	76.8	36.0
1876–80	20,722	21,705	42,427	32,160	7,334	39,484	86.5	50.5
1881–5	11,113	17,174	28,287	16,232	7,412	23,664	73.0	33.0
1886–90	7,640	14,414	22,054	13,072	5,516	18,228	73.5	29.8
1891–5	4,108	14,914	19,022	8,246	5,275	13,521	63.1	24.6
1896–8	1,831	10,989	12,820	4,926	3,139	8,065	56.7	21.6
TOTAL	97,228	146,001	243,229	119,985	73,472	193,457	65.9	37.8

* Includes men discharged after first period of service

**Estimated

Source: *General Annual Return of the British Army,* P.P., XLIII (c.1323), 1875, p.25; XLIII (c.6196), 1890, p.32; LIII (c.9246), 1899, p.34.

for having completed twenty-one years' service. The proportion of men who received a pension during these years declined if anything. Since every man who completed the maximum period of service was entitled to a pension, it is clear that an increasingly large number of those who were invalided from the army must have received no compensation whatsoever. Furthermore, a large proportion of the pensions which were granted were temporary in nature.

The pensions paid to police constables and to private soldiers were frequently compared between 1856 and 1899. As with wages, comparisons leave no doubt that the constable was much better off. Pension regulations varied somewhat between police forces, however it seems clear that throughout the whole of the period permanent pensions were awarded for twenty-five years' service, and for invalidity any time after fifteen years. In some forces there was no minimum period of service to qualify for a disability pension. Rates of payment varied, although it appears that in most instances long-service pensions amounted to at least two-thirds of daily pay. Minimum disability pensions varied from three-tenths of daily pay after fifteen years to two-thirds after twenty-five years. In some forces full pay was awarded after just fifteen years.[199] To take but one example therefore, the police constable and the infantry private discharged after the maximum period of service would each receive a permanent pension. The constable's might amount to 20s per week, but the soldier's would be no more than half this amount.

The insufficiency of army pensions, both in terms of the number and the size of the allowances awarded each year is nowhere better demonstrated than by the number of ex-soldiers reduced to destitution and to dependence on civilian institutions yearly. If a pensioner had to be lodged in an asylum for the mentally ill, the War Office undertook to pay the guardians of the institution 4s for his maintenance, yet deducted this amount from his pension, leaving in some cases only a few pence for the support of the man's wife and family.[200] Similar instances arose in cases where men for illness or other reasons were obliged to enter a workhouse, and the guardians of the institution took nearly the whole of his army pension, leaving him neither enough money for the support of relatives or to make a new start on his own.[201] The circumstances of the majority of ex-soldiers, some of them disabled, who had received no pension and who fell on hard times were even more distressing.[202] In December 1897 there were over 1,900 army pensioners in Britain in receipt of poor relief, and more than 6,600 other ex-servicemen in the same circumstances.[203] A return ordered from workhouses on a particular night in December of that year revealed that there were nearly 9,000 inmates who had previously done military service.[204] How many others, it might be wondered, living in desperation yet somehow managed to stay clear of the Poor Law?[205]

If the army did little to care for the soldier in his retirement, equally there were few attempts to prepare him for the transition to a self-sufficient civilian life. Few soldiers, with the exception of some engineers, gunners and cavalrymen, left the forces with any marketable skills. If they had a trade or calling before enlistment, seven or more years' service would be enough to ensure that they forgot much of what they knew and lost whatever connections they might have had.

The plight of the unemployed veteran was especially stressed in Parliament[206] and in military journals.[207] It was often emphasised how much they harmed recruitment and that practical benefits in terms of recruitment would arise from relieving their distress.[208] Government inaction was heavily criticised.[209] Colonel F. Chenevix Trench, in a highly-regarded essay, wrote in 1887:

> . . .every Reservist of good character and abilities who cannot get work, and who is starving. . .or is seen tramping about the country from village to village in search of work, or who becomes periodically an inmate of a charitable refuge or a workhouse, acts upon all of his own class in life as a distinct deterent to recruiting and lowers the character and reputation of the Service. Inherited traditions, as is well known, die hard, especially among the lower classes and the tradition among them that the army is a very undesirable calling for a young man. . .is not by any means dead yet. . .[210]

When seeking civilian employment, the ex-soldier was hindered by a number of factors. Not only did he have few marketable skills as we have said, but he was often handicapped by his age as well. After 1870 obligations for reserve service were another serious stumbling-block to re-employment. Reserve exercises were infrequent,[211] but because of recurrent manpower shortages reservists were called out several times between 1870 and 1899.[212] In the circumstances many employers were unwilling to accept government assurances that the reserve would be used only in times of extreme national emergency and were reluctant to hire ex-servicemen.[213]

Scepticism in military circles and among some civilian employers of the ex-soldier's abilities also limited his chances. This feeling was by no means universal, but there were a number of senior army officers, civil servants and private employers who felt that military service unfitted a man for certain types of subsequent employment. Lieutenant-Colonel E.Y. Walcott, Chief Commissioner of the Metropolitan Police, told a select committee in 1875 that he considered a minimum of military service was preferable in ex-soldiers since in many cases their training had dulled any powers of initiative and of independent action. William Cawkwell, a railway company official, supported this view and testified that in his experience ex-soldiers were frequently unused to heavy labour and were therefore not as useful as civilian workers. Nor did he feel that their habits of discipline made them any more valuable. Ralph Thompson, a chief clerk in the War Office, remarked that in general he had found soldiers employed in clerical positions less capable than civilians.[214] The Inspector-General of Recruiting, Major-General R.C.H. Taylor, was sceptical as well of the soldier's abilities and felt that even NCOs would have to be highly supervised to be of any value.[215]

The majority of opinion in the army rejected these views, as it seems did most civilian employers. The enquiries after 1875 into the re-employment prospects of ex-servicemen received evidence from private civilians, civil servants and army officers to the effect that there was a wide variety of positions in government and other work which could satisfactorily be filled by ex-servicemen.[216] Railway officials whose firms gave preference to former soldiers testified that they were pleased with the results.[217] Civil servants confirmed that in certain positions ex-servicemen were every bit as capable as civilians.[218] Senior army officers involved in schemes to help servicemen find work testified to the variety of jobs these men could perform.[219]

The introduction of short-service enlistment in 1870 had not only increased the need for recruits, but with more men being discharged yearly, accentuated the plight of the ex-soldier. The last three decades of the century therefore witnessed considerable efforts by reformers within the army and without to improve opportunities for the employment of ex-servicemen in the civil service, the obvious area in which the government could act and set an example to civilian employers.

There was a number of precedents for reserving positions for ex-soldiers in the government service; in Germany and France for instance military service was a major avenue to civil service employment.[220] In Britain pensioners had been called up several times to do non-combatant jobs during military campaigns,[221] and since 1858 a small number of clerkships in the War Office was reserved for ex-soldiers.[222] In general, however, opportunities for ex-servicemen were limited, and with its own house in disarray the War Office could hardly exert pressure on civilian employers.

In 1876 a select committee outlined several proposals which were to be revived by subsequent enquiries. The committee's recommendations called for the reservation of certain types of menial employments such as permanent messengers for ex-servicemen; for civil service examinations to include skills and branches of knowledge likely to be possessed by soldiers; and finally for a review of civil service regulations pertaining to age and marital status.[223] Later committees delineated the list of civil service jobs that could be reserved for and filled by ex-soldiers,[224] and proposed to replace in a number of cases the soldiers employed as clerks with military pensioners.[225] With regard to employment outside government, better provisions for instructing men in trades were urged,[226] as well as greater assistance to privately-run employment agencies and more cooperation with civilian employers through the maintenance by the army of local registers of available work.[227]

A number of factors helps to explain government inaction. There might be precedents for the employment of ex-servicemen in the civil service, but there was little precedent on the whole for large-scale government action against unemployment. Civilian labour exchanges originated in the 1880s but received little attention before 1905. In London quasi-official exchanges were set up in that year, but were regarded with some suspicion by trade unions, and it was not until 1910 that an effective national system of exchanges was established. The arguments of reformers also contributed to official intransigence. They clashed with the principle of open competition which practically excluded most ex-soldiers.[228] Many of those who wanted to widen employment in the civil service discouraged compromise by demanding that a clerical position be reserved for all ex-servicemen. This met with opposition from existing vested interests and from senior officials alarmed at what they saw as a threat to efficiency.[229] Though the Treasury recognised the feasibility of providing a much larger number of positions in the civil service for ex-soldiers,[230] it argued that this was unnecessary,[231] since most of those concerned were able to find other employment. It was also reluctant to assist them in their search for work since this would be expensive, and normally work was found in any case through private agencies or on their own initiative. It was also felt that the number of men discharged from the army annually was so large that places could not possibly be found for them all.[232]

Actual measures which were undertaken were recognised as slight.[233] Registers of employment were set up at army headquarters and at divisional stations in 1884, but in the absence of much encouragement and example from the government employers were reluctant to do their hiring from the barracks.[234] Moreover ex-servicemen were frequently itinerant while searching for work and often lost contact with official registers.[235] Edward Cardwell and subsequent Secretaries of State for War were anxious that more ex-servicemen be taken into the civil service, and there was a number of positions reserved for ex-servicemen in military departments, but in the absence of a unified governmental response, the War Office role *vis à vis* other departments was reduced to one of persuasion.[236] Secretaries of State circulated many of the other departments where it was suggested a number of ex-servicemen might be employed, but until the 1890s only the Post Office responded to any degree.[237] Then under pressure from the Wantage and other committees concerned with recruitment several other government departments agreed at last to reserve a number of positions each year for ex-soldiers, as customs and prison officials, park keepers, messengers and clerks.[238] But the number of positions set aside was modest, and the total number of ex-servicemen employed in government departments was, until the end of the century, well below what it might have been. In 1878 there were less than 230 men of the first-class army reserve employed in civil departments of the state.[239] Between 1876 and 1891, more than 4,700 minor positions in the civil service were filled, yet only 220 of these went to ex-servicemen.[240] Between 1894 and 1898, 26,947 men were discharged from the army upon completion of service or for medical reasons.[241] There were 40,393 applications for work through official employment registers in these years, but only 4,437 ex-soldiers were placed in government departments.[242] In 1894 more than 7,700 army reservists, 9.6 per cent of the total reserve force, were unemployed.[243] It is not known how many of the thousands of ex-soldiers who were not reservists were out of work as well.[244]

In the absence of adequate government measures to help the ex-serviceman after 1856, a number of private organisations sprang up to fill an obvious need. These included benevolent societies, employment agencies and paramilitary organisations, most of which were founded and directed by army officers. A number of schemes were unrealistic and never took hold,[245] but by 1900 there were nearly a dozen such organisations operating in Britain. Although there was a great deal of overlapping of functions and central coordination was needed, the record of the main ones at least was significant.[246]

The first of these organisations to be founded was the Army and

Navy Pensioner's and Time-Expired Men's Society in 1855. A similar institution was the National Association for the Employment of Reserve and Discharged Soldiers, established in 1885. Neither charged fees for assistance; after 1890 each received modest financial help from the government.[247] Many ex-soldiers obtained work on their own, but these and other private agencies were able to find positions for increasingly large numbers each year.[248] By 1900 the Pensioner's Society and the National Association had several branches throughout the country which together were helping more than 4,000 men to find work annually.[249] Civilian employers in the last decade of the century seem to have become more responsive to this problem, though how much they were influenced by the societies is difficult to say. Two main sources of employment were the railways and the police. In 1889 for instance, 766 former soldiers were hired by police forces in Britain bringing the number employed to over 8,000;[250] the following year 2,545 ex-soldiers were taken on by UK railways, making the total then employed in this line of work nearly 11,000.[251]

A third major body was the Corps of Commissionaires, founded in 1859 by Captain Edward Walter to provide employment for wounded soldiers. Sensing an opening in the labour market for ex-servicemen, Walter extended the membership of his organisation to include any pensioner or reservist with a good character record.[252] Regulations required that applicants pay a small fee to join, purchase their own uniform, and out of their earnings bank a certain amount each week.[253] Military organisation and discipline were maintained, and commissionaires were employed on a variety of jobs such as messengers, attendants, night watchmen and delivery agents. Average full-time earnings exceeded those of the private soldier,[254] although the Commissionaires had of course to meet their full living costs from these. From modest beginnings the Corps rose considerably in public estimation and by 1900 was responsible for providing steady employment for more than 3,000 men annually.[255] Kipling's Commissionaire is therefore not quite an accurate portrait, though it effectively contrasts military excitement and responsibility with the serious let-down of the menial duties of messenger and doorman:

> Oh, it drives me half crazy to think of the days I
> Went slap for the Ghazi, my sword at my side,
> When we rode Hell-for-leather
> Both squadrons together,
> That didn't care whether we lived or we died.

But it's no use despairin', my wife must go charin'
. . .I'm old and I'm nervis,
I'm cast from the Service,
And all I deserve is a shillin' a day.[256]

The agitation for better government pensions for the rank and file was perhaps bound to end in failure, since at this time official carelessness and disregard was more than matched by the absence of any governmental provision for the social security of the civilian worker, and in the end it was the state of the labour market that dictated employment opportunities for both. Certainly, however, ex-soldiers found the transition from army to civilian life a particularly trying one. The government's failure to make better provision for his welfare when the army was increasingly in the public eye and when recruitment was difficult at best, was serious and damaging.

4. Pensions for Widows and Families

Considering the inadequacy of measures taken to provide for the ex-serviceman in civilian life, it is not surprising that the soldier's family was a victim of the army's neglect as well. Where financial assistance was concerned, even those married on the strength were shabbily treated. The army might congratulate itself that short-service enlistment had reduced the number on the married roll,[257] but this was little consolation to the wives and children of enlisted men. For most of the period 1856 to 1899 the army made no provision for widows and orphans of regular soldiers.[258] Military pensions were often insufficient even for the needs of the ex-serviceman, not to mention his family; and to make matters worse, when a pensioner died his allowances were discontinued and his dependants left penniless. This reduced many a soldier's family to destitution, and was in turn another sharp discouragement to recruitment.[259]

The condition of the soldier's family was not a major issue even among reformers,[260] though it was the normal practice to give pensions to officers' widows,[261] and the Admiralty had a pension scheme for the dependants of ordinary sailors killed in the line of duty.[262] The only concessions the army was to make before the turn of the century came in the 1880s. In 1881 the War Office agreed to provide the widows of NCOs and men killed or mortally wounded on active service a gratuity of one year's pay,[263] and the following year ordered separation allowances of 6d per day plus 2d for each child to be paid when units were ordered abroad for active duty.[264] Later in 1882 a War Office committee recommended the establishment of a fund from monies obtained from the sale of unclaimed effects to provide pensions for the widows and families of enlisted men,[265] and a year later a second committee recommended the drawing up of a proper scheme of pensions, allowing at least £10 per year for the widow of a private plus £1 for each dependent child.[266] In neither of these cases was any action taken. The outbreak of the South African War in 1899 forced the army to look to its image, and revealed considerable public concern with the welfare of the families of men sent out to fight. The War Office's only answer, however, was a further increase in separation allowances.[267]

A major reason why successive administrations were able to evade responsibility was that there was already a number of private charities working to fill some of the needs of soldiers' families. The largest of these was the Royal Victoria Patriotic Fund. As we have seen, the fund was originally intended for the dependants of Crimean veterans, but in 1886 its terms of reference were extended to provide relief for widows and orphans of all wars.[268] A number of similar charities were established on subsequent occasions throughout the next forty-five years, and the majority of them were eventually incorporated into and administered by the Patriotic Fund.[269]

Charitable agencies provided relief only for the widows and orphans of men killed or dying of wounds or illness contracted on active service. Where military responsibility for the soldier's death was recognised, a widow in need of support could apply to the Royal Patriotic Fund, and if her case were accepted, as it was in most instances, a small pension, liable to forfeiture if she should remarry, would be settled upon her. Under the terms of this assistance widows of staff sergeants were allowed 7s per week, and up to 12s with four dependent children; at the lower end of the scale a private's widow might receive 5s per week or 9s 6d with four children.[270] These meagre allowances could hardly be considered adequate and were especially ungenerous considering that much of the Patriotic Fund's income went unspent because its Commissioners were so parsimonious.[271]

The outburst of patriotism that accompanied the South African War spurred the chartering of a large number of new foundations to provide pensions and gratuities for widows and orphans, for wives and families of men at the front, and for some of the casualties themselves. It also resulted in an increase in the pensions paid by existing agencies.[272] There was little cooperation between national funds on one hand and local officials and local funds on the other, and the proliferation of agencies led to a great deal of duplication of effort and to the mismanagement of monies.[273] In spite of this the War Office remained aloof, and continued to pay only separation allowances and single gratuities in the event of a soldier's death. It was not until after the War that serious consideration was given to bringing widows' pensions and allowances within the compass of a properly-established pension board.[274]

5. Conclusion

By concentrating on wages, career prospects, the problems of discharge, pensions for widows and families, those aspects of military service which might be expected to appeal most to potential working-class recruits on financial grounds, it has been shown how little progress was made in widening the army's attractions after 1856. Between 1856 and 1899 the military wages including the cash value of housing, clothing, and food were too low to appeal to any who could be certain of regular employment. Career prospects within the lower ranks of the army were adequate, but in spite of the abolition of purchase in 1871, the barriers to men rising from the ranks remained as effective as ever. The problems of discharge continued largely unabated. Military service was more hazardous than most other occupations, but there was no adequate system of pensions. Many soldiers by virtue either of their having been so long in the army or their obligations to the reserve, were hampered in finding subsequent employment.

Failure to take sufficient measures to remedy these problems can be traced to government reluctance to spend money, and, on the whole, short-sighted economy was pursued against all odds. This, as the following chapters will show, was a key to the army's ever-present recruiting difficulties.

Notes

1. See E.H. Hunt, *Regional Wage Variations in Britain, 1850–1914* (Oxford, 1973).
2. The military wage was normally held to include regular pay plus the cash value of food, clothing, lodgings and allowances.
3. The private's 1s 1d was made up of ordinary pay of 1s plus an allowance for beer of 1d.
4. *Report of the Committee on Working Pay,* WO.33/33.
5. See Rewards for Meritorious Service, WO.32/6312; and Gratuities for South African Service, WO.32/7912; also Anon., 'The British Soldier', *Colburn's,* II (1863), pp.71–83.
6. The Pay, Allowances and Stoppages of Privates of Infantry from 1660–1891, WO.33/51.

7. See Appendix IV, Table IVA–1.
8. See for instance Fraser, *Sixty Years in Uniform,* p.42; Mole, *A King's Hussar,* p.31.
9. G.R. Godley, *Memorandum on the Means of Recruiting the Army and on an Army of Reserve,* 22 March 1859, Panmure MSS., GD45/8/504.
10. Robertson, *From Private to Field-Marshal,* pp.4–5; Grenville Murray, *Six Months in the Ranks,* p.61.
11. *Report of the Committee on the Simplification of the Various Rates of Duty Pay,* WO.33/277.
12. *Report of the Select Committee on the Civil Employment of Ex-Soldiers and Sailors,* P.P., XIV (c.2991), 1906, pp.24–5; cited hereafter as *Report of the Committee on Civil Employment* (1906).
13. Stoppages for Rations, WO.33/6b; *Minutes of Evidence Taken before the Select Committee on the Army before Sebastopol,* P.P., IX (c.156), 1854–5, pp.191–2; cited hereafter as *Sebastopol Army Evidence* (1854–5).
14. Wyndham, *Following the Drum,* p.57.
15. Grenville Murray, *Six Months in the Ranks,* p.74; Mole, *King's Hussar,* p.31.
16. Wyndham, op.cit., p.57.
17. In an earlier period clothing had been supplied in the army by colonels of regiments who were given a fixed sum by the government known as the 'off-reckonings' for each man enrolled. The inefficiencies of this system were such that many COs made handsome personal profits. In 1855 great difficulties were encountered in the attempts to clothe the large number of recruits required for service in the East. A royal warrant issued in that year provided for government supply of clothing by public contract. *Report of the Committee on the Annual Clothing Issue,* WO.32/6333; *Report of the Commissioners Appointed to Inquire into the State of the Store and Clothing Departments at Weedon, Woolwich, and the Tower,* P.P., IX (c.2577), 1859, p.iii; *Sebastopol Army Evidence* (1854–5), p.185; Frederick Greenwood, 'Life in a Barrack', *The Cornhill Magazine,* VII (1863), pp.441–56.
18. *Report of the Army Clothing Committee,* WO.33/51.
19. *Report of the Committee on the Annual Clothing Issue,* WO.32/6333.
20. War Office files contain several itemised accounts of the money stopped from soldiers' pay for articles worn out in the pursuance of military duties. As late as 1895–6 there are instances of experienced soldiers having to pay £1 10s and more in a year for the upkeep of their kit. *Report of the Army Clothing Committee,* WO.33/51.
21. Anon., Experiences of a Soldier, Unpublished MS. (circa 1890), NAM., 7008–13.
22. Gore-Browne, *The Nineteenth Century,* XXVIII (1890), pp.840–53; Edmondson, *Is a Soldier's Life Worth Living?,* pp.52 et seq.
23. Pay, Allowances, and Stoppages of Privates of Infantry From 1660–1891, WO.33/51; Robertson, *From Private to Field-Marshal,* p.5.
24. Mole, *King's Hussar,* p.351; Robertson, *From Private to Field-Marshal,* p.5.
25. See for instance, Anon., 'Our Military Reforms of Late Years and What They Have Done for Us', *Colburn's,* III (1860), pp.475–86; Anon., 'A Voice from the Ranks', *Once a Week* (1867), p.697; Lieutenant-Colonel W. Underwood, *A Plea for Conscription in Britain* (1900); Hansard, CLXXVI (27 June 1864), cc.388–92; LIV (28 Feb. 1898), cc.187–94; *The Times,* 18 May 1867, 10 June 1892.
26. D.I.G., 'The Recruiting System', *Colburn's,* I (1862), p.161.
27. J.W. Crowe, *Our Army; Or Penny Wise and Pound Foolish* (1856); Archibald Forbes, 'The Limited Enlistment Act by One Who Has Served in

the Ranks', *The Cornhill Magazine,* X (1864), pp.213–14; An Officer, *Thoughts on Recruiting* (1866), p.4; A Soldier, *Thoughts on the Recruiting Question* (Edinburgh, 1875); General Sir J. Lintorn Simmons, 'The Weakness of the Army', *The Nineteenth Century,* XIII (1883), pp.529–42; *The Times,* 18 May 1867, 15 March 1892.

28. Hansard, CLXXVII (20 March 1865), cc.1955–77; CCVII (19 June 1871), c.244; CCCL (23 Feb. 1891), cc.1383–4.
29. *Report of the Commission on Recruiting* (1867), pp.3–4.
30. *Report of the Committee on the Terms and Conditions of Service in the Army,* P.P., XIX (c.6582), 1892, pp.157, 163; cited hereafter as *Report of the Wantage Committee* (1892).
31. Both Edward Cardwell and Henry Campbell-Bannerman voiced such views when Secretary of State for War, and similar opinions found expression in army circles. Edward Cardwell to W.E. Gladstone, 3 Jan. 1874, Cardwell MSS., PRO.30/48/2/10; Hansard, X (17 March 1893), cc.408–9; Lieutenant-Colonel W.T. Dooner, 'The Present System of Enlistment and Pay of Our Soldiers and Its Bearing on Recruiting', *JRUSI,* XXXV (1891), pp.207–38; Anon., 'The Real Position and Advantages of the Soldier: Increase of Pay and Pension', *Colburn's,* II (1866), pp.238–49.
32. This was a view held by many throughout the whole of the period. In 1855 Lord Panmure argued with critics to this effect, and in 1892, Redvers Buller, then Adjutant-General, assured the Wantage Committee that it would be preferable to give the soldier free groceries rather than increase his pay. See Lord Panmure to the Prince Consort, 31 May 1855, Panmure MSS., GD45/8/241; *Report of the Wantage Committee* (1892), pp.8, 36; *Report of the Commission on the War in South Africa* (1904), pp.193–4.
33. Anon., 'The British Soldier', *Colburn's,* II (1863), pp.71–83; Henry B. Lock, *Memorandum upon the Present Military Resources of England* (1870); An Officer, 'Regimental Depots and Recruits', *Colburn's,* I (1881), pp.228–42, 307–16; Miles, *Remarks on the Defence of the British Empire* (1889); Colonel W.T. Dooner, 'The Organisation of our Infantry with Reference to Foreign Reliefs', *Colburn's,* XIV (1897–8), pp.337–48; Arthur V. Palmer, 'A Recruiting Sergeant's Suggestions', *The Nineteenth Century,* XLIII (1898), pp.30–4; Colonel W.W. Knollys, 'The Recruiting Question II', *The United Services Magazine,* III (1891), pp.170–81; Anon., *Army Organisation* (1900), p.25.
34. Papers by General Lord Roberts on the Report on the Terms and Conditions of Service in the Army, WO.33/52; Frederick Roberts, 'Free Trade in the Army', *The Nineteenth Century,* XV (1884), pp.1055–74.
35. General Roberts to Edward Stanhope, 10 March 1891, 29 Nov. 1891, Stanhope MSS., 1401.
36. Some of the most important speakers were Henry Campbell-Bannerman, H.O. Arnold-Forster, and Sir Henry Havelock. See Hansard, CLXXVI (27 June 1864), cc.388–9; CLXXXV (7 March 1867), c.1500; CXCI (8 May 1868), cc.2003–4; CCXXII (8 March 1875), c.1459; CCXXXII (5 March 1877), c.1431; CCLXI (27 May 1881), c.1562; V (10 June 1892), cc.737–8, 763; LIV (25 Feb. 1898), cc.72, 119–20; also H.O. Arnold Forster, *Our Home Army* (1892), pp.35–6.
37. *The Times,* 18 May 1867; 9 March 1876; 10 June 1892.
38. *Report of the Commission on Recruiting* (1867), pp.59–62.
39. One of the most influential again was Lord Roberts, who argued strongly for increases of up to 4d per day for men on re-enlistment. See Papers of General Lord Roberts on the Report on the Terms and Conditions of Service in the Army, WO.33/52, pp.572–99; Roberts, *The Nineteenth*

Century, XV (1884), pp.1055–74. See also Hansard, LXXVII (21 Feb. 1865), cc.523–5; LXXVII (20 March 1865), c.1961; V (10 June 1892), cc.746–8; Captain Noake, 'On the Best Mode of Recruiting for the Army', *JRUSI,* XI (1868), pp.27–39; Lieutenant-Colonel J.R. Turnbull, *Essay on Recruiting on the System of Deferred Payments* (1875); Major-General Sir J. Lintorn Simmons, 'The Critical Condition of the Army', *The Nineteenth Century,* XIV (1883), pp.165–88.

40. Beedos, 'State of the Army II', *Colburn's,* XX (1899), pp.504–12; Lieutenant-General J. Sprot, *Incidents and Anecdotes in the Life of Lieutenant-General Sprot* (Edinburgh, 1906, 1907), II, p.18.
41. Hansard, CXXII (8 March 1875), c.1450; Anon., 'On Recruiting and Enlistment', *Colburn's,* II (1865), pp.1–15; A General Office, Royal Marines, 'Thoughts on Army Organisation and Discipline', *Colburn's,* II (1876), pp.101–5; Skene Dubh, 'A Solution of the Army Problem', *Colburn's,* XVI (1897–8), pp.572–99.
42. *Report of the Wantage Committee* (1892), pp.53–5, passim.
43. See for instance J.R. Godley, Assistant Under-Secretary of State for War, Memorandum on the Means of Recruiting the Army, WO.33/6b, pp.5–6; Simmons, *The Nineteenth Century,* XIII (1883), pp.529–42; Sprot, *Incidents,* II, p.8; *The Times,* 10 April 1876, 10 June 1892; J.C. Cameron, Deputy Inspector-General, 'Co-operative Enlistment', *Colburn's,* I (1874), pp.37–45.
44. The effect of military expenditure on the Treasury was usually immediate. In 1882, for instance, Gladstone's Cabinet was forced to push the income tax up to 6d in the pound. This was the year after Majuba Hill, and the year that an expedition was sent to Egypt to rescue Gordon.
45. Dooner, *JRUSI,* XXXV (1891), p.227.
46. An Ex-Non-Commissioned Officer, 'Weekly Payments to Soldiers', *Colburn's,* II (1868), pp.414–20; Anderson, *Political Science Quarterly,* LXXXII (1967), pp.526–45.
47. Hansard, X (17 March 1893), cc.408–9; Beedos, 'State of the Army II', *Colburn's,* XX (1899), pp.504–12.
48. For instance, Hansard, XCV (25 June 1901), cc.1370–3; *The Times,* 9 March 1876; Anon., 'On Recruiting', *Colburn's,* I (1865), pp.475–85; An Ex-Non-Commissioned Officer, 'Weekly Payments to Soldiers', *Colburn's,* II (1868), pp.414–20; Anon., 'The British Soldier', *New Monthly Magazine,* CXXI, p.133; Hardy, *Mr Thomas Atkins,* p.80.
49. The Papers and Memoranda of Sir Arthur Haliburton relative to the Wantage Committee Report, WO.32/52, p.570.
50. The Pay, Allowances, and Stoppages of Privates of Infantry from 1860–1891, WO.33/51.
51. *Report of the Commission on Recruiting* (1867), p.xiii.
52. *Report of a Committee on the Equalisation of Stoppages from the Soldier for Rations at Home, Abroad, in Hospital, and on Board Ship, and the Improvements Required in the Composition of his Ration,* P.P., XXXIX (c.197), 1871, pp.5–6; Richard L. Blanco, 'Army Recruiting Reforms, 1861–1867', *JSAHR,* XLVI (1968), p.222.
53. *Memorandum by the Inspector-General of Recruiting on Recruiting for the Regular Army,* P.P., XLII (c.57), 1870, p.1; The Pay, Allowances, and Stoppages of Privates of Infantry, from 1860–1891, WO.33/51.
54. *The Saturday Review,* XXII (1866), p.670.
55. *Fraser's Magazine,* LXXIV (1866), p.686.
56. Anon., 'How to Render the Army Popular as a Profession', *Colburn's,* II (1867), p.392.

57. Edward Cardwell to W.E. Gladstone, 1 Sept. 1872, 20 Dec. 1873, Gladstone MSS., 44120; Edward Cardwell to W.E. Gladstone, 3 Jan. 1874; Edward Cardwell to Lord Northbrook, 26 Sept. 1873, Cardwell MSS., PRO.30/48/2/10, 30/48/4/21.
58. W.E. Gladstone, Memorandum on Army Organisation, 5 Oct. 1871, Cardwell MSS., PRO.30/48/2/8.
59. Edward Cardwell, Memorandum, 3 Jan. 1874; Edward Cardwell to W.E. Gladstone, 9 Dec. 1871, Gladstone MSS., 44119–20.
60. Cardwell saw this measure as an incentive to good behaviour, but was able to secure Treasury support only by stopping the bounty paid to recruits on enlistment. Edward Cardwell to Robert Lowe, 12 April 1870, Cardwell MSS., PRO.30/48/5/22; The Pay, Allowances, and Stoppages of Privates of Infantry from 1860–1891, WO.33/51.
61. The allowance for beer was 1d per day. Until 1870 beer money was added to basic pay making it a total of 1s 3d per day. *Report of the Army Reorganisation Committee* (1881), pp.498–9.
62. The Duke of Cambridge to Edward Cardwell, 14 May 1870; Lord Northbrook to Edward Cardwell, 9 June 1873, 25 Aug. 1873, Cardwell MSS., PRO.30/48/3/13, 30/48/4/21.
63. *Report of the Committee on Recruiting,* WO.33/27.
64. Gathorne Hardy, Memorandum on Army Conditions and Recruitment, 8 Jan. 1876; Gathorne Hardy to the Duke of Richmond, 10 Jan. 1876, Hardy MSS., T501/16, T501/61.
65. *Report of the Inspector-General of Recruiting,* P.P., XIV (c.4314), 1884–5, p.16; J.B. Atlay, *Lord Haliburton* (1909), pp.205–6.
66. This kept the required period for the first badge at two years from the date of the last offence, but reduced that for subsequent badges to five, twelve, sixteen, eighteen, twenty-one, and twenty-six years. Reckoning of Service Towards Good Conduct Pay, WO.32/6666.
67. General Frederick Roberts to Edward Stanhope, 8 Aug. 1883; G. Salis Schwabe to Edward Stanhope, 23 Feb. 1891, Stanhope MSS., 1374, 1401.
68. Simmons, *The Nineteenth Century,* XIII (1883), pp.542–3.
69. The Papers and Memoranda of Sir Arthur Haliburton Relative to the Wantage Committee Report, WO.33/52, p.267.
70. The Rev George Wilde to W.H. Smith, 3 Nov. 1885, W. Cobrington to W.H. Smith, 2 Dec. 1885, Smith MSS., WO.110/3.
71. *Report of the Army Clothing Committee,* WO.33/51, passim.
72. Hansard, CCXVIII (30 March 1874), cc.467–9; CCXXII (8 March 1875), cc.1459–60; CCXXVII (2 March 1876), c.1258; CCXXII (5 March 1877), cc.1429–30; X (17 March 1893), cc.413–14; LIV (25 Feb. 1898), c.120.
73. Palmer, *The Nineteenth Century,* XLIII (1898), pp.30–4; Sir Arthur Haliburton, *Army Organisation: a Short Reply to Long Service* (1898), p.66.
74. Dooner, *JRUSI,* XXXV (1891), pp.207–38; Beedos, 'The State of the Army I', *Colburn's,* XIX (1899), pp.415–18.
75. The Duke of Cambridge had earlier gone on record advocating the abolition of deferred pay because it discouraged re-enlistment, but he was now supported by other senior officers like Redvers Buller and Evelyn Wood. *Second Report of the Select Committee on the Army Estimates,* P.P., VIII (c.212), 1888, p.38; *Report of the Wantage Committee* (1892), pp.6. 46, 76.
76. *Report of the Wantage Committee* (1892), pp.14–15.
77. Redvers Buller to Edward Stanhope, 29 Dec. 1891; Sir John Adye to Arthur Haliburton, 24 Feb. 1892; General Henry Brackenbury to Edward

Stanhope, 9 April, 1892, Stanhope MSS., 1349, 1359, 1389; E.G. Bulwer to Henry Campbell-Bannerman, 2 March 1892, Campbell-Bannerman MSS., 41233.

78. Revised Summary of the Recommendations of Lord Wantage's Committee and of Decisions Taken, WO.33/55.

79. *Report of the Committee on the Simplification of the Various Rates of Duty Pay*, WO.33/277.

80. *Report of the Commission on the War in South Africa* (1904), p.435.

81. *Report of the Committee on the Annual Clothing Issue*, WO.32/6333.

82. *Report of the Committee on Clothing for British Soldiers in Peace and War*, WO.33/210.

83. A.L. Bowley, *Wages and Incomes since 1860* (Cambridge, 1937), p.31.

84. Lord Panmure to the Prince Consort, 31 May 1855, Panmure MSS., GD45/8/241; Anon., 'Earnings of Soldiers compared with Civilians', *Colburn's*, II (1872), pp.1–8; G., 'Views on Army Reform: an Answer', *The United Services Magazine*, VI (1892–3), pp.469–75; Beedos, 'State of the Army II', *Colburn's*, XX (1899), pp.504–12.

85. *Second Report of the Committee on the Army Estimates*, P.P., VIII (c.212), 1888, pp.251 et seq.; Anon., 'Comparative Advantages of the French and British Non-Commissioned Officer', *Colburn's*, I (1877), pp.148–58.

86. D.I.G., 'The Recruiting System', *Colburn's*, I (1862), p.161; F.G. Le Cost Cockburn, 'The Soldier of the American Army', *Colburn's*, IV (1889–1890), pp.429–33; Don Rickey Jr., 'The Enlisted Men of the Indian Wars', *Military Affairs*, XXIII (1959), pp.91–6.

87. Statement of the Relative Pecuniary Position of the Soldier and of the Labourer, WO.33/18.

88. *Return Showing the Estimated Weekly Wage of a Private Soldier*, P.P., XLVII (c.182), 1878, p.2.

89. W.E. Cairnes, *The Army from Within* (1901), p.111; *Report of the Committee on the Soldier's Dietary*, P.P., XVII (c.5742), 1889, p.6. It might be argued that since retail prices had fallen, this figure should be even less.

90. Statement of the Relative Pecuniary Position of the Soldier and of the Labourer, WO.33/18.

91. Parliamentary returns place wages at approximately this level. It seems likely that information of this sort was the source for army calculations. In 1867 a Royal Commission on agricultural labourers reported the value of wages plus allowances throughout the United Kingdom, and their findings correspond approximately to these figures. Allowances might include room and board, cottages, fuel, gardens and grazing privileges. See *Return of the Average Weekly Wage of Agricultural Labourers in England During the Quarter Ending Christmas 1869*, P.P., L (c.371), 1868–9; *Return of the Average Weekly Wage of Agricultural Labourers in Ireland, 1861*, P.P., LX (c.2), 1862; Captain C.H. Malan, 'The Recruiting Difficulty', *The Fortnightly Review*, V (1866), pp.406–20; Anon., 'The Earnings of Soldiers Compared with the Wages of Civilians', *Colburn's*, II (1872), pp.1–8.

92. A Royal Commission on agricultural labourers in 1893 reported that salaries of 20s–21s per week for farm workers in Scotland were not uncommon. Economists in turn estimate that by 1900 regularly employed but lower paid agricultural labourers in England and Scotland received anywhere from 16s to 22s per week, a sum considerably below urban wages in the rest of the country yet higher than the military wage. *Report of the Royal Commission on Labourers: the Agricultural Labourer, Scotland,*

P.P., XXXVI (c.6894-XV), 1893, pp.79, 81; Bowley, *Wages and Incomes,* p.8.

93. Before the First World War for instance there are cases of married ploughmen in Aberdeenshire receiving in addition to their basic wage a house, sixty-five stones of oatmeal, two tons of coal, ten cwt of potatoes, and every day three pints of milk. See Transport and General Workers Union, *1912 Then And Now 1946* (Airdrie, Lanarkshire, 1946), p.1.

94. Statement of the Relative Pecuniary Position of the Soldier and of the Labourer, WO.33/18.

95. See Bowley, *Wages and Incomes,* p.10. Bricklayers are selected as an example of a semi-skilled occupation since the requirements of their trade varied little between 1856 and 1899.

96. The normal period of service in most police forces throughout the period was twenty-five years, although men could be invalided for sickness or injury or discharged for misconduct at any time. See for instance *Return of the Terms and Conditions of Employment of the Royal Irish Constabulary,* P.P., LXXIV, pt.II (c.281), 1893–4, p.6; *Reports of the Inspector of Constabulary,* P.P., XLVII (c.20), 1857–8.

97. In general the county police were not paid as well as those in boroughs or cities, or in London, and wages were often higher in other parts of the United Kingdom. See *Salaries and Allowances Paid to the Officers and Constables of Rural Police in England and Wales,* P.P., LVIII (c.326), 1866; *Return of the Terms and Conditions of Employment of the Royal Irish Constabulary,* P.P', LXXIV, pt.ii (c.281), 1893–4; *Forty-First Annual Report of Her Majesty's Inspector of Constabulary for Scotland,* P.P., XLII (c.9305), 1899.

98. *Reports of the Inspectors of Constabulary,* P.P., XLVII (c.20), 1857–8, pp.25–7.

99. One of the lowest paid, the Royal Irish Constabulary, started constables after six months' initial service at 20s per week. In many forces wages were very much higher. The starting salary for constables in the City of London force for example was 25s per week. See *Report of the Select Committee on the Employment of Soldiers, Sailors, and Marines in Civil Departments of the Public Service,* P.P., XLV (c.356), 1876, pp.145–6, 220–3; cited hereafter as *Report of the Committee on Civil Employment* (1876).

100. Some of the police forces in Scotland started men at no more than 20s per week, although this of course increased with length of service. The starting salary in the Metropolitan police force was 24s per week, the maximum for constables was 32s per week. See *Forty-First Annual Report of Her Majesty's Inspector of Constables for Scotland,* P.P., XLII (c.9305), 1899, pp.21–5; *Reports of the Inspectors of Constabulary,* P.P., XLII (c.157), 1899; *Extract from Police Order of December 1890, Announcing Increase in Pay to the Metropolitan Police Force,* P.P., LXIV (c.57), 1890–1, p.1.

101. It is just out of our period, but in 1906 the rates of pay for constables in the Metropolitan police force were 25s 6d to 33s 6d per week, and because of allowances of different kinds plus cooperative catering, living costs per man averaged only 15s to 16s per week. See *Report of the Committee on Civil Employment* (1906), pp.59–61; *Minutes of Evidence Taken before the Select Committee on the Civil Employment of Ex-Soldiers and Sailors,* P.P., XIV (c.2922), 1906, pp.70–4.

102. See for instance *Life in the Ranks of the English Army* (1883); *A British Soldier's Life in the Ranks* (1886).

103. *The Army and What It Offers* (circa 1910), p.1.

104. Colonel W.K. Stuart, *Reminiscences of a Soldier* (1874), II, p.274.

105. Heavy Drill 'Em, *Information for the Soldier* (1865), p.6; Anon., 'The Volunteer, the Militiaman and the Regular Soldier', *Colburn's* III (1873), pp.285–94, 490–7; Anon., 'The Cost of the British Army and Recruiting', *Colburn's,* I (1875), pp.497–507; Captain J.S.A. Herford, 'The Recruiting Question', *The United Services Magazine,* IV (1891–2), p.75; Arnold-Forster, *Our Home Army,* pp.34–7.
106. Anon., 'How to Render the Army Popular as a Profession', *Colburn's,* II (1867), pp.390–3; H.W.C.-B., 'Does it Pay to Enlist?', *Colburn's,* IX (1894), pp.229–40.
107. Charles Booth, *Life and Labour of the People in London,* II (1891), p.36.
108. B. Seebohm Rowntree, *Poverty–a Study of Town Life* (1900), pp.57, 144.
109. P.H. Mann's study of the village of Ridgemount, Bedfordshire, in 1904 shows that at that time 34.3 per cent of the population (41 per cent of the working class) were living in primary poverty, and an additional 11.3 per cent (13.6 per cent) respectively were living in secondary poverty. Furthermore, 25.9 per cent of the families above the poverty line would have been below were it not for supplementary earnings such as money sent by absent children. See P.H. Mann, 'Life in an Agricultural Village in England', *Sociological Papers,* I, 1904, pp.176–7, 189. A similar study of village life with comparable findings is M.F. Davies, *Life in an English Village* (1909), see particularly pp.138–91.
110. Grenville Murray, *Six Months in the Ranks,* p.62.
111. A Non-Commissioned Officer, 'Our Non-Commissioned Officers', *Colburn's,* III (1880), pp.98–113.
112. The normal ratio of NCOs to enlisted men was in the nature of one to six, and approximately one-third to one-half of these were sergeants of one grade or another. *Report of the Army Reorganisation Committee* (1881), pp.677–8; *General Annual Return of the British Army,* P.P., XLII (c.6196), 1890, p.10.
113. A Non-Commissioned Officer, op.cit.
114. Cairnes, *The Army from Within,* p.119; *The Advantages of the Army,* P.P., LIV (c.81), 1898, p.6; cited hereafter as *Advantages of the Army* (1898); The Recruiting of the British Army–the Old System and the New, WO.33/35.
115. *Report of the Committee on Short Service Conditions* (1881), p.15.
116. *Report of the Army Reorganisation Committee* (1881), pp.27–8.
117. *Report of the Committee on Short Service Conditions* (1881), pp.15–17; Improvements in the Pay and Position of Non-Commissioned Officers, WO.33/6673; An Officer, *Thoughts on Recruiting* (1866); A Non-Commissioned Officer, 'Our Non-Commissioned Officers', *Colburn's,* IV (1880), pp.98–113; A Troop Sergeant-Major of Dragoons, 'Our Non-Commissioned Officers', *Colburn's,* IV (1891–2), pp.361–7.
118. Hansard, CCXXII (8 March 1875), c.1450; CCXXVII (2 March 1876), c.1260–1; CCXLIV (3 March 1879), cc.63–7; *The Times,* 18 March 1881; *Report of the Committee on Recruiting,* WO.33/27, *Report of the Army Reorganisation Committee* (1881), pp.27–31; *Report of the Committee on Short Service Conditions* (1881), pp.15–17.
119. The Recruiting of the British Army–the Old System and the New, WO.33/35.
120. *Report of the Commission on Recruiting* (1861), p.210.
121. *Advantages of the Army* (1898), p.8.
122. A lance-corporal was not of course considered to be an NCO even though the step from the rank of private was a clear promotion.
123. Acland-Troyte, *Through the Ranks,* pp.53–4; John F. Lucy, *There's a Devil in the Drum* (1938), pp.63–4; *Report of the Wantage Committee*

(1892), p.19.

124. One step below them corporals messed with the lower ranks, yet drew equal pay. Greenwood, *The Cornhill Magazine,* VII (1863), pp.441–56.

125. *Report of the Inspector-General of Recruiting,* P.P., XVIII (c.1655), 1877, p.1.

126. Improvement in the Pay and Position of Non-Commissioned Officers, WO.32/6673; A Non-Commissioned Officer, 'Our Non-Commissioned Officers', *Colburn's,* III (1880), pp.98–113.

127. This was a step intended more to enhance the position of the NCO than to provide a transition to commissioned rank. A clear distinction was maintained between the warrant officer and the commissioned officer. Despite many appeals by interested parties, the War Office refused to allow warrant officers to appear in public in mufti. Sir Samuel Smith to W.H. Smith 10 Sept. 1886, 19 Sept. 1886; W. H. Smith to Sir Samuel Smith, 11 Sept. 1886, 21 Sept. 1886, Smith MSS., WO.110/3, 110/5; *Report of the Principal Changes in Army Organisation Effective 1 July 1881,* P.P., LVIII (c.2922), 1881, p.5.

128. Anon., 'Recruiting and Enlistment', *Colburn's,* II (1865), pp.1–15.

129. *Report of the Wantage Committee* (1892), pp.19–20; *Advantages of the Army* (1898), p.8.

130. Mole, *King's Hussar,* pp.335–6; Wyndham, *Queen's Service,* p.263.

131. A Lieutenant-Colonel, *The British Army* (1899), p.241.

132. *The Army and What It Offers* (circa 1910); Hardy, *Thomas Atkins,* p.244.

133. Mole, *King's Hussar,* p.353.

134. Sprot, *Incidents and Anecdotes in the Life of Lieutenant-General Sprot,* II (1907), p.18.

135. A Voice from the Ranks, *The British Army and What We Think Of It* (1871), p.14.

136. A Quartermaster, 'The Duties of Regimental Quartermasters Particularised', *Colburn's,* III (1880), pp.267–77, 389–400; Anon., 'The Position of Regimental Quartermasters Considered', *Colburn's,* I (1880), pp.403–18.

137. *Accounts of the System of Military Education in France, Prussia, Austria, Bavaria, and the U.S.,* P.P., XXV (c.47), 1870, p.237.

138. A Voice from the Ranks, *The British Army,* p.14.

139. See Brian Bond, *The Victorian Army and the Staff College, 1854–1914* (1972), pp.17–30.

140. Richards, *Old Soldier Sahib,* p.156 P.E. Razzell has shown that as late as 1912 more than 40 per cent of officers in the home army were landed gentry or aristocratic in background. See P.E. Razzell, 'Social Origins of Officers of the Indian and British Home Army, 1758–1962', *British Journal of Sociology,* XIV (1963), p.253.

141. W.E. Gladstone to Edward Cardwell, 4 Oct. 1870, Cardwell MSS., PRO.30/48/2/7; W.P.B. 'Army Reform', *Colburn's,* II (1855), pp.192–203; Anon., 'On Purchase in the Army and Promotion from the Ranks', *Colburn's,* II (1861), pp.14–25; Anon., 'The British Soldier', *New Monthly Magazine,* CXXI, p.133; W.W. Knollys, 'Risen from the Ranks', *Colburn's,* I (1864), pp.50–65; Anon., 'Promotion from the Ranks', *Colburn's,* II (1877), pp.410–18.

142. J.W. Crowe, *Our Army; Or Penny-Wise and Pound Foolish* (1856); General Sir J. F. Burgoyne, *Army Reform* (1857); Anon., 'Recruits without Compulsory Enlistment', *Colburn's,* II (1875), pp.49–67; Anon., 'Promotion from the Ranks', *Colburn's,* II (1877), pp.410–18; *Report of the Commission on the War in South Africa* (1904), p.556.

143. W.P.B., op.cit., pp.192–203; Knollys, op.cit., pp.50–65; Anon., 'Our Non-Commissioned Officers', *Colburn's,* I (1866), pp.166–77.

144. Lieutenant-General the Hon. C. Grey to Edward Cardwell, 24 Dec. 1869, Cardwell MSS., PRO.30/48/1/1.
145. Florence Nightingale to John Sutherland [?] 23 Nov. 1872, Nightingale MSS., 45753; Anon., 'On Purchase in the Army and Promotion from the Ranks', *Colburn's,* II (1861), pp.14–25; Anon., 'Promotion of the Non-Commissioned Officers of the Army', *Colburn's,* II (1874), pp.365–70; Knollys, op.cit., pp.50–65; Stuart, *Reminiscences,* p.276.
146. Anon., 'Soldiers', *Colburn's,* II (1866), pp.406–20.
147. Acland-Troyte, *Through the Ranks,* p.163.
148. Henry Curling, ed., *Recollections of Rifleman Harris* (1929), p.41.
149. A.F. Corbett, *Service through Six Reigns* (1953), p.47.
150. Wyndham, *Following the Drum,* p.63.
151. Acland-Troyte, *Through the Ranks,* p.163; Wyndham, *Queen's Service,* pp.248–9; *Report of the Wantage Committee* (1892), pp.410–11; A Sergeant, 'Prospects for Gentlemen in the Ranks', *Colburn's,* XVI (1897–8), pp.383–9; Hardy, *Thomas Atkins,* p.242; Richards, *Old Soldier Sahib,* p.272. The purchase and sale of commissions was of course abolished in 1871.
152. Acland-Troyte, *Through the Ranks,* pp.163–70; Robertson, *From Private to Field-Marshal,* p.30.
153. The army of course valued this type of recruit, and looked with favour upon their progress which could be pointed to as proof of the openness of the Service and of the fact that men of ability could always rise through the ranks. Edward Cardwell to W.E. Gladstone, 31 Aug. 1874, Gladstone MSS., 44210.
154. Robertson, *From Private to Field-Marshal,* p.30.
155. A.H.D. Acland-Troyte had been a volunteer officer before enlisting as a private soldier in the regular army in 1873. He argued that the examination he was required to pass for his commission demanded skills he could only have acquired as an officer. Acland-Troyte, *Through the Ranks,* p.166; see also Wyndham, *Queen's Service,* pp.248–9.
156. Anon., 'Promotion from the Ranks', *Colburn's,* III (1873), pp.322–6.
157. Robertson, op.cit., p.31.
158. Ibid., pp.31–3.
159. A committee on officers' expenses in 1903 found that an initial sum of at least £600 plus a minimum private income of £270 yearly was necessary to maintain a commission in the cavalry. Infantry regiments, especially country units, were less expensive, although still prohibitive in cost. *Report of the Committee on Officers' Expenses,* P.P., X (c.1421), 1903, p.8.
160. B. de Sales la Terriere, *Days That Are Gone* (1924), pp.110–11.
161. Victor Bonham-Carter, *Soldier True* (1963), p.30.
162. Robertson, op.cit., pp.29–31.
163. Knollys, *Colburn's,* I (1864), pp.50–65; A Common Soldier, *Army Misrule* (1860); Anon., 'The British Soldier', *New Monthly Magazine,* CXXI, p.133.
164. Mole, *King's Hussar,* p.355.
165. Hansard, CCCXV (16 May 1887), c.95; Anon., 'The Present Lack of Good Non-Commissioned Officers', *Colburn's,* II (1878), pp.474–85.
166. Hansard, CXLIV (12 March 1857), cc.2246–7; CLI (27 July 1858), cc.2238–9; CCXCIX (13 July 1885), c.468; Anon., *Army Reform: Its Tendency in the Future* (1875); Blatchford, *My Life in the Army,* p.256; Wyndham, *Following the Drum,* p.63.
167. Sir Charles Trevelyan, *The British Army in 1868* (1868); *Papers Relating to the Sale and Purchase of Commissions in the Army,* P.P., XXXVII (c.498),

1857–8, pp.409–505.
168. *Correspondence Relating to the Condition of the Regimental Quartermasters of the Army,* P.P., XXXIII (c.414), 1863, pp.285–301; Hansard, CLXX (15 May 1863), cc.1774–9; CLXXVI (21 June 1864), cc.92–4; CCXCV (19 March 1885), cc.1755–9; CCCXV (16 May 1887), c.71–2.
169. Hansard, CXLIV (12 March 1875), cc.2246–9; CLI (27 July 1858), cc.2238–9; VIII (20 Feb. 1893), c.1855.
170. Bond, *Staff College,* pp.29–30.
171. *General Annual Return of the British Army,* P.P., XLIII (c.1323), 1875, p.25; XLIII (c.6196), 1890, p.32; LIII (c.9426), 1899, p.34.
172. A free discharge might be granted to a recruit who could prove false or improper enlistment (by having been under age for instance) or who had failed to reach minimum physical standards within a certain time, or to others if a considerable reduction in establishment was contemplated. Edward Cardwell to Lord Kimberly, 14 April 1869, Cardwell MSS., PRO.30/48/5/31.
173. *First Report of a Committee on the Royal Hospitals at Chelsea and Kilmainham,* P.P., XII (c.191), 1870, p.i.
174. *Second Report of a Committee on the Royal Hospitals at Chelsea and Kilmainham,* P.P., XIV (c.275), 1871, p.v; Hansard, XXXIX (27 March 1876), cc.303–4.
175. *Report of the Committee on Chelsea and Kilmainham* (1883), p.59; the Duke of Cambridge to Edward Cardwell, 18 Nov. 1869, Cardwell MSS., PRO.30/48/3/12.
176. Memorandum on Half-Pay, Pensions, etc., WO.33/19.
177. *Report of the Committee on Disability Pensions,* WO.33/199.
178. *Report of the Wantage Committee* (1892), pp.17–18; Hansard, LX (5 July 1898), c.1113.
179. See George Ainley, Secretary of the Royal Hospital, Chelsea, to E.C. Fanshaw, 6 Nov. 1871, Cardwell MSS., PRO.30/48/2/8; Grant of Modified Pensions, WO.32/6681; Curling, *Recollections of Rifleman Harris,* p.124; Corbett, *Service through Six Reigns,* pp.55–6.
180. Grant of Modified Pensions, WO.32/6681.
181. *Report of the Army Reorganisation Committee* (1881), p.503; *Report of the Committee on Short Service Conditions* (1881), pp.18–19.
182. *Report of the Committee on the Regulations for Soldiers' Pensions,* WO.32/8794.
183. Troop Sergeant-Major Edwin Mole for instance lost 4d a day off his pension because his service was broken when he was convicted, wrongfully as it happens, on a charge of drunkenness. See Mole, *King's Hussar,* pp.201, et seq.
184. Payment of Soldiers' Pensions, WO.32/6506; Payment of Pensioners, WO.32/6504; Memorandum Relating to the Quarterly Payment of Soldiers' Pensions and Army Reserve Pay, WO.32/6508; Hansard, XXIII (10 April 1894), cc.12–13.
185. Regulations Relative to the Conveyance of Discharged Soldiers, WO.32/6682; Reckoning of Service Towards Good Conduct Pay, WO.32/6666. War Office records show clearly that many took the opportunity to emigrate to Canada, Australia or New Zealand. See Commutation of Pensions, WO.32/6546.
186. Hansard, CLVII (31 May 1860), c.1841; CCXVI (1 July 1873), cc.1619–20; Anon., 'Pensioners and Recruits', *Colburn's,* II (1867), pp.13–18.
187. Heavy Drill 'Em, *Information for the Civilian* (1856), c.6.

188. Hansard, CLXXVIII (6 April 1865), cc.853–4; CCXVI (1 July 1873), c.1620; CCXLIV (3 March 1879), cc.67–8; LIV (25 Feb. 1898), cc.82–6; Colonel James Lindsay, 'A Scheme for the Reorganisation, Recruiting, and Instruction of the Army', *JRUSI*, IV (1861), pp.73–83; Anon., 'The Real Position and Advantages of the Soldier', *Colburn's*, I (1866), pp.584–98; A General Officer, Royal Marines, 'Thoughts on Army Organisation and Discipline', *Colburn's*, II (1876), pp.101–5; Captain F. Chenevix Trench, *Short Service and Deferred Pay* (1876), passim; Skene Dubh, 'A Solution to the Army Problem', *Colburn's*, XVI (1897–8), pp.572–99.
189. In 1874 officers attending a discussion on recruitment at the Royal United Services Institution all agreed that the army's difficulties could be reduced to a question of finances and that the majority of whatever funds were available should be spent on augmenting pensions. In 1891 the Inspector-General of Recruiting, Major-General J.H. Rocke, told a similar group '. . .the real enemy at the gate of the recruiter is the discontented reservist'. See Adams, *JRUSI*, XVIII (1874), pp.55–98; passim; Dooner, *JRUSI*, XXXV (1891), pp.207–38; Lieutenant-Colonel de Mesurier to W.H. Smith, 6 Sept. 1886, 16 Oct. 1886, Smith MSS., WO.110/3, 110/5; also Hansard, CLXXVII (20 March 1865), cc.1961–3; CCXXVII (25 Feb. 1876), c.943; Archibald Forbes, 'The Limited Enlistment Act', *The Cornhill Magazine*, X (1864), pp.207–17; Anon., 'Recruits without Compulsory Enlistment', *Colburn's*, III (1875), pp.49–67; Lieutenant-Colonel J. McD. Moody, 'Recruiting for Her Majesty's Service', *JRUSI*, XXIX (1885), pp.565–628; Dooner, *Colburn's*, XVI (1897–8), pp.337–48.
190. The Papers of General Lord Roberts on the Report on the Terms and Conditions of Service in the Army, WO.33/52.
191. *Report of the Wantage Committee* (1892), pp.17, 563.
192. *The Times*, 15 Dec. 1898; *The Labour Leader*, 11 Aug. 1894, 28 Sept. 1895; *The Border Advertiser*, 8 June 1892, 2 Nov. 1892, 9 Nov. 1892; *The Scottish Border Record*, 4 June 1892; *The Northern Ensign and Weekly Gazette*, 22 Jan. 1857.
193. *The Glasgow Sentinel and Scottish Banner*, 2 May 1868.
194. *The Labour Leader*, 31 March 1894.
195. *The Advantages of the Army* (1898), p.10.
196. *Report of the Commission on the War in South Africa* (1904), p.556; *The Army and What It Offers* (circa 1910), passim.
197. *Report of the War Office Committee on the Treatment of Soldiers Invalided for Tuberculosis*, P.P., XI (c.3930), 1908, pp.3–5; *Report of the Committee on Disability Pensions*, WO.33/199.
198. Grant of Modified Pensions, WO.32/6681.
199. See *Return of the Scales for Ordinary Pensions Adopted under Section 3 of the Police Act*, 1890, P.P., LXIV (c.142), 1890–1, p.9; *Return of the Pension Scale under the Police Bill, 1894*, LXIII (c.67), 1884, p.1; *Return of the Terms and Conditions of Employment of the Royal Irish Constabulary*, P.P., LXXIV, pt.II (c.281), 1893–4, p.6.
200. Deductions from Army Pensions for Maintenance and Asylums, WO.32/6523.
201. Pensions and Parish Relief, WO.32/8788.
202. With the introduction of short-service enlistment in 1870, the strength of the total army reserve rose from a nominal 283 to more than 78,800 in thirty years, and as will be shown, the provisions the army made for its reservists were meagre. In many cases the benefit of the retaining fee was more than offset by the difficulty reservists encountered in finding work. *General Annual Return of the British Army*, P.P., XLIII (c.1323), 1875,

p.75; LII (c.9426), 1899, p.135.

203. *Return of the Number of Soldiers Dischargeable on the Poor Rates in December 1877,* P.P., LXXVIII (c.332), 1898, p.61.
204. Hansard, LXI (8 July 1898), c.317.
205. A number of serious cases of this sort is outlined in one of the appendices to the Wantage Committee Report for instance. See *Report of the Wantage Committee* (1892), pp.564–7.
206. Hansard, CCXXVII (25 Feb. 1876), cc.943–4; XII (29 May 1893), c.1472.
207. Anon., 'Our Non-Commissioned Officers', *Colburn's,* I (1861), pp.166–77; A Troop Sergeant-Major of Dragoons, 'Our Non-Commissioned Officers', *United Services Magazine,* IV (1891–2), pp.361–7; Beedos, 'The State of the Army I', *Colburn's,* XIX (1899), pp.415–19; Moody, *JRUSI,* XLI (1897), pp.125–66.
208. Anon., 'The Recruiting of the Army', *Colburn's,* II (1861), pp.159–70; Sir Charles E. Trevelyan, *The British Army in 1868* (1868), p.53; Phipps Onslow, 'The Philosophy of Recruiting', *The Contemporary Review,* XII (1869), pp.545–8; A Voice from the Ranks, *The British Army,* p.18; John Holms, *The British Army in 1875* (1875), pp.57–9; Captain R.J. Byford, 'The Civil Employment of Discharged Soldiers, a Suggestion', *Colburn's,* XIX (1899), pp.645–7; Arnold-Forster, *Our Home Army,* p.33.
209. Hansard, CCVII (19 June 1871), cc.238–45; CCXXVII (25 Feb. 1876), cc.941–4; CCXLVII (24 June 1879), c.576; CCCL (19 Feb. 1891), c.1069; XXV (13 June 1894), cc.1012–15; LXVII (3 March 1899), cc.1310–16; Adams, *JRUSI,* XVIII (1874), pp.55–98; Colonel G.H. Moncrieff, 'State and National Responsibility in regard to the Employment of Reserve Soldiers and their Transfer to Civil Life', *JRUSI,* XXIX (1885), pp.565–628; Knollys, *The United Services Magazine,* III (1891), pp.170–81.
210. Colonel F. Chenevix Trench, *The Dark Side of Short Service* (1887), pp.15–16.
211. The War Office recognised the desirability of annual reserve training, but was unwilling to insist upon it for fear that it would restrict the soldier's employment opportunities even further. Edward Stanhope to General Frederick Roberts, 29 May 1891, Stanhope MSS., 1401.
212. *Report of the Wantage Committee* (1892), p.533.
213. Trench, op.cit., pp.3–6; Hansard, CCCV (16 May 1887), c.71.
214. *Report of the Committee on Civil Employment* (1876), pp.iii, 21, 168–71.
215. *Report of the Select Committee on the Employment of Soldiers, Sailors, and Marines in Civil Departments of the Public Service,* P.P., XV (c.393), 1877, p.2; cited hereafter as *Report of the Committee on Civil Employment* (1877).
216. *Report of the Select Committee on Retired Soldiers' and Sailors' Employment,* P.P., XII (c.338), 1895, pp.1–56, passim; cited hereafter as *Report of the Committee on Civil Employment* (1895).
217. *Report of the Committee on Civil Employment* (1876), pp.172–5.
218. *Report of the Committee on Civil Employment* (1877), pp.21–2.
219. *Report of the Select Committee on Retired Soldiers' and Sailors' Employment,* P.P., XV (c.258), 1894, pp.18–21; cited hereafter as *Report of the Committee on Civil Employment* (1894), One of the most influential was the Duke of Cambridge, who underlined the need for a stimulus to recruitment, and stressed the suitability of ex-soldiers for clerical positions. *Report of the Committee on Civil Employment* (1877), pp.81–92.
220. Employment of Ex-Servicemen in the German Army, WO.33/54; *Second Report of the Select Committee on the Army Estimates,* P.P., VII (c.212),

1888, p.44; Anon., 'Comparative Advantages of the French and British Non-Commissioned Officer', *Colburn's,* I (1877), pp.148–58; A Staff Officer, 'The Backbone of an Army: I–Non-Commissioned Officers Abroad', *United Services Magazine,* IV (1891–2), pp.526–36.

221. *Appendix to the Report of the Commission into the Supplies of the British Army in the Crimea,* P.P., XX (c.2007), 1856, p.194.
222. Clerks in Military Staff Offices, WO.43/75.
223. *Report of the Committee on Civil Employment* (1877), pp.iii–vii.
224. *Report of the Committee on the Employment of Soldiers and Pensioners,* WO.33/53; *Report of the Committee on Employment in the Postmaster General's Department of NCOs and Men of the Royal Engineers Who Have Been Discharged from the Army or Who Have Passed into the Army Reserve.* WO.33/43; *Report of the Committee on Civil Employment* (1894), passim; *Report of the Wantage Committee* (1892), pp.18–19.
225. *Report of the Committee on the Employment of Military Clerks in the War Office,* WO.33/430.
226. *Report of the Committee on Civil Employment* (1895), p.vi; *Report of the Committee on Civil Employment* (1906), p.30.
227. *Report of the Committee on Civil Employment* (1906), pp.9–11; *Report of the Committee on Civil Employment* (1895), p.vi.
228. *Report of the Army Reorganisation Committee* (1881), pp.29–31.
229. Trench, *Dark Side of Short Service,* p.40; Hansard, XXXIX (12 April 1896), c.1426.
230. *Report of the Committee on Civil Employment* (1895), pp.iii–vii.
231. Civil Employment of Retired Soldiers and Sailors, WO.33/39.
232. *Report of the Wantage Committee* (1892), pp.59–60; Hansard, XXXIX (12 April 1896), c.1438; Colonel W.T. Dooner, 'The Civil Employment of Reserve and Discharged Soldiers', *Colburn's,* XX (1899), pp.196–200.
233. Sinclair, *Contemporary Review,* LVI (1889), pp.610–21; Rev. W. Le Grave, 'The Army Reserve Man', *United Services Magazine,* IV (1891–2), pp.452–8; Major F.N. Maude, 'The Training of Men with the Colours in Relation with their Subsequent Employment in Civil Life', *JRUSI,* XLI (1897), pp.1333–48.
234. *Report of the Inspector-General of Recruiting,* P.P., XVII (c.5652), 1889, p.14.
235. *Report of the Inspector-General of Recruiting,* P.P., XVI (c.8370), 1897, p.14.
236. See for instance Edward Cardwell to W.E. Gladstone, 11 Jan. 1869, 21 Dec. 1870, Gladstone MSS., 44119; W.E. Gladstone to Edward Cardwell, 12 Jan. 1869, 28 Dec. 1870, Cardwell MSS., PRO.30/48/2/6, 30/48/2/7; W.E. Smith argued that by finding employment for ex-soldiers in Ireland, the state would be assured of a hedge against any revolutionary movements. W.E. Smith to Sir Michael Hicks Beach, 5 Nov. 1886, Smith MSS., WO.110/5.
237. Civil Employment of Discharged Soldiers and Army Reserve Men, WO.33/70.
238. *Report of the Wantage Committee* (1892), pp.18–19, 28; Summary of the Recommendations of the Wantage Committee and of Action Taken, WO.33/52; *Report of the Inspector-General of Recruiting,* P.P., XIII (c.8770), 1898, pp.12–13.
239. *Return Showing the Number of Men of the Army Reserve Employed in Civil Departments of the State,* P.P., XLVII (c.323), 1878.
240. *Report of the Wantage Committee* (1892), p.18.
241. *General Annual Return of the British Army,* P.P., LIII (c.9426), 1899, p.34.

242. *Report of the Inspector-General of Recruiting,* P.P., XI (c.9185), 1899, p.22.
243. *Report of the Committee on Civil Employment* (1894), p.133.
244. Roberts, *The Nineteenth Century,* XV (1884), pp.1055–74, passim.
245. See for instance Commander Wallace B. McHardy, 'A Scheme for Establishing a Royal Army Society for Each County and Great City, in Order to Improve the Status of the British Soldier on his Return to Civil Life, *JRUSI,* XXXVII (1893), pp.361–86.
246. *Report of the Committee on Civil Employment* (1906), pp.9 et seq.
247. *Report of the Committee on Civil Employment* (1895), pp.iv–v.
248. *Annual Report of the Army and Navy Pensioners' and Time-Expired Men's Society for 1884,* Smith MSS., WO.110/1.
249. *Report of the Inspector-General of Recruiting,* P.P., IX (c.519), 1901, p.24.
250. *Report of the Inspector-General of Recruiting,* P.P., X (c.110), 1900, p.21.
251. *Report of the Inspector-General of Recruiting,* P.P., IX (c.519), 1901, p.23.
252. A.B. Tucker, *The Romance of the King's Army* (1908), p.308.
253. Anon., 'Hope for Discharged Soldiers–the London Commissionaires', *Colburn's,* III (1866), pp.337–43; *The Times,* 31 Jan. 1881.
254. Wages varied, depending on ranks, from £1 1s per week for privates to £1 8s or more for sergeants. Edgar R. Hawks, *Guide to Obtaining Civil Employment* (Chatham, 1887), p.28.
255. *Report of the Committee on Civil Employment* (1906), p.5; *The Times,* 21 Aug. 1876.
256. Rudyard Kipling, 'Shillin' a Day', in *Rudyard Kipling's Verse,* (1941), p.429.
257. Recruiting the British Army–the Old System and the New, WO.33/35.
258. Memorandum on Half-Pay, Pensions, Etc., WO.33/19.
259. There are few figures available, however returns indicate that between just 1873 and 1875 there were on the average 627 wives and 1,233 children of soldiers in receipt of poor relief in England and Wales each year. *Return from Each Union of England on the Number of Wives and Children of Soldiers in Receipt of Poor Relief at Any Time During the Parochial Year 1873,* P.P., LV (c.103), 1874, p.7; *Return of the Number of Wives and Children of Soldiers in Receipt of Poor Relief at Any Time During The Parochial Year 1874,* P.P., XLIII (c.359), 1875, pp.1–33; *Return of the Number of Wives and Children of Soldiers in Receipt of Poor Relief at Any Time During the Parochial Year 1875,* P.P., XLIII (c.329), 1876, pp.1–5.
260. See Anon., 'A Voice from the Ranks', *Once a Week* (15 June 1867), p.689. This was one of the few cases where the issue was raised before 1899.
261. *Army Estimates,* P.P., XLII (c.36), 1870, p.2.
262. *Report of the Joint Select Committee of the House Of Lords and the House of Commons on Charitable Agencies for Relief of Widows and Orphans of Soldiers and Sailors,* P.P., V (c.289), 1901, pp.v–ix; cited hereafter as *Report of the Committee on Charitable Agencies* (1901).
263. Hansard, CCLXIV (11 Aug. 1881), c.1534.
264. Hansard, CCLXXIII (28 July 1882), c.4.
265. *Report of the Committee on the Disposal of Funds from the Effects of Deceased Soldiers, Fines for Drunkenness, and Regimental Charitable Funds,* WO.33/39.
266. *Report of the Committee on the Grant of Pensions to the Widows of Non-Commissioned Officers and Men,* WO.33/40.
267. *Report of the Inspector-General of Recruiting,* P.P., X (c.110), 1900, p.8.

268. *Report of the Committee on Charitable Agencies* (1901), p.v.
269. *Eighteenth Report of the Royal Commissioners of the Patriotic Fund*, P.P., XIII (c.2675), 1880, pp.14–15.
270. *Papers Relating to the Royal Patriotic Fund*, P.P., XLII (c.230), 1870, p.3.
271. Hudson E. Kearley, 'The Royal Patriotic Fund', *The Fortnightly Review*, LV (1894), pp.634–44.
272. The Patriotic Fund for instance sent every soldier's widow a gratuity of £5 plus £1 for each child on being informed of her husband's death.
273. *Report of the War Relief Funds Committee*, P.P., XLII (c.196), 1900, pp.6 et seq.
274. *Report of the Committee on Charitable Agencies* (1901), pp.v–ix.

5 THE RECRUITING PROBLEM

> Outside the pages of popular fiction, the soldier as he really is, is scarcely heard of, and over his life hangs a veil of reserve that is but seldom lifted.
>
> Sergeant Horace Wyndham

> It is drink and being hard up which leads a great many to enlist.
>
> Maj.-Gen. Lord Wm. Paulet

Throughout the whole of the period 1856 to 1899, one of the biggest problems facing the regular army was to recruit men in sufficient numbers to meet its needs. It impinged upon most aspects of military life and overshadowed other contemporary issues. Changes in the terms and conditions of service were designed to improve the lives of the rank and file, to increase the efficiency of the forces, and in some cases to achieve certain strategic goals, such as the creation of an effective regular reserve. In nearly every instance, however, a major consideration was the effect these measures could be expected to have on recruitment. Essential to a discussion of the recruiting problem and the attempts made to find solutions is an understanding of the nature of the recruiting system, the obstacles to recruitment presented by the image of the army, recruiting appeals and inducements, and especially the effects of the changing terms of service. To an extent none of these can easily be separated from the question of the motives which men had for enlistment, though these are much more difficult to pin down.

The attempts to reform the machinery of recruitment and to change the army's image after 1856 achieved only a limited success. There was therefore a considerable debate about how to strengthen the inducements to enlist, and a great deal of experimentation with the conditions and terms of service. One main aspect of this was the controversy over long- versus short-term enlistment. A considerable volume of speculation as to why men enlisted can be obtained as a result from official enquiries and from the observations of officers concerned with recruitment. This is a major though indirect source of evidence about the reasons why men were attracted to the army. Although the army failed to solve its recruiting difficulties, it did not necessarily fail to put its finger on the chief impediments or to perceive the best methods of overcoming them.

Soldier's memoirs are a fund of information; but they are not numerous. From 1856 to 1899 there were in the neighbourhood of 1,125,000 men enlisted in the regular army[1] but few wrote memoirs. Nor can it necessarily be assumed that the writers were typical of the soldiers of their day. For one thing a high proportion reached non-commissioned rank and a very few rose even higher. Yet their initial reasons for enlistment and those of their immediate comrades may not have differed significantly from those of many others. The problems of evidence and interpretation perhaps cannot be fully resolved, but a reasonable estimate of men's motives for enlisting can certainly be obtained.

1. The State of Recruitment, 1856–99

Inadequate recruitment is clearly one of the biggest hazards confronting the voluntary service army. In spite of efforts to relieve deficiencies and to adapt to the difficulties of raising men the Victorian army faced severe manpower shortages throughout virtually the whole of the second half of the nineteenth century. A number of crises dotted the period. Close on the strains of the Crimean War and the Indian Mutiny followed the threat of war against France in 1859. The appointment of a Royal Commission on recruitment the following year was an attempt to find a solution to the shortage of men.[2] Prussian military successes against first the Danes in 1864 and then the Austrians in 1866 underlined Britain's insecure military position and the shortcomings of recruitment.[3] In Parliament the government was forced to admit that recruiting was a failure and to accede to pressure for a second Royal Commission.[4] Within four years mass armies were mobilised on the Continent again but despite the reforms instigated by Cardwell and subsequent Secretaries of State for War, enlistment continued to lag behind the army's needs. By 1890 it was clear that shortages were becoming crucial. The following year the government, admitting that the burden of foreign reliefs could no longer be met, appointed the Wantage Committee on the terms and conditions of service in the army.[5] Within ten years there was another massive shock comparable to that suffered during the Crimean War. Despite the accumulation of regular reserve forces of nearly 80,000 men by 1899,[6] militia, yeomanry, volunteers, and even colonial contingents had to be called upon to help the regular army settle a localised colonial conflict.

The many crises which erupted after 1856 were in some ways only symptoms of an ever-present recruiting problem. In fact, the army suffered from a chronic inability to raise sufficient men to meet its needs. This is clear from statistics which compare the establishment, i.e. the number of men voted by Parliament, with the actual number of NCOs and men serving on the first day of the year.[7] Because army estimates were not normally presented to Parliament until February or March these figures indicate fairly the situation at the end of each year, and reveal the army's failure either to raise or maintain the numbers voted.[8] In the majority of cases the establishment exceeded the number of effectives in spite of the fact that it was reduced each year between 1861 and 1882, and even in 1898 the numbers voted were not as high as during the years immediately following the Crimean War. For much of the period wastage remained constant while the establishment was reduced sharply. Although there was a substantial long-term increase in the numbers enlisted, however, recruitment was unable to keep pace. After 1876, the effects of short-service enlistment began to be felt, and during the next twenty-two years the number of men discharged annually all but doubled. Although recruitment was up in these years, for the most part it was insufficient to make good the wastage through discharge, death, desertion and other causes. As a result on occasions auxiliary forces had to be mobilised.

Claims by recruiting officers that recruitment was satisfactory cannot be supported.[9] The male population of the United Kingdom aged fifteen to twenty-four grew from approximately 2,523,100 in 1859 to 3,973,200 in 1901, an increase of 57.5 per cent.[10] Army recruitment on the other hand expanded by only 45 per cent during the same period. In 1859 the army enlisted 1.1 per cent of the men of this age group in Britain, in 1898 approximately 1.0 per cent.[11] Moreover exceptional methods had to be employed to obtain even these numbers.

A fruitful way of getting around the shortage of men was to lower minimum physical standards. This was strongly opposed by regular officers but was nevertheless resorted to frequently by the War Office.[12] In 1861 definite age limits for enlistment of seventeen to twenty-five and a minimum height of 5 feet 8 inches were laid down.[13] In 1868 the latter was lowered to 5 feet 5 inches. The following year regulations were altered again. In anticipation of a surge in recruiting because of the attractions of short-service enlistment[14] standards were raised first to 5 feet 7 inches, then to 5 feet 8 inches, and finally settled on 5 feet 7 inches. In the end optimism had to be abandoned in the face of reality. In January 1870 the army stood over 4,100 below establishment. Successive regulations of that year again lowered the minimum height to 5 feet 4½ inches. The popularity of short-service enlistment introduced later that year did have some effect, though by nowhere near what had been predicted, and allowed the army to be more discerning. In 1871 the minimum age was raised to eighteen, and the standard of height was raised an inch to 5 feet 5½ inches; 1878 brought it to 5 feet 6 inches. The secret behind cheerful recruiting figures for 1880–2, however, was another reduction in standards. During these years the minimum height was reduced progressively to 5 feet 4 inches, and in 1883 it dropped to the lowest it was ever to be, 5 feet 3 inches.[15] This standard was deviated from only marginally during the remainder of the century. In 1889 it was raised to 5 feet 4 inches, at which level it remained until 1897; in 1900 it was reduced first to 5 feet 3½ inches, then to 5 feet 3 inches. A minimum weight of 115 pounds was stipulated in 1884 and was not subsequently altered.[16] It is clear therefore, that while the health and almost certainly also the physical stature of the British people improved markedly between 1856 and 1899, the army was forced to lower physical standards in order to maintain a reduced establishment and to continue to attract to the colours a slightly smaller proportion of the nation's youth.

Nor was this the whole extent of the subterfuge. Not only were physical standards drastically reduced after 1856, but recruits were commonly taken who failed to come up to minimum levels. Before 1892 medical and recruiting officers were allowed, subject to the approval of the chief recruiting officer, to accept men who were slightly below minimum physical standards but who in their view promised to become efficient soldiers. In 1882 permission was given for medical officers to approve on their own authority any recruit who they estimated would, in the reasonably short period of a few months, grow into an efficient soldier. The Wantage Committee recorded a great deal of criticism of the practices which padded out enlistment figures and led to false claims that recruiting was soundly based,[17] and this forced the War Office to reveal the extent to which regulations had been bent. In 1892, the Inspector-General of Recruiting admitted that 'special enlistments' had made up 32 per cent of all recruitment annually in the past few years.[18] Between 1890 and 1898, when the minimum standards required recruits to be eighteen years of age, 115 pounds in weight, and of a height of 5 feet 3½ inches to 5 feet 4 inches, 26 per cent to 30 per cent of all those enlisted failed in at least one respect to meet minimum requirements.[19] Furthermore, just how many men slipped through medical examination with faults undetected is not known. Certainly it was common for recruits to conceal their age.[20] and in some cases, although not so much in later years, doctors were careless in their examination of recruits.[21]

The standards of men being recruited for the army were a cause of grave concern during the later years of the century especially and led to the belief in some quarters that the nation was degenerating physically owing to urbanisation. The basis of these accusations was the exceedingly high number of men who either failed army medical tests outright or who were discharged from the forces within a short period of their enlistment each year. In the seven years 1893 to 1899 alone, 2,887 recruits had to be released for medical reasons after just three months of service.[22] On 1 January 1899, there were 2,563 men in the army at home enlisted by special permission who after a similar length of service had not reached the required standard. In the ensuing controversy, in which alarm at the type of recruit being obtained was expressed by the Director-General of Army Medical Services, an Inter-Departmental Committee on Physical Deterioration was appointed and in 1904 presented its report. Fears of national physical deterioration were played down by emphasising that army recruits were 'rubbish', that 'under present conditions largely those who have failed in civil life offer themselves as recruits', and that in the circumstances it was not uncommon for large numbers to be rejected on medical grounds. Certainly there was no evidence to suggest that the physical standard of even a large proportion of the youth of the nation was deteriorating, yet it was clearly a cause for concern that so many had failed to pass the medical examination at a time when physical standards were at their lowest ever. What was obvious was that the army was able to draw the majority of its recruits from among the nation's poorest physical specimens only. This was bound to result in certain patterns of recruitment which were to have a serious effect on the army.[23]

2. The Recruiting System

A principal target of the efforts to improve recruitment was the recruiting system since it was felt that iniquitous and inefficient methods partly prevented the army from reaching its manpower objectives. At the outset of the period recruitment relied heavily upon a large staff of army pensioners and of soldiers seconded from regular and militia units. Each regiment recruited at its headquarters while, independent of this, the country was divided into several large districts centred around major cities, where fulltime recruiting staff were employed.[24] Regulations forbade units to recruit over their voted establishment, a practice surviving from earlier days when Parliament was eager to limit the size of the army. This meant that recruitment had to be turned off like a tap when the establishment was reached and back on when colonial drafts reduced the size of the home army.[25] Not infrequently potential recruits were turned away who would be urgently needed within a short period of time.[26] The decentralised administration limited supervision and control by the Adjutant-General's department. Both before and after the formalisation of the territorial ties of regiments in 1881 local connections were not fully exploited. Advertisements were rare and tended to be unimaginative notices in a local newspaper that a particular regiment was looking for recruits.[27]

There was a number of glaring abuses which went uncorrected as well. Cash bounties were sometimes used to attract men to the colours, the amount paid varying with the need for men. In 1859 during the threat of war with France, each recruit received £3. Substantial sums such as these encouraged drunkenness, desertion and fraudulent enlistment.[28] Recruiting officials received a fee for every man they enlisted. In 1859 again, £1 7s 6d was shared between the recruiting party and the superintending officer. This of course encouraged recruiters to employ every possible deception in securing recruits.[29] Vagabonds, thieves and other disreputable characters might be enlisted.[30] Other men might be tempted by false stories of high pay and luxurious conditions, and by the promise of a substantial cash bounty. A great deal of recruitment centred on drinking places where unscrupulous recruiting sergeants enveigled men fuddled by the influence of liquor and entraced by deceptive promises of military glory into taking the Queen's shilling. In 1862 Edwin Mole was enlisted while intoxicated and awoke the next morning to find himself a soldier.[31] Nearly ten years later Robert Blatchford, out of work and penniless, was enticed into the army when he encountered a recruiting sergeant who

> . . .slapped his back with his whip, curled his black moustache, like Porthos, and assured a sulky-looking chimney stack that, damme, it was no part of his duty to deceive any lad; that now the short-service Act was passed, a really superior young man might enjoy a six years' picnic at Her Majesty's expense; that we were getting a superior class of recruits now; quite a superior class; that the uniform, dammit, was the proper dress for a man; and the irresistible magnet for the women; that purchase was abolished, and

> any fine young fellow might win a commission; and that as I appeared to be a really very superior person indeed, what did I say to a drink at the King's Arms while he ran a tape over me?[32]

By 1856 the disrepute of such a system was widespread. In a memorandum on army recruitment in 1858, J.R. Godley, then Assistant Under-Secretary of State for War, wrote '. . .no thoughtful man can have observed the scenes that take place daily and nightly at the taverns frequented by our recruiting staff. . .without feeling shame and disgust that such proceedings should form part of the recognised machinery of the British Military Service'.[33]

There was some disagreement over the precise methods to be used by a reformed recruiting system, but at least the direction which improvement should take was clear. The general aim was 'to hold up the army as a profession which a fair proportion of those who are capable of bearing arms might well avail themselves',[34] and the general need was for honesty and propriety in recruiting procedures.[35] More especially, suggestions for improvement centred around three main aspects of the system: improved organisation, the need to eliminate dishonest techniques, and the need to establish better local connections. There was a multitude of detailed suggestions: a separate War Office department to superintend recruiting staffs and procedures;[36] the simplification of the enlistment process; an effort to make certain that each recruit's first few days in the Service were not discouraging;[37] legislation to ensure that soldiers received better treatment in public places;[38] a proposal that servicemen on furlough be given the means and encouragement to recruit among their friends;[39] recruiting marches and closer relations with local magistrates and churchmen in order to publish the attractions of the army and establish local connections;[40] and extensive advertising to banish local ignorance of and prejudices about the army.[41] 'The printer will get three times the number of men', a military journal remarked in 1872, 'for one-third of the money that the Sergeant Kites require to produce a worse article.'[42]

One curious source of opposition to change was concern that the army should continue to absorb and provide discipline and occupation for undesirable elements within society.[43] Senior officers such as Lord Wolseley, who suffered from no delusions as to the inadequacy of regular army recruitment and the need for attracting more men to the colours, nevertheless emphasised the value of this function. 'Civilisation in the United Kingdom', he wrote when

Commander-in-Chief, 'is *pro tanto* the gainer, for every one of those recruits when discharged will be a better man, a better citizen, than he was the day he first put on Her Majesty's uniform.'[44] Others were indifferent to reform because they believed that it would not be possible to change the bases of recruitment. 'The ranks in this country will always be filled, as they were filled in times past,' argued an article concerned with the Limited Enlistment Act of 1870, 'with the dissolute, the idle, and the unfortunate from among the humbler classes'.[45] But these views on their own scarcely damaged the case for reform.

The barriers to quick action lay partly in the political system. Secretaries of State for War often occupied a difficult position in the Cabinet, and faced opposition from colleagues. Many liberals in particular were doubtful about the benefits of a large regular army, and questioned the need to change the basis of recruitment. Old fears of militarism, and of the social instability of having too large a proportion of the population trained in the use of arms fostered such doubts.[46] An even greater stumbling block was the financial stringency which fear of galloping military expenditures encouraged. Because few politicians concerned themselves actively with military affairs, the Secretary of State for War might have little real interest in army reform or be the only one in the Cabinet with any detailed views on military questions. His Cabinet colleagues often tended to approach the army from a different angle activated only by a desire to effect as great a reduction in the Service estimates as possible. This accounts to some extent for the haphazard manner in which questions of army reform were handled, and the reluctance which governments of the period exhibited in contemplating any increase in military expenditure.[47]

In the end, a considerable amount was done if only gradually and slowly, and the large numbers of recruits being absorbed each year by the end of the period was an indication that the machinery was functioning more smoothly.[48] The power to hasten the transfer of men from the colours to the reserve enacted by the short-service legislation of 1870 somewhat mitigated the regulations which prohibited recruitment above the voted establishment.[49] However, these restrictions continued despite the representations of senior officers,[50] until they were withdrawn in 1893–4, after the Wantage Committee had condemned them.[51]

In 1867 recruitment was centralised in the office of an Inspector-General who was able to cut down irregularities and enforce a uniformity in recruiting methods.[52] Henceforth considerable efforts were made to make recruitment more open and above board.[53] The number of pensioners employed was greatly reduced,[54] and regulations provided that men must not be taken before a magistrate for attestation before a minimum of twenty-four hours or a maximum of ninety-six had elapsed, in order that recruits could reconsider and be sure about their intention to enlist.[55] Recruiting advertisements after 1870 set out the terms and conditions of service more clearly,[56] and recruiting officers were instructed to conduct their efforts with propriety and to remove their offices from inns and other public drinking places.[57] Any recruit who could prove he had been misled on enlistment was given a free discharge, and the expenses incurred were charged to the recruiter. Enlistment bounties which encouraged fraudulent enlistment and desertion were done away with in 1870,[58] and measures were taken to make medical examinations more rigid and searching.[59] In later years increasing importance was paid to publicity and advertising. Notices and brochures were displayed in post offices and other public places throughout the country,[60] and numbers of local recruiting marches were organised.[61] Public displays like the Royal Navy and Military Tournament were held annually after 1893. By 1881 advertisements were being run in 140 local and national newspapers, and within ten years the annual budget for newspaper advertisement had reached nearly £5,500.[62] The goal of this publicity was to present conditions in the army fairly but in the best light possible, in order to convince prospective recruits and their families that military service was an honourable and rewarding profession, and that its more odious aspects had been expunged.[63] Upon how successfully this was done would depend another important element in recruitment, the army's image.

3. The Image of the Army

Even a reformed recruiting system had to cope with the problem of the army's image. A critical factor in the success or failure of recruitment was the manner in which the forces were regarded by the British public. During the nineteenth century suspicion of, and disregard for, the army was widespread throughout all levels of society. This hostility had a number of sources. As has often been pointed out, traditional distrust of the standing army survived long into the last century, and after Waterloo there was no clear notion of its national role. The navy was regarded as the country's first line of defence, and had worldwide obligations to police shipping lanes; sailors were frequently away from their native shores, out of sight and out of mind. In contrast, as H.O. Arnold Forster wrote in 1898,

> there are probably few matters upon which it is harder to create and maintain general public interest than those which concern the Army. Popular sentiment has never attached itself to the Army to the same degree and in the same way as to the Navy. The value of the Navy is apparent to all sections of the community, and the services which it has rendered have been of a character very easily understood and appreciated. The Army, represented at home by its least efficient and least imposing detachments, has suffered somewhat in the popular estimation from the fact that it is, and must always be, a second line of defence only. . .No tradition is more deeply rooted in the minds of the poorer classes in all parts of the United Kingdom, than that which represents enlistment as the last step on the downward career of a young man.[64]

Another source of unpopularity was the way in which the army was employed internally. By 1856 with the organisation of local police forces, the army had largely been relieved of duties to enforce the law, but the obligation to come to the aid of the civil power remained, and during the rest of the century troops were used in strikes and to enforce evictions in Ireland.[65]

The army reacted by attempting to remain as uncontroversial and invisible as possible. This led to the Wellingtonian policy, only reversed by Cardwell, of hiding troops from the British public in garrisons around the globe.[66] Nevertheless it was necessary for troops to be quartered in the United Kingdom, and in the absence of proper barracks before 1850 they were billeted on innkeepers and even private householders.[67] In many cases billeting served to perpetuate hostility to the army and keep alive old dislikes. In 1857, a Select Committee into the procedures of billeting revealed the great opposition of innkeepers and others affected by the practice and recommended that alternative means of housing the soldier should be found.[68] In the end Britain's growing network of railways made feasible the concentration of troops in certain areas, and the situation was relieved by the construction of barracks. With alternative quarters available billeting all but disappeared after 1857 and the legal provisions supporting it fell into disuse. How long it took for the discredit it caused to disappear is difficult to say.

For the public in general, dishonest recruiting methods were a more lingering source of the stigma surrounding the army. It was difficult to break out of a vicious circle. The enlistment of doubtful characters, the notorious deceptions of the recruiting sergeant and repelling conditions of military service convinced many ordinary men that the army was the dustbin of the nation. In turn the army was forced to look to devious recruiting measures and to 'waifs and strays' to fill the ranks. The deceptions practised by recruiting officers led to disciplinary problems among those who felt themselves tricked. 'It is not seldom I have heard an intelligent recruit', argued an ex-soldier, 'who showed every appearance of making a good soldier, say that he had been enlisted under an entire misunderstanding, and that he was justified in releasing himself as soon, in any manner, as he could find the opportunity.'[69] At the same time a better class of recruit was discouraged.[70] 'There is no denying the fact', remarked a soldier in 1871, 'that in the present day the army, as a profession, finds small favour in the eyes of steady, intelligent, well-educated young men–the very stamp of men wanted in the service.'[71] Measures designed to prevent fraudulent enlistment and to expedite dishonourable discharges went far towards ridding the army of the habitual offender, but the notion that military service should be the reformatory school of the nation and that the forces were fit only for paupers and hardened criminals persisted. Such a system, argued a writer in *The Contemporary Review* in 1869, means that every 'reckless, wild, debauched young fellow, the refuse of the beershop, the sweepings of the gaol, every one who is too idle to work, too stupid to hold his place among his fellows, who had come into unwelcome contact with the law, or generally involved his fortunes in some desperate calamity, is considered, by general consent to have a distinct vocation to defend his country'.[72]

Public disdain was encouraged too by the kind of publicity the Service received.[73] Local newspapers seldom devoted space to comment on the regular army, and on the occasions that they did, it was often in the context of reporting the destitution of a pensioner or the capture of a deserter. Where enlistment and conditions of service were discussed, journalistic coverage was frequently critical.[74] This general neglect, broken by occasional unfavourable attention, contributed to the situation which John Holms described in 1878: 'The Army appears to be the only institution in the kingdom which is outside of the people. They know nothing of it, take no interest in it, and express no opinion on it.'[75]

There was an increasing reliance on advertisements to publicise the advantages of the military service after 1870, but most advertisements were unimaginative, merely setting forth the terms and conditions of service and making detached statements that men would find a career in the army attractive.[76] Little stress was placed on recent improvements and with the emphasis on honesty in recruitment after 1870, some of the conditions described may in fact have discouraged prospective recruits.[77] 'There can be no doubt at all', wrote H.O. Arnold-Forster in 1906, 'that hitherto we have failed to obtain full value for our money and our effort because we have not taken ordinary and reasonable means to explain to the people most concerned what we have done and what we are offering.'[78] Public relations may have improved by the last decades of the century as recruiting officers and others optimistically claimed,[79] but it is difficult to see specifically how this was so.[80]

The unpopularity of the army had obviously a serious effect on recruitment. Not only were prospective recruits wary of enlistment, but their relations and friends were often contemptuous of the Service and anxious that they stay clear of the recruiting sergeant.[81] Many youths found themselves cut off from friends and family by enlisting. E.C. Grenville Murray, who enlisted out of public school, was told 'Your father gave you an expensive education and you are turning it to no account. He put a costly steam engine in your hands, and you are using it to chop little bits of wood for your own amusement.'[82] When John Fraser joined the army in 1877, he found his father infuriated at his decision:

> To him my step was a blow from which he thought he would never recover, for it meant disgrace of the worst type. His son a soldier! He could not believe his ears. Rather would he have had me out of work for the rest of my life than earning my living in such a manner. More than that, he would rather see me in my grave.[83]

The reaction of William Robertson's parents to his enlistment in 1877 was another illustration of the low regard in which the army was held and the opposition within many families to any sons aspiring to a career in the ranks. On being informed of his enlistment, Robertson's mother wrote, '. . .there are plenty of things Steady Young Men can do when they can write and read as you can. . .[the army] is a refuge for all Idle people. . .I shall name it to no one for I am ashamed to think of it. I would rather Bury you than see you in a red coat. . .'[84]

'It is certainly remarkable', stated a War Office paper on recruitment in 1880, 'that whilst the army for a century past has engaged in military enterprises in every part of the world, conducted as a rule with great success, and of a character likely to inspire the enthusiasm of the youths of England. . .a Military career has hitherto been looked on. . .with dislike and dread.'[85] That same year a senior army officer in an article in *Colburn's United Services Magazine* argued 'The conviction that the soldier's life is one of unbridled debauchery and black-guardism; that "to go for a soldier" is to take a final plunge into the lowest depths of degradation is. . . almost universal'.[86]

Hostility towards the army also manifested itself in the treatment which the soldier received in public. In the last decades of the century particularly, the soldier became somewhat of a pet, popularised in music-hall songs and in romantic accounts of his bravery and skill in action; nevertheless he continued to be kept at arm's length and was treated as a pariah by much of the public. In 1872 the use of troops to help farmers complete their harvesting was met by violent objections, not all of which can be explained as opposition to cheap labour.[87] Proposals in 1874 to establish a military centre at Oxford under the provisions of the army localisation scheme brought fierce protest from university and public officials. In the House of Commons, Lord Randolph Churchill argued that Oxford would soon become a garrison town, 'the mingling of learned Professors and thoughtful students with roystering soldiers and licentious camp followers, tending to demoralise its ancient institutions'.[88] In fact, the reputation gained in war was soon forgotten in times of peace.[89] Soldiers were frequently excluded from parks and places of public amusement, restaurants and cafes, and even senior NCOs were on occasion prevented from travelling second-class on public transport, though their wives and families were allowed to do so.[90] Civilians were affected as well, and those who kept the company of soldiers often found themselves the victims of discrimination.[91] These slights were keenly felt in the ranks, lowered the position of the soldier in his own eyes, and must have severely limited the army's appeal.[92]

4. Motives for Enlistment

'We can only expect to get Recruits', argued the report of the Royal Commission on Recruitment in 1861,

> from among those few who may, naturally, have a predilection for a Soldier's life, or those who may be induced to adopt it either for domestic reasons, or when, by the fluctuations of trade, or the adverse influence of the seasons on agricultural operations, they are deprived of other employment; our recommendations must, in

> consequence, be chiefly confined to the removal of any obstacles which may hitherto have impeded this mode of Recruiting.[93]

Probably, as this seems to imply, economic pressure was the principal impetus to recruitment. Throughout the period many soldiers and civilians were convinced that most of the recruits obtained each year came to the Service not entirely willingly. In the most dire instances of high unemployment, it was argued, men were driven into the army as a last resort short of the workhouse, and even under less desperate conditions economic pressure was a factor in encouraging men to enlist.[94] By comparison those with 'a natural predilection for a soldier's life' were few. In 1859 Lieutenant-General Sir G.A. Wetherall, then Adjutant-General, told the Royal Commission on recruiting, '. . .there are very few men who enlist for the love of being a soldier; it is a very rare exception'. He added that 'they are starving, or they have quarrelled with their friends, or their masters, or there are cases of bastardy, and all sorts of things'.[95] Six years later Brigadier-General George Campbell, a brigade commander at Aldershot, observed '. . .men who have no option left them. . .go into the army'.[96] During the next forty years official enquiries continued to record the view that the pressure of necessity drove men into the army.[97]

The most frequent observation was that recruiting was brisk when unemployment was high, and slow when trade picked up.[98] In 1890 the War Office attempted to substantiate the connection by producing a graph of exports and imports, pauperism, and army and militia recruitment.[99] This purported to show a strong correlation between recruitment and civilian unemployment, but the statistics did not completely prove the case, and there were substantial difficulties involved in producing such a graph, and basing this kind of argument upon it. Pauperism, the state of trade, and recruitment differed considerably from region to region and these variations were unaccounted for. Other factors to which recruitment was sensitive, such as alterations in the terms and conditions of service and the establishment voted were ignored. In any case the correlation was only rough; for example the graph showed an all-time low in pauperism, circa 1877–8 matched by relatively high recruitment.

Soldiers' memoirs show that most recruits enlisted either because they were forced to,[100] or because they could find no other employment or at least none that they preferred.[101] 'At the age of eighteen,' wrote Sergeant Taffs, a veteran of the Crimea and of subsequent campaigns, 'I found myself by force of circumstances, starving in the streets of London, and determined to tramp to Chatham and enlist as a soldier.'[102] Sergeant J. MacMullen, writing a few years earlier, estimated that three-quarters of those who enlisted each year were forced by circumstances to do so.[103] Robert Blatchford found himself penniless and unemployed in London in 1871 when he first spotted the recruiting sergeant;[104] Sergeant Robert Edmondson, who at the end of the period estimated that 70 to 80 per cent of the British Army was drawn from the unemployed,[105] asserted 'Empty pockets and hungry stomachs are the most eloquent and persuasive of recruiting sergeants'.[106]

If this was the case, it was nevertheless true that sometimes soldiers enlisted for a number of causes which were quite unconnected with economic necessity. For those running from the law, from family or friends, or from the boring sameness of civilian life and a menial occupation, the army provided a ready means of escape.[107] Some were deceived through the use of alcohol and false promises. Impulse too had a part to play. Evidently a considerable number of soldiers joined the army each year simply because it struck their fancy at the time.[108] And there was always a large number of men who enlisted either to be with family or friends,[109] for the opportunity to travel, or out of a desire for the glamour or excitement of a soldier's life.[110] A veteran of the war in the Crimea recalled in his memoirs, 'My father was a soldier at the time of the battle of Waterloo. . .As a boy, I always had a desire to see a battlefield, and made up my mind to enlist in a cavalry regiment.'[111] This latter group of recruits, although not the most numerous, were among the most highly valued.[112] They included auxiliary forces personnel who had acquired a taste for military service[113] and the sons of men who were soldiers themselves such as the boys at the Royal Military Asylum and the Royal Hibernian Military School. They were of course a minority among recruits as a whole, and their motives for enlistment were minority ones.

5. Short Service and Recruitment

Given the nature of the army's image and the motives for enlistment, even a reformed recruiting system was faced with a major task in trying to raise sufficient men to meet military needs. There were a number of ways the problem could be approached, and one of the most obvious was through the conditions of service.

It was felt that improvements in accommodation, education and other aspects of the soldier's life in the army could attract recruits; it was expected that at least they would lessen markedly the discouragements to enlistment.[114] But in fact, the results scarcely bore out these expectations. For those who were aware of them, unhealthy living conditions undoubtedly deterred enlistment, and in some instances their amelioration may have influenced a decision to enlist, but it is unlikely that in the majority of cases this had much effect, especially in an era when standards of civilian health were rising rapidly as well. There is no evidence that better food and clothing was an important factor, particularly as improvement was far from universal throughout the forces. The influence of army education is equally dubious, for if it was of only limited importance to the man in the ranks, it is improbable that it furnished much of an attraction to prospective recruits. It is reasonable to suggest that fewer men may have been discouraged from enlistment as a result of the easing of disciplinary restrictions and the more realistic punishments which were introduced,[115] but again it would be difficult to argue that such measures provided any definite incentive towards recruitment.

An allied problem in each case was lack of publicity. Insufficient efforts were made before 1900 to publicise improvements, and, as we have noted, not a great deal was achieved in changing the army's image. An exception may possibly be the improvements in provisions for recreation. In the later years of the nineteenth century recruiting posters and brochures did emphasise sports, schools, libraries and reading rooms as major attractions of military service.[116]

It was most widely accepted that the surest way of increasing recruiting inducements was through an improvement in rates of pay, pensions, and opportunities for re-employment.[117] As we have seen, although after 1856 net pay in particular increased, there was no striking improvement in the soldier's long-or short-term financial prospects because a sizable and direct increase in expenditure of public funds was unacceptable to all governments. Economy therefore prevented the measures which might have been cheaper in the long run, and have been the most effective. In the circumstances, it is not surprising that the emphasis changed to a less directly expensive method of solving the manpower problem: through alterations in the terms of service.

A variety of proposals were entertained, some of them suggesting only a slight degree of change, others root and branch reform. Those which were taken most seriously drew inspiration from practices employed in the navy and some foreign armies. Successive governments experimented with reform and many of their measures were to prove highly controversial. The recruiting problem was a major impulse behind the changes and its continued presence afterwards was an important strand in the dissatisfaction which grew up around the Cardwell reforms. But the question of the terms of service was inextricably linked with strategic considerations and with the role of the army, and it is not therefore possible to separate clearly the issue of recruitment from other aspects which aroused dispute. To explain the course of events, one needs to look at the whole controversy.

The most important of the changes which had been made by 1900 involved specific alterations to the terms of service, the formalisation of local ties, and the linking or pairing of regular battalions. Because there was a number of different stages reached between 1856 and 1899 the period is conveniently divided into two parts: the years until the introduction of the Cardwell reforms, 1856 to 1870; and the years afterwards, 1870 to 1899.

In the first period reformers argued that terms of enlistment restricted the army's appeal and ensured that only a certain type of recruit would enlist voluntarily,[118] and that a lengthy period of service, much of it overseas in a debilitating climate, reduced the usefulness of the man in the ranks.[119] Shorter periods of enlistment were looked to, to provide more and better recruits and the basis for establishing an effective reserve.[120] In addition, it was suggested that these reforms might lead to financial savings in that with fewer men serving for twenty-one years, the pension list could be substantially reduced and less provision made for a married establishment.[121] This promised reduction of spending was one of the attractions of the Cardwell reforms.[122]

Until 1847 enlistment in the army was for life or until a discharge on medical grounds was granted.[123] In that year enlistment was limited to twenty-one years in the infantry, twenty-four in other corps; and a first period of service in the infantry of ten years and in the cavalry and artillery of twelve years was introduced. Re-engagement for a second term was with the understanding that men would be awarded a pension after completing twenty-one or twenty-four years.[124] The exigencies of the Crimean War and the Indian Mutiny highlighted the army's inability to provide adequate reinforcements to sustain a lengthy campaign. Wartime military expansion was also made more difficult by expanding economy.[125] In the 1860s Continental wars and the American Civil War seemed to accentuated Britain's military weaknesses, and efforts to form a reserve during the war scares of 1859 and 1867 proved abortive because the terms of service were still deterrent.[126]

The Duke of Cambridge and other conservatives claimed that limited enlistment in terms of the 1847 Act was unpopular and ineffective in that it had not solved the army's shortage of men.[127] They argued that the insecurity of short service with no guarantee of re-engagement for a second term discouraged many prospective recruits who would otherwise have enlisted if the prospect for a pension had been certain.[128] There was also a considerable fear that many NCOs and other experienced soldiers were being lost simply because they were allowed to leave the Service after ten or twelve years, although the findings of a Royal Commission on Recruitment in 1867 ultimately discounted this.[129] *The Times* argued in 1861 that 'an army can never be relied upon unless a certain proportion of it consists of well-trained men with that fellow-feeling and that professional spirit which belong only to the soldier who sees in arms the calling of his entire life'.[130] Only long service could provide this cadre.[131]

The reports of the 1859 and 1865 Royal Commissions on Recruitment were deeply influenced by the arguments against short service. Few witnesses advocated a return to enlistment for twenty-one years, but most urged the lengthening of the first term of service for the infantry to twelve or even fifteen years on the grounds that men who had completed ten years with the colours were just entering their prime.[132] The Duke of Cambridge and others claimed that an extra few years would deter no one, and that many more would re-engage if the second period of service were a short one.[133] Although in the end both Commissions supported this principle of limited enlistment, each rejected short service as understood and practised in continental armies. The 1861 report recommended that a variety of enlistment periods be considered (this was an early example of the proposals mooted by H.O. Arnold-Forster and others at the end of the century);[134] the second report six years later called for a first term of service of twelve years, and this recommendation was enacted by legislation that same year.[135] When Edward Cardwell became Secretary of State for War in 1868, the whole question of short service and of a reserve therefore remained unsolved. Moreover, a substantial body of military opinion had grown up, resentful of civilian tampering with the army and ready to blame any defects on limited enlistment.

In 1870 Cardwell introduced the first of a series of measures associated with his name which altered the terms of service and the organisational basis of the army; their propriety and success was still being hotly debated when war broke out in South Africa nearly thirty years later. Although the first steps were not taken until 1870 the bases for and the direction of these reforms had been decided upon even earlier.[136] By 1868 the establishment of the army had reached a new low; and it was no longer possible to disguise falling enlistments by reducing the size of the forces each year. Using the Prussian army as a model a compromise was evolved. Short service was accepted in principle,[137] but the initial period of enlistment was longer than in the major Continental armies. The Army Enlistment Act of 1870 kept the initial term of service in the regular army at twelve years, but it provided that under normal circumstances the first six years might be served with the colours and the second with the regular reserve. Soldiers of every corps were to be allowed to extend their service with the colours to twenty-one years but it was expected that most would elect to pass out of the regular army at the end of the minimum period. The War Office reserved the right, if recruitment was adequate, to reduce the first period of colour service to three years.[138] In subsequent measures regiments were linked in pairs and assigned territorial recruiting areas, and steps were taken to withdraw as many regiments as possible from colonial duty.[139]

Considerations of recruitment were central to these changes. By shortening the period of colour service the War Office hoped to stimulate enlistment.[140] Since no man need feel that by joining the army he took a decision that would affect him for the rest of his life, shorter service was expected to attract a better quality of recruit and to reduce wastage from desertion and other offences.[141] Regular and medical officers had argued that the physical and mental condition of soldiers deteriorated remarkably after eight or nine years abroad.[142] The recall of units from overseas and the ending of the army's virtual exile were seen as hitting at a major source of its unpopularity.[143] The linking of battalions and assignment of territorial recruiting areas were designed to strengthen the local ties and feelings which would both encourage more to enlist and again help to draw a better class of recruit.[144] 'It is intended to associate every regiment and battalion of the Army with some particular district of the country,' Cardwell informed the House of Commons in 1872, 'in order that the ties of kindred and of locality may bring into the army a better class of men and a greater number than now present themselves.'[145] If local ties could be strengthened, predicted a military journal in 1875,

> . . .country folk would be attracted to the service, companions at the plough, or loom, well fed, well dressed, with ample leisure and

> few cares, and admired by the village lasses, would be objects of envy; the display of the parade and its martial music would inflame them with military ardour, and there would be no difficulty in filling the ranks with good material.[146]

Time revealed that the Cardwell reforms contained a number of serious flaws, which were accentuated by the parsimonious handling the army received from successive administrations. By 1876 the stresses that had been placed on the already shaky recruiting system were becoming apparent. Cardwell's loose linking of the regular infantry battalions presupposed an equal balance between those at home and those abroad in order that units in Britain could recruit for and reinforce those stationed overseas. Although the regiments were roughly balanced in 1872 with seventy battalions at home and seventy-one abroad, there was no account taken of the possibility that conditions might require more troops to be sent overseas. When this occurred the balance was destroyed. By February 1879 there were eighty-two battalions abroad but only fifty-nine at home.[147] Small colonial wars alone strained the recruiting system which even in peacetime could not effectively handle the burden of foreign reliefs and provide sufficient men for the formation of a reserve.[148] Short service, as conservatives had partly foreseen, had two faults: it allowed experienced men to leave the army sooner, and it required more recruits yearly. Under pressure the battalions of the home army shrank to inadequate size and in order to maintain establishments, standards were lowered. The youth and physical inadequacies of many recruits rendered them unfit for active service or colonial duty even when fully trained, and when a battalion stationed in Britain came up on the roster for foreign service it was often found that the only way of raising it to fighting strength was to take volunteers from other regiments.[149]

It is hardly surprising that in the second period from 1870 to 1899 Cardwell's organisational reforms resulted in controversy. There was opposition at two levels: from government military advisers, and less officially, from many soldiers and civilians.

Much of the debate was conducted without any reference to recruitment, but this was a major issue and it was often implicit in much of the discussions of other problems. The drastic reduction in colonial garrisons was suspect in many quarters. At the War Office Lord Northbrook argued that Cardwell was overestimating the additional inducement to recruitment to be gained from diminishing the force in the colonies without reducing the extent of Indian service.[150] The Duke of Cambridge opposed any reduction in establishment[151] and looked upon Cardwell's measures as threatening to put too great a strain on imperial forces.[152] Rather than conceding that foreign service had its disadvantages, he argued that it was beneficial to officers and men by the experience and expertise it created.[153] Moreover, he felt the government was endangering the safety of the colonies and that of coaling stations and trading routes, and by unfairly burdening colonial governments was destroying any prospect of joint imperial-colonial military cooperation.[154]

Advisers also had doubts about the suitability of short service to Britain's military needs and the requirements of army organisation.[155] The Adjutant-General and other officers repeatedly charged that the army was filling with young immature boys, incapable of standing up to the duties required of them.[156] The Duke of Cambridge feared that short-term enlistments would overstrain the recruiting system, argued that there could be no effective reduction in the pension list as long as troops were required for India,[157] and in company with other senior officers questioned the value of a reserve and its usefulness in war.[158]

The number of official enquiries showed the influence of this body of opinion. In 1875 a War Office Committee under Major-General R.C.H. Taylor, the Inspector-General of Recruiting, warned that the demands of short service were so great that unless inducements were considerably increased, sufficient men would not be obtained after 1876 to keep up the establishment of the army.[159] In 1879 a committee of general officers under Lord Airey suggested that the demand for men was so great recruits were being insufficiently trained, and that the necessity of transferring the best men from battalions at home to those overseas was damaging *esprit de corps* and dangerously weakening the home army.[160] The Ashanti campaign of 1874 had been seen as successful vindication of the Cardwell reforms, but it had really been fought with a force of picked professionals and it was not until the Zulu War of 1879 that short service was put to the test. The results were far from satisfactory. Young recruits were unable to bear the strain of the campaign, but the reserves who had been called out a year earlier could not be mobilised again.[161] The Airey Committee pointed to a considerable body of opinion in the army which was critical of the results of short service, and Lord Chelmsford, who had commanded the army in Zululand, was quoted as arguing:

> . . .now-a-days when the home duty is so severe, and when it is so very difficult really to give the soldier an adequate amount of training, he does not develop into a man you can really trust under three years, and the consequence is that if you deprive us of his services at six years, it is just when he is at his prime, and just at the time, if he is fit for the work, that you would like to make use of him as a non-commissioned officer. . .I should like to see a man live and die in the army, so to speak, so long as he conducted himself satisfactorily and was physically fit to do duty either abroad or at home.[162]

The Committee's recommendations would have entailed the virtual abandonment of short service, so F.A. Stanley, the Secretary of State for War, delayed publication of the report. In 1881 a committee considering the effect of short service on the forces reported. It re-emphasised the burden short-term enlistments were throwing on the recruiting system.[163] That same year the high point in official opposition to the Cardwell reforms was reached with government publication of the Airey report. However, instead of abandoning short service, localisation and the two-battalion regiment as so many wished, the government acted to preserve them, arguing that these reforms were still the most acceptable answers to the army's needs.[164] Though less vocal than were their opponents, there were many supporters of the principles of short service. The length of the first term of colour service was increased to seven years and reserve service reduced to five in 1881 but the principle of short-service enlistment (in so far as seven years can be called short) remained.[165] That same year, H.C.E. Childers, the Secretary of State for War, pushed reform a step further by fusing the linked battalions of the army and adding two militia battalions to form a territorial regiment, abolishing the old numbers and severing many historical traditions.

Government reaffirmation of the principles of short service effectively silenced much of the opposition at the official level; but it did not still the controversy at a lower level.[166] There was considerable resentment to meddling by the 'uninformed civilians of Whitehall'.[167] Even civilian experts such as H.O. Arnold-Forster criticised civilian control of the forces, and he and others hoped the army would be left alone to manage itself.[168] 'The thing that puzzles us and vexes us most of all', wrote a soldier in 1884, 'is, that every one of these so-called reforms and alterations originate among the civilian clerks in the War Office. We believe that if the Duke and his military advisers had their way, the army would be a man's home as it used to be in the old. . . 'corrupt'. . .days.[169] Regimental officers resented the linking of battalions and the loss of traditions, such as the old regimental numbers replaced by territorial titles.[170] Opposition to localisation held up the establishment of local depots,[171] and *esprit de corps* in the linked battalions was supposed to be fragile.[172] Regimental officers had also to train more recruits each year, and because of the loss of experienced soldiers to the reserve, had fewer 'handsome showy' men in their battalions.[173] Finally short service obviously aggravated the problem of finding employment for the discharged soldier.[174]

Above all there was the continued failure to recruit sufficient men.[175] In addition there was the increasing proportion of youth in the ranks, which supposedly struck deeply at efficiency.[176] As the century wore on the average age of the man in the ranks dropped significantly. The transfer of men to the reserve after a short period of duty with the colours had the effect of decreasing the proportion of older men with the regular army, and it is also clear that younger men made up a higher proportion of each year's recruits in later years. In 1862 for example, 34.1 per cent of the recruits enlisted were aged nineteen or less, in 1898 49.2 per cent were in this group.[177] There is no doubt, as critics charged, that seasoned soldiers of thirty years of age or more were scarce by 1900. It is questionable, of course, how serious this was. In the army as a whole there was very little increase in the proportion of men aged less than twenty. There were considerably more men aged between twenty and thirty, but for reasons of physical capability this age group was surely the most desirable. The military policy of concentrating the younger men in the home army made the army appear more youthful than it was.

This policy was an outcome of the warnings by medical officers that little reliance could be placed upon the physical capabilities of soldiers under the age of twenty.[178] As the effects of short service began to be felt, army doctors repeatedly expressed the reservations which they had always had about youthful troops 'unfit for carrying the weight of a soldier's equipment on marches or other active exercises, for enduring the effects of severe and frequent drills, of broken sleep, exposure to cold, bad and indifferent food, reverses or other depressing influences'.[179] For the remainder of the century they continued to harbour these doubts[180] which were shared by a wide range of opinion both outside and inside the army.[181]

Two problems were intertwined: the continued need to attract recruits and the need to counter the supposedly harmful effects of short service on the army's efficiency. In these circumstances a number of changes were canvassed. An outright return to long service was urged although this was less popular after 1881.[182] To meet shortages the War Office frequently encouraged soldiers, especially NCOs, to extend their colour service to twelve and even twenty-one years, and there were many who felt that this practice should be continued.[183] A disadvantage was that if this were to spread much further, it would cripple the development of an effective reserve. The introduction of very much shorter terms of enlistment to encourage recruitment was argued for in some quarters,[184] but its most obvious disadvantage was that it would make even more difficult the provision of troops for foreign service. Prevailing military opinion held that Britain could not afford to send men overseas for less than six or seven years.[185] Advocates of shorter service would have provided foreign drafts by voluntary re-engagement, but could never be certain how many soldiers would be willing to extend their service each year.

Wider currency was given to the suggestion that a combination of long and short service be introduced.[186] This concept went back at least as far as the Royal Commission on recruitment in 1861,[187] and in the later decades of the century it was championed by H.O. Arnold-Forster and Charles Dilke in Parliament[188] and in the army by Lord Roberts.[189] They argued that the foreign service army should be recruited for long service but that very short service of (say) two or three years with the colours should be offered for service in Britain. This implied the development of two different types of armies and possibly the separation of one from the other, but it was confidently expected that the best of each system could be achieved.[190] Flexible terms of enlistment were expected to be a considerable inducement to prospective recruits. The danger of course was that the long-term army could become too separate and might develop and preserve skills and techniques which would render it wholly unsuited for a conflict with European powers should its presence be required.[191] Arnold-Forster tried to introduce a combination of long and short service when Secretary of State for War in 1903, but his proposals never met with much support, and in the end his scheme was not given an adequate trial.[192]

With the government committed to the Cardwell reforms, a wide range of military opinion gradually marshalled behind short service.[193] One of the chief exponents of the terms of enlistment favoured by successive governments was the Inspector-General of Recruiting.[194] The office changed hands several times between 1867 and 1899, yet the Inspector-General's annual reports to the Secretary of State are invariably models of optimism given the actual state of enlistment.[195] It is not surprising that in time these reports came to be regarded with considerable scepticism.[196]

There were other prominent apologists with less specialised knowledge. Major-General Sir John Adye for example strongly praised the effects of short service and the measures that accompanied it on several occasions, and argued against any change in policy.[197] The most eloquent and effective support for the current terms of service came from a civilian member of the War Office, the Assistant Under-Secretary of State for War, Sir Arthur Haliburton. Haliburton made his debut as a government spokesman when serving as a member of the Wantage Committee. By the last decade of the century malignant recruiting problems caused even the normally optimistic Inspector-General of Recruiting to admit that enlistment was faltering,[198] as the army seemed increasingly unable to meet the requirements for Indian and Colonial drafts.[199] It was this which forced the appointment of the committee under the chairmanship of Lord Wantage to look into the problem of foreign drafts.[200] Its report and evidence published in 1892 created considerable stir.[201] Lord Wolseley's famous statement that the battalions of the home army were 'squeezed lemons' was a point upon which most opposition factions within the army joined in agreement.[202] The main report emphasised the failings of recruitment and the unsatisfactory condition of the home army, but Haliburton wrote a dissent which was every bit as lengthy as the original. In his discussion he produced evidence to show that recruitment was no worse than it had ever been and that by relying on its reserve as the creators of short service had intended, the home army would prove to be every bit as efficient as was required.[203] The government might deny that Haliburton was put on the Committee to 'wreck the ship', but he did greatly weaken the impact of its findings. His objections provided reassurance that the army was capable of any task for which it might be required,[204] and a convenient excuse for government inaction.[205] Haliburton went on to become Permanent Under-Secretary of State for War in 1895 and was always one of the chief defenders of short service. In 1897–8 he waged a campaign in the press against detractors of the Cardwell reforms, particularly Arnold-Forster.[206] In 1898 he published his *Army Organisation: a Short Reply to Long Service,* a long and detailed answer to the arguments of War Office critics.

Finally as reverence for Cardwell grew, it was argued that if there were problems these arose because his reforms had not been allowed to function as their designer had intended.[207] Major-General P.L.

MacDougall and Lord Wolseley both spoke in this way,[208] and these views also appeared in the report of the Wantage Committee. 'The whole weight of the evidence', the Commission reported,

> has fully sustained the conviction that the question of long service, in the common acceptation of the term, as opposed to short service, is not now open to argument. . .The present difficulties are not attributable to short service as such, but to the failure of successive Governments to carry out the principles accepted in 1872, upon which the short-service organisation adopted in that year was based.[209]

These attitudes discouraged any fundamental departure from the *status quo.*

For all these reasons there was no alteration of the basic terms of service introduced by the Cardwell reforms in spite of their disappointing failure to deal with the manpower shortage in the long run. The withdrawal of troops from overseas and the shortening of initial periods of enlistment probably helped to remove the impression that military service meant virtual exile in an unhealthy climate and prolonged absence from family and friends, but there is no evidence that this had a significant effect on recruitment. Localisation helped recruiting drives to reach areas which were hitherto inadequately tapped and the association of units with particular regions may have proved an incentive to recruitment,[210] but the shift of population from rural to urban areas served to limit success. In the face of the rapid increase in the urban population of Britain, success on the scale that Cardwell and others had hoped for was probably impossible. There was an initial concentration upon areas no longer able to provide the number of men required from them each year and in the end the army was forced to look beyond local connections for recruits. In 1874 83.8 per cent of that year's 20,312 recruits were raised in local recruiting districts centred on large urban areas.[211] In 1898 by contrast, local districts and regimental HQs accounted for only 63.3 per cent of the men enlisted.[212]

Short-term enlistment was clearly more popular than was long service. The choice of either was open to recruits, but by 1872 most were opting for short service, and within six years fewer than one man in ten elected to serve the full period with the colours. In later years this proportion was even less.[213]

However, in spite of what Cardwell and others claimed[214] short service as defined by the 1870 Act does not appear to have been a significant attraction on its own.[215] Perhaps this was because it was at best a compromise; colour service of ten years in 1856 differed from short service of seven or eight years in 1899 only in degree. Repeated changes in the length of service also discouraged potential NCOs from re-enlisting.[216] Despite encouragements to stay with the regular army, there was little significant variation in the number or proportion of soldiers between 1856 and 1899 who agreed to do so. The principal encouragement was the bounty.[217] As a temporary expedient, it was often given when recruiting shortages were especially acute to induce men about to leave the army to extend their stay for a period of active service. This of course tended to nullify the terms of short service. Moreover their failure in a number of instances was particularly obvious. Attempts had been made in 1859 to encourage men in India to re-engage for service in China, but few could be induced to come forward. Similar measures were tried in 1881 and again in 1891 but with little success.[218] Statistics clearly show that in the long term the proportion of the forces re-engaging each year varied little between 1857 and 1898.[219] A large number was reported in 1867, 31,476 as compared to an average of 3,000–4,000 in previous years, but these resulted from increased bounties designed to ease the recruiting difficulties emphasised by the Royal Commission report of that year. By 1879, when the first lots of men enlisted under the terms of the Army Enlistment Act of 1870 had completed their initial terms of service, re-engagements had dropped sharply. This decline and the continued low rate of re-engagement in subsequent years reflects two things: the efforts that were made to maintain the growth of the first-class reserve by encouraging the transfer of men from the colours, and the steady but high proportion of recruits who preferred short service but were reluctant, even after several years of service, to serve more than a minimum term with the regular forces.

Short service in spite of its defects was in fact the most plausible of any of the measures designed to get around the shortage of recruits. As well as promising to stimulate enlistment, it held a second fascination for army reformers. The development of a sizable reserve was perhaps its most significant achievement, and to some extent allowed the army to make better use of the numbers it was able to attract. Short service had the additional advantage of working within the already established ground rules of voluntary enlistment.

6. Boy Enlistment and Proposals for Conscription

The lingering problem of attracting enough suitable recruits each year led to proposals aimed at solving the manpower shortage by other means than a direct inducement to recruitment. The use of mercenaries which reached its peak during the Napoleonic Wars, was not seriously considered after 1856 although units of German troops had been raised during the Crimean War. Efforts to recruit men in the United States at this time met with severe protests from Washington. In response the British government was forced to deny any knowledge of the actions of its agents, realising nevertheless that the day of the foreign mercenary had passed.[220] Future efforts directed as easing the army's recruiting needs would of necessity be more introspective. Two such proposals were an increased recruitment of boys, and the introduction of some form of conscription. A model for the first could be found in the navy, and foreign armies provided a wide variety of forms of conscription.

Boy enlistment was a traditional method of augmenting recruitment. Regiments consisting entirely of boys had been formed at an earlier date, but the last had disappeared in 1802.[221] Between 1856 and 1899 regulations specified that the number was not to exceed 2 per cent per establishment.[222] Boys were taken on from the age of fifteen and served an apprenticeship until they reached the normal age of enlistment. During this time they were taught one of two or three trades. Nearly three-quarters of the boys recruited underwent training as musicians (i.e. drummers and buglers), the remainder as tailors and shoemakers. On reaching the minimum age for enlistment, boys formally joined the regiment to which they were attached. What was new was the suggestion inspired by the practices of the Royal Navy, of a comprehensive training scheme.[223] Borrowing directly from the navy's experience, many advocated that special training schools be set up, and that the establishment of boys at the Royal Military Asylum and the Royal Hibernian Military School be substantially increased.[224] A variation called for the introduction in the normal curriculum of industrial and Poor Law schools of a measure of military training,[225] and the compulsory enlistment of schoolboys in these institutions or in reformatories.[226] There was less hesitation felt in turning to conscription in this instance. In 1875 the superintendent of a major industrial school argued:

> My experience is that these boys become manageable and tractable, and acquire habits of industry; and I call it a shame that the country should permit them to be trained and taught and made efficient, and then that these wretched parents should be allowed to step in and take them back to their miserable homes and afterwards let them

again become gutter Arabs.[227]

Those who urged an increase in the proportion of boys taken into the army each year were confident this would guarantee the Service a steady supply of recruits whose quality was expected to be much above average.[228] It might well have done so if the proposals had been put into effect, but a number of difficulties were anticipated. One was the extra expense that would be involved.[229] 'There has never been any lack of boys to fill the vacancies occurring in the service,' argued the Inspector-General of Recruiting in 1875, 'but I am afraid the question of £sd is one we must get put forward by some one who can persuade those who hold the purse strings to let us have something given towards the necessary expenditure.'[230] Another difficulty concerned their serviceability, since military authorities argued that they would be unable to find employment in the army for more than the present proportion of men under the age of eighteen.[231] In the end, there was little action taken to increase the proportion of boys with the colours. Boy soldiers continued to provide a steady source of recruits throughout the whole of the period, but the proportion taken into the forces increased only slightly between 1856 and 1899, and not significantly so.[232]

Conscription had been involved in some of the discussion of boy soldiers. After the example afforded by conscript-based continental armies in the 1860s and 1870s, compulsory service in Britain was strongly favoured by a number of soldiers and civilians as an immediate solution to otherwise insoluble recruiting difficulties and as an answer to the country's need for a large reserve force.[233] Conscription was also urged on grounds of its being cheaper than a large standing army,[234] and for the moral and social benefits that might be expected by having a large proportion of the nation receive a short period of military training.[235] For others less keen on its merits, conscription was an unwelcome but last resort in the face of faltering voluntary enlistment.[236] J.R. Godley, for instance, an Assistant Under-Secretary of State for War, told the Royal Commission on army recruitment in 1861 that compulsory service was the only method of obtaining a good army unless the terms and conditions of service were made very much more attractive.[237] Because recruitment continued to falter during the whole of the rest of the century, many others came to feel that a form of coercion might be inevitable. Lord Roberts[238] and Lord Wolseley[239] each took up this view, and the army reforms introduced by St John Brodrick during the Boer War clearly threatened conscription unless the necessary men could be raised by voluntary means.[240]

In the event opposition to conscription was much stronger than any movement for its introduction. Conservatives, liberals, the majority of army reformers, and indeed the army itself were strongly opposed to any form of compulsory military service.[241] Politicians rightly believed that any attempts to introduce legislation embodying conscription would be political suicide.[242] The country's natural disinclination to military service,[243] the unsuitability of conscription to its military needs,[244] the damage that would be done through loss of labour,[245] and the personal injustices and hardships that would be suffered, were all emphasised.[246] None of the major enquiries which looked into the question of army recruitment during the latter half of the century even considered conscription as a reasonable alternative to voluntary enlistment, although forces in favour of its institution gathered momentum after the Boer War, and this is exampled in the National Service League. Nevertheless it was not until the First World War and the failure of voluntary enlistment in the face of an extreme national emergency that recourse was had to coercion. The impossible situation in which the Victorian Army found itself arose not only from enforced reliance on voluntary enlistment without sufficient efforts being made to render the Service more attractive, but also from the requirement, especially after 1870, that despite extensive commitments overseas, it produced a large and effective reserve force. It was to take involvement in a major colonial war at the end of the century to prove that the warnings and fears of army reformers were not unfounded.

7. Conclusion

Because there were so many facets to the recruiting problem a wide variety of solutions were considered after 1856. In the end not all were attempted, nor were all of those which were experimented with successful. One difficulty was the machinery of recruitment, and this was tackled with considerable success. The image which the army projected was a more thorny problem, and one which seems to have defied solution. Although there was an improvement in public relations between 1856 and 1899, it is clear that the ordinary soldier was virtually ostracised in some circumstances, and that in many circles his profession was not considered a respectable alternative to other types of employment. Part of the reason for this of course was the failure to make sufficient improvements to the terms and conditions of service, and to publicise adequately those improvements which had been made. A great deal of attention was devoted to changes in the terms of service, but the compromise solutions settled upon proved, in an atmosphere of heightened international tension and increasing military involvement abroad, to be an insufficient answer to the army's needs.

It would be a mistake nevertheless not to realise that throughout the whole of the period the army did recruit substantial numbers each year. Its share of the available civilian male population may have been no greater in 1899 than in 1856, as we have seen, but the numbers recruited each year at the end of the century were very much higher than they had been forty or fifty years earlier. Between 1856 and 1899 something in excess of one million men were enlisted, a sizable number by any estimate. The following chapter is concerned with these men rather than those that never were, and it discusses the patterns of recruitment that emerged in this period.

Notes

1. *Report of the Commission on Recruiting* (1861), p.326; *General Annual Return of the British Army*, P.P., XLIII (c.1323), 1875, p.20; XLIII (c.6196), 1890, p.28; LIII (c.9426), 1899, p.30.
2. *Report of the Commission on Recruiting* (1861); *The Times*, 4 April 1859.
3. *The Times*, 18 Feb. 1867, 16 March 1867; Hansard, CLXXIV (11 April 1864), cc.809–11; CLXXIV (15 April 1864), cc.1064–72; CLXXVI (27 June 1864), cc.387–90; CLXXVII (21 Feb. 1865), c.516; CLXXVII (16 March 1865), cc.1791–3; CLXXXI (5 March 1866), cc.1547–8.
4. Hansard, CLXXXI (5 March 1866), c.1532.
5. *The Times*, 16 March 1870, 29 May 1890, 28 July 1890, 25 Sept. 1890; Hansard, CCCXXXIII (5 March 1889), cc.1458–9; CCCXLVII (22 July 1890), c.578; CCCXLVII (28 July 1890), cc.1005–9: CCCL (19 Feb. 1891), cc.1089–93.
6. *Report of the Inspector-General of Recruiting*, P.P., X (c.110), 1900, p.39.
7. Estimates of what were the army's requirements varied of course, and were often a source of conflict between the Secretary of State for War and the Horse Guards. The Duke of Cambridge and other military advisers consistently opposed reductions. The opposite reaction could be expected from many Liberals. The establishments put forward by governments and voted by Parliament were inevitably a result of compromise. See Lord Panmure to the Duke of Cambridge, 15 March 1857; Lord Panmure, Minute on Army Establishments, 8 Dec. 1857, Panmure MSS., GD45/8/153, 45/8/474.
8. See Appendix V, Table VA–1.
9. See for example, *Report of the Inspector-General of Recruiting*, P.P., XIV (c.495), 1872, p.1; XIII (c.4677), 1886, p.15.
10. B.R. Mitchell, *Abstract of British Historical Statistics* (1962), pp.12–14.
11. *Report of the Commission on Recruiting* (1861), p.326; *General Annual Return of the British Army*, P.P., LII (c.9426), 1899, p.30.
12. Lord Palmerston to Lord Panmure, 18 July 1857, Panmure MSS., GD45/8/150; Lord Roberts to Edward Stanhope, 8 May 1883, Stanhope

MSS., 1401.
13. *Report of the Army Medical Department,* P.P., XXXIV (c.3233), 1863, p.32.
14. *Memorandum by the Inspector-General of Recruiting,* P.P., XLII (c.57), 1870, p.1.
15. *Report of the Wantage Committee* (1892), pp.520–1.
16. *Report of the Commission on the War in South Africa* (1904), p.139.
17. See for instance *Report of the Wantage Committee* (1892), pp.10, 166, 170, 315.
18. *Report of the Inspector-General of Recruiting,* P.P., XX (c.6597), 1892, p.5.
19. *Report of the Inspector-General of Recruiting,* P.P., XVIII (c.7659), 1895, p.6; XI (c.9185), 1899, p.9: *General Annual Return of the British Army* P.P. LIII (c.9426), 1899, p.26; *Report of the Commission on the War in South Africa* (1904), p.253.
20. Robertson, *From Private to Field-Marshal,* p.2.
21. Regulations allowed the enlistment of men who were blind in one eye, provided the physical requirements of height, weight, age and physique were met. Surgeon-General T. Longmore, *Manual of Instructions for the Guidance of Army Surgeons in Testing the Range and Quality of Vision of Recruits, and in Distinguishing the Causes of Defective Vision in Soldiers* (1875), pp.61 et seq.; see also Wyndham, *Following the Drum,* p.6.; Blatchford, *My Life in the Army,* pp.24–5.
22. Hansard, LXXIII (3 July 1899), c.1271.
23. *Memorandum by the Director-General, Army Medical Service, on the Physical Unfitness of Men Offering Themselves for Enlistment in the Army,* P.P., XXXVIII (c.1501), 1903; *Report of the Physical Deterioration Committee* (1904), pp.2, 5, 96.
24. *Report of the Commission on Recruiting* (1861), pp.iii–v.
25. Edward Cardwell to Lieutenant-General the Hon. C. Grey, 7 Jan. 1868; Edward Cardwell to Robert Lowe, 9 Aug. 1870; Cardwell MSS., PRO.30/48/1/1, 30/48/5/22.
26. *Report of the Wantage Committee* (1892), p.7.
27. See for instance *The Border Advertiser,* 5 March, 19 Nov. 1884, 6 July 1892.
28. *Report of the Commission on Recruiting* (1861), p.xiii.
29. Ibid., *Report of the Committee on Short Service Conditions* (1881), p.21.
30. The practice of pardoning criminals on condition of their serving abroad was a frequent resort in times of emergency. See The Recruiting of the British Army–the Old System and the New, WO.33/35; Charles M. Clode, *The Military Forces of the Crown* (1869), II, pp.1, 37
31. Mole, *King's Hussar,* p.29.
32. Blatchford, *My Life in the Army,* p.16.
33. Memorandum on the Means of Recruiting the Army, WO.33/6b.
34. *Report of the Commission on Recruiting* (1867), p.viii.
35. See for instance *Report of the Commission on Recruiting* (1867), p.vii–ix; An Ex-Non-Commissioned Officer, 'Recruiting as a Profession', *Colburn's,* I (1870), pp.346–53; Malan, *The Fortnightly Review,* V (1866), pp.406–20; *The Times,* 14 Dec. 1867, 10 June 1892; *The Reformer,* 9 July 1870; Hansard, CL (10 May 1858), c.363; CLXXVII (21 Feb. 1865), c.516; CLXXXVII (16 May 1867), c.674; CCCV (16 May 1887), cc.74–5; CCCL (19 Feb. 1891), cc.1095–8.
36. *Report of the Commission on Recruiting* (1867), p.x.
37. Anon., 'Our Military Administration–the Recruiting of the Army', *Colburn's,* I (1859), pp.505–18; Anon., 'How to Reform the Recruiting

System of the Army', *Colburn's,* II (1866), pp.317–18; James Johnston, *How to Reform the Recruiting System of the British Army* (1866).

38. Noake, *JRUSI,* XI (1868), pp.27–39; Anon., *Our Increasing Military Difficulty and One Way of Dealing With It* (1876); W. Sidney Randall, 'The Recruiting Question II', *Colburn's,* III (1891), pp.278–88; Palmer, *The Nineteenth Century,* XLIII (1898), pp.30–4; Anon., *Army Reorganisation* (1900); *The Times,* 10 May 1892, 9 June 1892; Hansard, CCXXIV (20 May 1875), c.707.
39. J.A. Skene Thomson, 'Military Enthusiasm as a Means of Recruiting', *The Westminster Review,* CXXXVI (1891), pp.624–42.
40. General Sir Neville Lyttelton, a strong advocate of regular manoeuvres to familiarise local people with the sight of the army, once recalled having met an elderly parish clerk in Wiltshire in 1869 who vowed he had not seen a red coat since 1805 when he witnessed French prisoners being marched under escort to Dartmoor. General Sir Neville Lyttelton, *80 Years* (1876), p.71.
41. An Ex-Non-Commissioned Officer, 'Recruiting as a Profession', *Colburn's,* I (1870), pp.346–53; A Soldier, *Thoughts on the Recruiting Question* (Edinburgh, 1875), pp.13–14; Joseph Byrne, 'The Recruiting Question', *Colburn's,* IV (1891–2), pp.170–5; Beedos, 'The Recruiting Question', *Colburn's,* XVIII (1898–9), pp.86–8; Hansard, CLII (4 March 1859), cc.1325–6.
42. Anon., 'How Soldiers May Be Procured', *Colburn's,* II (1872), p.71.
43. W.R. Greg, 'Popular versus Professional Armies', *The Contemporary Review,* XVI (1871), pp.351–71; Hansard, LXXIV (13 July 1899), c.685. The Queen's private secretary for instance remarked that he found nothing wrong with the present class of recruits, that the men who came forward made excellent soldiers. See Lieutenant-General the Hon. C. Grey, Memorandum on Regimental Organisation, circa December 1869, Cardwell MSS., PRO. 30/48/1/1.
44. Field-Marshal Viscount Wolseley, 'War and Civilisation', *Colburn's,* XIV (1896–7), p.568.
45. Anon., 'The Army Enlistment Act', *Blackwood's Edinburgh Magazine,* CVIII (1870), p.18.
46. See for instance Hansard, CCXII (15 July 1872), cc.1209–11; CCXXVII (6 March 1876), c.1440; CCLXXVII (12 March 1883), cc.262–7; XXXIX (21 April 1896), c.1426.
47. See for instance Lord Panmure to the Prince Consort, 31 May 1855, Panmure MSS., GD45/8/33; W.E. Gladstone to Sidney Herbert, 19 Dec. 1859, 31 March 1860, 21 Jan. 1861, Gladstone MSS.44211; Edward Cardwell, 11 Jan. 1869, 24 July, 1 Aug. 1870, 7 June, 11 Dec. 1871, 15 Oct. 1872, Cardwell MSS., PRO.30/48/2/6–9; Gladstone MSS., 44119; Stafford Northcote to Gathorne Hardy, 29 Jan. 1875, 18 Jan., 16 Oct., 24 Oct. 1876, Hardy MSS., T501/271; H.C.E. Childers to W.E. Gladstone, 4 June 1880, Gladstone MSS., 44129; Lord Reay to Henry Campbell-Bannerman, 19 Jan. 1886, Campbell-Bannerman MSS., 41232; Randolph Churchill to Edward Stanhope, 25 May 1887, Stanhope MSS., 1392.
48. In 1861, 10,918 recruits joined the forces, by 1898 nearly four times that number were taken annually. See *General Annual Return of the British Army,* P.P., XLIII (c.1323), 1875, p.20; LIII (c.9426), 1899, p.30.
49. W.H. Smith to Lord Wolseley, 28 Dec. 1886, Smith MSS., WO.110/6.
50. The Duke of Cambridge to Edward Cardwell, 22 June 1870, Cardwell MSS., PRO.30/48/3/13.
51. Revised Summary of the Recommendations of Lord Wantage's Committee

and of Actions Taken WO.33/55.

52. *Memorandum by the Inspector-General of Recruiting,* P.P., XLII (c.57), 1870, pp.1–2; cited hereafter as *Memorandum on Recruiting* (1870).
53. Papers on Illegal Recruitment, WO.32/6992; *The Queen's Regulations and Orders for the Army* (1883), pp.432–7; W.E. Gladstone, Memorandum on Army Reorganisation, 5 Oct. 1871, Cardwell MSS., PRO.30/48/2/8.
54. *Memorandum on Recruiting* (1870), pp.3–4.
55. Papers on Illegal Recruitment, WO.32/6992.
56. See for instance, *Life in the Ranks of the English Army* (1883); *A British Soldier's Life in the Ranks* (1886), *The Advantages of the Army,* P.P., LIV (c.27), 1898.
57. *Memorandum on Recruiting* (1870), p.3; *Report of the Army Reorganisation Committee* (1881), pp.495–6; *Reports and Other Documents Relating to Army Organisation: General Order 32 of 1873,* P.P., XXI (c.2792), 1881, pp.63–77.
58. Edward Cardwell to Robert Lowe, 12 April 1870, 15 April 1870, Cardwell MSS., PRO.30/48/5/22; Edward Cardwell, The Army In 1872, November 1872, Gladstone MSS., 44120.
59. *Memorandum on Recruiting* (1870), p.2.
60. Papers on Illegal Recruitment, WO.32/6692; *Report of the Inspector-General of Recruiting,* P.P., XX (c.2832), 1881, p.7; XVII (c.3911), 1884, p.7; XIII (c.4677), 1886, p.8; XVI (c.6906), 1893–4, pp.3–4.
61. *Report of the Inspector-General of Recruiting,* P.P., XVI (c.6906), 1893–4, p.5; XVIII (c.7890), 1896, p.15. It was still argued as late as 1893 however that country people rarely saw and knew little of the regular army. G.C. Campbell to E. Majoribanks MP, 24 Nov. 1893, Campbell-Bannerman MSS., 41233.
62. WO.32/6886; Report on the Account of Army Expenditure for 1891–2, WO.33/53.
63. See *Life in the Ranks of the English Army* (1883), p.3; *The Army and What It Offers* (circa 1910), p.1.
64. H.O. Arnold-Forster, 'The Army and the Government's Opportunity', *The Nineteenth Century,* XLII (1898), pp.345–6.
65. In 1888 the government for the first time formally set out the army's duties. This recognised its principal obligation as one of providing effective support of the civil power in all parts of the United Kingdom. It was not until the end of the South African War that there was any serious reconsideration of these priorities. See *Report of the Commission on the War in South Africa* (1904), pp.224–5.
66. Hansard, CXCIX (3 March 1870), c.1204.
67. For 10d per man and upon very little notice landlords were expected to provide a hot meal of meat and vegetables and accommodation for the night.
68. One licensed victualler argued for instance that the men he was required to put up '. . .are so often in so dirty a state that they are really not fit to have in a respectable person's house. . .they imagine, with a great deal of intolerance, that they are qualified to have any accommodation and their general conduct is very disreputable indeed'. *Report of the Select Committee on the Billeting System,* P.P., X (c.363), 1857–8, pp.iv, 99; cited hereafter as *Report of the Committee on the Billeting System* (1857–8).
69. John Pindar, *Autobiography of a Private Soldier* (Cupar, Fife, 1877), p.164; *Report of the Commission on Recruiting* (1867), pp.viii,xi.

70. Grenville Murray, *Six Months in the Ranks,* p.263; *Report of the Army Reorganisation Committee* (1881), p.256.
71. A Voice from the Ranks, *The British Army and What We Think on the Subject* (1871), p.6.
72. Phipps Onslow, *The Contemporary Review,* XII (1869), p.548.
73. Anon., 'The Recruit of the Period', *Colburn's,* II (1871), pp.323–8; Randall, *Colburn's,* III (1891), pp.278–88; A British Field Officer, *The Army and the Press in 1900* (1901).
74. See for instance, *The Border Advertiser,* 5 Aug. 1870, 14 Nov. 1888, 18 April 1899; *The Dunfermline Journal,* 1 June 1874, 24 Aug. 1878; *The Northern Ensign and Weekly Gazette,* 20 March 1856; *The Scottish Border Record,* 16 Feb. 1895, 16 March 1895.
75. John Holms, 'Our Army and the People', *The Nineteenth Century,* III (1878), p.47.
76. 'Anyone may notice the crowd which always collects in front of the windows of a picture shop displaying any stirring episode of military life', complained a writer in 1891, 'but I doubt whether the magnetic attraction inspired by the highly coloured and insipid recruiting placards which we see at the local post-office has ever been found sufficient to enflame the enthusiasms of one hesitating enquirer.' Thomson, *The Westminster Review,* CXXXVI (1891), p.629.
77. For instance a recruiting pamphlet published in 1883 remarks that soldiers are at liberty to buy butter, cheese or bacon to help down the dry bread served for breakfast. Recruits, it states, may go directly to their depots, and thus avoid associating with other recruits who may be of low character. See *Life in the Ranks of the English Army* (1883), pp.4, 11.
78. H.O. Arnold-Forster, *The Army in 1906* (1906), p.139.
79. *Report of the Inspector-General of Recruiting,* P.P., XII (c.939), 1874, p.4; XVI (c.3169), 1882, pp.1, 4; XVIII (c.7659), 1895, p.6; *The Times,* 8 Feb. 1879; Hansard, XXXIX (21 April 1869), c.1421.
80. For a statement that prejudice had not in fact abated, see Randall, *Colburn's,* III (1891), pp.278–88; Beedos, 'The Recruiting Question', *Colburn's,* XVIII (1898–9), pp.86–8.
81. Malan, *The Fortnightly Review,* V (1886), p.407; Captain R.D. Gibney, Superintendent of Recruiting, Salisbury Sub-District, 'Recruiting', *Colburn's,* I (1874), pp.344–50; Ryder, *Four Years' Service in India,* p.3.
82. Grenville Murray, *Six Months in the Ranks,* p.257.
83. Fraser, *Sixty Years in Uniform,* p.42.
84. Quoted in Bonham-Carter, *Soldier True,* p.5.
85. The Recruiting of the British Army – the Old System and the New, WO.33/35.
86. Lieutenant-Colonel W.W. Knollys, 'The Position and Condition of the British Soldier', *Colburn's,* III (1880), p.344.
87. Edward Cardwell to W.E. Gladstone, 25 Oct. 1872, W.E. Gladstone to Edward Cardwell, 27 Oct. 1872, Cardwell MSS., PRO.30/48/2/9.
88. Hansard, CCXIX (22 May 1874), cc.713–14.
89. Hardy, *Thomas Atkins,* p.xi; John G. Gollan, *Twelve Years in the Army; Or the Incidents in a Soldier's Life* (Elgin, 1864), p.38; Lieutenant-General Sir Francis Tuker, ed., *The Chronicle of Private Henry Metcalfe, H.M. 32nd Regiment of Foot* (1953), p.89.
90. *Report of the Committee on Short Service Conditions* (1881), p.17; *The Times,* 22 Jan. 1876; *The Regiment,* 25 July 1896; Fuller, *The Army in My Time,* pp.5–6.
91. Knollys, *Colburn's,* III (1880), p.344.

92. Anon., *Recollections of an Old Soldier* (Birmingham, 1886), p.107; A Voice from the Ranks, *The British Army and What We Think on the Subject* (1871), p.10.
93. *Report of the Commission on Recruiting* (1861), p.iii.
94. James Pyne to Fox Maule, 2 Feb. 1849, Panmure MSS., GD45/8/57; Lieutenant-Colonel de Mesurier to W.H. Smith, 16 Oct. 1886, Smith MSS., WO.110/5; Anon., 'Our Military Reforms of Late Years, and What They Have Done for Us', *Colburn's,* III (1860), pp.475–9; Anon., 'Long versus Short Enlistment', *Colburn's,* II (1869), p.484; Anon., 'A Plea for a Veteran Soldiery', *Colburn's,* II (1871), pp.224–8; Brigade Surgeon William Curran, 'A Medical View of Recruiting', *Colburn's,* I (1885), pp.421–34; Anon., 'The Recruiting Question V', *Colburn's,* III (1891), pp.471–5; A Soldier, 'About Soldiers', *Blackwood's Edinburgh Magazine,* CLI (1892), p.880; Lieutenant-Colonel C.M. Douglas, 'Recruiting from a Depot Medical Officer's Point of View', *JRUSI,* XLIV (1900), pp.5–7; *The Times,* 4 April 1867; Hansard, CLXXVII (21 Feb. 1865), cc.516–17; LXVIII (14 March 1899), cc.813–14.
95. *Report of the Commission on Recruiting* (1861), p.2.
96. *Report of the Commission on Recruiting* (1867), p.39.
97. Ibid., p.101; *Report of the Army Reorganisation Committee* (1881), pp.32–3, 137; *Report of the Wantage Committee* (1892), pp.8, 193, 472.
98. Strikes did not normally provide a bonus for the army, since workers seldom deserted their pickets to enlist. Lord de Grey, Memorandum on Army Recruitment, circa 1866, Panmure MSS., GD45/8/517; *Report of the Commission on Recruiting* (1867), pp.130–2; *Report of the Inspector-General of Recruiting,* P.P., XXV (c.1435), 1876, p.1; XIII (c.4677), 1886, p.15; XIX (c.5953), 1890, p.4; XVI (c.6906), 1893–4, p.7; *Report of the Physical Deterioration Committee* (1904), p.8.
99. See *Report of the Committee on Certain Questions Relative to the Militia,* P.P., XIX (c.5922), 1890, p.491.
100. A Voice from the Ranks, *The British Army and What We Think on the Subject* (1871), p.6; Anon., Experiences of a Soldier, unpublished MS., NAM. (circa 1890), p.1; Fraser, *Sixty Years in Uniform,* p.38.
101. Daniel Reid, *Memorials of the Life of a Soldier* (1864), pp.1–3; Grenville Murray, *Six Months in the Ranks,* p.263; Sergeant John Menzies, *Reminiscences of an Old Soldier* (Edinburgh, 1883), pp.4–7.
102. Sergeant Taffs, 'Alma, Inkermann, and Magdala', in E.M. Small, ed., *Told from the Ranks* (1897), p.87.
103. MacMullen, *Camp and Barrack-Room* (1846), p.311.
104. Blatchford, *My Life in the Army,* pp.11–12; A. Neil Lyons, *Robert Blatchford* (1910), p.36.
105. Edmondson, *Is a Soldier's Life Worth Living?,* p.5; Edmondson, *John Bull's Army from Within,* p.3.
106. Edmondson, *Is a Soldier's Life Worth Living?,* p.5.
107. Anon., 'On Recruiting and Enlistment', *Colburn's,* II (1865), pp.1–2; Anon., 'The Real Position and Advantages of the Soldier', *Colburn's,* I (1866), pp.586–90; Anon., 'Rank and File', *Colburn's,* II (1866), pp.394–6; Red Coat, 'A Voice from the Ranks', *Colburn's,* II (1884), pp.1–10; Grenville Murray, *A Voice from the Ranks,* p.1; *Report of the Wantage Committee* (1892), p.59.
108. *Report of the Commission on Recruiting* (1867), p.12.
109. Ryder, *Four Years' Service in India,* pp.1–3; Thomas McKiernan, *Experiences of a Veteran British Soldier* (Aberavan, 1892), p.7; Corbett, *Service through Six Reigns,* p.5; Tuker, *The Chronicle of Private Henry*

Metcalfe, p.12; Hardy, *Thomas Atkins,* p.23.

110. Gollan, *Twelve Years in the Army,* pp.1–3; One of the Rank and File, *Recollections of an Old Soldier* (Birmingham, 1886), pp.1–2; J.W. Moodie, *A Soldier's Life and Experience* (Ardrossan, 1887), p.2; James O'Malley, *The Life of James O'Malley* (1893), p.3; J.W.F., 'How May the Army Be Made More Popular and Recruiting More Efficient?', *Colburn's,* I (1858), pp.1–3; Linesman, 'The British Soldier', *Colburn's,* XIX (1899), pp.306–10; Pindar, *Autobiography of a Private Soldier,* p.5; Marquess of Anglesey, ed., *Sergeant Pearman's Memoirs* (1968), pp.2–8. The stress that must be placed on adventure as a drawing-card for recruitment is well recognised today. The opportunity for travel is no longer so important an attraction, but it certainly was until Britain's involvement overseas declined significantly. See Colonel J.D. Lunt, 'Another Angle on Recruiting', *JRUSI,* CVI (1961), p.58; Major G. Hatch, 'Adventure Training and Recruiting–Some Suggestions', *JRUSI,* CVI (1961), pp.486–90.

111. Joseph Gregg, 'The Charge of the Six Hundred', in Small, ed., *Told from the Ranks,* p.61.

112. *Report of the Inspector-General of Recruiting,* P.P., XV (c.1149), 1875, p.2; *Report of the Commission on Recruiting,* (1867), p.xi.

113. *Report of the Wantage Committee* (1892), p.19. In 1875 alone, at least 15 per cent of that year's recruits were former militiamen. *Report of the Committee on Certain Questions Relative to the Militia and Present Brigade Depot System,* P.P., XVIII (c.1654), 1877, p.499.

114. This argument was used even with efforts to improve army barracks. 'Nothing can more effectively assist recruiting', H.O. Arnold-Forster wrote, 'than the substitution of healthy and attractive buildings for the sombre, inconvenient, and often unsanitary barracks in which our troops are too frequently lodged. See H.O. Arnold Forster, *The Army in 1906* (1906), p.31; also Moody, *JRUSI,* XXIX (1885), pp.605–7; Hansard, CXLII (19 June 1856), c.1711; CCCXLVI (26 June 1890), c.102.

115. Lieutenant-General the Hon. C. Grey to Edward Cardwell, 24 Dec. 1869, Cardwell MSS., PRO.30/48/1/1; Hansard, CLXXXI (5 March 1866), c.1572; CLXXXV (15 March 1867), cc.1974–5; CCLIX (17 March 1881), cc.1336–7; CCCIII (25 March 1886), c.1809–16; *The Times,* 3 Sept. 1859, 30 March 1867, 30 Dec. 1875, 19 July 1879, 30 July 1890.

116. See for instance *The Advantages of the Army,* P.P., LIV (c.81), 1898, p.9.

117. *Report of the Commission on Recruiting* (1861), pp.xiv–vi; *Report of the Commission on Recruiting* (1867), pp.x, xiii; Memorandum on the Means of Recruiting the Army, WO.33/6b; *Report of the Committee on Recruiting,* WO.33/27; *Report of the Committee on Short Service Conditions* (1881), pp.4–8; *Report of the Army Reorganisation Committee* (1881), pp.35–6; *Report of the Wantage Committee* (1892), p.27.

118. Hansard, CXLII (16 June 1856), c.1551; CLVIII (1 June 1860), c.1911; CLXXIV (15 April 1864), cc.1068–71; CXCIV (11 March 1869), c.1166; *The Times,* 27 Aug. 1859; Spencer Walpole, 'Army Reform', *The Cornhill Magazine,* XVIII (1868), pp.671–85.

119. *Report of the Commission on Recruiting* (1861), p.189.

120. Hansard, CLXXVII (16 March 1865), cc.1794–5.

121. General C. Grey to the Prince Consort, 21 July 1855, Panmure MSS., GD45/8/241; *The Times,* 14 July 1859.

122. See for instance Edward Cardwell to W.E. Gladstone, 9 Jan. 1869; General Edwards, Memorandum on Army Reform, 21 Jan. 1869, Cardwell MSS., PRO.30/48/2/6, 30/48/3/11; Anon., 'The Pension Difficulty', *Colburn's,* I (1873), pp.297–300; Lieutenant-General Sir John Adye, 'The British

Army', *The Nineteenth Century,* VI (1879), pp.354–60.

123. *Report of the Commission on Recruiting* (1861), p.v.
124. *Report of the Commission on Recruiting* (1867), p.xi.
125. The Duke of Cambridge to Lord Panmure, 28 Aug., 23 Oct., 1857; Lord Panmure to the Duke of Cambridge, 6 Oct. 1857, Panmure MSS., GD45/8/152–3.
126. *Report of the Commission on Recruiting* (1867), p.xii.
127. *Report of the Commission on Recruiting* (1867), pp.65, 69; Hansard, CLXXIV (15 April 1864), cc.1064–7.
128. Noake, *JRUSI,* XI (1868), pp.35–9; *Report of the Commission on Recruiting* (1861), p.165; *Report of the Commission on Recruiting* (1867), pp.1, 112; Hansard, CLXXIV (11 April 1864), c.827; CLXXVI (27 June 1864), c.388; CLXXVII (21 Feb. 1865), c.523; CLXXXI (5 March 1866), c.1546.
129. *Report of the Commission on Recruiting* (1861), p.vi; *Report of the Commission on Recruiting* (1867), p.xii; Anon., 'The Army Enlistment Act', *Blackwood's Edinburgh Magazine,* CVIII (1870), pp.1–5; Hansard, CLXXIV (17 March 1864), c.163; CLXXVII (16 March 1865), c.1791.
130. *The Times,* 22 June 1861.
131. Anon., 'On Army Organisation', *Blackwood's Edinburgh Magazine,* CV (1869), pp.152–60; Anon., 'On the Limitation of Enlistment and Army Reserves', *Blackwood's Edinburgh Magazine,* CVI (1869), pp.279–89; *Report of the Commission on Recruiting* (1861), p.65; Hansard, CLXXVII (21 Feb. 1865), cc.520–5; CLXXVII (16 March 1865), cc.1784–5, 1809; CLXXXI (5 March 1866), c.1558.
132. *Report of the Commission on Recruiting* (1861), pp.227, 231; Anon., 'Re-Enlistment of Time-Expired Men', *Colburn's,* II (1864), pp.1–15; Forbes, *The Cornhill Magazine,* X (1864), pp.214–17.
133. *Report of the Commission on Recruiting* (1867), pp.xii, 65; Anon., 'The Army', *Blackwood's Edinburgh Magazine,* CI (1867), p.447; Hansard, CLXXXV (14 March 1867), c.1790.
134. *Report of the Commission on Recruiting* (1861), p.vi.
135. *Report of the Commission on Recruiting* (1867), p.xii.
136. Edward Cardwell to W.E. Gladstone, 9 Jan. 1869, Gladstone MSS., 44119; the Duke of Cambridge to Edward Cardwell, 20 Oct., 19 Dec. 1868, 3 Aug. 1869; Lord Northbrook, Memorandum on Auxiliary Forces, 29 Jan. 1869; Lieutenant-General the Hon. C. Grey, Memoranda on Regimental Organisation, circa December 1869, Cardwell MSS., PRO.30/48/1/1, 30/48/3/11, 30/48/4/18.
137. Edward Cardwell to W.E. Gladstone, 22 Sept. 1870, W.E. Gladstone to Edward Cardwell, 23 Sept. 1870, Cardwell MSS., PRO.30/48/2/7.
138. *An Act to Shorten the Time of Active Service in the Army, and to Amend in Certain Respects the Law of Enlistment,* 33 and 34 Vict. (9 Aug. 1870); General Edwards, Memorandum on Army Reform, 21 Jan. 1869, Cardwell MSS., PRO.30/48/3/11.
139. *Report of the Committee on the Formation of Territorial Regiments,* P.P., XX (c.2793), 1881, pp.4–10; see also Brian Bond, 'The Effect of the Cardwell Reforms in Army Organisation, 1874–1904', *JRUSI,* CV (1960), pp.515–24.
140. Edward Cardwell to W.E. Gladstone, 9 Jan. 1869, 10 Oct. 1871, 20 Dec. 1873, Gladstone MSS., 44119–20; Hansard, CCIV (16 Feb. 1871), c.333.
141. Anon., 'Army Organisation', *Westminster Review,* XCVI (1871), p.140; Hansard, CCIX (22 Feb. 1872), c.895; CCIII (18 July 1870), cc.445–6.
142. Short Service and Indian Requirements, WO.33/28; Surgeon G.J.H. Evatt,

Short Service for the English Soldier in India (Simla, 1876), Parkes Pamphlets, VII.

143. Cardwell considered the withdrawal of troops from foreign stations to be a key to the whole question of army reform. Not only did he believe foreign service to be a considerable hindrance to recruitment, but he held that unless such obligations were reduced, there would be little hope of shortening the term of regular service. Edward Cardwell to W.E. Gladstone, 9 Jan. 1869, Cardwell MSS., PRO.30/48/2/6; Edward Cardwell to W.E. Gladstone, 1 Sept. 1892, Gladstone MSS., 44120.
144. Particular emphasis was placed upon the need to reverse the decline in enlistments from rural areas. Edward Cardwell to Queen Victoria, 18 Dec. 1872, Cardwell MSS., PRO.30/48/1/3; Hansard, CCXIII (29 July 1872), cc.92–5.
145. Hansard, CCIX (22 Feb. 1872), c.901.
146. Anon., 'The Provision of Recruits and Formation of Reserves for the Army', *Colburn's,* II (1875), p.168; see also *Final Report of the Committee on the Organisation of the Various Military Land Forces of the Country,* P.P., XVIII (c.712), 1873, p.11.
147. *Report of the Army Reorganisation Committee* (1881), p.10.
148. *Report of the Wantage Committee* (1892), pp.2–3. Between 1856 and 1899 the only years in which British forces were not engaged in some part of the world were 1869 and 1883.
149. *Report of the Army Reorganisation Committee* (1881), pp.iv, 10–11; *Report of the Committee on the Effects of Short Service,* WO.32/6882; Minutes on the Condition of The Army, WO.33/35; *Report of the Wantage Committee* (1892), pp.5, 10.
150. Lord Northbrook to Edward Cardwell, 15 Jan. 1869; Lord Northbrook, Memorandum on Army Organisation, circa January 1869, Cardwell MSS., PRO.30/48/4/18.
151. The Duke occasionally went directly to the Prime Minister or the Queen in opposing troop reductions. See his correspondence with Edward Cardwell and Cardwell's rejoinders to Gladstone in the Cardwell MSS., PRO.30/48/3/11, 30/48/3/14 and 30/48/2/7. See also the Duke of Cambridge, Memorandum on Army Establishments, 5 Dec. 1863, Ripon MSS., 43511; the Duke of Cambridge to Gathorne Hardy, 23 Feb. 1878, 16 Sept. 1881, Hardy MSS., T501/264; the Duke of Cambridge to W.H. Smith, 26 Dec. 1885, Smith MSS., WO.110/3; the Duke of Cambridge to Edward Stanhope, 30 Jan. 15 March 1887, 14 Jan. 1888, 3 Jan. 1890, Stanhope MSS., 1368; H.C.E. Childers to W.E. Gladstone, 12 Oct. 1880, 27 Dec. 1881, Gladstone MSS., 44129.
152. The Duke of Cambridge to Edward Cardwell, 1 Feb. 1869, Cardwell MSS., PRO.30/48/3/12; the Duke of Cambridge to Lord de Grey and Ripon, 25 March 1881, 3 Feb. 1882, Ripon MSS., 43511.
153. The Duke of Cambridge to Edward Cardwell, 3 Aug. 1869, Cardwell MSS., PRO.30/48/3/11.
154. The Duke of Cambridge to Edward Cardwell, 19 Dec. 1868, 3 Aug. 1869, Cardwell MSS., PRO.30/48/3/11.
155. Anon., 'The New Law of Enlistment', *Colburn's,* II (1870), pp.358–65; M. Laing Meason, 'Our Military Mistakes', *Colburn's,* I (1881), pp.137–41, 307–15.
156. *Draft Report of a War Office Committee on the Effects of Short Service on the Preparedness for War of the Army,* WO.33/33; *Reports on the Effects of Short Service,* WO.32/6882; Minutes on the Condition of the Army, WO.33/35.

157. The Duke of Cambridge, Memorandum on Army Reform, 2 Feb. 1869; the Duke of Cambridge to Edward Cardwell, 16 Feb. 1869, 2 Jan. 1870, 4 March 1871, Cardwell MSS., PRO.30/48/3/11, 30/48/4/15; the Duke of Cambridge to Gathorne Hardy, 30 Nov. 1874, Hardy MSS., T501/264.
158. The Duke of Cambridge, Memorandum on Infantry Establishments, 22 Dec. 1868; the Duke of Cambridge to Edward Cardwell, 11 Jan. 1870, Cardwell MSS., PRO.30/48/3/11, 30/48/3/13; Lord Strathnairn to Lord Derby, 1 April 1876, Hardy MSS., T501/105.
159. *Report of the Committee on Recruiting,* WO.33/27, pp.240 et seq. This led Gathorne Hardy as Secretary of State for War to take steps to improve recruitment for the Guards by granting a number of special privileges, including a small increase in pay. Gathorne Hardy, Memorandum on Army Conditions and Recruitment, 8 Jan. 1876, Gathorne Hardy to the Duke of Richmond, 10 Jan. 1876, Hardy MSS., T501/61, T501/16.
160. *Report of the Army Reorganisation Committee* (1881), p.10.
161. *The Times,* 14 July 1879; *Report of the Army Reorganisation Committee* (1881), pp.3–4, 369–400.
162. *Report of the Army Reorganisation Committee* (1881), p.398.
163. *Report of the Committee on Short Service Conditions* (1881), pp.3, 15–17.
164. Hansard, CCLIX (3 March 1881), cc.1340–6.
165. *Revised Memorandum on the Principal Changes in Army Organisation Effective 1 July 1881,* P.P., LVIII (c.2922), 1881, pp.1–2.
166. 'Officers in the Army must be far greater grumblers and *croakers* than formerly,' Lord Malmesbury was to remark to Gathorne Hardy, 'or else Cardwell must have left the Service in a very distorted state.' Lord Malmesbury to Gathorne Hardy, 4 March 1878, Hardy MSS., T501/264.
167. Hansard, CCLXXX (29 June 1883), cc.1839–43. See also Hamer, *Civil Military Relations,* pp.23 et seq.
168. H.O. Arnold-Forster, 'Parliamentary Misrule of Our War Services', *The Nineteenth Century,* XXVI (1889), pp.523–44; Anon., 'Army Vivisection', *Blackwood's Edinburgh Magazine,* CXXXV (1884), pp.289–91.
169. Red Coat, 'A Voice from the Ranks', *Colburn's,* II (1884), p.10.
170. *Report of the Committee on the Formation of Territorial Regiments,* WO.33/35; Lieutenant-Colonel A.A.D. L'Estrange, 'The Comic Army List', *Colburn's,* I (1885), pp.209–22.
171. It was contended that men enlisted to get away from their native areas, but not necessarily to travel abroad. I have found no evidence to suggest that recruits selected particular regiments for this reason. An Officer, *A Few Remarks on Mr. Cardwell's Army Reorganisation Bill* (1871); *Report of the Committee on Certain Questions Relative to the Militia and Present Brigade Depot System,* P.P., XVIII (c.1654), 1877, pp.3–5; Lieutenant-General the Hon. C. Grey to Edward Cardwell, 24 Dec. 1869, Cardwell MSS., PRO.30/48/1/1.
172. There is a great deal of correspondence relating to these matters in the Cardwell MSS., PRO.30/48/1/3–4, and in the Campbell-Bannerman MSS., 41218, 41227, 41209 and 41233. I have discussed this in greater detail in my own thesis. See A.R. Skelley, 'The Terms and Conditions of Service and Recruitment of the Rank and File of the British Regular Home Army, 1856–1899', unpublished Ph.D thesis, Edinburgh University (1975), p.401.
173. A Regimental CO and Past Assistant Adjutant-General, On Short Service and Division Depots, Official War Office Papers of General Viscount Wolseley, W.33.
174. See for instance Trench, *The Dark Side of Short Service,* passim.
175. This of course was one of the principal weaknesses picked out by critics.

See the Duke of Cambridge to Edward Cardwell, 4 July 1870, Cardwell MSS., PRO.30/48/3/14; the Duke of Cambridge, Memorandum on Army Establishments, December 1881; Henry Campbell-Bannerman to W.E. Gladstone, 1 Nov. 1892, Gladstone MSS., 44117, 44130; Lord Wolseley to Henry Campbell-Bannerman, 6 Dec. 1892; Redvers Buller to Henry Campbell-Bannerman, 1 Jan. 1893, Campbell-Bannerman MSS., 41233, 41212; Anon., 'Inefficiency of the British Army', *The Quarterly Review,* CXXIX (1870), p.524; Lieutenant-Colonel W.W. Knollys, 'What Sort of an Army Have We Got?', *Colburn's,* II (1883), pp.659–70; Hanbury, *The Fortnightly Review,* LI (1892), pp.850–7; Colonel A.M. Brookfield, Major F.C. Rasch et al., 'The War Office and its Sham Army', *The Nineteenth Century,* XLIII (1898), p.11; *The Times,* 15 July 1879, 30 June 1879; Hansard, CCLXXVII (12 March 1883), cc.226–9, 241–4; CCCIII (25 March 1886), c.1822; IX (9 March 1893), cc.1464–77.

176. It was common to regard this as a recent development, but in fact criticism of the proportion of youth in the army was not new. Many of the reinforcements sent out to the War in the Crimea were under age, and at one stage in the campaign Lord Raglan refused a group of 2,000 reinforcements who he argued were too young. (The Recruiting of the British Army: the Old System and the New, WO.33/35.) In 1892 Lord Wolseley wrote, 'I joined at Chatham, in 1852, and it was full of recruits all waiting for conveyance to India. As regards age, they were nearly all boys, and not nearly such nice looking, or such good boys as those we get now. I was nearly nineteen myself, and thought myself a man; but I remember that I regarded the recruits around me as boys, that is, as much younger than I was. We never did enlist men in this century.' Quoted in Atlay, *Lord Haliburton,* p.109.

177. *Report of the Army Medical Department,* P.P., XXXVI (c.3404), 1864, p.33; LIII (c.9453), 1899, p.41.

178. Henry Marshall, Surgeon to the Forces, *Hints to Young Medical Officers of the Army on the Examination of Recruits* (1828); Anon., 'A Few Remarks on Recruiting, and the Limited Service Act of 1847', *Colburn's,* I (1861), pp.84–7; William Aitken MD, *On the Growth of the Recruit and the Young Soldier* (1862).

179. *Report of the Army Reorganisation Committee* (1881), p.16. In 1881 the War Office ordered that no men should be sent overseas on colonial duty unless they had either reached the age of twenty or had completed one year of service. This of course exacerbated the plight of the home army.

180. Aitken, *Growth of the Recruit;* Brigade Surgeon Lieutenant-Colonel William Hill-Climo, 'The Recruit and his Training', *Colburn's,* XII (1895–6), pp.247–60; idem, 'A Substitute for Conscription', *Colburn's,* XVI (1897–8), pp.259–63; Surgeon-Captain J. Will, 'The Recruit and His Physical Training', *Colburn's,* XVII (1898), pp.628–40.

181. Among the more influential senior officers were Sir J. Lintorn Simmons, Lord Roberts and Lord Wolseley. See for example, J.L.A. Simmons, Table of Discharge Rates, WO.33/32; idem, 'The Inefficiency of the Army', *The Nineteenth Century,* XXXI (1892), pp.885–98; Lord Roberts to Edward Stanhope, 8 May 1883, Stanhope MSS., 1401; Papers by General Lord Roberts on the Report on the Terms and Conditions of Service in the Army, WO.33/52; G.J. Wolseley, Memorandum on the Infantry Establishment, Official War Office Papers of General Viscount Wolseley, W.21; *Report of the Wantage Committee* (1892), pp.153–68. H.O. Arnold-Forster, Sir Charles Dilke and John Holms were the leading politicians. See H.O. Arnold-Forster, *Our Home Army* (1892); idem, *The War Office, the Army, and*

the Empire (1900); *The Times,* 26 Feb. 1876, 22 April 1892, 31 March 1899; Hansard, CCIX (4 March 1872), cc.1328–37, CCXXXVII (4 March 1878), cc.682–90, LIV (25 Feb. 1898), cc.60–71, LXVII (2 March 1899), cc.1097–8; Sir Charles W. Dilke, *The British Army* (1888); idem, *Army Reform* (1898); John Holms, *The Nineteenth Century,* III (1878), pp.97–115, 355–70.

182. See for example Major Charles G.C. Norton, *The Reorganisation of the British Infantry and How to Employ Our Volunteers* (1871); Major R. Compton Noake, *The British Army, 1875: a Challenge to the War Office Actuaries* (1875); A. Allison, 'On Our Army', *Blackwood's Edinburgh Magazine,* CLI (1892), pp.475–87; Moody, *JRUSI,* XXIX (1885), pp.621–8; Hansard, CXCIX (3 March 1870), cc.1190–7; CCXVI (1 July 1873), cc.1612–14; CCXXVII (25 Feb. 1876), cc.1213–17; *The Times,* 28 Oct. 1870, 28 July 1890.

183. *Report of the Committee on the Effects of Short Service Enlistment,* WO.32/6882; *Report of the Committee on the Inducements for Re-Enlistment,* WO.33/32; Reckoning of Previous Service on Re-Enlistment, WO.32/6693; *Memorandum on Extension of Service and Enlistment in the Brigade of Guards,* P.P., XXXIX (c.3638), 1883; Major North Dalrymple Hamilton, 'Organisation and Training of Our Land Forces', *Colburn's,* XV (1897), pp.193–5; Hansard, CCLIX (17 March 1881), cc.1279–80, 1291.

184. Holms, *The Nineteenth Century,* III (1878), pp.360–70; *The British Army in 1875* (1875), pp.59–61; Captain H.M. Hozier, 'The German and British Armies: a Comparison', *The Nineteenth Century,* XIV (1883), pp.210–21; Thomson, *The Westminster Review,* CXXXVI (1891), pp.640–2; Major H.W. Pearse, 'Squeezed Lemons', *Colburn's,* X (1894–5), pp.190–5; Colonel W.T. Dooner, 'The Recruiting Problem', *Colburn's,* XIV (1896–7), pp.170–6.

185. G.J. Wolseley, *Troops for India,* Official War Office Papers of General Viscount Wolseley, W.35; Hansard, CCXXVII (25 Feb. 1876), cc.950–1.

186. An Officer, *A Practical Scheme for the Reorganisation of the Armies of England* (1871); J.N.F., 'The Army of the Future', *Colburn's,* II (1872), pp.323–35; Knollys, *The Nineteenth Century,* VI (1879), pp.8–9; G.R. Gleig, 'Short Service: one Cause of its Failure', *The Nineteenth Century,* XIV (1883), pp.648–53; Palmer, *The Nineteenth Century,* XLIII (1898), pp.30–4; *The Times,* 5 Dec. 1870; Hansard, CCXXXVII (4 March 1878), cc.654–8; CCLXXXVI (17 March 1884), cc.53–5; CCCXXXIII (5 March 1889), cc.1435–41; LIV (28 Feb. 1898), cc.199–200.

187. *Report of the Commission on Recruiting* (1861), p.vi.

188. See for instance H.O. Arnold-Forster, *Army Letters, 1897–98* (1898), pp.119–20; Dilke, *The British Army,* pp.54, 85–6; idem, *Army Reform* (1898), pp.270–81.

189. Lord Roberts to Edward Stanhope, 8 May 1883, 8 Aug. 1883, Stanhope MSS., 1401; Lord Roberts to H.O. Arnold-Forster, 20 Jan. 1904, Roberts MSS., R/7101–23–3; The Papers and Memoranda of General Lord Roberts on the Report on the Terms and Conditions of Service in the Army, WO.33/52; *The Times,* 9 June 1892.

190. Major J. Brown, *A National Army, or How to Solve the Problem of the Day* (1871); Anon., 'The British Army', *Fortnightly Review,* XLIII (1888), pp.180–6.

191. Schemes of this nature were mooted when Edward Cardwell was at the War Office, but he strongly opposed them on the grounds that they would destroy the recruiting system. Edward Cardwell to W.E. Gladstone, 24 Oct. 1870, Gladstone MSS., 44119.

192. Arthur Haliburton to Henry Campbell-Bannerman, 2 May 1905; Henry Campbell-Bannerman to Arthur Haliburton, 7 May 1905, Campbell-Bannerman MSS., 41218; H.O. Arnold-Forster, *The Army in 1906* (1906), pp.28 et seq., idem, *Military Needs and Military Policy* (1909), pp.11–18.
193. Even the Duke of Cambridge reluctantly lent his support. See the Duke of Cambridge to Gathorne Hardy, 4 March 1878, Hardy MSS., T501/264; The Recruiting of the British Army–The Old System and the New, WO.33/35, p.75. Also 'B', 'Our Army and its Detractors', *Fortnightly Review*, L (1892), pp.773–92; 'G', 'Views on Army Reform: an Answer', *Colburn's*, VI (1892–3), pp.469–75; Brigade Surgeon F.P. Staples, 'The Age and Physique of Our Recruits', *Colburn's*, VI (1892–3), pp.251–60; Vinculum, 'The Recruiting Problem (Another View)', *Colburn's*, XIV (1896–7), pp.550–8.
194. Edward Cardwell to W.E. Gladstone, 20 Dec. 1873, Gladstone MSS., 44120.
195. See for example *Report of the Inspector-General of Recruiting*, P.P., XIV (c.495), 1872, pp.1–5; XVI (c.3169), 1882, pp.1–8; XIX (c.5953), 1890, pp.1–11.
196. *The Times*, 18 March 1870, 22 Feb. 1877, 5 June 1883, 3 March 1899; Hansard, LXVII (3 March 1899), cc.1290–1, 1306–19.
197. Major-General Sir John Adye, Memorandum on Indian Establishments, 12 Aug. 1880, Gladstone MSS., 44129; Major-General Sir John Adye, *The British Army in 1875: a Reply to Mr John Holms MP* (1876); Adye, *The Nineteenth Century*, VI (1879), pp.344–50; General Sir John Adye, 'The British Army, Past and Present', *Fortnightly Review*, XLI (1887), pp.499–515; idem, 'In Defence of Short Service', *The Nineteenth Century*, XXXII (1892), pp.358–69; *The Times*, 24 May 1890.
198. *Report of the Inspector-General of Recruiting*, P.P., XIX (c.6275), 1890–1, pp.6–7.
199. Hansard, CCCXXXIII (5 March 1889), cc.1458–9; CCCXLVII (22 July 1890), c.578; CCCXLVII (28 July 1890), cc.1005–9; CCCL (19 Feb. 1891), cc.1089–93; *The Times*, 6 March 1870, 29 May 1890, 28 July 1890, 25 Sept. 1890.
200. Wantage recognised that to be of value his committee must be given the power to inquire into the minimum age for service in India and to suggest methods of improving recruiting. Stanhope refused at first to allow any extension of the terms of reference, arguing that Parliament would never agree to an increase in the army establishment, and that he himself regarded such a measure as distasteful. Disagreement between Wantage and Stanhope led to a heated correspondence in which the Secretary of State not only tried to limit the jurisdiction of the committee, but refused initially to make the report public. Nevertheless Wantage proceeded as if he had been given a *carte blanche*, arguing that any restrictions were emasculating, and that if the evidence was to show that the effect of foreign drafts was to injure the home army, then the present system was faulty and in need of consideration. Stanhope eventually withdrew his restrictions, although his hostility to the committee's report was ill-disguised. See their correspondence in the Stanhope MSS., 1313.
201. Cato, 'Lord Wantage's Report and Public Opinion', *Colburn's*, V (1892), pp.77–95; *The Times*, 25 Feb. 1892; Hansard, V (10 June 1892), cc.701–7, 711–15.
202. *Report of the Wantage Committee* (1892), pp.1–16, 71–83, 167, 181–8, 389–95; Brookfield et al., *The Nineteenth Century*, XLIII (1898), p.11.
203. *Report of the Wantage Committee* (1892), pp.33–62.

204. *The Times,* 15 March 1892, 10 March 1892, 28 May 1892, 4 June 1892.
205. This is pointed out by Brian Bond in 'Recruiting the Victorian Army 1870–92', *Victorian Studies,* V (1962), p.337. Sir John Adye wrote to congratulate Haliburton on his dissent, confident that it would 'squash' the committee report. Sir John Adye to A. Haliburton, 24 Feb. 1892, Stanhope MSS., 1349. General G.C. Chesney predicted in a letter to Lord Roberts that with Haliburton's rider on top, virtually nothing would come of the Wantage report. G.C. Chesney to Lord Roberts, 11 March 1892, Roberts MSS., R14/298. No doubt Stanhope was pleased as well, but there is no indication of this in his correspondence.
206. See for instance *The Times,* 6 Jan. 1898, 11 Jan. 1898, 7 March 1898.
207. See for instance Hansard, CCLXXIX (1 June 1883), cc.1546–56.
208. P.L. MacDougall, Confidential Note on Recruiting, WO.33/26; idem, 'Have we an Army?' *The Nineteenth Century,* XIV (1883), pp.501–2; idem, 'The Inefficiency of the Army: a Reply', *Blackwood's Edinburgh Magazine,* CLII (1892), p.268; *The Times,* 17 Jan. 1881, 28 Jan. 1881.
209. *Report of the Wantage Committee* (1892), p.3. Lord Wantage expressed this view himself. Lord Wantage to Edward Stanhope, 24 Dec. 1891, Stanhope MSS., 1331.
210. Edward Cardwell, The Army in 1872, Nov. 1872, Gladstone MSS., 44120; *Report of the Inspector-General of Recruiting,* P.P., XIX (c.5953), 1890, p.7; XVI (c.3169), 1882, p.1.
211. *General Annual Return of the British Army,* P.P., XLIII (c.1323), 1875, p.13.
212. *General Annual Return of the British Army,* P.P., LIII (c.9426), 1899, p.16.
213. See Appendix V, Table VA–2.
214. Cardwell argued that his measures had led to a considerable improvement in the numbers enlisted, and had helped the army to attract a higher quality of recruit than ever before. See Edward Cardwell to W.E. Gladstone, 23 Sept. 1871, Cardwell MSS., PRO.30/48/2/8; Edward Cardwell to Henry Campbell-Bannerman, 23 Jan. 1875, Campbell-Bannerman MSS., 41214; See also *Report of the Inspector-General of Recruiting,* P.P., XIV (c.495), 1872, p.1; XVIII (c.1655), 1877, p.1; *The Times,* 15 March 1886.
215. *Report of the Inspector-General of Recruiting,* P.P., XIV (c.495), 1872, p.2; XVIII (c.718), 1873, p.4; XII (c.939), 1874, p.3; Edward Cardwell to W.E. Gladstone, 24 Oct. 1870, Gladstone MSS., 44119.
216. Brian Bond, 'The Effect of the Cardwell Reforms in Army Organisation, 1874–1904', *JRUSI,* CV (1960), p.519.
217. See *Report of a Committee on Inducements for Re-Enlistment,* WO.33/32; *Memorandum on Extension of Service and Enlistment in the Brigade of Guards,* P.P., XXXIX (c.3638), 1883.
218. Senior officers often looked with anxiety on the offering of bounties, convinced that the most effective answer to the shortage of men was a reform of the terms and conditions of service. See Lord de Grey and Ripon to General Mansfield, 19 Sept. 1859, General Mansfield to Lord de Grey and Ripon, 31 Oct. 1859, Ripon MSS., 43619; Lord Roberts to Edward Stanhope, 9 Aug. 1883, 10 March 1891, Stanhope MSS., 1401.
219. See Appendix V, Table VA–3.
220. See the official papers and correspondence in the Panmure MSS., GD45/8/165, 45/8/228.
221. Recruitment of Boys, WO.32/6881, pp.2–3.
222. Army returns for 1875 for instance show that on 1 January of that year there were 3,031 boys in the forces. *Report of the Committee on Boy Enlistment,* P.P., XVIII (c.1677), 1877, p.3; cited hereafter as *Report of*

the Committee on Boy Enlistment (1877).

223. Boy service formed a major part of the navy's annual recruiting efforts. Young lads were taken on at an early age, underwent instruction in special training ships, and when old enough were placed on active service with the fleet. In this way the navy was guaranteed a steady supply of well-trained recruits. See R. Taylor, 'Manning the Royal Navy: the Reform of the Recruiting System, 1852–1862', *Mariners' Mirror,* XLIV (1958), pp.302–13; XLV (1959), pp.46–58, passim.

224. J.T.W. Bacot, 'Boy Soldiers', *Colburn's,* III (1873), pp.294–300; Anon., 'The Provision of Recruits and Formation of Reserves for the Army', *Colburn's,* II (1875), pp.161–75; A General Officer, Royal Marines, 'Thoughts on Army Organisation and Discipline', *Colburn's,* II (1876), pp.103–5; *Report of the Commission on Recruiting* (1867), p.ix; *The Times,* 6 Jan. 1876, 10 Jan. 1876, 11 June 1883, 7 Sept. 1883, 11 Sept. 1883.

225. T. St. L. Alcock, *The Relative Power of Nations* (1875), p.3; H.M. Havelock-Allen, 'A General Voluntary Training to Arms versus Conscription', *The Fortnightly Review,* LXI (1897), pp.91–7; Hansard, CCXXIII (19 April 1875), cc.1202–3.

226. Major-General E.A. Saunders, *Recruiting without Conscription* (1875), p.23; John MacGregor, Chairman of the Industrial Schools Committee of the London School Board, 'On Training Boys for Soldiers', *JRUSI,* XIX (1875), pp.399–418; Sir Walter Crofton, 'Recruiting for the Army', *The Contemporary Review,* XXVII (1875–6), pp.460–70; Colonel M.J. King Harman, 'How to Make the Army Popular', *The United Services Magazine,* II (1890–1), pp.400–6; *The Times,* 17 June 1871.

227. Major H.L. Geary, 'On the Employment of Boys in the Army', *JRUSI,* XXI (1877), p.153.

228. *Report of the Committee on Boy Enlistment* (1877), p.4.

229. Hansard, CLXXXV (7 March 1867), p.1460.

230. MacGregor, *JRUSI,* XIX (1875), p.418.

231. Edward Cardwell to Henry Campbell-Bannerman, 27 Jan. 1876, Campbell-Bannerman MSS., 41212.

232. See Recruitment of Boys, WO.32/6881; Terms of Service for Boy Recruits, WO.32/6897.

233. J.E. Cairnes, 'Our Defences: a National or a Standing Army?', *The Fortnightly Review,* IX (1871, pp.166–98; Captain Totton Brown, *Suggestions for a National Army on an English System* (1872); Major C.E.D. Telfer-Smollet, 'The Relative Advantages and Disadvantages of Voluntary and Compulsory Service Both From a Military and a National Point of View', *JRUSI,* XLI (1897), pp.919–68; Anon., 'National Defence', *The Edinburgh Review,* CLXXXV (1900), pp.507–39; R. Lowe to Edward Cardwell, 20 Dec. 1870, Cardwell MSS., PRO.30/48/5/22.

234. Edwin Chadwick, 'On the Chief Economic Principles for Consideration in Relation to National as Against Standing Armies, as Displayed in the Present War on the Continent', *Transactions of the National Association for the Promotion of Social Science* (1900), pp.500–16.

235. Colonel F. Maurice, 'The Zeit-Geist Under Drill', *The Fortnightly Review,* XLV (1889), pp.711–26; Lieutenant-Colonel W. Underwood, *A Plea for Conscription in Britain* (1901).

236. An English Company Officer, 'How the German Soldier Is Made'. *Macmillan's Magazine,* LIX (1888), pp.95–106; A Patriotic Soldier, *England's Phantom Army: the Unrealities, Delusions, and Imperfections of the Brodrick Scheme* (1901); Anon., 'Efficiency in the Services', *The*

Quarterly Review, CXCVI (1902), pp.269–94.
237. *Report of the Commission on Recruiting* (1861), pp.104–5.
238. The Papers and Memoranda of General Lord Roberts on the Report of the Committee on the Terms and Conditions of Service in the Army, WO.33/52.
239. *Report of the Wantage Committee* (1892), p.158.
240. Edward M. Spiers, 'The Reform of the Front-Line Forces of the Regular Army in the United Kingdom, 1895–1914', unpublished Ph.D thesis, Edinburgh University (1974), p.11–27.
241. Cardwell argued that conscription was neither wise nor necessary. Edward Cardwell to Queen Victoria, 1 Dec. 1870, Cardwell MSS., PRO.30/48/1/2. General Sir Ian Hamilton's *Compulsory Service* (1911), was one of the classic rebuttals of the need for conscription. See also J.L.A. Simmons, Table of Discharge Rates, WO.32/32.
242. Field-Marshal Sir William Robertson, *Soldiers and Statesmen 1914–1918,* I (1923), pp.36–7; Brian Bond, 'The Introduction and Operation of Short Service Localisation in the British Army, 1868–1892', unpublished MA thesis, University of London (1962), p.120.
243. F.G. Wallace-Goodbody, 'Would Conscription Be Suitable to England?', *Colburn's,* IV (1889–90), pp.409–18; Havelock-Allan, *The Fortnightly Review,* LXI (1897), pp.85–97; A.W. Livesay, 'The Case against Conscription', *The Westminster Review,* CLIV (1900), pp.260–75; Arthur Griffiths, 'Our Military Needs', *The Fortnightly Review,* LXVII (1900), pp.527–36.
244. Saunders, *Recruiting without Conscription,* passim; Captain D. Henderson, 'The Relative Advantages of Voluntary and Compulsory Service, both from a Military and a National Point of View', *JRUSI,* XLI (1897), pp.563–95; Hansard, CCXXIII (20 April 1875), cc.1303, 1305; Lieutenant-General the Hon. C. Grey to Edward Cardwell, 24 Dec. 1869, Cardwell MSS., PRO.30/48/1/1.
245. Anon., 'Army Organisation', *The Westminster Review,* XCV (1871), pp.485–512; Anon., 'Compulsory or Voluntary Service', *Macmillan's Magazine,* XXXVIII (1878), pp.452–8.
246. Major W.P. Jones, 'Compulsory Military Service', *Colburn's,* I (1872), pp.40–3; Henderson, op.cit., pp.563–95; Livesay, op.cit., pp.260–75.

6 PATTERNS OF RECRUITMENT

> My opinion is that the recruits are very much of the same description as the men we have always had.
>
> The Duke of Cambridge

> The line recruit of today has, as a rule, the physical equivalent of a schoolboy between sixteen and seventeen years of age. He is unfit for active service and incapable of doing a hard day's work in England. . .Some of the recruits that I have had during the last few months were unable to hold the magazine rifle steadily. . . A few years ago when we had a little war we would take the troops at Aldershot and send them out, but I am of the opinion now that there is not more than one battalion that is fit for active service abroad.
>
> Lieutenant-General Sir Evelyn Wood, V.C.

We have observed that the recruiting problem was one of the major difficulties facing army administrators after 1856, and that it was a consideration in nearly every aspect of reform affecting the terms and conditions of service of the rank and file. The concern of this chapter is the patterns of recruitment and their effect on the forces. It looks specifically at recruits in terms of age, physique, nationality, urban/rural background, and occupations prior to enlistment. This provides the most systematic insight available into the type of men who chose to join the army, and sheds light therefore upon the character of the army itself.

An important but rarely used source of statistics is the census for Scotland. Scottish returns alone permit comparisons to be made and conclusions to be drawn over the forty-year period between 1851 and 1891, and there is no reason to suspect that the groups stationed in Scottish command were not in most respects a fair sampling of the home army.[1] English infantry, cavalry units and artillery are included in the survey and in some cases outnumber the men in the native Scots units. Moreover, as was the case in England, Scotland's recruits were drawn from both rural and urban districts and regiments had to be filled when necessary with men from outside the local recruiting area.

Official army figures showing the nationality of recruits and census returns indicating places of birth may mislead to an extent unless it is realised that some recruits may have grown up and enlisted in a different area than that in which they were born. The proportion of soldiers at any time who were of Irish extraction may therefore have been greater than statistics would indicate, and some of those singled out as having come from rural areas may in fact have lived most of their lives in towns or cities. There is also the problem of defining precisely what is meant by urban and rural. Similarly, there are limitations to statistics which indicate the previous occupations pursued by army recruits. Army statistics do not distinguish between urban and rural labourers, and the census listed occupations in the returns of 1851 and 1861 only. Furthermore, while it is unlikely that those who said they were unskilled labourers before enlistment were anything else, some of those who claimed to be skilled or semi-skilled might not in fact have been anything but unskilled. It is impossible to say what proportion of men might be affected by any of these reservations, but if the qualifications are assumed to apply equally throughout the period (a reasonable enough assumption), the trends which emerge are valid.

1. Age and Physical Standards

One of the clearest patterns to emerge from statistics is the progressive drop in the physical stature of the army recruit. Table 6–1 shows the age, weight and height of recruits between 1861, when first figures are available, and 1898. In the long run, there was a significant increase in the proportion of younger, lighter and smaller men enlisted. This was obviously a result of lowering physical standards, but in addition may be connected with a decline in recruitment in rural areas.

The effect of such trends on the regular forces was significant. Scottish census returns show that there was a substantial increase between 1851 and 1891 in the proportion of younger men serving with the army stationed in Scotland. (Complete tables are provided in Appendix VI, Table VIA–1.) While the proportion of men under the age of seventeen remained substantially the same throughout the period, there was after 1851, and again after 1881, by which time the effects of short service could be felt, a considerable increase in the percentage of those between the ages of seventeen and nineteen. This suggests that there was a significant loss of men from the home army after seven or eight years by either discharge or by transfer to foreign service. This had reached such a point by 1891 that over 85 per cent of the rank and file of the army in Scotland were twenty-five years of age or younger, an increase of 20 per cent on 1851. There was a corresponding decrease in the age of NCOs.

Table 6—1 Physical Standards of Recruits Approved for the Regular Army, 1861—98

Year	Age (Percent)				Weight (Percent)				Height (Percent)		
	Under 17	17 & 18	19 & 20	Over 20	Under 100	100 & 110	120 & 130	140 & Over	Under 5'3"	5'3"—5'5"	5'6" & Over
1861	2.05	32.14	25.69	39.85	2.09	20.16	51.20	26.55	2.01	18.75	79.24
1862	4.39	29.75	29.44	36.42	4.11	13.00	52.99	29.90	4.19	6.58	89.23
1864	2.82	35.18	30.96	31.04	2.64	16.45	60.15	20.76	2.67	4.23	93.10
1866	1.63	36.70	30.01	31.66	0.99	23.87	58.59	16.55	1.40	14.31	84.29
1868	2.87	35.82	29.16	32.15	1.53	19.66	54.70	24.11	2.60	6.29	91.11
1870	1.72	40.48	32.34	25.46	1.13	23.72	56.66	18.49	1.39	14.46	84.15
1872	2.70	31.57	38.75	26.98	2.87	20.73	57.89	18.51	2.43	12.08	85.49
1874	2.24	31.54	37.86	28.36	2.34	11.38	58.45	27.83	2.11	16.37	81.52
1876	1.87	26.72	23.66	37.75	2.19	12.87	55.27	29.67	1.77	14.94	83.29
1878	1.89	24.93	33.31	39.87	2.10	12.42	54.05	31.43	1.75	10.50	87.75
1880	2.45	29.10	33.07	35.38	2.57	10.60	57.26	29.57	2.17	9.66	88.17
1882	2.80	4.42	62.23	28.55	2.56	14.58	61.28	21.58	2.71	25.08	73.21
1884	2.37	34.44	36.80	26.39	2.13	24.35	55.76	17.76	3.70	31.72	64.58
1886	2.04	41.67	31.20	25.09	1.85	27.51	54.27	16.37	2.78	31.27	65.95
1888	4.64	43.06	31.20	21.20	3.76	17.54	59.50	19.20	4.08	28.32	67.60
1890	3.95	50.36	29.04	16.65	3.26	25.19	57.41	14.14	4.07	31.76	64.17
1892	3.35	45.75	29.73	21.17	2.72	25.13	55.64	16.51	3.59	29.74	66.66
1894	3.92	43.25	31.31	21.52	3.00	20.95	58.58	17.47	3.36	28.18	68.46
1896	4.36	43.67	31.59	20.38	3.56	19.18	58.86	18.40	3.95	26.36	69.69
1898	3.91	45.36	31.48	19.25	3.25	25.88	54.36	16.51	3.93	30.45	65.62

Source: *Annual Reports of the Army Medical Department,* P.P.

Statistics for the whole of the army present much the same sort of picture. Table 6–2 illustrates the proportion of men of various age groups serving with the army between 1866, when statistics were first available, and 1898. During these years there was no significant increase in the percentage of men under the age of eighteen; but there were increases in the proportions of soldiers aged eighteen to twenty, and more especially twenty to twenty five. Conversely the percentage of those aged between twenty-five and forty declined substantially.

Table 6–2 Ages of NCOs and Men Serving with the Regular Army, 1866–98

	Percentage					
Year	Under 18	18–20	20–25	25–30	30–40	Over 40
1866*	1.8	11.5	27.5	35.6	22.5	1.1
1871	2.9	16.1	27.3	21.7	30.0	2:0
1875	1.7	8.0	34.3	22.0	30.5	3.5
1879	1.6	9.0	37.5	25.8	20.5	3.6
1883	1.5	7.4	42.7	27.8	19.2	1.4
1887	1.7	15.1	48.9	21.1	11.9	1.3
1891	1.7	14.1	49.3	25.5	8.4	1.0
1895	1.7	14.0	52.8	22.5	8.2	0.8
1898	1.8	14.9	48.1	25.7	8.9	0.6

* Infantry of the line only

Source: *General Annual Return of the British Army*, P.P., XLIII (c.1323), 1875, p.54; XLIII (c.6196), 1890, p.78; LIII (c.9426), 1899, p.88.

2. Nationality

At the mid-point of the century, the army relied heavily upon Irish enlistment to fill the ranks. Massive unemployment and social disruption on a scale rarely experienced in the rest of the country, rendered Ireland fertile for recruitment,[2] and Irishmen not only predominated in the Irish regiments of the army but enlisted in large numbers in English and Scottish units as well. As the century wore on however, Irish enlistments fell drastically, forcing the army to look elsewhere for more of its recruits. Large-scale emigration after the famine of 1846 substantially reduced the surplus population of Ireland; its effect on recruitment was multiplied by the fact that emigrants were most often young men who otherwise might have looked to the British army for a career.[3] By 1900 Ireland's population had fallen by 32 per cent, and this had gone a long way to drying up the reservoir of recruits.[4] In the later years of the century opposition from nationalists to army recruiting drives proved to be another, if less serious obstacle.[5]

Table 6–3 shows the proportion of English and Welsh, Scottish and Irish recruits who were examined and enlisted during certain years between 1862, the first year for which figures of this sort are available, and 1899. Although there was somewhat of a resurgence in 1874–81, it is clear that on the whole Irish enlistment decreased sharply after 1860. The most marked decrease took place in the decade 1862–72. On the other hand the proportion of Scots recruited remained fairly constant throughout the period, and the difference seems to have been made up by the enlistment of larger numbers of Englishmen. During 1874 to 1881, the only years in which English and Scottish enlistment fell, they dropped by approximately the same amount while Irish recruitment underwent a corresponding increase. This suggests that the factors which influenced recruiting, such as unemployment, affected England and Scotland to approximately the same extent. Because Ireland was predominantly rural, the oscillating fortunes of industry had less effect on the labour market.

These trends were obvious to contemporaries. In February 1859 an editorial in *The Times* regretted that Ireland was no longer the great reserve of soldiers it had once been.[6] A year later a pamphlet observed:

> Ireland has ceased to offer an inexhaustible, *corps de reserve.* Ireland thrives apace. Not a trace of dust and ashes, the famine, the squalor, the mortal agony of 1846 visible on that gladsome green robe of hers. An hungering, redundant population no longer affects her. Ever-flowing emigration keeps up the price of labour, and the peasantry having at last a fair day's wage for a fair day's work, (thank God!) listen mockingly to Sergeant Kite's romances.[7]

This falling Irish enlistment was seized upon by many as a non-controversial explanation for the unhealthy state of recruiting. In 1864 both Earl de Grey and Ripon and the Earl of Dalhousie suggested to the Lords that the decreasing availability of Irish recruits was a major cause of the army's shortage of men.[8] Later Edward Cardwell and Henry Campbell-Bannerman each emphasised the declining proportions of Irish soldiers in the ranks and stressed the importance of emigration in shrinking the pool of prospective recruits.[9] In 1874 a medical officer involved with recruiting told a gathering at the Royal United Services

Institution that emigration had 'thinned the superstratum of stalwart youths, who in rags and tatters, were wont to crowd the barrack gates, begging for military service'.[10] A year later Lord Sandhurst, then GOC the forces in Ireland, argued in a memorandum to a War Office Committee that the decent men who wanted to better their condition did not now think of entering the army as had been the case before the great famine of 1846–7.[11] Lord Wolseley, speaking before the Wantage Committee in 1892, pointed out that Irish enlistment had declined to such an extent that much greater efforts were necessary to boost recruitment.[12]

Table 6–3 Recruitment by Nationality, 1862–99

	(Percentage of Total Recruitment)					
	English & Welsh		Scottish		Irish	
Year	Examined	Passed	Examined	Passed	Examined	Passed
1862	54.6	53.9	15.1	15.8	30.3	28.3
1865	69.8	64.7	7.8	10.2	21.9	25.1
1868	72.6	73.8	7.6	9.4	16.8	16.8
1870	89.1	82.1	6.8	6.8	11.1	11.1
1872	82.5	82.4	10.2	10.2	7.3	7.4
1874	71.6	91.4	9.0	9.1	19.4	19.5
1876	72.8	72.4	9.3	9.6	17.9	18.0
1878	69.9	69.6	9.8	10.0	20.3	20.4
1881	73.7	73.3	8.9	9.2	17.4	17.5
1883	78.1	77.6	9.2	9.3	12.7	12.9
1885	76.5	75.7	9.9	9.9	13.6	13.4
1887	77.2	76.7	9.7	10.0	13.1	13.3
1891	79.9	79.4	8.3	8.6	11.8	12.0
1893	78.9	78.5	8.5	8.8	12.6	12.7
1895	79.1	78.6	8.6	8.9	12.3	12.5
1897	77.2	76.7	9.8	10.0	13.0	12.3
1899	77.4	77.1	10.6	10.8	12.0	12.1

Source: *Annual Reports of the Army Medical Department,* P.P.

The emphasis placed on falling Irish enlistment was a rather facile explanation for the army's recruiting problems, since after 1860 the proportion of Irish recruited kept pace with Ireland's share of the United Kingdom population. Moreover, it did so despite the effects of emigration and a falling birthrate which made the Irish an ageing population, more so than the rest of the United Kingdom. In 1861 29.3 per cent of all recruits and 22.8 per cent of the male population of the United Kingdom between the ages of fiteen and twenty-four were Irish; in 1901 Ireland made up 12.1 per cent of the recruits enlisted in that year, and 11.4 per cent of the male population of military age. Ireland was in fact over-represented in recruitment throughout the period, and although Irish enlistments dropped sharply, so did the Irish population.

Table 6–4 shows the nationality of men serving with the colours between 1868, when the first such figures are available, and 1898. If, as it might be argued, there are such things as national characteristics, then the character of the army was changing.

Table 6–4 Nationalities of Men Serving with the Colours, 1868–98

Year	English and Welsh	(Percentage) Scottish	Irish
1868	59.5	9.5	31.0
1870	61.8	9.7	28.5
1872	66.3	8.9	24.8
1874	68.1	8.3	23.6
1876	69.4	8.1	22.5
1878	70.1	8.0	21.9
1880	70.3	8.4	21.3
1882	71.2	7.8	21.0
1884	73.8	8.0	18.2
1886	74.9	8.1	17.0
1888	75.8	8.6	15.6
1890	76.9	8.3	14.8
1892	78.2	8.0	13.8
1894	78.7	8.2	13.1
1896	79.0	8.0	13.0
1898	78.2	8.2	13.6

Source: *General Annual Return of the British Army,* P.P., XLIII (c.1323), 1875, p.56; XLIII (c.6196), 1890, p.83; LIII (c.9426), 1899, p.91.

The Scottish census returns not only demonstrate the effect of declining Irish enlistments after 1850, but also provide a wealth of additional information on how the army was constituted by nationality. Detailed figures are to be found in Appendix VI, Table VIA–2. From these statistics the proportion of Irish in the ranks of the army in Scotland appears to have been the highest throughout the period in units of English infantry, cavalry and artillery. The latter two recruited throughout the United Kingdom. However, it is not clear why there were fewer Irish in Scots than English infantry regiments. There may have been a higher proportion of English regiments stationed in Ireland at any time, which therefore may have attracted more recruits. It is also possible that the Irish preferred English regiments, or that there was less attempt made to recruit in Ireland for Scottish infantry units. No Irish regiments of course were stationed in Scotland, and it may be too that Irishmen more frequently enlisted for units serving or being posted overseas. Whatever the cause, there had been by 1891 a very substantial decrease in the proportion of Irishmen serving with all units of the army in Scotland, fewer than might have been expected from figures for Irish recruitment.

On the reasonable assumption that the Scottish regiments represented in these returns are typical of Scottish regiments in general, the proportion of Scots was highest throughout the period taken as a whole in their own regiments, a fact which shows the strength of some form of local attachments. However, despite relatively steady recruitment of Scots after 1860, it is clear from these figures that the proportion of Scots in their own units declined somewhat between 1851 and 1891. Their places in the ranks, like those of the Irish, were taken by English (and Welsh) soldiers. This clearly throws some doubt on the success of Cardwell's localisation of recruitment.

Whether recruitment in Scotland differed from that in other parts of the country is difficult to say. Certainly there were special difficulties encountered in recruitment. It was particularly difficult to attract men in the depopulated northern counties,[13] and there was a frequently observed refusal of a group of Scots to enlist unless each and every member was accepted.[14] Celebrated Highland regiments contained a large share of English, Irish and Lowland Scots in their ranks; how many is not clear. H. J. Hanham has pointed out that Scottish recruitment was unable to keep up with the demand for Scottish soldiers. Of this there can be little doubt. He goes on to argue however that out of nineteen such regiments in 1878, only three drew 60 per cent or more of their NCOs and men from Scotland.[15] The source of his information is unclear certainly, and to generalise on its basis would be misleading. High as it was, the proportion of soldiers other than native Scots should not be overstressed. A.V. Tucker's assertion for instance that in 1892 60 per cent of the Cameron Highlanders were 'Whitechapel Highlanders' must be questioned.[16] Returns for 1891 show 673 men of the Camerons stationed at Glencorse and Leith, 514 or 76.4 per cent of whom were Scots, 19 per cent English and 3.4 per cent Irish.[17]

Census returns, unlike other figures, provide a certain amount of separate information on the non-commissioned officer. For the most part, the nationality of NCOs varied with that of the rank and file, as might be expected. It is significant however that in most cases there were relatively more English NCOs and fewer Scottish and especially Irish. This suggests that either the English soldier was more successful in obtaining promotion than was the Scot or the Irishman, or that the others had less desire to gain advancement.[18]

3. The Effect of Urbanisation

Between 1850 and 1900 there was a considerable shift of population from the farms to the towns and cities resulting in rural depopulation and the rapid growth of urban areas.[19] The migration of the primarily rural population of Ireland to the industrial areas of Britain and America was a facet of this. The rest of the United Kingdom was affected as well, and in the end the army was forced to react by shifting the basis of its recruitment.

It was commonly believed during the 1850s that most army recruits came from rural areas. A regular officer, testifying before the Barrack Accommodation Committee in 1854, for example, remarked that he would 'have nothing complicated about barracks, because generally speaking the soldiers came from the farm yard, where they never saw a pump or anything like a drain'.[20] In fact population changes were well under way by 1850, and if the majority of recruits were at one time taken from entirely rural areas, this was clearly no longer the case by the middle of the century. Olive Anderson has argued that rural depopulation in England and Scotland as well as in Ireland contributed to the breakdown of the recruiting system during the Crimean War,[21] a contention which is supported by Scottish census returns. Table 6–5 gives a breakdown of the backgrounds of men stationed with the army in Scotland in 1851. Because exact birthplaces were not provided in every case, the proportions indicated are only of those men for whom information was precise. Cities are classified as those areas with a population of 10,000 or more when the census was taken, towns of 2,000–10,000, and rural areas of less than 2,000. Even if these constitute a rather arbitrary classification (particularly the definition of 'city' perhaps) it seems in general to define urban as distinct from rural areas.[22]

Although by 1851 a minority of soldiers came originally from rural areas, it is nevertheless clear that they formed an important part of infantry units particularly. It is interesting that a large majority of cavalrymen came from urban areas. Men from rural areas may have preferred not to work with horses, or there may have been a preference in the cavalry for small light men which resulted in more men being recruited from London and the other industrial centres. In all units a high percentage of Irish soldiers came from rural communities, which reflects the intensely rural character of Ireland. In contrast soldiers from more heavily populated England appear to have come principally from urban centres, and those from Scotland from small towns and from cities slightly more than from rural areas. Whatever their nationality, a substantially higher proportion of NCOs than rank and file came from the larger towns and cities. By the standards of the time rural recruits made good soldiers, but they more often did not, it appears, make the best NCOs.

This must throw doubt on the opinion widely held by military authorities that recruits from farming communities were the best material. Countrymen were not seen as more intelligent than those from towns or cities, but their value was felt to lie in their supposed good health and physical superiority. 'Those men who come from the manufacturing districts and large towns', a writer argued in 1855, 'are too frequently the most idle and dissolute; they require all the means in the power of their officers to correct the intemperate and vicious habits in which they have indulged, and to teach them that subordination is the first duty in the profession into which they have entered.'[23]

These views were current throughout the century. In 1863 Army Medical Department regulations observed that 'recruits from country districts are far preferable to those from towns'.[24] A few years later a London journal remarked:

> The country lout, stolid chaw-bacon, with his splay feet, and his loutish gait offers much more favourable material for soldier-making than the shrewd, quick-witted Londoner bred and born. The lout is preferable from every point of view. In the first place, he has vastly more of genuine 'stuff' in him—more bone and muscle. He has sounder lungs, and his stock is altogether healthier. His thick head too, and his slowness of comprehension are pristine advantages rather than drawbacks. The process of converting a civilian into a soldier is almost entirely a mechanical process, and one that a

Table 6–5 The Birthplace of Men Serving with the Army Stationed in Scotland on Census Day, 1851

Unit	Scots				English and Welsh				Irish				Total of Whole			
		Percentage				Percentage				Percentage				Percentage		
	Number	Rural	Towns	Cities	Number	Rural	Towns	Cities	Number	Rural	Towns	Cities	Number	Rural	Towns	Cities
Scottish Infantry																
Ranks	639	27.5	39.8	32.7	19	63.2	5.3	31.5	178	80.9	7.3	11.8	836	39.7	32.1	28.0
NCOs	88	28.4	45.5	26.1	11	45.4	27.3	27.3	19	63.2	15.8	21.0	118	35.6	38.9	25.5
English Infantry																
Ranks	115	19.1	27.8	53.1	197	39.1	12.7	48.2	328	77.4	9.8	12.8	640	55.2	13.9	30.9
NCOs	9	—	33.4	66.6	45	28.9	20.0	51.1	32	56.3	21.9	21.8	86	36.0	22.1	41.9
Cavalry																
Ranks	16	12.5	25.0	62.5	185	16.2	9.7	74.1	90	33.3	20.0	46.7	291	21.3	13.9	64.8
NCOs	1	—	100	—	37	18.9	2.7	78.4	4	25.0	50.0	25.0	42	19.0	9.5	71.5
Royal Artillery																
Ranks	15	26.6	33.4	40.0	57	70.2	5.3	24.5	46	84.8	6.5	8.7	118	70.4	9.3	20.3
NCOs	1	—	100	—	6	33.4	16.6	50.0	5	80.0	—	20.0	12	50.0	16.6	33.4
TOTAL*																
Ranks	791	25.9	37.4	36.7	462	34.6	11.8	53.6	638	73.2	9.2	17.6	1891	44.0	21.3	34.7
NCOs	99	25.2	45.5	29.3	99	27.3	14.1	58.6	60	58.3	20.0	21.7	258	33.7	27.5	38.8

*Includes Military Prison at Greenlaw

Source: Enumerators' Workbooks for the Census of Scotland, 1851.

creature of low degree of intellect has much more chance of emerging from in a satisfactory manner than one possessed of an uncommon amount of brains, and, consequently, of sensitiveness.[25]

Table 6–6 A Comparison between Recruitment in Six Rural and Six Urban Districts, 1873–98

Year	Total UK Recruitment	Percentage From 6 Rural Areas	Percentage From 6 Urban Areas
1873	6,160	3.2	13.4
1874	11,052	5.7	17.4
1875	9,414	5.3	17.6
1876	16,878	5.1	16.3
1877	17,380	4.9	11.9
1878	17,181	4.4	13.7
1879	15,915	4.3	13.6
1880	16,727	4.0	15.4
1881	18,227	4.6	18.1
1882	16,464	5.4	19.0
1883	23,096	5.8	20.3
1884	24,561	5.7	20.0
1885	27,681	5.0	20.2
1886	26,155	5.5	19.8
1887	20,472	5.8	20.5
1888	16,620	4.9	18.5
1889	19,195	4.5	21.7
1890	19,920	4.1	24.8
1891	22,791	3.6	24.4
1892	23,954	4.9	18.7
1893	19,133	5.7	15.2
1894	18,041	5.6	15.5
1895	19,905	5.7	17.0
1896	16,619	5.7	14.0
1897	19,099	6.1	16.9
1898	22,359	5.9	17.3

Source: *Annual Reports of the Inspector-General of Recruiting,* P.P.

In 1875 army officers in the House of Commons warned against the reliance on recruits who were '. . .the scum of the cities, sons of infirm parents, brought up in vice and crime, breathing foul air, morally and physically inferior'.[26] Before the Wantage Committee Colonel Upcher, of the Durham Light Infantry, was asked how town recruits compare in physique to farm boys, and observed: 'They are not so good, as a rule. I have seen a good many of the recruits who passed through for the West Riding Regiment and they looked very poor'.[27] Colonel Trotter of the Grenadier Guards remarked, 'I think, speaking generally, the country recruits turn out better than other men.'[28] By the conclusion of the South African War, the value of intelligence and resourcefulness was no longer to be quite so discounted, yet the conviction remained strong that men from rural areas made the best soldiers. What was an apparent contradiction was resolved without difficulty. To the Royal Commission on the war in South Africa Lieutenant-General Sir Archibald Hunter observed:

> . . .you could teach such men as the Imperial Light Horse anything in one teaching, the same as you could any well-educated, intelligent, active young man. But if you get a town-bred population, as most of ours are that enlist now, you have to take them out into the country and show them what is what and try and teach them what is on the other side of a hill. . .Intellect and physique march side by side; the development of the brain and the development of the body generally go together.[29]

Given such feelings, it is not surprising that any decline in the proportion of rural enlistment should be singled out as one of the ills inflicting the recruiting system and should be viewed with alarm.[30] Cardwell's localisation of recruitment aimed to attract more of the agricultural population to the colours,[31] but with a shifting population the army was concentrating its efforts on a depleting resource. Much as it might regret it, the army had eventually to look increasingly to the urban areas to supply the men needed each year. Already in 1865, Colonel H. Graham, the inspecting field officer of an army recruiting district, told the Royal Commission on Recruiting, 'I never see what I used to see, namely the chaw-bacon fellow in a smock frock.'[32] In 1875 the Inspector-General of Recruiting reported that the recruiting districts 'which comprise sections of the country in which the population is chiefly employed in agricultural pursuits have not contributed recruits in numbers equivalent to those raised in the manufacturing and mining districts'.[33] Subsequent reports told the same story,[34] and the Wantage Committee report of 1892 provided further evidence. The Duke of Connaught for instance informed the Committee that '. . .the number of recruits coming in from an agricultural district is very small in proportion to the total number we get; it is only one-sixth or one-eighth'.[35]

Table 6–7 The Birthplaces of Men Serving with the Army Stationed in Scotland on Census Day, 1851 and 1891

Unit	1851 Rural Areas	1851 Towns	1851 Cities	1891 Rural Areas	1891 Towns	1891 Cities
Scots Infantry						
Rank and File	39.7	32.1	28.0	15.8	20.4	63.8
NCOs	35.6	38.9	25.5	26.8	25.5	47.6
English Infantry						
Rank and File	55.2	13.9	30.9	5.6	11.1	83.3
NCOs	36.0	22.1	41.9	27.3	9.1	63.6
Cavalry						
Rank and File	21.3	13.9	64.8	—	—	—
NCOs	19.0	9.5	71.5	—	—	—
Artillery						
Rank and File	70.4	9.3	20.3	13.8	13.8	72.4
NCOs	50.0	16.6	33.4	16.7	50.0	33.3
Total						
Rank and File	44.0	21.3	34.7	15.7	20.1	64.2
NCOs	33.7	27.5	38.8	26.6	25.4	47.9

Source: Enumerators' Workbooks for the Census of Scotland, 1851 and 1891.

Because there are no comprehensive army statistics to illustrate the decline in recruitment from rural areas, the best that can be done is to look at the results achieved by the recruiting districts. Only a few comprised entirely rural or urban areas. In Table 6–6, twelve such districts are randomly selected and the results of recruitment compared over a period of years. Six of them comprise essentially rural areas, the remaining six urban industrial areas. Three of each set are in England, two each in Scotland and one each in Ireland.[36] The first figures were available in 1873. The results are by no means conclusive, but they do show that on the whole the proportion of recruits from the six urban districts to those from the rural areas remained constant after 1873 at three or four to one.

Scottish census returns illustrate more clearly the decrease in recruitment from agricultural areas. Table 6–7 compares the birthplaces of men serving with the army in 1851 and 1891. Cities, towns and villages are defined as above. By this latter date a very substantial decrease in the proportion of soldiers from the country had taken place. Rural enlistment was highest in the Scottish infantry regiments, perhaps because of the influence on the one hand of local attachments, and on the other of restricted employment opportunities. The distribution of the birthplaces of non-commissioned officers conforms very closely with that of the rank and file, although it seems clear that by 1891 more NCOs came from small towns and rural areas. This may be the result of a time-lag since NCOs would normally be older men who enlisted at a time when recruitment from rural areas was heavier.

4. The Occupational Background

The occupation the soldier pursued before enlistment may tell something about his character, his reasons for enlistment, and about the army of which he was a part. Throughout the period it was the unskilled labourers who most frequently enlisted and industrial workers outnumbered farm labourers. The earliest statistics available are the Scottish census returns of 1861. There is information for only a limited number of men stationed in Scotland in that year and no similar data for subsequent years; however it is clear that the majority of soldiers in this category had been unskilled workers before enlistment.[37] The number who declared themselves to have been rural workers before they joined the army is far less than the 44.0 per cent of the army in Scotland in 1851 who apparently came from a rural background, but it is not to be expected that every recruit from a farming area would have worked only as an agricultural labourer. Some may have pursued a different type of rural occupation, or moved to a town or city and worked there before enlisting.

This information may be compared with official statistics showing the previous occupations of men serving in the ranks of the army on 1 January 1860. Industrial workers clearly predominated, while those with any sort of trade or skill made up less than one-third of the rank and file.

Table 6–8 The Occupation before Enlistment of Men Serving with the British Regular Army on 1 January 1860

	Number	Percent
Rural workers	31,802	15.5
Artisans	26,959	13.1
Domestic workers	12,942	6.3
Professional/semi professional	4,922	2.4
Industrial workers	74,305	37.6
Semi-skilled tradesmen	30,894	14.8
Other	20,684	10.1
None	—	—
TOTAL	202,508	100.0

Source: *Report of the Army Medical Department,* P.P., XXIV (c.3233), 1863, p.35.

From other official returns there is no doubt that this pattern continued. In 1864 it was estimated that of the 78,695 rank and file of the home army, 23,174 or fewer than one-third had learned any sort of a trade before enlistment.[38] After 1862 Army Medical Department reports provided annual statistics showing the civilian occupations of all recruits passed for military service. Although farm labourers are not distinguished from urban workers, the figures indicate what class of working men were enlisted and whether there was any discernible change in later years. We have seen that one of the claims of short service and of several of the army reforms introduced after 1870 was that it attracted men of better quality to the ranks.[39] This is not supported by these statistics. Table 6–9 shows that while the proportion of shopmen/clerical and professional occupations enlisted did not positively decline, neither did it increase between 1862 and 1898. Throughout the period the percentage of mechanics (i.e. workmen who at the very least were semi-skilled) fell by 13 per cent. The percentage of ordinary labourers appears to have risen by an equal amount. Artisans, who may be loosely defined as non-industrial craftsmen, and who certainly had a degree of skill and training, remained a fairly constant proportion of recruits.

Table 6–9 The Previous Civilian Occupations of Recruits Approved by the Army Medical Department for Military Service, 1862–98

	Expressed as a Percentage of the Total Accepted for Military Service					
Year	Labourers	Artisans	Mechanics	Shopmen/ Clerks	Professional	Boys
1862	52.8	9.9	22.9	7.5	1.3	5.6
1865	61.0	14.9	15.1	6.3	0.9	1.8
1868	57.2	13.9	18.6	7.1	0.8	2.3
1871	63.9	8.0	18.2	7.7	0.8	1.4
1874	61.9	11.6	17.6	5.8	0.8	2.2
1877	62.0	10.8	17.7	6.9	1.1	1.6
1880	62.5	12.8	16.7	6.7	1.0	2.2
1883	59.6	14.2	16.0	5.3	1.3	3.7
1886	63.6	14.4	12.1	5.8	1.3	2.9
1889	64.2	15.0	11.7	6.2	1.4	3.7
1892	65.9	13.1	11.2	5.3	1.1	3.4
1895	64.4	14.0	10.2	6.2	1.3	3.9
1898	65.7	12.9	9.5	7.0	0.9	3.9

Source: *Annual Reports of the Army Medical Department,* P.P.

Clearly then the call to arms during the second half of the century was answered increasingly by the unskilled working man. At the very end, as Richard Price has recently shown, the patriotic response to the Boer War was largely a middle-class one.[40] The contradiction is more implied than real, however, because the principal motives which encouraged men to choose the army as a career and those which led thousands of others to enlist in time of national emergency were entirely dissimilar. The previous occupations of recruits were those which one would expect given the way in which the army was regarded by British society and the influence of unemployment and other economic pressures on the decisions of many recruits to enlist.

5. Conclusion

Where does the balance lie? Among the army's achievements by the end of the century was the creation of regular reserves of nearly 80,000 men, the number of recruits enlisted yearly was several times greater than in 1856, and the army was able to keep up its share of the labour market. Yet the kernel of failure lies in the fact that throughout the period the army was unable to attract a bigger share of the male population, and that to achieve even the number that it did, physical standards had to be lowered ruthlessly. Even then, with the increased demands of empire and the burden of short service the numbers who could be attracted to the colours were not adequate.

The lowering of minimum physical standards, the introduction of short-service enlistment, and demographic changes in Britain altered traditional patterns of recruitment and had a profound effect on the social composition of the army. In 1856 the army recruit was likely to have come from a small town or farming community, a third or more were Irish, and nearly half had some sort of trade or calling before enlistment. In addition the army contained a high percentage of older soldiers. By 1899, the recruit was likely to be smaller and physically more immature, and to come from an industrial centre of England where his occupation had been that of an unskilled labourer. This was reflected in the ranks of the army which were now younger, contained fewer Irish, and fewer men from either small towns or farming communities.

Notes

1. Since unpublished material relating to the English census cannot be obtained until the documents are one hundred years old, returns for 1881 and 1891 are not available at present.
2. Parnell for instance argued that recruiting sergeants in Ireland appealed to a poor and starving peasantry grasping at a chance of life. Hansard, CCXLIV (17 March 1879), c.1091.
3. Between 1848 and 1855 emigration reached two million, by 1914 an additional three and one-half million had left. During the ten years 1863 to 1873 alone, emigration totalled nearly 800,000, considerably more than that from England during the same period. Joseph Lee, *The*

Modernisation of Irish Society, 1848–1918 (Dublin, 1973), p.6; *Thirty-Third General Report of the Emigration Commissioners,* P.P., XVIII (c.768), 1873, p.1.

4. Mitchell, *Abstract of Statistics,* p.9.
5. *Report of the Inspector-General of Recruiting,* P.P., XX (c.6597), 1892, p.3; *The Times,* 8 March 1890; Anon., 'Desertion and Recruiting', *Colburn's,* I (1874), pp.301–7.
6. *The Times,* 14 Feb. 1859.
7. A Soldier, *The Army, the Horse Guards, and the People* (1860), p.30.
8. Hansard, CLXXIV (15 April 1864), cc.1071–3.
9. Edward Cardwell to Earl Granville, 7 Dec. 1872, Cardwell MSS., PRO.30/48/5/30; Hansard, XVI (18 Aug. 1893), c.517.
10. Adams, *JRUSI,* XVIII (1874), p.57.
11. *Report of the Committee on Recruiting,* WO.33/27, p.240.
12. *Report of the Wantage Committee* (1892), p.286.
13. The War Office argued, and possibly with some justification, that Highlanders were reluctant to enlist for fear that they would be called upon to enforce evictions in the Highlands as in Ireland. Gilbert Beith to A. Cameron Corbett MP, 5 Jan. 1893, Campbell-Bannerman MSS., 41233.
14. 'J.A.', 'Population and Recruiting', *Colburn's,* IX (1894), pp.241–9; Lieutenant-Colonel J.H.E. Austin, 'Recruiting in Scotland', *Journal of the Royal Army Medical Corps,* XXIII (1914), pp.216–18.
15. Hanham, in Foot, ed., *War and Society,* pp.165–6.
16. Tucker, *Journal of British Studies* (1963), p.136.
17. The case of the Cameron Highlanders is an interesting one. In 1892–3 the War Office proposed amalgamating the Cameron Highlanders, then the only single-battalion regiment, with the Scots Guards in order to restore the balance between the units stationed at home and those abroad. In the ensuing controversy, the difficulties the regiment experienced in recruiting only from Scotland were emphasised. W. Fielding, the Inspector-General of Recruiting, argued that until English districts were opened, the Camerons had been unable to recruit up to strength. Lord Sandhurst asserted that only 21 per cent of the men in the regiment came from its own recruiting district and that 60 per cent were 'Whitechapel Highlanders'. Campbell-Bannerman, the Secretary of State, argued that the Camerons poached in the territory of other Highland regiments, all of whom had a difficult time maintaining themselves, and that of the last 936 recruits that had been raised for the regiment, nearly two-thirds had come from England. If such was the case, and yearly army recruiting figures are not detailed enough to substantiate such a claim, the ranks of the regiment itself did not in 1891 at least reflect such a heavy reliance on recruitment from outside Scotland. W. Fielding to Henry Campbell-Bannerman, 27 Dec. 1892; Lord Sandhurst to Henry Campbell-Bannerman, 6 Dec. 1892; Henry Campbell-Bannerman to G.C. Campbell, 23 Jan. 1893, Campbell-Bannerman MSS., 41227, 41233.
18. It was suggested by Lieutenant-Colonel C.G. Mort (The Gordon Highlanders, ret'd), that Scottish regiments deliberately recruited a proportion of English soldiers to provide a cadre of good NCOs, a position for which the average Scottish recruit was unfit. There is no evidence to substantiate this theory, but it may well have been true in some cases.
19. Between 1851 and 1901 the population of England and Wales increased by 81.3 per cent; in the same period that of Greater London on the other hand grew by 145.7 per cent. The conurbations of Greater London, south-east Lancashire, west Midlands, west Yorkshire, Merseyside, and Tyneside constituted 36.8 per cent of England and Wales by population in 1871; by

1901 they together made up 41.1 per cent. Mitchell, *Abstract of Statistics*, pp.9, 19.
20. *Report of the Barrack Accommodation Committee* (1854–5), p.153.
21. Olive Anderson, 'Early Experiences of Manpower Problems in Industrial Society at War: Great Britain, 1854–6', *Political Science Quarterly*, LXXXII (1967), p.541.
22. For the population of towns and cities at this time see *Ordnance Gazetteer of Scotland* (Edinburgh, 1901); *Reports of the Registrar-General of Births, Deaths, and Marriages In Scotland* (Edinburgh, 1851, 1861, 1871, 1881, and 1891).
23. H. Byerley Thomson, *The Military Forces and Institutions of Great Britain and Ireland: Their Constitution, Administration, and Government, Military and Civil* (1855), p.xviii.
24. *Report of the Army Medical Department*, P.P., XXXVI (c.3404), 1864, p.535.
25. Anon., 'Enlisting for the British Army', *Hours At Home*, VII (1868), p.484.
26. Hansard, CCXXII (8 March 1875), c.1463.
27. *Report of the Wantage Committee* (1892), p.151.
28. Ibid., p.365.
29. *Report of the Commission on the War in South Africa* (1904), p.43.
30. See for instance Hansard, CLII (4 March 1859), cc.1331–2; CCXXVII (2 March 1876), c.1275.
31. Edward Cardwell to Queen Victoria, 18 Dec. 1871, Cardwell MSS., PRO.30/48/1/3; *Report of the Army Reorganisation Committee* (1881), p.31.
32. *Report of the Commission on Recruiting* (1867), p.7.
33. *Report of the Inspector-General of Recruiting*, P.P., XV (c.1435), 1876, p.2.
34. *Report of the Inspector-General of Recruiting*, P.P., XIX (c.6275), 1890–1, p.6; XX (c.6597), 1892, p.3.
35. *Report of the Wantage Committee* (1892), p.311.
36. The six essentially rural recruiting areas were: Wiltshire, Cornwall, Brecon, Ayrshire, Orkney and Shetland, and Galway; the six essentially urban ones: Warwickshire, Gloucestershire, Yorkshire, Lanark, Perthshire and Belfast. Urban and rural areas are best defined on the basis of population density.
37. See Appendix VI, Table VIA–3.
38. *Return of the Number of NCOs and Men at Home Who Have Learned Some Trade before Enlistment and Showing Whether They Have Worked at Their Trades since They Entered the Army*, P.P., XXXII (c.13), 1865, pp.6–7.
39. Edward Cardwell to Henry Campbell-Bannerman, 23 Jan. 1875, Campbell-Bannerman MSS., 41212; Hansard, CCXXII (8 March 1875), cc.1429–31; *Memorandum on Recruiting* (1870), p.1; *Report of the Inspector-General of Recruiting*, P.P., XIX (c.1945), 1878, p.1; XV (c.3503), 1883, pp.5, 11.
40. Richard Price, *An Imperial War and the British Working Class* (1972), pp.47–177, passim.

7 CONCLUSION: REFORM AND ITS LIMITATIONS

Early in October 1899 the British army, supremely confident in its own capabilities, embarked upon what was expected to be a brief campaign designed to restore British interests in South Africa, to reassert British supremacy, and to revenge the humiliations of previous defeats. By the time peace was restored however the small campaign had become a major war, and it was the British army that had been taught the lessons. The Boer War pinpointed faults in training and organisation which revealed that the army was unprepared for the type of war it was required to fight. The majority of these faults were only apparent under active service conditions and were not particularly a feature of the home army in peace. Medical services were unprepared for and unable to deal with the large number of casualties from wounds and sickness;[1] transport arrangement was inadequate, as was the supply of ammunition, and the soldier himself was found to be improperly trained for a war requiring a high degree of personal initiative.[2] An overriding problem and one which was within the province of the home army, was of course the manpower shortage. This was a difficulty which, as we have seen, had not been solved between 1856 and 1899, and in this, the first war in which Britain would employ huge numbers of men, it was to show the limitations of the regular army and of its traditional means of recruitment. Between the outbreak of war and the cessation of hostilities, more than 448,000 men were employed in South Africa; 238,000 were regulars and reservists from Britain, and 18,000 were regulars sent from India. The remainder consisted of colonial contingents (30,000), men raised in South Africa itself (52,000) and militia, yeomanry and volunteers, that is Britain's home defence forces (110,000).[3]

In fixing the terms of service for the regular forces and in improving the conditions of service, the army faced a number of problems after 1856 which, if they had been solved, might have led in turn to a solution to the recruiting problem. There were special difficulties associated with the army's image and with the recruiting system, and these were complicated by the necessity of retraining voluntary enlistment while at the same time finding the answer to certain strategic considerations. As if this were not enough, there was the additional caveat of economy, which limited the scope of any possible reform.

This is not to argue by any means that there was no improvement in the conditions of military service between 1856 and 1899. The private soldier at the end of the century was a different man than his predecessor had been forty-five years earlier. He may have enlisted for what amounted to the same reasons, but for the most part his background was different, and he came into the Service with different expectations about what conditions would be like. His life in the army would be a mixture of the old and the new. The tenor of military service was essentially unchanged: discipline was severe and a myriad of minute regulations governed the soldier's everyday conduct. His financial position relative to that of the civilian had not improved, nor had career prospects or the provisions which the army made for the discharged soldier. With the increasing youth of the army after 1870, it is not surprising that the incidence of desertion, insubordination and similar offences remained high. On the other hand, however, there was a number of respects in which changes had transformed the regular army. One of the most obvious was health, an improvement in which had been brought about largely by better barracks, medical facilities, physical training, and to an extent, better food and clothing as well. Provisions for recreation and education proliferated, although technical education was neglected. Military punishments were both less harsh and more realistic, and this was reflected in a significant decrease in the incidence of most crimes.

The period between 1902 and the outbreak of the First World War in 1914 is perhaps best known for the reforms of R.B. Haldane, who was one of the first to foresee Britain's involvement in Continental warfare. When Haldane took office in 1905, reconstruction of the military system along the lines of the Esher Committee Report had already begun,[4] but he was responsible for its implementation, and his term of office saw extensive War Office reorganisation, the creation of a general staff, and official definition of staff responsibilities and procedures as well as the reorganisation of the home field army and the reserve system.

While the inter-war years witnessed considerable organisational reform therefore, this was not altogether the case with the terms and conditions of service of the rank and file. Most of the trends established by 1900 were pursued, and there was a continued improvement in many of the conditions of military service, but this was change on established lines which did not amount to any significant innovation or departure from accepted practice. Barrack renovation and construction continued, khaki service dress was introduced along with a proper working dress for the army, and army meals were improved. The experiences of the South African War also led to increased employment of female nurses in army hospitals.[5] Trends towards more humane punishments and a slight easing of disciplinary restrictions were certainly not reversed; while a scheme for education was embarked upon in 1907, the pay of army privates with two years' service or more was increased to 1s 6d per day clear of regular stoppages in 1904,[6] and modest steps were taken to improve army pensions. Yet where it probably mattered the most, reform was either neglected or largely ineffectual. The increase in pay to 1s 6d per day was not enough to provide a significant new inducement to recruitment, there was no increase in the proportion of men commissioned from the ranks, and throughout the Edwardian period there was only a marginal increase in the opportunities open to ex-soldiers for employment in the civil service.[7] One finds in 1903 senior officers critical of the type of recruit being attracted to the colours and concerned with inadequate numbers just as they had been for years previously.[8] The same type of arguments as to the wisdom of directly increasing pay and other inducements or of altering the terms of service were current, and although Haldane was to increase greatly the army's effectiveness through his reorganisation of the home field army and the reserve, there is no evidence to suggest that recruitment for the regular army was any more satisfactory in (say) 1912 than it had been in 1898, or that efforts to alter the bases of recruitment had been any more successful. In an age of national armies and approaching mass warfare, it was often questioned whether voluntary enlistment would be enough. Events after 1914 were to prove conclusively that it would not.

There is a great deal that is known about the terms and conditions of military service during the period between the Crimean and South Africa Wars, but less that can be said about the character of the man in the ranks. Certain things can be inferred from what is known about the make-up of the army and the backgrounds of recruits. The conditions of life in the regular army add something to the picture since they must have shaped the character of the rank and file. Desertion was high throughout the period, and there were many unable or unwilling to cope with the demands of military service, yet in spite of low wages and other conditions which conspired to turn men away, there was something about a soldier's life, intangible perhaps but real none the less, that affected men deeply. For many of those who came to terms with military life and served the full period of their enlistment, be it seven or twenty-one years, it retained an incredible hold on them, a feeling that perhaps only those who have experienced it themselves can fully appreciate. The regiment to many soldiers was their first and only home, and its honour was to be preserved above all else. Coulson Kernahan, a recruiting officer during the First World War, re-enlisted an ex-soldier in a workhouse, and the man expressed a widely-held feeling. 'My name isn't Wilson, sir,' he confessed 'and I've told you a lie. But this is a workhouse. . .and I remembered the old regiment, and I didn't want them to know me here by the name they knew me there. . . for the old regiment's sake.'[9]

Regardless of the reason for enlistment, the excitement of military service, the comradeship and the discipline all made for something that many could not find the equal of in civilian life, although this was often not apparent until one had actually left the army. 'Such are the attractions of army service, so strong is the hold which the barracks fasten upon the heart of a man', wrote Captain W.E. Cairnes in 1901, 'that the large majority of soldiers have hardly shaken the dust of the parade ground from their feet ere they pine for the sound of the bugles and long to be back once more in the regiment which for twelve years has been their home.'[10] Frank Richards, who took his discharge before the First World War, recalled in his memoirs:

> Every quarter-day, or pension-day as it was called, a number of us reservists and service-pension-wallahs would have a day off from our work to spend it together. . .By stop-tap most of us had said what utter fools we had been to leave the Service, and that if we had our time over again, we would not leave the Army until we were damned well kicked out of it.[11]

There is a number of difficulties in making any sweeping generalisations about the character of the British soldier, and this is a task that historians have usually left to more popular writers. For one thing, a very large number of men passed through the ranks between 1856 and 1899, and it would be difficult if not impossible to generalise more than vaguely on their characteristics. For another, conditions in the army varied greatly from unit to unit as well as from year to year, a fact which army memoirs make very clear. These same memoirs tell a great deal about army life, but as has been said, it is not clear how closely their authors typified the men in the ranks, or to what extent their experiences were exceptional. For the most part the soldier in the later Victorian army was healthy, literate and highly disciplined, although not always well-behaved. More than that it would be difficult to say with any certainty. Nevertheless it is reasonable to admire the soldier for the characteristics which the rank and file as a whole seemed to have possessed in large amounts, although of course these were not characteristics possessed by all. It was not just heroism and bravery that gave the army its reputation, but the stoicism and tenacity of its men, their endurance and adaptability, and above all, their utter dependability.

One cannot come away from any examination of the conditions under which these men served with anything but a deep affection for them.

Notes

1. See *Report of the Royal Commission on the Care and Treatment of the Sick and Wounded During the South African Campaign*, P.P., XXIX (c.453), 1901; *Report of the Royal Commission on the Nature, Pathology, Causation, and Prevention of Dysentery and Its Relationship to Enteric Fever*, P.P., X (c.1498), 1903; Anon., 'The Sick and Wounded in South Africa', *The Edinburgh Review*, CXCII (1900), pp.505–25; Lieutenant-Colonel R.J.S. Simpson, *The Medical History of the War in South Africa*, (1911).
2. *Report of the Commission on the War in South Africa* (1904), pp.43–8, 84–8, 97–9.
3. Ibid., p.35.
4. See *Report of the War Office (Reconstruction)Committee*, P.P. VIII (c.1932), 1904.
5. *Recommendations of the Royal Commission on the Care and Treatment of the Sick and Wounded in South Africa, and the Actions Taken*, P.P., XLVI (c.2440), 1905.
6. *Minutes of Evidence Taken before the Commission on the War in South Africa*, P.P., XLI (c.1791), 1904, p.556.
7. Edward M. Spiers, 'The Reform of the Front-Line Forces of the Regular Army in the United Kingdom, 1895–1914', unpublished Ph.D thesis, University of Edinburgh (1974), p.v–40.
8. *Report of the Commission on the War in South Africa* (1904), pp.41–5, 193–5, 225–8.
9. Coulson Kernahan, *The Experiences of a Recruiting Officer* (1915), p.22; see also Baynes, *Morale*, pp.43,163.
10. Cairnes, *The Army from Within*, p.15.
11. Richards, *Old Soldier Sahib*, p.341.

Appendix I

Table 1A–1 Height and Chest Measurement NCOs and Men, Regular Army, 1866–99

Year	Height: Percent Under 5'7"	Height: Percent Over 5'7"	Chest Measurement: Percent Under 37"	Chest Measurement: Percent Over 37"
1866	49.1	50.9	—	—
1874	39.6	60.4	—	—
1876	40.5	59.5	57.7	42.3
1878	42.9	57.1	58.2	41.8
1880	39.8	60.2	56.2	43.8
1882	40.8	59.2	56.2	43.8
1884	43.7	56.3	59.2	40.8
1886	47.3	52.7	63.8	36.2
1888	48.4	51.6	65.2	34.8
1890	48.5	51.5	65.7	34.3
1892	49.1	50.9	68.0	32.0
1894	48.8	51.2	68.4	31.6
1896	47.2	52.8	67.8	32.2
1898	46.1	53.9	67.7	32.3
1899	47.4	52.6	67.8	32.2

Source: *General Annual Return of the British Army,* P.P., XLIII (c.1323), 1875, pp.53–4; XLIII (c.6196), 1890, pp.78–9; and LIII (c.9426), 1899, pp.88–9.

Table 1A–2 Percentages of Each Year's Recruits Rejected in Medical Examinations, 1860 and 1899

Reason for Failure*	Percentage 1860	Percentage 1899
Syphilis	1.2	0.26
Other Zymotic Diseases	0.09	N/A
Scrofula	1.9	0.9
Phthisis	0.4	
Other Constitutional Diseases	2.6	0.6
Diseases of Brain, Spine, Nerves	0.08	0.1
Diseases of Eyes and Eyelids	4.5	0.2
Diseases of Nose and Mouth	0.2	0.06
Diseases of Ears	0.3	0.2
Deafness	0.2	0.2
Speech Impediment	0.2	0.09
Diseases of Heart	1.8	1.7
Diseases of Arteries	0.07	0.01
Diseases of Veins	4.4	1.15
Diseases of Lungs	0.2	0.08
Small Malformed Chest or Curvature of Spine	3.3	N/A
Loss or Decay of Many Teeth	1.7	2.6
Hernia	1.8	0.8
Laxity of Abdominal Rings	1.3	0.1
Haemorrhoids	0.6	0.1
Diseases of Urinary Organs	0.03	0.06
Varicocele	1.8	1.2
Hydroule	0.4	N/A
Diseases of Genital Organs	0.5	0.2
Muscular Tenuity	3.5	N/A
Debility	0.7	0.6
Defects of Upper Extremities	1.7	0.6
Defects of Lower Extremities	4.2	1.4
Diseases of Joints	0.2	0.2
Other Affectations of Bone and Muscle	0.1	0.2
Ulcers, Wounds, Cicatrices	1.2	0.1
Other Affectations of Cutaneous System	0.9	0.3
Weakness of Intellect	0.3	0.2
Malformation of Ears	0.01	0.007
Malformation of Nose and Mouth	0.1	0.01
Malformation of Chest and Spine	1.1	0.6
Malformation of Urinary and Genital Organs	0.1	0.05
Marks of Punishment	0.7	N/A
Unsound Health, Cupping, Blistering	4.5	N/A
Defective Vision	N/A	4.2
Flat Feet	N/A	1.3
Under Height	N/A	2.0
Under Chest Measurement	N/A	6.6
Under Weight	N/A	3.4
Wrong Age	N/A	0.6
Not Likely to Become Efficient	N/A	0.5
Over Height	N/A	0.08
TOTAL	47.9	33.1

*Where disease is marked not applicable, there was no classification with this heading.

Source: *Report of the Army Medical Department,* P.P., XXXIII (c.3051), 1862, p.36; XXXIX (c.521), 1901, p.39.

Table 1A–3 Estimated Expenditure for Barrack Construction and Repairs in the United Kingdom, 1857–98

Fiscal Year	New Works and Improvements	Ordinary Repairs	Total Expenditure
	£	£	£
1857–8	404,142	75,607	479,749
1858–9	433,617	154,753	588,370
1860–1	456,680	153,626	610,306
1864–5	179,147	133,965	313,112
1868–9	107,208	138,469	245,677
1872–3	124,846	143,463	268,309
1876–7	187,335	173,804	361,139
1880–1	158,210	193,140	351,350
1884–5	132,796	184,948	317,744
1888–9	158,830	188,266	347,096
1892–3	130,730	201,153	331,883
1894–5	111,720	210,281	322,001
1896–7	153,094	216,952	370,046
1898–9	206,527	219,900	426,427

Source: *Army Estimates,* P.P.

Appendix II

Table IIA–1 The Percentage of Literates among Recruits for the Regular Army, 1861–99

Year	Percentage Unable to Read or Write	Percentage Able to Read Only	Percentage Able to Read and Write	Percentage Possessing a Superior Education
1861	20.3	21.2	58.5	—
1864	22.2	11.2	66.6	—
1867	20.6	8.7	70.7	—
1870	18.6	10.5	70.9	—
1874	15.9	12.2	71.9	—
1877	16.3	7.8	75.9	—
1880	13.9	9.5	76.6	—
1883	12.4	7.8	71.9	7.9
1885	9.0	8.6	75.2	7.2
1888	5.9	3.8	80.3	10.0
1891	3.4	2.2	88.5	5.9
1894	2.5	1.4	89.9	6.2
1897	1.7	1.4	92.3	4.6
1899	1.7	1.3	89.9	7.1

Source: *Reports of the Army Medical Department,* P.P.

Table IIA–2 The Percentages of Rank and File in Possession of Army Education Certificates, 1871–96

Year	1st Class	2nd Class	3rd Class	4th Class	None
1871	0.5	3.1	5.4	0.6	90.4
1873	0.6	7.6	10.4	8.4	73.0
1877	0.6	12.1	13.6	22.4	51.3
1880	0.5	14.3	14.3	27.1	43.8
1882	0.5	15.2	15.9	29.9	38.5
1884	0.5	17.1	16.3	33.9	32.2
1886	0.6	17.4	16.7	33.7	31.6
1887	0.6	17.6	17.0	34.4	30.4
1888*	0.7	19.2	18.3	–	61.8
1892	1.4	20.4	15.6	–	62.6
1896	2.1	21.2	14.8	–	61.9

*4th class certificate abolished.

Source: *Reports of the Director-General of Military Education*, P.P.; *Report of the Committee on Army Schools and Schoolmasters*, WO.33/47, p.1179; *Report of the Committee on the Royal Hospitals and the Royal Military Asylum, Chelsea and the Royal Hibernian Military School, Dublin*, P.P., XV (c.3679), 1883, p.363.

Table IIA–3 Recruits Joining the Army from RMA and RHMS, 1856–95

	RMA Recruits Joined Yearly			RHMS Recruits Joined Yearly			Total No. from Both Institutions
Year(s)	No.	%	Avg. No.	No.	%	Avg. No.	
1856	30	69.7	30	27	36	27	57
1858	42	75	42	43	59.7	43	85
1860	77	67	77	159	71	159	236
1862–3	151	73.3	76	199	88.5	100	350
1864	55	66.2	55	58	77	58	113
1865	46	73	46	48	75	48	94
1866–7	180	63	90	148	82	74	328
1868–9	120	81.2	61	121	80.7	61	242
1870–1	140	82.8	70	128	75.7	64	268
1872–3	116	84.1	58	128	78.5	64	244
1874–6	245	84.8	82	189	69.7	63	434
1884–8	374	Not Known	75	372	Not Known	74	746
1889–92	430	70.7	108	273	67.4	101	703
1893–5	296	70.3	99	117	47.8	39	413

Source: Lefroy, *Report on Army Schools,* pp.73, 79; *Reports of the Council of Military Education,* P.P.; *Reports of the Director-General of Military Education,* P.P.

Appendix III

Table IIIA–1 Numbers of Courts-Martial for Specific Offences, Proportions Relative to the Strength of the Whole Army, 1865–98

Offence	Year									
	1865	1869	1872	1876	1880	1884	1888	1892	1896	1898
Mutiny	— —	2 (0.0)	5 (0.0)	— —	1 (0.0)	— —	— —	5 (0.0)	5 (0.0)	— —
Desertion	1914 (0.97)	1855 (1.05)	2365 (1.29)	2776 (1.57)	1740 (0.96)	1540 (0.88)	1821 (0.90)	2071 (1.01)	1611 (0.76)	1819 (0.84)
AWOL	3779 (1.91)	3273 (1.85)	2909 (1.59)	2730 (1.54)	2948 (1.62)	2261 (1.29)	2062 (1.02)	1552 (0.76)	722 (0.34)	890 (0.41)
Fraudulent Enlistment	N/A	N/A	N/A	N/A	1243 (0.67)	786 (0.45)	725 (0.36)	1145 (0.56)	1229 (0.58)	1296 (0.60)
Disobedience, Insubordination, etc.	1726 (0.87)	2106 (1.19)	1687 (0.92)	1630 (0.92)	2824 (1.56)	3172 (1.81)	4304 (2.12)	4213 (2.05)	4189 (1.98)	4005 (1.85)
Quitting or Sleeping on Post	475 (0.24)	552 (0.23)	420 (0.23)	466 (0.26)	600 (0.33)	574 (0.33)	407 (2.0)	280 (0.14)	160 (0.06)	197 (0.09)
Drunkenness (all kinds)	8656 (4.37)	5675 (3.22)	3289 (1.79)	3873 (2.20)	4148 (2.29)	3102 (1.77)	2581 (1.27)	1764 (0.86)	1639 (0.77)	1784 (0.83)
Disgraceful Conduct	728 (0.37)	761 (0.43)	728 (0.40)	861 (0.49)	773 (0.43)	625 (0.36)	944 (0.46)	882 (0.43)	791 (0.37)	773 (0.36)
Making Away With Equpt.	2685 (1.36)	2695 (1.53)	2662 (1.45)	4424 (2.50)	3451 (1.90)	2913 (1.66)	3493 (1.72)	3432 (1.67)	2224 (1.05)	2239 (1.04)
Other	5122 (2.57)	5226 (2.96)	2623 (1.43)	3802 (2.16)	4065 (2.24)	2762 (1.56)	2291 (1.13)	2018 (0.98)	1093 (0.52)	1036 (0.48)

Note: Figures in parentheses indicate the proportion of the regular forces tried for each offence. No category for the offence of fraudulent enlistment existed before 1880.

Source: *General Annual Return of the British Army*, P.P., XLIII (c.1323), 1875, pp.38–9; XLIII (c.6196), 1890, p.54; LIII (c.9426), 1899, p.56.

Table IIIA–2 Desertion from the Regular Army, 1868–98

Year	Number of Recruits Annually	Total Number Deserted before Joining Regiment	As Percent of Total Regiment	Percentage Under 3 Mo.	Percentage 3–6 Mo.	Percentage 6–12 Mo.	Percentage Under 1 Yr	Percentage 1–2 Yrs	Percentage Over 2 Yrs	Percentage Not Known	Total Number Deserted	As Percent of Regular Army
1861	19,747	1,005	5.1	· · not reported · ·			· · · · · · · · · not reported · · · · ·				· · · not reported · · ·	
1865	25,495	1,166	4.6	· · not reported · ·			· · · · · · · · · not reported · · · · ·				· · · not reported · · ·	
1868	25,376	577	2.3	11.5	12.3	13.4	37.2	15.6	46.5	0.7	3011	1.6
1872	35,185	941	2.7	10.7	9.6	15.5	35.8	25.6	38.2	0.4	5861	3.2
1876	44,713	1,626	3.6	27.1	14.0	14.9	56.0	14.8	29.2	–	4835	2.7
1880	44,298	1,963*	4.4*	23.7	11.6	17.6	52.9	14.6	28.7	3.8	4833	2.6
1884	65,300	2,648*	4.1*	30.6	16.6	20.9	68.1	12.5	19.0	0.4	4478	2.5
1888	47,503	1,684*	3.5*	17.8	12.2	19.2	49.2	24.1	26.7	–	4430	2.1
1892	77,874	2,555*	3.3*	30.9	15.3	21.7	67.9	19.0	13.0	0.1	4962	2.4
1896	66,237	2,198*	3.3*	22.9	14.4	21.4	58.7	20.5	20.8	–	3367	1.6
1898	84,626	3,693*	4.4*	32.0	17.5	21.4	70.9	15.4	12.6	1.1	4074	1.9

*Estimated

Source: *General Annual Return of the British Army,* P.P., XLIII (c.1323), 1875, p.26; XLIII (c.6196), 1890, p.33; LIII (c.9426), 1899, p.35.

Table IIIA–3 Comparisons between Military Prisoners and the Regular Army in Terms of Nationality, Religion, Age, and Length of Service, 1856–98

Year	Nationalities of Military Prisioners (Percent)				National Make-Up of Regular Army (Percent)				Religion of Prisoners (Percent)			Religion of Regular Army (Percent)		
	Eng.	Scots.	Irish	Other	Eng.	Scots.	Irish	Other	Protestant (Anglican)	Presbyt. & Other Prot.	Roman Catholic	Protestant (Anglican)	Presbyt. & Other Prot.	Roman Catholic
1856	57.9	10.2	31.9	—	not reported				62.7	6.5	30.8	not reported		
1859	60.0	8.1	31.9	—	not reported				59.7	6.1	34.2	not reported		
1862	61.0	6.8	32.2	—	not reported				59.1	6.8	34.1	57.7	13.2	29.1
1865	56.8	10.8	32.4	—	not reported				54.9	10.4	34.7	not reported		
1868	59.9	7.3	32.8	—	59.3	9.4	30.8	0.5	62.2	1.5	36.3	58.6	12.7	28.7
1872	70.7	7.7	21.4	0.2	66.3	8.9	24.8	—	62.3	8.7	29.0	64.8	12.2	23.0
1876	63.1	10.3	25.7	0.9	69.3	8.0	22.4	0.3	55.2	10.4	34.4	65.4	11.8	22.8
1880	62.0	10.9	26.2	0.9	69.7	8.1	20.9	1.3	50.4	12.5	37.1	64.6	12.0	23.4
1884	66.2	10.9	21.4	1.5	73.0	7.8	17.8	1.4	53.3	11.8	34.9	66.2	12.1	21.7
1888	69.2	8.3	20.2	2.3	75.1	8.4	15.2	1.3	54.0	11.2	34.8	67.2	13.4	19.4
1892	76.3	7.8	14.3	1.6	77.2	7.8	13.4	1.6	58.5	9.8	31.8	68.7	13.3	18.0
1896	67.4	8.6	22.9	1.1	78.0	7.9	12.6	1.5	51.4	11.1	37.5	68.9	13.7	17.4
1898	75.5	7.5	16.6	0.4	77.2	8.1	13.2	1.5	56.8	10.6	32.6	68.3	13.4	18.3

Note: Figures for the whole army were quoted as of 1 January in the original reports and in this table have been entered as the previous year's figures.

Source: *Reports on the Discipline and Management of Military Prisons; General Annual Returns of the British Army*, P.P.

Table IIIA–3 Continued

Year	Total Men in Prison	Percentage of Reg. Army	Ages of Prisoners (Percent)				Ages NCOs and Men as Percent Reg. Army				Length of Service of Prisoners (Percent)					Length of Service Regular Army (Percent)				
			Under 20	20–30	30–40	40+	Under 20	20–30	30–40	40+	2 yrs & less	6 yrs & less	7–14	14–21	21+	2 yrs & less	6 yrs & less	7–14	14–21	21+
1856	6,376	2.6	22.5	67.4	9.8	0.5	not reported				64.9	19.7	11.4	3.7	0.3	not reported				
1859	6,348		21.9	70.4	7.2	0.5	not reported				65.3	26.8	5.6	2.2	0.1	not reported				
1862	5,341	2.5	9.6	77.9	12.2	0.3	not reported				23.6	54.7	17.5	3.9	0.3	not reported				
1865	6,390	3.2	12.5	69.0	18.1	0.4	13.3	63.1	22.5	1.1	25.3	36.4	33.9	4.0	0.4	12.4	43.4	33.0	9.0	2.2
1868	7,553	4.0	11.1	63.9	24.3	0.7	not reported				27.4	24.8	42.9	4.3	0.6	not reported				
1872	4,723	2.6	19.8	66.2	13.3	0.7	15.5	52.5	29.8	2.2	51.0	27.9	14.7	6.3	0.1	20.3	31.8	26.9	19.5	1.5
1876	4,703	2.7	12.6	77.0	9.5	0.9	9.7	57.4	28.7	4.2	39.0	42.5	12.3	6.0	0.2	22.5	34.9	21.2	19.5	1.9
1880	3,447	1.9	11.0	79.9	8.6	0.5	10.0	66.4	20.7	2.9	40.7	42.6	13.3	3.2	0.2	23.3	41.6	22.0	10.7	2.4
1884	5,804	3.3	18.6	75.7	5.5	0.2	11.9	69.9	16.8	1.4	56.9	34.7	6.4	2.0	0.0	32.0	42.0	14.4	8.9	2.7
1888	6,772	3.3	13.9	82.4	3.6	0.1	15.6	72.0	11.1	1.3	38.1	54.3	6.5	1.1	0.0	24.1	56.5	13.4	4.9	1.0
1892	7,393	3.6	26.4	71.5	2.1	—	17.8	73.3	8.1	0.8	53.0	40.4	6.4	0.2	0.0	30.0	50.8	14.6	3.2	1.4
1896	6,665	3.1	17.3	80.8	1.8	0.1	14.5	76.4	8.4	0.7	37.0	57.7	5.0	0.3	0.0	23.4	56.0	15.7	3.5	1.4
1898	8,672	4.0	28.3	69.0	2.6	0.1	15.3	75.3	8.7	0.7	55.0	39.1	5.6	0.3	0.0	28.3	49.5	17.3	3.8	1.1

Source: *Reports on the Discipline and Management of Military Prisons; General Annual Returns of the British Army*, P.P.

Table IIIA–4 The Level of Education of Those Confined in Military Prisons, 1856–98

A. Of Those Who Had Been Sent to Military Prisons Previously, 1856–66

Year	Percentage Unable to Read and Write	Percentage Unable to Write	Percentage Literate
1856	21.2	34.7	44.1
1858	30.6	23.6	45.8
1860	30.6	36.9	32.5
1862	22.9	27.4	49.7
1864	23.0	26.7	50.3
1866	17.6	20.4	62.0

B. Of All Those Sent to Military Prisons, 1870–98

Year	Percentage Unable to Read	Percentage Unable To Write	Percentage Able to Read	Percentage Able to Write
1870	14.9	17.8	85.1	82.2
1874	15.6	17.6	84.4	82.4
1878	8.9	10.3	91.1	89.7
1882	10.0	11.4	90.0	88.6
1886	7.7	8.2	92.3	91.8
1890	5.5	6.0	94.5	94.0
1894	3.7	3.8	96.3	96.2
1898	2.7	2.7	97.3	97.3

Source: *Report on the Discipline and Management of Military Prisons,* P.P.

Table IIIA–5 Punishments Inflicted in the Regular Army, 1868–98

Year	Total Punishments Summary and Courts-Martial	Percentage Which Were Summary Punishments	Courts-Martial
1870	238,732	94.7	5.3
1875	265,088	95.1	4.9
1880	230,598	93.7	6.3
1885	297,819	95.3	4.7
1890	221,816	93.8	6.2
1895	217,059	95.9	4.1
1898	226,459	95.9	4.1

Source: *General Annual Return of the British Army,* P.P., XLIII (c.1323), 1875, pp.40, 43; XLIII (c.6196), 1890, pp.56–7; LIII (c.9426), 1899, pp.58–9.

Table IIIA–6 Number and Percentage of Offenders Previously Convicted for Each Crime Committed to Prison, 1856–97

Year	Desertion	AWOL	Drunkenness	Disgraceful Conduct	Insubordination	Other	Percentage Men Who Had Been Court-Martialled More Than Once
1856	580 (9.1%)	1,106 (17.3%)	1,035 (16.2%)	111 (1.7%)	—	619 (9.7%)	23.4
1860	1,162 (17.3%)	1,836 (27.3%)	1,108 (16.3%)	143 (2.1%)	—	1,187 (17.9%)	35.4
1865	1,112 (17.4%)	2,273 (35.5%)	2,878 (45.0%)	201 (3.1%)	—	1,869 (29.2%)	16.3
1873	267 (11.3%)	157 (5.4%)	166 (5.0%)	11 (1.5%)	126 (7.5%)	89 (1.6%)	11.9
1878	239 (7.3%)	116 (3.1%)	298 (7.3%)	11 (1.1%)	70 (3.0%)	100 (.9%)	13.1
1881	204 (7.3%)	129 (3.9%)	220 (4.6%)	30 (4.5%)	135 (4.3%)	210 (2.4%)	12.1
1885	125 (3.9%)	133 (5.7%)	167 (5.1%)	6 (0.6%)	95 (2.5%)	193 (2.8%)	12.0
1897	175 (7.1%)	83 (7.9%)	69 (4.6%)	1 (0.1%)	146 (3.9%)	73 (2.1%)	11.2

Source: *Annual Reports of the Discipline and Management of Military Prisons,* P.P.

Appendix IV

Table IVA–1 Number and Proportion of Privates in Possession of Good Conduct Badges, 1870–99

On 1 January	One	Two	Three	Four	Five	Six	Total One or More
*1870 No.	34,801	29,607	10,822	3,154	712	165	79,261
%	(22.2)	(18.9)	(6.9)	(2.0)	(0.5)	(0.1)	(50.5)
1874 No.	41,584	22,736	17,187	6,485	215	8	88,215
%	(25.7)	(14.0)	(10.6)	(4.0)	(0.1)	(0.004)	(54.4)
**1878 No.	34,697	25,707	9,849	9,738	308	11	80,310
%	(20.9)	(15.5)	(5.7)	(5.9)	(0.2)	(0.007)	(48.3)
1882 No.	45,722	18,959	8,177	3,582	583	41	77,064
%	(27.6)	(11.4)	(4.9)	(2.2)	(0.4)	(0.02)	(46.5)
1886 No.	47,465	15,764	5,271	3,405	345	95	72,345
%	(26.8)	(8.9)	(3.0)	(1.9)	(0.2)	(0.05)	(40.9)
1890 No.	67,539	19,112	2,240	1,950	405	117	91,363
%	(36.4)	(10.3)	(1.2)	(1.1)	(0.2)	(0.06)	(49.3)
1894 No.	64,826	24,610	2,686	971	289	117	93,499
%	(33.4)	(12.7)	(1.4)	(0.5)	(0.1)	(0.06)	(48.2)
1898 No.	74,215	24,480	2,951	1,264	158	125	103,193
%	(38.1)	(12.6)	(1.5)	(0.6)	(0.8)	(0.06)	(53.0)
1899 No.	70,071	29,335	3,279	1,363	140	121	104,309
%	(34.3)	(14.4)	(1.6)	(0.7)	(0.07)	(0.06)	(51.7)

*After 1870 badges in 2, 6, 12, 18, 23 and 28 years.

**After 1876 badges in 2, 5, 12, 16, 18, 21 and 26 years.

Source: *General Annual Return of the British Army,* P.P., XLIII (c.1323), 1875, p.49; XLIII (c.6196), 1890, p.67; LIII (c.9426), 1899, p.69.

Appendix V

Table VA–1 Establishments, Increase and Decrease in Forces, 1859–98

Year	Establishment as of 1 January	Effectives on 1 January	Number Wanting to Complete	Number Supernumary	Number Recruits Joined During Each Year	Exceptional Increases from Other Sources	Deaths	Discharges Including Reserves	Desertion and Other	Total Decrease
1859	217,726	204,079	13,647	–	28,137	–	not reported			
1861	202,040	201,015	1,025	–	10,918	–	4,290	14,875	5,021	24,186
1862	194,271	189,968	4,303	–	8,814	14,211[1]	3,450	12,231	2,895	18,576
1864	192,153	188,025	4,128	–	16,323	–	3,373	13,118	3,622	20,113
1866	182,468	176,731	5,737	–	15,277	–	2,730	14,323	4,144	21,197
1868	172,633	172,014	619	–	17,060	–	2,685	16,419	3,431	22,535
1870	161,150	157,017	4,133	–	24,594	–	2,508	15,720	3,332	21,560
1872	171,029	166,985	3,044	–	17,791	–	2,546	11,570	6,602	20,718
1874	161,031	162,079	–	1,048	20,640	–	2,011	13,999	6,770	22,780
1876	160,537	159,640	897	–	29,370	–	1,998	16,921	6,516	25,435
1878	164,877	166,366	–	1,489	28,325	34,853[2]	2,171	54,532*	7,493	64,196
1880	164,115	167,909	–	3,794	25,622	–	3,186	20,802	5,903	29,891
1882	163,401	165,655	–	2,254	23,802	10,840[3]	2,140	24,591	5,351	32,163
1884	165,386	158,029	7,357	–	35,653	1,415[3]	1,521	24,874	4,762	31,157
1886	180,130	176,865	3,265	–	39,409	–	2,721	25,108	5,897	33,726
1888	186,180	186,839	–	659	25,153	–	1,852	20,822	4,484	27,218
1890	189,426	185,432	3,994	–	31,407	–	1,738	26,579	4,411	32,728
1892	191,348	186,447	4,901	–	41,659	–	1,859	30,261	5,424	37,544
1894	190,690	193,896	–	3,206	33,698	–	1,792	27,353	4,034	33,179
1896	192,054	195,980	–	3,926	28,532	–	1,769	26,021	3,637	31.427
1898	195,304	194,705	599	–	40,729	4,578[3]	2,578	29,892	4,646	37,116

1. East India Company troops transferred to regular army.
2. Transferred from Army and Militia Reserve
3. From Army Reserve.

*Includes 21,637 returned to militia reserve.

Source: *General Annual Return of the British Army,* P.P., XLIII (c.1323), 1875, p.20; XLIII (c.6196), 1890 pp.24–5; LIII (c.9426), 1890, pp.26–7.

Table VA–2 Proportion of Men Enlisting for Long or Short Service, 1870–98

Year	Long Service (12 Years)	Short Service
1870*	90.2	9.8
1872	42.3	57.7
1874	37.7	62.3
1876	18.7	81.3
1878	9.1	90.9
1880	7.3	92.7
1882	5.3	94.7
1884	5.1	94.9
1886	4.3	95.7
1888	5.9	94.1
1890	4.8	95.2
1892	5.9	94.9
1894	5.1	95.3
1896	5.7	95.3
1898	6.1	93.9

*Short Service not introduced until later in the year.

Source: *General Annual Return of the British Army,* P.P., XLIII (c.1323), 1875, p.21; XLIII (c.6196), 1890, p.26; LIII (c.9426), 1899, pp.28–9.

Table VA–3 The Number of Men Re-Engaging for a Second Period of Colour Service, 1857–98

Year	After 6 Years' Service	After 7–10 Years' Service	After 11 Years' Service	On Completing First Term of Service	After Discharge	Total	Percentage of Re-engagements to Number of Men Serving
1857–60	–	–	–	3,845	650	4,495	–
1861	–	–	–	2,093	192	2,285	1.1
1864	–	–	–	3,742	228	3,970	1.9
1867*	1,346	18,416	1,056	10,026	632	31,476	16.6
1870+	1,405	2,762	150	1,836	136	6,289	3.7
1873	1,270	1,839	182	–	6	3,297	1.8
1876	55	4,817	265	–	111	4,618	2.6
1879**	14	1,065	792	–	8	1,879	1.0
1882	–	212	1,720	–	–	1,932	1.1
1885	–	207	1,357	–	–	1,564	0.8
1888	–	664	1,802	–	–	2,466	1.2
1891	–	498	1,347	–	–	1,845	0.9
1894	–	858	1,684	–	–	2,542	1.2
1897	–	800	1,945	–	–	2,745	1.3
1898	–	931	2,050	–	–	2,981	1.4

* Men permitted to re-engage after two-thirds of their first term of service.
\+ Re-engagements restricted to men in the last year of their first term of service.
** Re-engagements after discharge discontinued.

Source: *General Annual Return of the British Army,* P.P., XLIII (c.1323), 1875, p.24; XLIII (c.6196), 1890, p.31; LIII (c.9426), 1899, p.33.

Appendix VI

Table VIA–1 Ages of Soldiers Stationed with the Army in Scotland, 1851–91

1. 1851

Unit	Number	Percentage						
		Under 17	17–19	20–25	26–30	31–35	36–40	40+
Scottish Infantry								
Rank and File	904	0.9	17.8	47.3	16.4	9.5	5.8	2.3
NCOs	129	–	1.6	20.2	24.8	15.5	24.8	13.1
English Infantry								
Rank and File	696	0.9	10.5	45.4	24.9	12.8	4.5	1.0
NCOs	89	–	–	15.8	44.9	20.2	13.5	5.6
Cavalry								
Rank and File	304	1.6	7.2	42.4	23.0	12.2	7.2	6.4
NCOs	44	–	–	6.8	27.3	18.2	15.9	31.8
Artillery								
Rank and File	119	–	5.0	58.0	12.6	13.4	7.6	3.4
NCOs	12	–	–	25.0	8.4	33.2	25.0	8.4
Subtotal* English Infantry Cavalry Artillery								
Rank and File	1,136	0.9	9.1	46.2	22.9	12.8	5.5	2.6
NCOs	145	–	–	13.8	36.6	20.7	15.2	13.7
Total*								
Rank and File	2,040	0.9	12.9	46.7	20.0	11.3	5.7	2.5
NCOs	274	–	0.7	16.8	31.0	18.2	19.7	13.6

* Includes Military Prison at Greenlaw.

Table VIA–1 Continued

2. 1861

Unit	Number	Percentage Under 17	17–19	20–25	26–30	31–35	36–40	40+
Scottish Infantry								
Rank and File	1,979	2.6	38.3	32.8	10.6	9.0	5.0	1.7
NCOs	165	–	6.1	21.8	16.4	29.0	21.2	5.5
English Infantry								
Rank and File	751	–	9.2	52.6	14.2	16.8	5.6	1.6
NCOs	80	–	1.2	26.3	21.2	31.3	12.5	7.5
Cavalry								
Rank and File	431	1.9	12.3	65.4	12.5	4.4	2.1	1.4
NCOs	68	–	–	33.8	29.4	22.1	10.3	4.4
Royal Artillery								
Rank and File	185	1.1	2.2	65.9	22.7	4.9	1.6	1.6
NCOs	30	–	–	40.0	23.3	23.3	6.7	6.7
Subtotal* English Infantry Cavalry Royal Artillery								
Rank and File	1,441	0.7	9.4	57.8	14.8	11.4	4.4	1.5
NCOs	196	–	0.5	28.6	24.5	26.0	11.2	9.2
Total*								
Rank and File	3,420	1.8	26.1	43.4	12.4	10.0	4.7	1.6
NCOs	361	–	3.0	25.5	20.8	27.4	15.8	7.5

* Includes Greenlaw Military Prison and Glasgow Recruit Barracks.

Table VIA–1 Continued

3. 1871

Unit	Number	Percentage						
		Under 17	17–19	20–25	26–30	31–35	36–40	40+
Scottish Infantry								
Rank and File	630	2.5	17.1	30.0	17.4	21.4	8.9	2.7
NCOs	62	–	1.6	17.7	37.1	22.6	19.4	1.6
English Infantry								
Rank and File	1,305	1.9	24.7	34.9	13.8	19.9	4.0	0.8
NCOs	195	–	1.0	20.5	29.8	34.4	9.7	4.6
Cavalry								
Rank and File	479	1.3	13.9	49.2	18.6	13.2	2.5	1.3
NCOs	86	–	1.2	8.1	29.1	36.1	17.4	8.1
Royal Artillery								
Rank and File	130	0.7	17.7	13.1	6.9	26.2	30.0	5.4
NCOs	30	–	–	10.0	3.3	53.3	26.7	6.7
Subtotal*								
English Infantry								
Cavalry								
Royal Artillery								
Rank and File	1,951	1.6	21.7	37.2	14.5	18.4	5.4	1.2
NCOs	311	–	0.9	16.1	27.0	36.7	13.5	5.8
Total*								
Rank and File	2,581	1.9	20.6	35.4	15.2	19.1	6.3	1.5
NCOs	373	–	1.0	16.4	28.7	34.3	14.5	5.1

* Includes Greenlaw Military Prison and Glasgow Recruit Barracks.

Table VIA–1 Continued

4. 1881

Unit	Number	Percentage						
		Under 17	17–19	20–25	26–30	31–35	36–40	40+
Scottish Infantry								
Rank and File	1,719	1.9	19.2	35.7	15.7	13.2	11.5	2.8
NCOs	253	0.3	2.4	16.6	17.4	24.1	26.1	13.1
English Infantry								
Rank and File	211	2.8	25.1	34.1	19.4	10.0	5.7	2.9
NCOs	31	–	9.7	58.1	16.0	–	9.7	6.5
Cavalry								
Rank and File	372	0.8	15.3	60.8	16.9	2.2	1.1	2.9
NCOs	68	–	–	35.3	26.5	17.6	5.9	14.7
Royal Artillery								
Rank and File	88	6.8	17.1	47.7	6.8	8.0	5.7	7.9
NCOs	22	–	4.5	18.2	18.2	9.1	27.3	22.7
Subtotal* English Infantry Cavalry Royal Artillery								
Rank and File	715	2.1	18.3	51.0	16.5	5.6	3.3	3.2
NCOs	129	–	3.1	35.7	21.7	10.9	12.4	16.2
Total*								
Rank and File	2,434	1.9	18.9	40.2	15.9	11.0	9.2	2.9
NCOs	382	0.3	2.6	23.0	18.8	19.6	21.5	14.2

* Includes Greenlaw Military Prison and Glasgow Recruit Barracks.

Table VIA–1 Continued

5. 1891

Unit	Number	Percentage Under 17	17–19	20–25	26–30	31–35	36–40	40+
Scottish Infantry								
Rank and File	2,065	1.2	44.9	40.4	7.8	2.5	1.8	1.4
NCOs	424	–	1.7	36.3	21.0	20.8	11.1	9.1
English Infantry								
Rank and File	690	3.2	40.1	47.8	5.4	1.2	1.7	0.6
NCOs	160	–	3.8	51.9	19.4	10.6	11.9	2.4
Cavalry								
Rank and File	210	0.9	22.9	52.4	18.1	1.9	3.3	0.5
NCOs	60	–	–	35.0	26.7	13.3	16.7	8.3
Royal Artillery								
Rank and File	79	13.9	22.8	32.9	10.1	6.3	11.5	2.5
NCOs	26	–	3.8	26.9	23.1	23.2	11.5	11.5
Subtotal English Infantry Cavalry Royal Artillery								
Rank and File	979	3.6	35.0	47.6	8.5	1.7	2.9	0.7
NCOs	246	–	2.8	45.2	21.5	12.6	13.0	4.9
Total								
Rank and File	3,044	1.9	41.8	42.6	8.0	2.3	2.2	1.2
NCOs	670	–	2.1	39.6	21.2	17.7	11.8	7.6

Source: Enumerators' Workbooks for the Census of Scotland, 1851, 1861, 1871, 1881 and 1891.

Table VIA–2 Nationalities of the NCOs and Men of the Army Stationed in Scotland on Census Day, 1851–91

1. 1851

Unit	Total Number Men	Total Scots (%)	Total English (%)	Total Irish (%)	Born Milit. Stns. Overseas (%)
Scottish Infantry					
1st Royal Scots 93 Sutherlands					
Rank and File	904	640 (70.8)	36 (4.0)	221 (24.4)	7 (0.8)
NCOs	129	88 (68.2)	16 (12.4)	24 (18.6)	1 (0.8)
English Infantry					
21st Fusiliers					
Rank and File	696	124 (17.8)	211 (30.3)	358 (51.4)	3 (0.5)
NCOs	89	9 (10.1)	45 (50.6)	34 (38.2)	1 (1.1)
Cavalry					
13th Dragoons					
Rank and File	304	16 (5.2)	185 (60.9)	90 (29.6)	13 (4.3)
NCOs	44	1 (2.3)	37 (84.1)	4 (9.1)	2 (4.5)
Royal Artillery					
Rank and File	119	15 (12.0)	57 (47.9)	46 (38.7)	1 (1.4)
NCOs	12	1 (8.3)	6 (50.0)	5 (41.7)	— —
Subtotal* English Infantry Cavalry Royal Artillery					
Rank and File	1,136	161 (14.2)	457 (40.2)	500 (44.0)	18 (1.6)
NCOs	145	11 (7.6)	88 (60.7)	43 (29.7)	3 (2.0)
Total The Army in Scotland, 1851*					
Rank and File	2,040	801 (39.3)	493 (24.1)	721 (35.3)	25 (1.3)
NCOs	274	99 (36.1)	104 (37.9)	67 (24.5)	4 (1.5)

* Includes also prisoners at Greenlaw Military Prison.

Table VIA–2 Continued

2. 1861

Unit	Total Number Men	Total Scots (%)	Total English (%)	Total Irish (%)	Born Milit. Stns. Overseas (%)
Scottish Infantry					
42nd, 74th, 72nd, 78th, 93rd					
Rank and File	1,970	1,459 (75.9)	264 (13.8)	176 (9.2)	21 (1.1)
NCOs	162	117 (72.2)	32 (19.8)	10 (6.2)	3 (1.8)
English Infantry					
76th					
Rank and File	751	10 (1.3)	428 (56.9)	309 (41.3)	4 (0.5)
NCOs	80	3 (3.8)	43 (53.8)	32 (40.0)	2 (2.4)
Cavalry					
13th Dragoons					
Rank and File	473	56 (11.8)	294 (62.2)	119 (25.2)	4 (0.8)
NCOs	68	2 (2.9)	54 (79.4)	9 (13.2)	3 (4.5)
Royal Artillery					
Rank and File	201	21 (10.4)	124 (61.7)	56 (27.9)	– –
NCOs	32	3 (9.4)	19 (59.4)	10 (31.2)	– –
Subtotal*					
English Infantry					
Cavalry					
Royal Artillery					
Rank and File	1,439	134 (8.9)	857 (57.2)	499 (33.3)	9 (0.6)
NCOs	198	12 (6.0)	110 (55.6)	71 (35.9)	5 (2.5)
Total					
The Army in Scotland, 1861*					
Rank and File	3,419	1,593 (46.6)	1,121 (32.8)	675 (19.7)	30 (0.9)
NCOs	360	129 (35.8)	142 (39.5)	81 (22.5)	8 (2.2)

* Includes Military Prison at Greenlaw, Glasgow Recruit Barracks.

Table VIA–2 Continued

3. 1871

Units	Total Number Men	Total Scots (%)	Total English (%)	Total Irish (%)	Born Milit. Stns. Overseas (%)
Scottish Infantry					
93rd					
Rank and File	576	498 (86.5)	45 (7.8)	21 (3.6)	12 (2.1)
NCOs	51	51 (82.3)	8 (12.9)	2 (3.2)	1 (1.6)
English Infantry					
5th, 32nd, 90th					
Rank and File	1,305	270 (20.7)	807 (61.8)	224 (17.2)	4 (0.3)
NCOs	195	14 (7.2)	138 (70.8)	41 (21.0)	2 (1.0)
Cavalry					
13th, 15th					
Rank and File	535	98 (18.3)	328 (61.3)	108 (20.1)	2 (0.3)
NCOs	86	9 (9.3)	65 (75.6)	12 (13.9)	1 (1.2)
Royal Artillery					
Rank and File	130	17 (13.1)	83 (63.8)	30 (23.1)	– –
NCOs	30	3 (10.0)	17 (56.7)	19 (30.0)	1 (3.3)
Subtotal*					
English Infantry					
Cavalry					
Royal Artillery					
Rank and File	2,008	401 (19.9)	1,235 (61.6)	366 (18.2)	6 (0.3)
NCOs	311	25 (8.0)	220 (70.8)	62 (19.9)	4 (1.3)
Total					
The Army in Scotland, 1871*					
Rank and File	2,584	899 (34.8)	1,280 (49.6)	387 (14.9)	18 (0.7)
NCOs	373	76 (20.4)	228 (61.1)	64 (17.2)	5 (1.3)

* Includes Military Prison at Greenlaw.

Table VIA–2 Continued

4. 1881

Unit	Total Number Men	Total Scots (%)	Total English (%)	Total Irish (%)	Born Milit. Stns. Overseas (%)
Scottish Infantry					
1st, 74th, 91st 42nd, 78th, 93rd, 71st, 99th					
Rank and File	1,712	982 (57.4)	506 (29.6)	192 (11.2)	32 (1.8)
NCOs	242	154 (63.7)	61 (25.2)	24 (9.9)	3 (1.2)
English Infantry					
21st					
Rank and File	211	86 (40.8)	76 (36.0)	43 (20.4)	6 (2.8)
NCOs	31	8 (25.8)	12 (38.7)	10 (32.3)	1 (3.2)
Cavalry					
21st Hussars					
Rank and File	372	59 (15.8)	283 (76.1)	27 (7.3)	3 (0.8)
NCOs	68	3 (4.4)	58 (85.3)	6 (8.8)	1 (1.5)
Royal Artillery					
Rank and File	95	47 (49.5)	28 (29.5)	15 (15.8)	5 (5.2)
NCOs	33	2 (6.1)	24 (72.7)	6 (18.2)	1 (3.0)
Subtotal*					
English Infantry					
Cavalry					
Royal Artillery					
Rank and File	722	217 (30.1)	299 (55.3)	92 (12.7)	14 (1.9)
NCOs	140	17 (12.1)	98 (70.0)	22 (15.7)	3 (2.2)
Total					
The Army in Scotland, 1881*					
Rank and File	2,434	1,199 (49.3)	904 (37.1)	284 (11.7)	46 (1.9)
NCOs	382	171 (44.8)	159 (41.6)	46 (12.0)	6 (1.6)

* Includes Greenlaw Military Prison and Glasgow Recruiting Barracks.

Table VIA–2 Continued

5. 1891

Unit	Total Number Men	Total Scots (%)	Total English (%)	Total Irish (%)	Born Milit. Stns. Overseas (%)
Scottish Infantry					
Royal Scots					
Seaforths					
HLI, RHR,					
Camerons, Gordons					
Cameronians					
Argyll and					
Sutherlands					
Rank and File	2,076	1,278 (61.5)	683 (32.9)	89 (4.3)	26 (1.3)
NCOs	429	231 (53.9)	149 (34.7)	30 (7.0)	19 (4.4)
English Infantry					
Lancashire Fusiliers					
Rank and File	690	18 (2.6)	618 (89.5)	39 (5.7)	15 (2.2)
NCOs	160	11 (6.9)	123 (76.8)	18 (11.3)	8 (5.0)
Cavalry					
13th Hussars					
Rank and File	202	31 (15.3)	153 (75.7)	11 (5.5)	7 (3.5)
NCOs	60	2 (3.3)	53 (88.4)	2 (3.3)	3 (5.0)
Royal Artillery					
Rank and File	76	29 (38.1)	31 (40.8)	12 (15.8)	4 (5.3)
NCOs	29	6 (20.7)	17 (58.6)	5 (17.2)	1 (3.5)
Subtotal					
English Infantry					
Cavalry					
Royal Artillery					
Rank and File	968	78 (8.1)	802 (82.9)	62 (6.4)	26 (2.7)
NCOs	249	19 (7.6)	193 (77.5)	25 (10.1)	12 (4.8)
Total					
The Army in Scotland, 1891					
Rank and File	3,044	1,356 (44.5)	1,485 (48.8)	151 (5.0)	52 (1.7)
NCOs	678	250 (36.9)	342 (50.4)	55 (8.1)	31 (4.6)

Source: Enumerators' Workbooks for the Census of Scotland, 1851, 1861, 1871, 1881 and 1891.

Table VIA–3 The Previous Occupations where Known of Soldiers Serving with the Army Stationed in Scotland on Census Day, 1851

	Total Ranks	Percent Ranks	Total NCO	Percent NCO
Rural Workers:				
Agricultural Labourers	78	16.7	6	8.6
Fishermen	1	0.2	–	–
Artisans:				
Cloth Trade	48	10.4	5	7.1
Carter	1	0.2	–	–
Cabinet Maker	8	1.7	1	1.4
Saddler	1	0.2	3	4.3
Domestic:				
Servant	11	2.4	2	2.9
Groom	12	2.6	1	1.4
Gardener	3	0.6	1	1.4
Professional/Semi-Professional:				
Clerk	10	2.2	8	1.4
Schoolmaster	1	0.2	–	–
Industrial Workers:				
General Labourer	165	35.4	16	22.9
Semi-Skilled Trade:				
Shoemaker	21	4.5	8	11.4
Tailor	1	0.2	–	–
Butcher	–	–	1	1.4
Painter	–	–	–	–
Skilled	28	6.0	5	7.1
Other	61	13.1	7	10.0
None	16	3.4	6	8.0
TOTAL	466	100	70	100

Source: Enumerators' Workbooks for the Census of Scotland, 1851.

SELECT BIBLIOGRAPHY

In case of published material, the place of publication, unless otherwise specified, is London. Within their own classification, official army publications, parliamentary papers and statutes are listed chronologically. Other material is arranged alphabetically.

I PRIMARY SOURCES

1. Manuscript Collections

A. Official

P.R.O., London

Cabinet Papers

CAB.37 Cabinet Memoranda, 1856–1900.

CAB.41 Royal Correspondence, 1856–1900.

War Office Papers

WO.3 Out-Letters, 1856–68.

WO.32 Registered Papers, General Series, 1855–1900.

WO.33 Reports and Miscellaneous Papers, 1856–96.

WO.43 Selected Correspondence, 1850–7.

WO.84 Judge Advocate–General's Office, Charge Books, 1856–74.

WO.86 Judge Advocate-General's Office, Court-Martial Records, 1856–74.

WO.91 Judge Advocate-General's Office, Court-Martial Records, 1856–74.

Central and Army Library, London

Wolseley Papers. Official War Office Papers of General Viscount Wolseley.

Register House, Edinburgh

Census of Scotland. Enumerators' Workbooks for the Census of Scotland, 1851, 1861, 1871, 1881 and 1891.

Registrar-General's Reports. Annual Reports of the Registrar-General of Births, Deaths and Marriages in Scotland, 1851, 1861, 1871, 1881 and 1891.

B. *Private*

British Museum, Additional Manuscripts, London
- Campbell-Bannerman Papers. The Papers of Sir Henry Campbell-Bannerman.
- Gladstone Papers. The Papers of W.E. Gladstone.
- Nightingale Papers. The Papers of Florence Nightingale.
- Ripon Papers. The Papers of Earl de Grey and Ripon.

P.R.O., London
- Cardwell Papers. The Papers of Edward Cardwell.
- Smith Papers. The Papers of W.H. Smith.

National Army Museum, London
- Roberts Papers. The Papers of Field-Marshal Earl Roberts.
- Experiences of a Soldier. Unpublished Anonymous Memoirs, 7008–13 (circa 1890).

Royal Army Medical College, London
- Longmore Papers. The Papers of Surgeon-General Thomas Longmore.
- Parkes Pamphlets. A Collection of Pamphlets Pertaining to Army Health belonging to E.A. Parkes.

United Services Museum, Edinburgh
- Calder Papers. The Letters of Private William Calder to His Mother.

County Record Office, Ipswich, Suffolk
- Cranbrook Papers. The Papers of Gathorne Hardy, Viscount Cranbrook.

County Record Office, Maidstone, Kent
- Stanhope Papers. The Papers of Edward Stanhope.

Hove Public Library, Hove
- Wolseley Papers. The Papers of Field-Marshal Viscount Wolseley.

Register House, Edinburgh
- Panmure Papers. The Papers of Fox Maule, Baron Panmure.

2. Official Army Publications

A. *Regulations, Orders, Circulars*

Queen's Regulations and Orders for the Army. 1856–1900.
King's Regulations and Orders for the Army. 1901.
O'Byrnes Collection of Army Circulars and General Orders. 1867–75.
Standing Orders of the 48th Regiment. 1 August 1857.
Standing Orders of the 73rd or Perthshire Regiment. 1871.
Standing Orders of the 42nd Royal Highlanders. 1880.

Standing Orders of the 1st Battalion, The Gordon Highlanders. 1890.
Standing Orders and Regulations for the 1st Battalion, The Black Watch. 1906.
Royal Warrants, Circulars, General Orders and Memoranda. 1856–64.

B. *Manuals, Returns, Advertisements*

Marshall, Surgeon Henry. *Hints to Young Medical Officers of the Army on the Examination of Recruits.* Burgess & Hull, 1828.
Malton, Captain William D. *Company and Battalion Drill.* W. Clowes, 1862.
A Series of Exercises for the Regulation Clubs, HMSO, 1863.
Longmore, Surgeon General T. *Form of Exercise for the Examination of Recruits.* Southampton: J.J. Bennett, 1863.
Wolseley, General Viscount. *The Soldier's Pocket Book.* Macmillan,1869.
Longmore, Surgeon General T. *Manual of Instruction for the Guidance of Army Surgeons in Testing the Range and Quality of Vision of Recruits, and in Distinguishing the Causes of Defective Vision in Soldiers.* HMSO, 1875.
Guide to Obtaining a Second Class Certificate of Education. Chatham: Gale & Polden, 1884.
Guide to Obtaining a First Class Certificate of Army Education. Chatham: Gale & Polden, 1886.
Guide to Obtaining Civil Employment. Chatham: Gale & Polden, 1887.
The Third Class Army School Certificate Made Easy. Chatham: Gale & Polden, 1889.
Instructions for the Physical Training of Recruits at Regimental Districts. HMSO, 1896.
Infantry Drill. HMSO, 1897.
Manual of Military Law. HMSO, 1899.
The Army Handbook of Physical Training. Aldershot: Gale & Polden, 1900.
Instructions in the Care of Barracks. HMSO, 1901.
The Non-Commissioned Officer's Guide to Promotion. Aldershot: Gale & Polden, 1903.
Fuller, Captain J.F.C. *Training Soldiers for War.* Hugh Rees, 1914.
Mortality of the British Army at Home and Abroad and During the Russian Wars, as Compared with the Mortality of the Civil Population in England. Harrison & Sons, 1858.
Life in the Ranks of the English Army. HMSO, 1883.
A British Soldier's Life in the Ranks. HMSO, 1886.
The Army and What It Offers. HMSO, circa 1910.

3. Parliamentary Debates

Hansard, 3rd series, 1856–91.
Hansard, 4th series, 1892–1905.

4. Parliamentary Papers

A. Royal Commissions

First Report of the Royal Commission into the Supplies of the British Army in the Crimea. XX (c.2007), 1856.

Second Report of the Royal Commission into the Supplies of the British Army in the Crimea. XX (c.422–I), 1856.

Appendix to the Report of the Royal Commission into the Supplies of the British Army in the Crimea. XX (c.2007–I), 1856.

Report of the Sanitary Commission Dispatched to the Seat of War in the East. IX (c.2196), 1st session, 1857.

Report of the Royal Commission on the Purchase and Sale of Commissions in the Army. XVIII (c.2267), 2nd session, 1857.

First Report of the Royal Commissioners of the Patriotic Fund. XIX (c.163), 1857–8.

Second Report of the Royal Commissioners of the Patriotic Fund. XIX (c.164), 1857–8.

Report of the Commissioners Appointed to Enquire into the Regulations Affecting the Sanitary Condition of the Army, the Organisation of Military Hospitals, and the Treatment of the Sick and Wounded. XVIII (c.2318), 1857–8.

Report of the Commissioners appointed to Enquire into the State of the Store and Clothing Depots at Weedon, Woolwich, and the Tower, Etc. IX (c.2577), 2nd session, 1859.

Report of the Commissioners Appointed to Enquire into the Present System of Recruiting in the Army. XV (c.2762), 1861.

Report of the Barracks and Hospital Improvement Commission. XVI (c.2839), 1861.

Third Report of the Royal Commissioners of the Patriotic Fund. XIII (c.313), 1863.

Report of the Barracks and Hospital Improvement Commission. XIII (c.3084), 1863.

Appendix to the Report of the Commission for Improving the Sanitary Condition of Barracks and Hospitals. XIII (c.3085), 1863.

Report of the Barrack and Hospital Improvement Commission on the Ventilation of Cavalry Stables. XVI (c.3290), 1864.

Report of the Royal Commission on Recruiting for the Army. XV (c.3752), 1867.

First Report of the Royal Commission on the Constitution and Practice of Courts-Martial in the Army and the Present System of Punishment for Military Offences. XII (c.4114), 1868–9.

Second Report of the Royal Commission on the Constitution and Practice of Courts-Martial in the Army, and the Present System of Punishment for Military Offences. XII (c.4114–1), 1868–9.

Second Report of the Royal Commission on the Present State of Military Education. XXIV (c.214), 1870.

Report of the Royal Commission upon the Administration and Operation of the Contagious Diseases Acts. XIX (c.408), 1871.

Report of the Royal Commission on Wellington College. XIII (c.2650), 1880.

Twentieth Report of the Royal Commissioners of the Patriotic Fund. XVI (c.3404), 1882.

Report of the Royal Commission on the Civil and Professional Administration of the Naval and Military Departments. XIX (c.5979), 1890.

Report of the Royal Commission on Labourers: the Agricultural Labourers: Scotland. XXXVI (c.6894–XV), 1893.

Thirty-Seventh Report of the Royal Commissioners of the Patriotic Fund. XI (c.9316), 1899.

Report of the Royal Commission on the Care and Treatment of the Sick and Wounded During the South African Campaign. XXXIX (c.453), 1901.

Appendix to the Report of the Royal Commission on the Care and Treatment of the Sick and Wounded During the South African Campaign. XXX (c.454, 455), 1901.

Report of the Commission on the Nature, Pathology, Causation, and Prevention of Dysentery and its Relationship to Enteric Fever. X (c.1498), 1903.

Report of the Royal Commission on the War in South Africa. XL, XLI, XLII (c.1789), 1904.

Report of the Royal Commission on the Militia and Volunteers. XXX (c.2061), 1904.

Recommendations of the Royal Commission on the Care and Treatment of the Sick and Wounded in South Africa and Actions Taken. XLVI (c.2440), 1905.

B. Select Committees

Proceedings of the Select Committee on the Army before Sebastopol.

IX, pt.III (c.86), 1854–5.

Minutes of Evidence Taken before the Select Committee on the Army before Sebastopol. IX, pt.III (c.247), 1854–5.

Fifth Report of the Select Committee Appointed to Enquire into the Condition of the Army before Sebastopol. IX, pt.III (c.318), 1854–5.

Report of the Select Committee on the Medical Department (Army). XIII (c.331), 1856.

Report from the Select Committee on the Billeting System. X (c.363), 1857–8.

Report of the Select Committee on the Employment of Soldiers, Sailors, and Marines in Civil Departments of the Public Service. XIV (c.356), 1876.

Report of the Select Committee on the Employment of Soldiers, Sailors, and Marines in Civil Departments of the Public Service, XV (c.383), 1877.

Report of the Select Committee on the Mutiny and Marine Mutiny Acts. X (c.253), 1878.

Report from the Select Committee on the Contagious Diseases Acts. XIII (c.323), 1878–9.

Second Report of the Select Committee on the Army Estimates. VIII (c.212), 1888.

Third Report of the Select Committee on the Army Estimates. VIII (c.225), 1888.

Fourth Report of the Select Committee on the Army Estimates. IX (c.269), 1888.

Fifth Report of the Select Committee on the Army Estimates. IX (c.285), 1888.

Report of the Select Committee on Retired Soldiers' and Sailors' Employment. XV (c.258), 1894.

Report of the Select Committee on Retired Soldiers' and Sailors' Employment. XII (c.338), 1895.

Report of the Select Committee on the Royal Patriotic Fund. XIII (c.368), 1896.

Report of the Joint Select Committee of the House of Lords and the House of Commons on Charitable Agencies for Relief of Widows and Orphans of Soldiers and Sailors. V (c.289), 1901.

Minutes of Evidence Taken before the Select Committee on Civil Employment of Ex-Soldiers and Sailors. XIV (c.2992), 1906.

C. *Inter-Departmental and Other Committees*

Report of the Committee on Barrack Accommodation for the Army. XXXII (c.405), 1854–5.

Evidence Taken before the Committee on Barrack Accommodation for the Army. XXXII (c.406), 1854–5.

Report of the Committee on Foreign Military Education and on the Education and Training of Officers for the Scientific Corps. XL (c.406), 1856.

Report of the Committee on the Pathology of the Diseases of the Army in the East. XVIII (c.2229), 2nd session, 1857.

Report of a Board of Medical Officers upon the Plans of a Proposed Hospital for Aldershot. XXXVII (c.361), 1857–8.

Report to the Director-General of the Army Medical Department on the Sanitary Condition of the Army in the East. XXXVII (c.425), 1857–8.

Report on the Site of the Royal Victoria Hospital, Netley. XIX (c.2401), 1857–8.

Report of the Committee on the Preparation of Army Medical Statistics. XXXVII (c.366), 1861.

Report on the Soldiers' Institutes at Aldershot and at Portsmouth. XXXII (c.126), 1862.

Report of a Committee on the Present State and on the Improvement of Libraries, Reading Rooms, and Day Rooms. XXXII (c.2920), 1862.

Report of the Committee on the Construction, Repair, and Maintenance of Works and Buildings. XXXIII (c.3041), 1862.

Report of a Committee on the Proper Means for the Instruction and Employment of Soldiers and Their Children in Trades. XXXII (c.3133), 1863.

Report on the Herbert Hospital at Woolwich. XXVI (c.3579), 1865.

Report on the Late Epidemic of Scarlet Fever among Children in Aldershot Camp. XVIII (c.3708), 1866.

Report of a Committee into the Equalisation of Stoppages from the Soldier for Rations at Home, Abroad, in Hospital, and on Board Ship, and the Improvements Required in the Composition of His Ration. XLI (c.130), 1867.

Report of the Committee on the Pathology and Treatment of the Venereal Disease, with the View to Diminish Its Inurious Effects on the Men of the Army and Navy. XXXVII (c.4031), 1867–8.

First Report of a Committee on the Royal Hospitals at Kilmainham and Chelsea. XII (c.191), 1870.

Report of the Committee on Fines for Drunkenness. XII (c.199), 1870.
Report of a Committee on the Equalisation of Stoppages from the Soldier for Rations at Home, Abroad, in Hospital, and on Board Ship, and the Improvements Required in the Composition of His Ration. XXXIX (c.197), 1871.
Second Report of a Committee on the Royal Hospitals at Chelsea and Kilmainham. XIV (c.275), 1871.
Report of a Committee on the Organisation of the Various Military Land Forces of the Country. XXXVII (c.493), 1872.
Report on the Moral Effects of the Contagious Diseases Acts. XL (c.209), 1873.
Final Report of the Committee on the Organisation of the Various Military Land Forces of the Country. XVIII (c.712), 1873.
Report of the Committee on Certain Questions Relative to the Militia and the Present Brigade Depot System. XVIII (c.1654), 1877.
Report of the Committee on Boy Enlistment. XVIII (c.1677), 1877.
Report of the Committee on Candidature for the Army Medical Department. XLIV (c.2200), 1878–9.
Reports by Sir Garnet Wolseley on the Conduct of the Troops in South Africa. XLII (c.74, 220, 95), 1880.
Report of a Committee of General and Other Officers of the Army on Army Reorganisation. XXI (c.2791), 1881.
Report of the Committee on the Formation of Territorial Regiments. XX (c.2793), 1881.
Report of the Committee on the Conditions of Service as Affected by the Short Service System. XX (c.2817), 1881.
Report of the Committee on Contagious Diseases Acts. IX (c.340), 1882.
Report of the Cavalry Organisation Committee. XVI (c.3167), 1882.
Report of the Committee on Artillery Localisation. XVI (c.3168), 1882.
Extracts from the Report of the Committee on Musketry Instruction in the Army. XXXIX (c.3522), 1885.
Report of the Colour Committee. XV (c.3536), 1883.
Report of the Committee on the Organisation of the Army Hospital Corps, Hospital Management and Nursing in the Field, and the Sea Transport of Sick and Wounded. XVI (c.3607), 1883.
Report of the Committee on the Royal Hospitals at Chelsea and Kilmainham and on the Educational Establishments at the Royal Military Asylum, Chelsea and the Royal Hibernian Military School, Dublin. XV (c.3679), 1883.

Report on the Prevalence of Enteric Fever in the Royal Barracks, Dublin. XXV (c.5292), 1888.

Report of the Committee on the Organisation of the Royal Artillery. XXV (c.5491), 1888.

Interim Report on the Sanitary Condition of the Royal Barracks,Dublin. XVII (c.5653), 1889.

Report of the Committee on Soldiers' Dietary. XVII (c.5742), 1889.

Report of the Committee on the Pay, Status, and Conditions of Service of Medical Officers of the Army and Navy. XVII (c.5810), 1889.

Report of the Committee on Certain Questions Relative to the Militia. XIX (c.5922), 1890.

Report of the Committee on the Terms and Conditions of Service in the Army. XIX (c.6582), 1892.

Report of the Committee on the Condition of the Yeomanry. XX (c.6675), 1892.

Report of the War Relief Funds Committee. XLII (c.196, 248), 1900.

Report of the Committee on War Office Organisation. XL (c.580), 1901.

Report of a Committee on the Reorganisation of the Army Medical Services. X (c.791), 1902.

Report of the Committee on Officers' Expenses. X (c.1421), 1903.

Report of the Committee on the Existing Conditions under Which Canteens and Regimental Institutes Are Conducted. X (c.1424), 1903.

Reports of the War Office (Reconstruction) Committee. VIII, pts. I–III (c.1932, 1968, 2002), 1904.

Report of the Inter-Departmental Committee on Physical Deterioration. XXXII (c.2175), 1904.

Report of the Committee on the Civil Employment of Ex-Soldiers and Sailors. XIV (c.2991), 1906.

Report on the Steps Taken to Provide Technical Instruction to Soldiers. XLIV (c.3511), 1907.

Report of the War Office Committee on the Treatment of Soldiers Invalided for Tuberculosis. XI (c.3930), 1908.

War Office Report on the Steps Taken During 1907 to Provide Technical Instruction to Soldiers to Fit Them for Civilian Life. XI (c.4059), 1908.

D. Regular Reports

Report on the Discipline and Management of the Military Prisons. Annual Reports, 1854–1900.

Reports of the Inspectors of Constabulary. XLVII (c.20), 1857–8.
Statistical Report on the Health of the Army. XXXVII (c.2853), 1861.
First Report by the Council of Military Education on Army Schools, Libraries, and Recreation Rooms. XXXII (c.2957), 1862.
Statistical Report on the Health of the Army. XXXIII (c.3051), 1862.
[Statistical, Sanitary, and Medical] Report of the Army Medical Department, Annual Reports, 1863–1901.
Second Report by the Council of Military Education on Army Schools, Libraries, and Recreation Rooms. XXXIV (c.3422), 1865.
Third Report by the Council of Military Education on Army Schools, Libraries, and Recreation Rooms. XLIV (c.3604), 1866.
Fourth Report by the Council of Military Education on Army Schools, Libraries, and Recreation Rooms. XLIV (c.3737), 1866.
Fifth Report by the Council of Military Education on Army Schools, Libraries, and Recreation Rooms. XXII (c.4108), 1868–9.
Memorandum by the Inspector-General of Recruiting. XLII (c.57), 1870.
Sixth Report by the Council of Military Education on Army Schools, Libraries, and Recreation Rooms. XXV (c.131), 1870.
Report of the Director of Gymnastics, on the Gymnastic Instruction of the Army. XLII (c.265), 1870.
Report of the Inspector-General of Recruiting [on Recruiting for the Regular Army]. Annual Reports, 1871–1901.
First Report by the Director-General of Military Education on Army Schools, Libraries, and Recreation Rooms. XIV (c.654), 1872.
Second Report by the Director-General of Military Education on Army Schools, Libraries, and Recreation Rooms. XII (c.1085), 1874.
Third Report by the Director-General of Military Education on Army Schools and Libraries. XXX (c.1885), 1877.
Reports of the Inspectors of Constabulary. XLII (c.157), 1899.
Statistical Report of the Health of the Navy for the Year 1898. LV (c.311), 1899.
Report of the Inspector-General of Military Education on Army Schools, Libraries, and Reading Rooms. XVII (c.5805), 1889.
Fifth Report by the Director-General of Military Education on Army Schools, Libraries, and Reading Rooms. XVI (c.7017), 1893–4.
Sixth Report on Army Schools by the Director-General of Military Schools. XVIII (c.8421), 1896.
Forty-First Annual Report of Her Majesty's Inspector of Constabulary for Scotland. XLII (c.9305), 1899.

E. Returns and Other Papers

Return of the Names of All NCOs of the Army Who Were Promoted to Commissions While Serving in the Field with the Army of the East, 1 May 1854–1 August 1856. XXVII (c.188), session II, 1857.

Papers Relating to Military Bands, Etc. XXXVII (c.128), 1857–8.

Returns Relating to Mortality in the Foot Guards. XXXVII (c.211), 1857–8.

Correspondence Relating to Barrack Improvements, Etc. XXXVII (c.300), 1857–8.

Papers Relating to the Purchase and Sale of Commissions in the Army. XXXVII (c.498), 1857–8.

Copy of Correspondence on the Subject of the Employment of Soldiers in Trades. XXXII (c.181), 1863.

Papers Relating to Soldiers' Institutes. XXXIII (c.332), 1863.

Correspondence Relating to the Condition of the Regimental Quartermasters of the Army. XXXIII (c.414), 1863.

Return on the Numbers and Religious Denominations of All Soldiers in H.M. Land Forces. XXXV (c.382), 1864.

Return on the Number of NCOs and Men at Home Who Have Learned Some Trade before Enlistment and Showing Whether They Have Worked at Their Trades since They Entered the Army. XXXII (c.13), 1865.

Dispositions of Witnesses and Verdict of the Jury upon the Inquest Held into the Death of Private Robert Slim by Flogging. XLI (c.202), 1867.

Papers Relating to Recruiting for the Army. XLI (c.203), 1867.

Return of the Equivalent Weekly Wage of a Private Soldier. XXXIX (c.192), 1871.

Tables Relative to the Working of the Contagious Diseases Act as Regards the Army. XL (c.208), 1873.

Return of the Number of Soldiers under Twenty Years of Age Left at the Depot by Units Embarking for Abroad, and the Number of Men Transferred from the Units. XLIII (c.339), 1875.

General Annual Return of the British Army. XLIII (c.1323), 1875.

Return Showing the Estimated Weekly Wage of a Private Soldier. XLVII (c.182), 1878.

Return Showing the Number of Men of the Army Reserve Employed in Civil Departments of the State. XLVII (c.323), 1878.

Rules for Summary Punishments under the Army Discipline and Regulation (Annual) Act, 1881. LVIII (c.368), 1881.

Reports and Other Documents Relating to Army Organisation: General Order 32 of 1873. XXI (c.2792), 1881.
Revised Memorandum on the Principal Changes in Army Organisation Effective 1 July 1881. LVIII (c.2922), 1881.
Return of the Ages, Length of Service, and Transfers of the Men Serving at Tel-el-Kebir. XXXIX (c.78), 1883.
Memorandum on Extension of Service and Enlistment in the Brigade of Guards. XXXIX (c.3638), 1883.
Return of all Officers Commissioned from the Ranks of the Army Since 31 January 1880. XLVI (c.90), 1884–5.
Returns Relating to Contagious Diseases. LXVII (c.245), 1888.
Return on the Total Amount of Stoppages from the Pay of Privates Stationed at Aldershot, 1890. L (c.209), 1890–91.
General Annual Return of the British Army. XLIII (c.6196), 1890.
Return of the Number of First Commissions (Exclusive of Quartermasters and Ridingmasters). LII (c.189), 1893–4.
Return of the Number of Men of Each Unit Which Has Embarked for or Sent Drafts to India, Who Were Unfit to Proceed Thither, and Reasons for Such Unfitness. LII (c.399), 1893–4.
Return of all Discharged Soldiers Chargeable on the Poor Rates. LXVI, pt.I (c.89), 1897.
Return on Hospital Admissions Relative to Contagious Diseases. LIV (c.140), 1897.
Return of the Persons Employed on the Fixed Establishment of the House of Commons. LXXII (c.209), 1898.
Return of Discharged Soldiers Chargeable on the Poor Rates in December 1897. LXXVIII (c.332), 1898.
Memorandum Issued by the Commander-In-Chief. LIV (c.9019), 1898.
Return of the Number of Commissions Granted During Each of the Years 1885 to 1898 Inclusive. LIII (c.281), 1899.
General Annual Return of the British Army. LIII (c.9426), 1899.
Memorandum by Field Marshal Viscount Wolseley Relative to the Control of the Army, With Replies by the Marquis of Lansdowne and Mr. Brodrick. XXXIX (c.512), 1901.
Paper by the Secretary of State on the Requirements of the Army. XXXIX (c.607), 1901.
Account of Expenditure under the Barrack Act. LVI (c.969), 1902.
Memorandum by the Director-General, Army Medical Services, on the Physical Unfitness of Men Offering Themselves for Enlistment in the Army. XXXVIII (c.1501), 1903.

5. Statutes

An Act for the Prevention of Contagious Diseases at Certain Naval and Military Stations. 27 & 28 Vict. (29 July 1864).

An Act for the Better Prevention of Contagious Diseases at Certain Naval and Military Stations. 29 & 30 Vict. (11 June 1866).

An Act to Amend the Contagious Diseases Acts. 32 & 33 Vict. (11 August 1869).

An Act to Shorten the Time of Active Service in the Army, and to Amend in Certain Respects the Law of Enlistment. 33 & 34 Vict. (9 August 1870).

An Act to Provide During Twelve Months for the Discipline and Regulation of the Army. 43 Vict. (19 March 1880).

An Act to Amend the Prison Acts. 61 & 62 Vict. (12 August 1898).

6. Published Memoirs, Correspondence

Acland-Troyte, A.H.D. *Through the Ranks to a Commission.* Macmillan, 1881.

Adams, B. *The Narrative of Private Buck Adams.* Cape Town: The Van Riebeck Society, 1941.

Adye, General Sir John. *Recollections of a Military Life.* Smith, Elder, 1895.

Adye, General Sir John. *Soldiers and Others I Have Known.* Herbert Jenkins, 1925.

Alexander, Lieutenant-Colonel W. Gordon. *Recollections of a Highland Subaltern.* Edward Arnold, 1898.

Anglesey, Marquess of, ed. *Sergeant Pearman's Memoirs.* Jonathan Cape, 1968.

Anon. *Recollections of an Old Soldier.* Birmingham: J.C. Aston, 1886.

Anthony, Francis. *A Man's Man.* Duckworth, 1932.

Bell, Major-General Sir George. *Soldier's Glory.* G. Bell, 1956.

Barwick, T. *To India in the Crocodile.* Poole, 1883–90.

Barwick, T. *Under Arms in India.* Poole, 1883–90.

Barwick, T. *Through the Jungle to Delhi.* Poole, 1883–90.

Barwick, T. *The Last of the Seven.* Poole, 1883–90.

Barwick, T. *Memories of Ireland.* Poole, 1883–90.

Blatchford, Robert. *My Life in the Army.* Clarendon Press, circa 1870.

Blatchford, Robert. *Tommy Atkins of the Ramchunders.* Edward Arnold, 1895.

Blood, General Sir Bindon. *Four Score Years and Ten.* G. Bell, 1933.

Buckle, George Earle, ed. *The Letters of Queen Victoria, 1837–1901.* 4 Vols. John Murray, 1907, 1926, 1928, 1931.

Butler, Robert. *The Narrative of the Life and Travels of Sergeant B.* Edinburgh: David Brown, 1823.

Cairnes, W.E. *The Army from Within.* Sands, 1901.

Clarke, Colour-Sergeant John. *Adventures of a Leicestershire Veteran.* Leicester: S. Barker, 1893.

Clifford, A.M. *On the March.* Madras: Higginbothan, 1904.

Clifford, Henry. *Henry Clifford V.C., His Letters and Sketches from the Crimea.* Michael Joseph, 1956.

Corbett, A.F. *Service Through Six Reigns.* Privately Printed, 1953.

Curling, Henry, ed. *Recollections of Rifleman Harris.* Peter Davies, 1929.

Donaldson, Joseph. *The Eventful Life of a Soldier.* Charles Griffin, 1863.

Douglas William. *Soldiering in Sunshine and Storm.* Edinburgh: A. & C. Black, 1865.

Edmondson, Robert. *Is a Soldier's Life Worth Living?* Twentieth Century Press, circa 1902.

Edmondson, Robert. *John Bull's Army from Within.* Francis Griffiths, 1907.

Faughnan, Thomas. *Stirring Incidents in the Life of a British Soldier.* Picton, Ontario: Thomas Faughnan, 1888.

Featherstone, Donald F. *All for a Shilling a Day.* Jarrolds, 1966.

Faber, M.A. *Recollections of Indian Life.* Chiswick Press, 1900.

Ferrar, Major M.L., ed. *The Diary of Colour Sergeant George Calladine 19th Foot 1793–1837.* Edwin Fisher, 1922.

Field, Cyril. *Old Times under Arms.* William Hodge, 1939.

Flockhart, Robert. *The Street Preacher.* Edinburgh: A. & C. Black, 1858.

Fraser, John. *Sixty Years in Uniform.* Stanley Paul, 1939.

Fuller, Major-General J.F.C. *The Army in My Time.* Rich & Cowan, 1935.

Fuller, Major-General, J.F.C. *Memoirs of an Unconventional Soldier.* Ivor Nicholson & Watson, 1936.

Gollan, John G. *Twelve Years in the Army, or the Incidents of a Soldier's Life.* Elgin: J.M'Gillivray, 1864.

Gowing, T. *A Soldier's Experience, or a Voice from the Ranks.* Nottingham: Thomas Forman, 1885.

Graham, Stephen. *A Private in the Guards.* Macmillan, 1919.

Grenville Murray, E.C. *Six Months in the Ranks or the Gentleman Private.* Leipzig: Bernard Tauchnitz, 1882.

'H'. *Reminiscences of a Redcoat.* Harrison, 1895.

Hall, J.H.W. *Scenes in a Soldier's Life.* Montreal: R. and C. Chalmers, 1848.

Hay, Ian. *The King's Service.* Methuen, 1938.

Hutton, George A. *Reminiscences in the Life of a Surgeon-Major.* H.K. Lewis, 1907.

Ives, J.C. *Six Years with the Colours.* Canterbury: E. Milton Small, 1891

Kernahan, Coulson. *The Experiences of a Recruiting Officer.* Hodder & Stoughton, 1915.

La Terriere, B. De Sales. *Days That Are Gone.* Hutchinson, 1924.

Lucy, John F. *There's a Devil in the Drum.* Faber & Faber, 1938.

Lyttelton, General Sir Neville. *80 Years.* Hodder & Stoughton, 1876.

McKiernan, Thomas. *Experiences of a Veteran British Soldier.* Averavon: T. Major Jones, 1892.

MacMullen, J. *Camp and Barrackroom, or the British Army As It Is.*, Chapman and Hall, 1846.

Malan, C.H. *A Soldier's Experience.* James Nisbet, 1874.

Mays, Spike. *Fall Out The Officers.* Eyre & Spottiswoode, 1969.

Menzies, Sergeant John. *Reminiscences of an Old Soldier.* Edinburgh: Crawford and M'Cabe, 1883.

Mole, Troop Sergeant-Major. *A King's Hussar.* Cassell, 1893.

Moodie, J.W. *A Soldier's Life and Experience.* Ardrossan: A. Guthrie, 1887.

O'Malley, James. *The Life of James O'Malley.* Montreal: Desaulniers' Printing Co., 1893.

Ouvry, M.H. *A Lady's Diary.* Lymington: Charles T. King, 1892.

Baget, Mrs Leopold. *Camp and Cantonment.* Longman, Green, Robert, and Green, 1865.

Patterson, J. Brunlees. *Life in the Ranks of the British Army.* John & Robert Maxwell, 1883.

Pindar, John. *Autobiography of a Private Soldier.* Cupar, Fife: Fife News, 1877.

Rankin, Sir Reginald. *A Subaltern's Letters to his Wife.* Longmans, Green, 1901.

Rawlins, J.P. *Under the Indian Sun.* Lahore: Civil and Military Gazette Press, 1897.

Reid, David, *Memorials of the Life of a Soldier.* Edinburgh: W.L. Rollo, 1864.

Reitz, Deneys. *Commando.* Faber & Faber, 1929.

Reitzel, William. *The Progress of a Plough-Boy to a Seat in Parliament.* Faber & Faber, 1933.

Richards, Frank. *Old Soldier Sahib.* Faber & Faber, 1936.

Roberts, Robert. *The Classic Slum.* Manchester: University Press, 1971.
Robertson, Field Marshal Sir William. *From Private to Field-Marshal.* Constable, 1921.
Robertson, Field Marshal Sir William. *Soldiers and Statesmen 1914–1918.* 2 Vols. Cassell, 1926.
Ryder, John. *Four Years' Service in India.* Leicester: W.H. Burton, 1853.
Sandes, Elise. *Enlisted; Or, My Story.* S.W. Partridge, 1896.
Scott, William. *In a Scarlet Coat.* Edinburgh: H. and J. Pillans and Wilson, 1911.
Shipp, John. *The Military Bijou.* 2 Vols. Whittaker Treacher, 1831.
Small, E. Milton, ed. *Told from the Ranks.* Andrew Melrose, 1897.
Somerville, Alexander. *Autobiography of a Working Man.* Turnstile Press, 1848, 1951.
Sprot, Lieutenant-General J. *Incidents and Anecdotes in the Life of Lieutenant-General Sprot.* 2 Vols. Edinburgh: Gordon Wilson, 1906, 1907.
Swinson, Arthur and Scott, Donald. *The Memoirs of Private Waterfield.* Cassell, 1968.
Tucker, A.B. *The Romance of the King's Army.* Henry Frowde and Hodder and Stoughton, 1908.
Tuker, Lieutenant-General Sir Francis, ed. *The Chronicle of Private Henry Metcalfe, H.M. 32nd Regiment of Foot.* Cassell, 1953.
Tyrrell, Isaac. *From England to the Antipodes and India–1846–1902.* Madras: Thompson and Co, 1902.
Whale, H.J. *Sword and Surplice.* David Bogue, 1880.
White, Sergeant William, ed. *Memorials of Sergeant William Marjouram.* James Nisbet, 1861.
Williamson, John. *The Narrative of a Commuted Pensioner.* Montreal: J. Starke, 1938.
Wolseley, Field-Marshal Viscount. *The Story of a Soldier's Life.* 2 Vols. Archibald Constable, 1903.
Wood, Field-Marshal Sir Evelyn. *From Midshipman to Field-Marshal.* 2 Vols. Methuen, 1906.
Wood, Field-Marshal Sir Evelyn. *Winnowed Memories.* Cassell, 1918.
Wyndham, Horace. *Following the Drum.* Andrew Melrose, 1914.
Wyndham, Horace. *The Queen's Service.* William Heinemann, 1899.
Wyndham, Horace. *Soldiers of the Queen.* Sands, 1899.

7. **Newspapers**

The Border Advertiser.

The Dunfermline Journal.
The Examiner.
The Galashiels Record.
The Glasgow Sentinel.
The Glasgow Sentinel and Scottish Banner.
The Glasgow Sentinel and Journal of Industrial Interests.
The Labour Leader.
The Manchester Guardian.
The Northern Ensign and Weekly Gazette.
The Reformer.
The Scottish Border Record.
The Times.

8. Journals and Periodicals

Army Education.
Blackwood's Edinburgh Magazine.
Colburn's United Services Magazine.
The Contemporary Review.
The Cornhill Magazine.
The Covenanter.
Dublin University Magazine.
The Edinburgh Review.
The Fortnightly Review.
Fraser's Magazine.
Good Words and Sunday Magazine.
The Green Bag.
Journal of the Military Services Institution.
Journal of the Royal United Services Institution.
Journal of the Royal Army Medical Corps.
Journal of the Statistical Society.
The Lancet.
Macmillan's Magazine.
The National Review.
New Monthly Magazine.
The Nineteenth Century.
Once a Week.
Punch.
The Quarterly Review.
The Regiment.
The Saturday Review.
The Soldiers' and Sailors' Almanack.

Transactions of the National Association for the Promotion of Social Science.
The Twentieth Century.
The United Services Magazine.
The Westminster Review.

9. Books, Pamphlets, Lectures

A British Field Officer. *The Army and the Press in 1900.* F.F. Robinson 1901.

A British Officer. *Social Life in the British Army.* John Long, 1900.

A Common Soldier. *Army Misrule.* Saunders, Otley, 1860.

Adye, Major-General Sir John. *The British Army in 1875, a Reply to Mr. John Holms, M.P.,* John Murray, 1876.

Aitken, William, M.D. *On the Growth of the Recruit and the Young Soldier.* Griffin, Bohn, 1862.

Aitken, William, M.D. *On the Growth of the Recruit and the Young Soldier.* Macmillan, 1887.

Alcock, T.St.L. *The Relative Power of Nations.* Frederick Norgate, 1875.

A Lieutenant-Colonel in the British Army. *The British Army.* Sampson, Low, Marston, 1899.

AMD. *The Army Medical Service in the Past and Future.* J. & A. Churchill, 1875.

A Soldier. *Thoughts on the Recruiting Question.* William Blackwood, 1875.

A Voice from the Ranks. *The British Army and What We Think on the Subject.* W. Mitchell, 1871.

Blake, W.A. and Sandwith, J.W.F. *With the Troops in Zululand. A Narrative of the Work Done by the Army Scripture Readers Despatched to the Seat of War in South Africa.* Army Scripture Readers and Soldiers' Friend Society, 1879.

Brown, Captain Tatton. *Suggestions for a National Army on an English System.* W. Mitchell, 1872.

Bull, Paul B. *God and Our Soldiers.* Methuen, 1904.

Burgoyne, General Sir John F. *Army Reform.* W. Skeffington, 1872.

'C'. *The Army in its Medico-Sanitary Relations.* Sutherland & Knox, 1859.

Clode, Charles M. *The Military Forces of the Crown.* 2 Vols. John Murray, 1869.

Constitutionalist [Sir Arthur Haliburton]. *Army Administration in Three Centuries.* Edward Stanford, 1901.

Crowe, J.W. *Our Army; or Penny Wise and Pound Foolish.*

T. Hatchard, 1856.
Daniell, G.F.S. *Aldershot: a Record of Mrs. Daniell's Work Amongst Soldiers, and Its Sequel.* Hodder & Stoughton, 1879.
De Ros, General Lord. *The Past and Future of the British Army.* Edward Stanford, 1872.
Dilke, Sir Charles W. *Army Reform.* Service & Paton, 1898.
Dilke, Sir Charles W. *The British Army.* Chapman & Hall, 1888.
Edwards, Major T. Bevan. *A National Army: Or How to Solve the Problem of the Day.* W. Mitchell, 1871.
Evatt, Surgeon G.J.H. *Short Service for the English Soldier in India.* Simla: Qayum Buksh, Parkes Pamphlets, VII, RAMC, 1876.
Forrest, Surgeon-Captain J.R. *The Soldier's Health and How to Preserve It.* Gale & Polden, 1896.
Gleig, Rev J.R. *Religion in the Ranks.* Religious Tract Society, 1856.
An Officer. *A Few Remarks on Mr. Cardwell's Army Reorganisation Bill.* Edward Stanford, 1871.
An Officer. *Fifteen Years of Army Reform.* William Blackwood, 1884.
An Officer. *A Practical Scheme for the Reorganisation of the Armies of England.* W. Mitchell, 1871.
An Officer from the Ranks. *Private Soldiers, Non-Commissioned Officers, and Candidates for Commissions.* Dublin: John Robertson, 1847.
An Officer. *Thoughts on Recruiting.* William Ridgeway, 1866.
Anon. *The Army Bill of 1871.* Harrison, 1871.
Anon. *Army Reform: Its Tendency in the Future.* William Clowes, 1875.
Anon. *The Dress and Accoutrements of Our Soldiers.* Parkes Pamphlets, V, RAMC, 1871.
Anon. *Our Increasing Military Deficiency and One Way of Meeting It.* Henry S. King, 1876.
Anon. *Report of the Army Sanitary Commissioners.* Parkes Pamphlets, II, RAMC, 1858.
Anon. *The Sanitary Reform of the British Army.* Hatchard, 1858.
Anon. *Soldiers' Grievances.* Kegan Paul, Trench, Trubner, 1891.
A Patriotic Soldier. *England's Phantom Army; the Unrealities, Delusions, and Imperfections of the 'Brodrick' Scheme.* Sands, 1901.
A Regimental Officer. *A Few Remarks about the British Army.* W. Clowes, 1857.
Arnold-Forster, H.O. *The Army in 1906.* John Murray, 1906.
Arnold-Forster, H.O. *Army Letters, 1897–1898.* Edward Arnold, 1898.

Arnold-Forster, H.O. *Military Needs and Military Policy*, Smith, Elder, 1909.

Arnold-Forster, H.O. *Our Home Army*. Cassell, 1892.

Arnold-Forster, H.O. *The War Office, the Army, and the Empire*. Cassell, 1900.

A Soldier. *The Army, the Horse Guards, and the People*. Charles J. Skeet, 1860.

Gordon, Deputy Inspector-General C.A. *A Lecture on Some Points for Comparison between the French and British Soldier*. Parkes Pamphlets, V, RAMC, 1872.

Haliburton, Sir Arthur. *Army Organisation: a Short Reply to Long Service*. Edward Stanford, 1898.

Hall, Sir John. *Rejoinder to Dr. Sutherland's Reply to Observations on the Report of the Sanitary Commissioners*. W. Clowes, 1858.

Hamilton, General Sir Ian. *Compulsory Service*. John Murray, 1911.

Hardy, Rev E.J. *Mr. Thomas Atkins*. T. Fisher Unwin, 1900.

Hatton, Captain E. Finch. *The Militia and the Recruiting Service*. Bosworth & Harrison, 1859.

Heavy Drill 'Em. *Advice to the Soldier*. Alfred W. Bennett, 1865.

Heavy Drill 'Em. *Information for the Civilian*. Alfred W. Bennett. 1865.

Hills, R.J.T. *Something About a Soldier*. Lovat Dickson, 1914.

Hime, Captain H.E.L. *Universal Conscription; the Only Answer to the Recruiting Question*. Harrison & Sons, 1875.

Holms, John. *The British Army in 1875*. Longmans, Green, 1876.

Johnston, James. *How to Reform the Recruiting System of the British Army*. 1866.

Lefroy, Brevet-Colonel J.H. *Report on the Regimental and Garrison Schools of the Army*. George E. Eyre and William Spottiswoode, 1859.

Loch, Henry Brougham. *Memorandum upon the Present Military Resources of England*. John Murray, 1870.

MacDougall, D. *The Sanitary Reform of the British Army*. Hatchard, 1858.

Miles. *Remarks on the Defence of the British Empire*. Roper & Drowley, 1889.

Milroy, Galvin, M.D. *The Health of the Royal Navy Considered*. Robert Hardwicke, Parkes Pamphlets, II, RAMC, 1862.

Musketeer. *Concerning the Employment of Soldiers in Useful Acts*. William Ridgeway, 1865.

Nightingale, Florence. *Notes on Matters Affecting the Health*

Efficiency, and Hospital Administration of the British Army. Harrison, 1858.
Nightingale, Florence. *Note on Supposed Protection Afforded against Venereal Disease, by Recognising Prostitution and Putting it Under Police Regulation.* 1863.
Noake, Major R. Compton. *The British Army, 1875; a Challenge to the War Office Actuaries.* Chapman & Hall, 1875.
Norton, Major Charles G.C. *The Reorganisation of the British Infantry and How to Employ Our Volunteers.* R. Hardwicke, 1871.
Philo-Medicus. *The Reorganisation of the Medical Department of the Army, a Letter to the Right Honourable Lord Panmure, Minister of War.* James Ridgeway, 1855.
Pincoffs, P., MD. *Militaria Sanitoria.* James Ridgeway, 1856.
Redford, George. *Memorandum of Improvements Suggested in the Medical Service of the Army.* John Churchill, 1858.
Roberts, Staff Surgeon Frederick. *Cursory Remarks on Recruiting and Recruits.* Parker, Furnivall & Parker, Parkes Pamphlets, II, RAMC, 1852.
Roberts, Staff Surgeon Frederick. *On the Development of Military Offences in Camps and Quarters.* Parker, Furnivall & Parker, Parkes Pamphlets, II, RAMC, 1853.
Russell, Colonel Sir William. *A Scheme for the Reorganisation of the Land Forces.* Edward Stanford, 1871.
Saunders, Major-General E.A. *Recruiting without Conscription.* W. Mitchell,1875.
Shipp, John. *Flogging and Its Substitutes.* Whittaker, Treacher, 1831.
Simmons, Captain Thomas Frederick. *Remarks on the Constitution and Practice of Courts-Martial.* John Murray, 1863.
Stanhope, Edward. *The British Army.* Kegan Paul, Trench, Trubner, 1892.
Stocqueler, J.A. *The British Soldier.* William S. Orr, 1857.
Thomson, H. Byerley. *The Military Forces and Institutions of Great Britain and Ireland: Their Constitution, Administration, and Government, Military and Civil.* Smith, Elder, 1855.
Trench, Captain F. Chenevix. *The 'Army Enlistment Bill of 1870'.* Macmillan, 1870.
Trench, Captain F. Chenevix. *Short Service and Deferred Pay.* W. Mitchell, 1876.
Trench, Colonel F. Chenevix. *The Dark Side of Short Service.* William Clowes, 1887.
Trevelyan, Sir Charles E. *The British Army in 1868.* Longmans,

Green, 1868.
Turnbull, Lieutenant-Colonel J.R. *Essay on Recruiting on the System of Deferred Payments.* W. Mitchell, 1875.
Two Musketeers. *A Comprehensive Scheme for Reorganising the Army.* W. Mitchell, 1871.
Underwood, Lieutenant-Colonel W. *A Plea for Conscription in Britain.* Forster, Groom, 1901.
'Union'. *Concerning the Army Medical Department.* Jubbulpore: Indian Railway Service Press, Parkes Pamphlets, VII, RAMC, 1875.
Wilkinson, Henry Spenser. *The Brain of an Army.* Macmillan, 1890.
Wilkinson, Henry Spenser. *Citizen Soldiers.* Kegan Paul, Trench, Trubner, 1884.
Wright, H.P. *The Church in the Army.* James Parker, 1875.

10. Reports of Societies

Army Scripture Readers and Soldiers' Friend Society. *Annual Reports.* 1876, 1877, 1878, 1879 and 1880.
Army Temperance Association. *Report and Statement of Accounts from 6 November 1893 to 31 March 1895.* 1895.

II SECONDARY SOURCES

1. Unpublished Theses

Bond, Brian James. 'The Introduction and Operation of Short Service Localisation in the British Army, 1868–1892'. Unpublished MA Thesis, University of London, 1962.
Spiers, Edward M. 'The Reform of the Front-Line Forces of the Regular Army in the United Kingdom, 1895–1914'. Unpublished Ph.D Thesis, University of Edinburgh, 1974.

2. Biographies

Atlay, J.B. *Lord Haliburton.* Smith, Elder, 1909.
Bonham-Carter, Victor. *Soldier True.* Frederick Muller, 1963.
Cook, Sir Edward. *The Life of Florence Nightingale.* 2 Vols. Macmillan, 1913.
Erickson, Arvel B. *Edward T. Cardwell: Peelite.* Philadelphia: Transactions of the American Philosophical Society, XLIX, 1959.
Lambert, Royston. *Sir John Simon 1816–1904 and English Social Administration.* MacGibbon & Kee, 1963.
Lehmann, Joseph H. *All Sir Garnet.* Jonathan Cape, 1964.

Lindsay, Harriet L., Baroness Wantage. *Lord Wantage: a Memoir by his Wife.* Smith, Elder, 1907.
Lyons, A. Neil. *Robert Blatchford.* The Clarion Press, 1910.
Maurice, Major-General Sir F. and Arthur, Sir George. *The Life of Lord Wolseley.* William Heinemann, 1924.
Melville, Colonel C.H. *Life of the Right Hon. Sir Redvers Buller, VC, GCB, GCMG.* Edward Arnold, 1923.
St. Aubyn, Giles. *The Royal George.* Constable, 1963.
Soyer, Alexis. *Soyer's Culinary Campaigns.* G. Routledge, 1857.
Thomas, Donald. *Charge! Hurrah! Hurrah!* Routledge & Kegan Paul, 1974.
Thompson, Laurence. *Robert Blatchford: Portrait of an Englishman.* Victor Gollancz, 1951.
Tisdall, E.E.P. *Mrs. Duberly's Campaigns.* Jarrolds, 1963.
Verner, William Willoughby Cole. *The Military Life of HRH George, Duke of Cambridge.* John Murray, 1905.
Woodham-Smith, Cecil. *Florence Nightingale 1820–1910.* Collins, 1969.

3. Articles

Anderson, Olive. 'Early Experiences of Manpower Problems in an Industrial Society at War: Great Britain, 1854–56.' *Political Science Quarterly,* LXXXII (1967), pp.526–45.
Anderson, Olive. 'The Growth of Christian Militarism in Mid-Victorian Britain.' *The English Historial Review,* LXXXVI (1971), pp. 46–72.
Blanco, Richard L. 'Army Recruiting Reforms, 1861–1867.' *JSAHR,* XLVI (1968), pp.217–24.
Blanco, Richard L. 'Attempts to Abolish Branding and Flogging in the Army of Victorian England before 1881.' *JSAHR.* XLVI (1968), pp.137–45.
Blanco, Richard L. 'The Attempted Control of Venereal Disease in the Army of Mid-Victorian England.' *JSAHR.* XLV (1967), pp.234–41.
Blanco, Richard L. 'Education Reforms for the Enlisted Man in the Army of Victorian England.' *History of Education Quarterly,* VI (1966), pp.61–72.
Blanco, Richard L. 'Reform and Wellington's Post Waterloo Army.' *Military Affairs,* XXIX (1965), pp.123–31.
Bond, Brian. 'The Effect of the Cardwell Reforms in Army Organisation, 1874–1904.' *JRUSI,* CV (1960), pp.515–24.
Bond, Brian. 'Prelude to the Cardwell Reforms, 1856–68.' *JRUSI*

CVI (1961), pp.229–36.

Bond, Brian. 'The Late Victorian Army.' *History Today*, XI (1961), pp. 616–24.

Bond, Brian. 'Recruiting the Victorian Army 1870–92.' *Victorian Studies*, V (1962), pp.331–8.

Bond, Brian. 'The Retirement of the Duke Of Cambridge.' *JRUSI*, CVI (1961), pp.544–53.

Bowyer-Bower, Major T.A. 'Some Early Educational Influences in the British Army.' *JSAHR*, XXXIII (1955), pp.5–12.

Coffman, Edward M. 'Army Life on the Frontier.' *Military Affairs*, XX (1956), pp.193–201.

Denholm, Anthony. 'Lord de Grey and Army Reform, 1859–1866. '*The Army Quarterly and Defence Journal*, CII (1971), pp.57–64.

Erickson, Arvel B. 'Abolition of Purchase in the British Army.' *Military Affairs*, XXIII (1959), pp.65–76.

Gatrell, V.A.C. and Hadden, T.B. 'Criminal Statistics and their Interpretation.' *Nineteenth Century Society, Essays in the Use of Quantative Methods for the Study of Social Data.* Edited by E.A. Wrigley. Cambridge: University Press, 1972.

Hanham, H.J. 'Religion and Nationality in the Mid Victorian Army.' *War and Society*. Edited by M.R.D. Foot. Paul Elek, 1972.

Hargreaves, Major Reginald. 'Poor Profligate Wretch.' *The Quarterly Review*, XXXV (1967), pp.318–29.

L'Esperance, Jean. 'The Work of the Ladies' Association for the Repeal of the Contagious Diseases Acts.' *Bulletin of the Society for the Study of Labour History*, XXVI (1973), pp.13–15.

Maitland, Major D.D. 'The Case of the Soldier's Family.' *The Royal Army Medical Corps Journal* (Aug. 1950), pp.107–25.

Mann, P.H. 'Life in an Agricultural Village in England.' *Sociological Papers*, I (1904), pp.163–93.

Nol. 'Regular Recruiting.' *JRUSI*, XCVII (1952), pp.533–7.

Razzell, P.E. 'Social Origins of Officers in the Indian and British Home Army: 1758–1962.' *British Journal of Sociology*, XIV (1963), pp.248–60.

Sigsworth, E.M. and Wyke, T.J. 'A Study of Victorian Prostitution and Venereal Disease.' *Suffer and Be Still, Women in the Victorian Age.* Edited by Martha Vicinus. Bloomington: Indiana University Press, 1972.

Smith, Frederick B. 'Ethics and Disease in the Later Nineteenth Century: the Contagious Diseases Acts.' *Historical Studies*, XV (1971), pp.118–35.

Sullivan, A.E. 'Married Quarters–a Retrospect.' *Army Quarterly* (1951), pp.113–19.

Taylor, R. 'Manning the Royal Navy: The Reform of the Recruiting System, 1852–1862.' *Mariners' Mirror,* XLIV (1958), pp.303–13; XLV (1959), pp. 46–58.

Tucker, Albert V. 'Army and Society in England, 1870–1900: a Reassessment of the Cardwell Reforms.' *Journal of British Studies* (May 1963), pp.110–41.

Tylden, Major G. 'The Accoutrements of the British Infantryman, 1640–1940.' *JSAHR,* XLVII (1969), pp. 5–22.

Webb, R.K. 'Literacy among the Working Classes in Nineteenth Century Scotland.' *Scottish Historical Review,* XXXIII (1954), p. 100–14.

4. Books, Pamphlets, Lectures

Abel-Smith, Brian. *A History of the Nursing Profession.* Heinemann, 1960.

Abel-Smith, Brian. *The Hospitals, 1800–1948.* Heinemann, 1964.

Anglesey, The Marquess of. *A History of British Cavalry 1816–1919.* I, II, Leo Cooper, 1973, 1975.

Barnett, Correlli. *Britain and Her Army, 1509–1970.* Allen Lane the Penguin Press, 1970.

Baynes, John. *Morale.* Cassell, 1967.

Biddulph, General Sir Robert. *Lord Cardwell at the War Office.* John Murray, 1904.

Bond, Brian. *The Victorian Army and the Staff College, 1854–1914.* Eyre Methuen, 1972.

Bond, Brian, ed., *Victorian Military Campaigns.* Hutchinson, 1967.

Booth, Charles. *Life and Labour of the People in London.* 15 Vols. Williams & Norgate, 1889–1903.

Bowley, A.L. *Wages and Incomes since 1860.* Cambridge: University Press, 1937.

Bowley, A.L. *Wages in the United Kingdom in the Nineteenth Century.* Cambridge: University Press, 1972.

Brand, Jeane L. *Doctors and the State.* Baltimore: John Hopkins Press, 1965.

Childers, Major E.S.E. and Stewart, R. *The Story of the Royal Hospital, Kilmainham.* Hutchinson, 1921.

Claver, Scott. *Under the Lash.* Torchstream Books, 1954.

Cole, Lieutenant-Colonel Howard N. *The Story of Aldershot.* Aldershot: Gale & Polden, 1951.

Cole, Major D.H. and Priestly, Major E.C. *An Outline of British Military History, 1660–1936.* Sifton Praed, 1936.

Davies, M.F. *Life in an English Village.* T. Fisher Unwin, 1909.

De Watteville, Colonel H. *The British Soldier: His Life from Tudor to Modern Times.* J.M. Dent, 1954.

Dunlop, Colonel John K. *The Development of the British Army, 1899–1914.* Methuen, 1938.

Fortescue, John. *The Royal Army Service Corps.* Cambridge: University Press, 1930.

Fortescue, John. *A Short Account of Canteens in the British Army.* Cambridge: University Press, 1928.

French, Major H.C. *Syphilis in the Army.* John Bale, Sons & Danielsson, 1907.

Gorell, Colonel Lord. *Education and the Army.* Oxford University Press, 1921.

Greenhill-Gardyne, Lieutenant-Colonel C. *The Life of a Regiment, the History of the Gordon Highlanders from 1816–1898.* 2 Vols. Edinburgh: David Douglas, 1903.

Grünhut, Max. *Penal Reform.* Oxford: Clarendon Press, 1948.

Haley, A.H. *The Crawley Affair.* Seeley, Service, 1972.

Hamer, W.S. *The British Army: Civil-Military Relations, 1885–1905.* Oxford: Clarendon Press, 1970.

Hargreaves, Reginald. *This Happy Breed.* Skeffington, 1951.

Harrison, Brian. *Drink and the Victorians.* Faber & Faber, 1971.

Hawkins, Major T.H. and Brimble, L.J.F. *Adult Education: the Record of the British Army.* Macmillan, 1947.

Hunt, E.H. *Regional Wage Variations in Britain, 1850–1914.* Oxford: Clarendon Press, 1973.

Kruger, Rayne. *Good-Bye Dolly Gray.* Cassell, 1956.

Luvaas, Jay. *The Education of an Army.* Chicago: University of Chicago Press, 1964.

Mason, Philip. *A Matter of Honour, an Account of the Indian Army, Its Officers and Men.* Jonathan Cape, 1974.

Melville, Brevet-Colonel C.H., Leishman, Brevet-Colonel Sir William, and Pollock, Major C.E. *A Manual of Venereal Diseases.* Henry Frowde, Hodder & Stoughton, 1913.

Melville, Colonel C.H. *Military Hygiene and Sanitation.* Edward Arnold, 1912.

Moran, Lord. *The Anatomy of Courage.* Constable, 1945.

Oldfield, Lieutenant-Colonel E.A.L. *History of the Army Physical Training Corps.* Aldershot: Gale & Polden, 1955.

Omond, Lieutenant-Colonel J.S. *Parliament and the Army 1642–1904.* Cambridge: University Press, 1933.

Pinker, Robert. *English Hospital Statistics, 1861–1938.* Heinemann, 1966.

Porter, Major-General Whitworth. *History of the Corps of Royal Engineers.* Longmans, Green, 1889.

Price, Richard. *An Imperial War and the British Working Class.* Routledge & Kegan Paul, 1972.

Radzinowicz, Leon. *Ideology and Crime.* Heinemann, 1966.

Rowntree, B. Seebohm. *Poverty, a Study of Town Life.* Thomas Nelson, 1900.

Rule, William Harris. *An Account of the Establishment of Wesleyan Methodism in the British Army.* T. Woolmer, 1883.

Saville, John. *Rural Depopulation in England and Wales, 1851–1951.* Routledge & Kegan Paul, 1957.

Scott, George Ryley. *This History of Corporal Punishment.* T. Werner Laurie, 1938.

Simpson, Lieutenant-Colonel R.J.S. *The Medical History of the War in South Africa.* HMSO, 1911.

Smith, Colonel Frederick. *A Short History of the Royal Army Medical Corps.* Aldershot: Gale & Polden, 1929.

Spencer, John C. *Crime and the Services.* Routledge & Kegan Paul, 1954.

Sturt, Mary. *The Education of the People.* Routledge & Kegan Paul, 1967.

Sutherland, Gillian. *Policy-Making in Elementary Education, 1870–1895.* Oxford: University Press, 1973.

Tobias, J.J. *Crime and Industrial Society in the Nineteenth Century.* Penguin, 1972.

Tropp, Asher. *The School Teachers.* William Heinemann, 1957.

Van Yelyr, R.G. *The Whip and the Rod.* Gerald G. Swan, 1941.

Vold, Goerge B. *Theoretical Criminology.* New York: Oxford University Press, 1958.

Walker, Nigel David. *Crime and Punishment in Britain.* Edinburgh: University Press, 1965.

Watson, Colonel Sir Charles M. *History of the Corps of Royal Engineers.* III. Chatham: The Royal Engineer Institute, 1915.

Webb, R.K. *The British Working Class Reader, 1799–1848.* George Allen & Unwin, 1955.

White, Colonel A.C.T. *The Story of Army Education, 1643–1963.* George G. Harrap, 1963.

Williams, Colonel N.T. St John. *Tommy Atkins' Children.* HMSO, 1971.

INDEX